Immigration Policy and the American Labor Force

Immigration Policy and the American Labor Force

VERNON M. BRIGGS, JR.

The Johns Hopkins University Press
BALTIMORE AND LONDON

The Johns Hopkins University Press, Baltimore, Maryland 21218
The Johns Hopkins Press Ltd., London

The paper in this book is acid-free and meets the guidelines for permanence and durability of the Committee on Production Guidelines for Book Longevity of the Council on Library Resources.

Library of Congress Cataloging in Publication Data

Briggs, Vernon M.
Immigration policy and the American labor force.

Includes bibliographical references and index.
1. United States—Emigration and immigration—
Government policy—History.   2. Alien labor—United
States—History.   I. Title.
JV6493.B74   1984   353.0081'7   84–7850
ISBN 0–8018–3168–7 (alk. paper)

To Martijna

Contents

Preface

In the study of the economics of labor markets, there are few areas in which public policy is seen to exert as great an influence as it does in the effort to regulate immigration between nations. There can be debate over the effectiveness, intentions, and omissions of particular government actions, but there cannot be any serious argument that in the late twentieth century the immigration policies of nations exert powerful effects on international labor patterns and population mobility.

This book examines U.S. immigration policy and the evolution of its influence on the American labor force. The primary focus of this study is policy development and the effects of policymaking since the end of World War II, not immigration per se or the multifaceted effects of immigration on American society. No attempt is made to prove or disprove any of the numerous and often contradictory theoretical explanations of the immigration process. Immigration theories are mentioned, but only as they relate to particular policy initiatives. The questions that are asked are What has been done? Why has it been done? How has it been done? and What else might be done in the future? For better or worse, the events that govern policymaking in labor economics usually dwarf the usefulness of available theoretical expositions. It is hoped, however, that this study—this focus on immigration policy—will prod other scholars to seek a better theoretical basis for explaining the phenomenon of immigration than those that currently exist, and to conduct more conclusive research on the multiple institutional factors that govern the effects of immigration and its influence on the labor force—factors that today remain largely speculative.

Public policy is not made; it evolves. This truism applies to all important issues that compete for a government's attention. Given the complexities, uncertainties, and political and emotional pressures that surround many subjects of public debate at any moment in history, policy initiatives represent a tentative approach to a perceived problem. Progress toward resolution of such concerns is by continuous trial and error. The policy that is ultimately adopted at any particular time often results from compromises between divergent political opinions and prevailing economic circumstances. Actions are based largely upon an understanding of what has already happened or is thought to have happened. Sometimes the analysis of the past proves to be faulty, and thus limits the effectiveness of new initiatives. Even when the diagnosis of the past is correct, political views and economic circumstances usually change. As a result, policies that are in place at any given time generally prove to be inadequate as time passes. Thus, policymaking is a never-ending process of refinement and correction. Sometimes it even involves purposeful inaction. Given the range of institutional factors that influence immigration policy, an awareness of past developments is essential to an understanding of existing immigration policy and its contemporary implications for the labor force. These insights, in turn, may provide a glimpse of future needs and issues.

Likewise, the labor force trends of a nation also change over time. Policy measures that seem to be appropriate at one point in a nation's history may prove to be unsatisfactory once significant structural changes in employment patterns have occurred. In the 1970s and early 1980s just such a conflict began to develop in the United States between the emerging and demonstrated needs of the labor market and the seeming indifference and counterthrusts of prevailing immigration policy. This divergence is the subject of the present inquiry. Immigration has reemerged as a phenomenon of major importance in American life. As will be shown, however, in recent years immigration policy has been allowed to fall into a state of shocking disrepair, in part because political leaders have been unwilling to commit the needed resources and to enact the legislation that is required to make the immigration laws and the enforcement agencies capable of accomplishing their assigned missions. More fundamentally, immigration policy itself has been allowed to become a hodgepodge of legalistic precepts that have resulted from several decades of tinkering for often dubious political purposes. Short-term political expediency—not congruence with economic trends and an assessment of long-run consequences—has been allowed to dominate the policymaking process. As will be shown, the stakes associated with this quest to redirect immigration policy are high. It remains to be demonstrated, therefore, whether immigration policy can guide the immigration process, as it is supposed to do, or will merely continue to respond to circumstances with ad hoc remedies that largely ratify events that have already taken place.

It is necessary to mention that for the past several years Congress has sought to enact a series of immigration reforms. The rallying point for these efforts has been a proposal known as the Simpson-Mazzoli bill. At the time that this manuscript was completed, the fate of the bill was unknown. Given the fact that Congress has on several occasions raised the nation's expectations that it was going to act, only to back away each time at the last moment, it was decided that publication of the book should not be postponed any longer. The key issues raised by the various provisions of this bill are discussed here, and if the bill does pass, the rationale for its provisions will be understood by the reader even though the exact legislative response is not specified. If the bill does not pass in 1984, all the problems it seeks to correct will remain to be addressed in the future. In either event, it should become apparent to the reader that the Simpson-Mazzoli bill touches only the tip of the iceberg. The real issue, which is the thesis of this book, is that the immigration policy of the United States has been allowed to function without regard to its economic consequences. The Simpson-Mazzoli bill addresses only a few of the most blatant abuses of the existing immigration system. As essential as it is to correct these shortcomings, this legislation represents only the beginning of an immigration reform process, not its conclusion.

Acknowledgments

I wish to thank Chris Smith, Jo Churey, and Pat Mayo for patiently and efficiently typing the numerous drafts of each chapter. Without their cheerful and professional assistance, the manuscript would have taken many more months to complete than I care to imagine.

I also wish to acknowledge the encouragement provided by the National Council on Employment Policy during the course of this study. The council is in no way accountable for my views and interpretations, but it cannot escape responsibility for the pragmatic orientation toward human resource policy development that it has advocated and that I have come to accept.

CHAPTER 1

The Study of
U.S. Immigration Policy

Throughout the history of the United States few influences have been more important to the development of its population and labor force than immigration. The descriptive phrase "a nation of immigrants" is no mere cliché. It correctly portrays the quantitative magnitude of the numbers of people who have come and are still coming to the United States, and it calls to mind the vital qualitative characteristic of their coming—the skills they brought with them and contributed to the building of the nation. The fact that the United States continues to receive substantial inflows of immigrants remains a feature that distinguishes this nation from all other countries of the world. In the 1970s and early 1980s, the United States legally admitted twice as many immigrants in absolute numbers as did all of the remaining nations of the world combined.

No subject touches the essence of the American experience more fundamentally than immigration, for our history is that of a heterogeneous people in quest of a homogeneous national identity. In its evolving and often controversial role, immigration policy has served as a foundation stone for numerous components of public policy. In addition to playing a vital human resource role, immigration has often become intertwined with such diverse public concerns as foreign policy, labor policy, family reunification, agricultural policy, national security, and racial policy.

The human resource aspects of contemporary immigration into the United States are the focus of the present study. Of necessity, mention will be made of all the other concerns that impinge upon immigration policy, but the human resource aspects will be stressed. Human resource policy is primarily concerned with the development of the employment and income potential of the nation's population in general and its labor force in particular. Obviously, immigration policy is only one dimension of a nation's comprehensive human resource policy. Immigration policy pertains to the regulation of persons who are or have been citizens of foreign countries and who seek to work, to live, or to visit the United States on either a permanent or a temporary basis.

There are only two ways for a nation to acquire its labor force: its people are born within its boundaries or they immigrate from other nations. Throughout most of the nineteenth century and the early twentieth century, immigration was

1

perhaps the most important factor in the human resource policy of the United States. Imposition of the nation's first numerical ceilings in the 1920s was followed by several decades of depression, war, and their respective aftermaths, however, and immigration receded dramatically in terms of its human resource potential. Then, in the mid-1960s, immigration—in all its diverse forms—began to increase dramatically. It is believed that more people immigrated to the United States (legally and illegally) during 1980 than in any previous single year in the nation's history. The 1980 census confirmed the reemergence of immigration as a critical national development. It revealed that since 1970 "the number of foreign born Americans has increased sharply after declining [each decade] since 1920" and noted that "one of every 10 people reported speaking a language other than English at home."[1] Commenting on the emerging trend, the demographer Leon Bouvier observed in 1981: "Immigration now appears to be almost as important as fertility insofar as U.S. population growth is concerned."[2] Because the labor force is the principal means by which population changes are transmitted to the nation's economy, he warned, "there is a compelling argument for close coordination between the formulation of employment and immigration policy."[3]

The labor force implications of immigration transcend concerns over aggregate numbers. They also involve such key factors as the employment adjustment process of immigrants, the postentry employment status of illegal immigrants, the permission given to some nonimmigrants to work in a country, the impact of commuting workers on border communities, the clustering of refugees in selected labor markets, and the effects of all these considerations on the income and employment opportunities for native-born citizens.

The revival of immigration as an important, even critical, aspect of American life has yet to be fully recognized by most of the populace or by many of the nation's policymakers. Aware of this lag, a presidential commission—the Select Commission on Immigration and Refugee Policy—stated in 1981 that the nation must confront "the reality of limitations on immigration."[4] The commission's final report read in part as follows:

> If it is truism to say that the United States is a nation of immigrants, it is also a truism that it is one no longer, nor can it become a land of unlimited immigration. As important as immigration has been and remains to our country, it is no longer possible to say as George Washington did that we welcome all of the oppressed of the world, or as the poet Emma Lazarus, that we should take all of the huddled masses yearning to be free.
> The United States of America—no matter how powerful and idealistic— cannot by itself solve the problems of world immigration. This nation must continue to have some limits on immigration.[5]

The commission's findings testified to the fact that the nation's immigration policy was in total disarray. The report was a manifestation of discontent over the seeming inability of policymakers to accomplish the stated objectives of immigration legislation.[6]

It thus seems timely to review the forces that have contributed to the revival of immigration as a critical issue in American economic life, to discuss the multiple aspects of contemporary immigration policy, to outline the available research on the human resource potential of the new immigrants, and to indicate the nature of the various reform measures that are likely to be debated and possibly enacted within the foreseeable future. As stated earlier, this study will consistently focus on the human resource dimensions of immigration policy. By the very nature of the topic, however, a discussion of immigration cannot totally avoid the political and social aspects of the subject. In fact, in the past, political and social factors have often been the dominant forces in shaping America's immigration policy. Unlike most other immigrant-receiving nations, the United States has generally shunted aside human resource considerations as vital aspects of policymaking. Hence, labor force impact is given priority in this study in an effort to highlight this critical feature of the nation's immigration policy, this feature that policymakers frequently lose sight of when other, more subjective, influences come to the forefront of discussion.

The Primacy of National Borders in Economic Policymaking

The borders of a nation are set by a number of different processes. Sometimes they have a geographical rationale—for example, if the land forms an island or is set apart by mountains or divided by rivers. More often they are the result of historical quirks that socially isolate a group of people, or they are the products of past political compromises that stemmed from the threat or exercise of military power. Geographic, political, and social considerations explain most existing national borders better than pragmatic economic factors do. Consequently, when implementing economic policies, nation-states must adjust to the institutional realities of a world divided by boundaries.

Political boundaries define nation-states. Borders are a way of maintaining specific differences between nations. These differences are reflected in the economic, social, linguistic, cultural, ideological, and political factors that shape the institutions of each nation. Policymakers must contend with the institutional restraints imposed by borders. Within the confines of these boundaries most of the crucial government policies that affect the quality of life of the citizens of each nation are made. Nominally there may be a world community, but the economic welfare of most people depends upon the decisions of a given government, and, typically, nation-states act to further their own interests. Hence, the study of the political economy of any and all nations begins with the existence of defined political borders.

From time to time, of course, these boundaries change; some borders are constantly disputed. Nevertheless, border changes are rare among the highly industrialized nations of the world. Territorialism is so strong among them, in fact, that changes or the threat of change in their borders can be counted upon to threaten or disrupt international order.

The emergence of nation-states brought forth numerous restrictions on the movement of people, products, capital, and natural resources. In this regard, each nation has a formal immigration policy that seeks to regulate the inflow of foreigners whether they be visitors, workers, businessmen, representatives of other governments, or would-be settlers. Most nations also seek to control the exit of citizens from their country. The United States does not. Periodic international efforts have been made to endorse the right of persons to move between nations. Most prominent of these is the Universal Declaration of Human Rights, which was set forth by the United Nations in 1948.[7] The declaration specifies that no nation shall inhibit its citizens from permanently leaving. But this pronouncement is essentially meaningless because it does not mandate any reciprocal obligation on the part of other nations to admit those persons who choose to leave the country where they were born. Even if permitted to do so, people cannot emigrate if there is no place to immigrate. Most of the people of the world are probably content or resigned to stay where they are, but because so few nations are willing to accept immigrants, most people are de facto prisoners of the nations of their birth.

As of the early 1980s only a handful of nations were willing to accept immigrants in substantial numbers and on a continual basis, and even they uniformly attempt to regulate entry. In most of the nations that accept immigrants, labor market considerations are paramount. In some instances, race and religion are. Virtually alone, the United States has since 1965 shelved these concerns and adopted a legal immigration policy that is governed primarily by the principle of family reunification.

Despite the fact that the immigration policies of most nations have sought to restrict the inflow of persons, these attempts have often failed. Illegal immigration has become a common phenomenon on virtually every continent. Sometimes, during periods of labor shortages, governments decide to supplement their domestic labor forces temporarily with nonimmigrant foreign workers. It is estimated that in 1980 some 20 million persons lived and worked in countries of which they were not citizens, nor did they intend, or would they usually be allowed, to become citizens.[8]

People also emigrate involuntarily. Various political actions in many nations continue to cause millions of citizens to flee (some have actually been expelled) from their homeland. In turn, humanitarian pressures have led other nations to accept these persons despite the strictures of their immigration policies. As the frequency and size of these movements increases, the importance of refugee accommodation to immigration policy also grows.

Thus, for most nations of the world, immigration is not a passive form of public policy. On the contrary, it is an active policy concern that requires daily monitoring as well as short-term adjustments, which often have long-term consequences. The primary effects of immigration are economic, but the content and character of immigration policy usually transcend these concerns and are intertwined with numerous other noneconomic policies that manifest perceived national interests.

The Components of Immigration Policy

In the 1980s the nature and characteristics of the formal immigration policy of the United States flow from several sources. Chief among these, of course, are statutory laws. These laws are subject to the vicissitudes of the political bodies that write the laws as well as those of the government agencies that interpret and enforce them. As will soon be apparent, the immigration policy of the United States is exceptionally legalistic compared to that of other nations.[9] This legalism derives from the fact that since 1940 the U.S. Department of Justice has been assigned primary responsibility for enforcing the nation's immigration laws. Congress, in turn, has assigned jurisdiction for immigration legislation to the judiciary committees of the House of Representatives and the Senate, since these committees are responsible for supervising Justice Department affairs. Traditionally, both committees have been composed exclusively of lawyers. Only on rare occasions have nonlawyers been permitted to serve on the judiciary committees—and then only as token members. As a result, "as immigration problems arise, be they major or minor, perceived or real, the response of lawyer-legislators is that the law should be changed."[10] Consequently, immigration law in the United States has been sarcastically described as second only to Internal Revenue codes in terms of its complexity. On occasion Congress has enacted major immigration legislation that completely by-passed the normal immigration policymaking channels. For example, the Mexican Labor Program (1942–1964) was authorized by legislation that was entirely independent of the existing body of immigration laws. In addition, world events—especially those that precipitate refugee accommodation—have required ad hoc policy revisions in order to permit large numbers of persons to enter the country through other than the normal immigration channels.

Historically, many U.S. presidents have differed strongly with the legislative branch over immigration policy. The uses of presidential veto power have been numerous. So have the congressional overrides of vetoes. One would be hard-pressed, in fact, to name any other subject of public policy in which legislative overrides have been so frequent and so far-reaching in their consequences. The executive branch has often sent Congress immigration legislation that was more liberal and humane than the legislative branch was willing to adopt. At other times the end result has been "a stand-off" between the two branches over the appropriateness of immigration reform measures.

A number of federal agencies are involved in various aspects of the nation's immigration policy. By far the most important of these is the Immigration and Naturalization Service (INS), which, since 1940, has been part of the U.S. Department of Justice. Like most government agencies, it is authorized to write the rules, regulations, and guidelines that are needed to make a statutory law operational. The INS is also responsible for the day-to-day enforcement of ap-propriate statutes and related administrative regulations.

The U.S. Department of Labor and the U.S. Department of State also have been assigned specific roles in administering the immigration system. The for-mer is responsible for issuing labor certifications to would-be immigrants who do not have familial ties to current citizens of the United States. It also plays an important role in the administration of various aspects of the nation's nonim-migrant-worker policy. The Department of State is responsible for issuing visas to all foreign visitors and aspiring legal immigrants.

As always, the final authority on the meaning of the statutes, the appropri-ateness of the rules, and the fairness of the enforcement procedures rests with the nation's courts. A body of judicial interpretations of immigration matters has evolved as a result of human encounters with the legal aspects of the system. As immigration laws and rules have changed over time, so judicial interpretations have changed in response to changing perspectives and circumstances.

Thus the nation's immigration system is dynamic, but like all institutional arrangements, it represents at any given time only a snapshot of an ever-evolving process. Prevailing institutional practices—which were set up in one era and were adapted to past circumstances—often lag behind the rapidly changing conditions of a later era. As will be shown, just such a situation developed in the United States in the 1970s. The nation's immigration system became obsolete because the laws and the associated administrative machinery were no longer operative. As the Select Commission on Immigration and Refugee Policy ob-served, by the early 1980s, "U.S. immigration policy was out of control."[11] In 1982, a comprehensive immigration bill was introduced to address some—but not all—of the more blatant policy deficiencies. The bill was known as the Immigration Reform and Control Act (or, popularly, the Simpson-Mazzoli bill). It passed the Senate in 1982 but died on the floor of the House of Representatives in the waning hours of the Ninety-seventh Congress. In February 1983, the same versions of the bills that had cleared the judiciary committees of both houses the previous year were reintroduced by the same sponsors in both chambers. The bill again passed the Senate overwhelmingly in May 1983 and was forwarded to the House, where an extensively amended form of the bill passed by a narrow vote in June 1984. It remains to be seen if the major differences in the respective versions of the bill that passed each house of Congress can be reconciled in a form that will be acceptable to President Reagan. Indeed, the day after the House passed its version, Speaker of the House Thomas P. O'Neill warned that final approval of the bill was still in doubt. He stated, "Its got a long, tough road ahead of it."[12]

The Inadequacy of Critical Data

As will quickly become apparent to anyone who wishes to study the critical effects of immigration on the American population and labor force, the available data are grossly deficient. This inadequacy can be attributed in part to the long lapse in the relative importance of immigration to the nation between 1924 and 1965. Since 1965, a myriad of international issues and a number of domestic labor market concerns (e.g., the military draft, unemployment among the nation's youth, automation, minority employment patterns, inflation, women in the labor market, poverty, and regional employment shifts) have diverted the attention of policymakers and human resource scholars from the gradual reemergence of immigration as a critical concern.[13] As a result there has been little pressure for better collection and dissemination of immigration data, despite major improvements in most other labor force indicators during this interval. Information on the effects of immigration on the American labor force is the weakest link in the nation's contemporary labor market statistics system.[14]

Immigration data first became available in 1820. In 1819 Congress passed legislation requiring the captains of all ships coming from foreign ports to prepare and submit lists of their passengers to U.S. port authorities. These lists became the basis for the annual reports on the age, sex, occupation, citizenship, and intended state of residence of all passengers—most of whom were immigrants—that the U.S. Department of State was required to make to Congress until 1870. Congress also mandated that the census of 1820 include other, more general, information on immigrants. Beginning in 1850, such questions were added to the census questionnaire. Responsibility for collecting specific data on immigrants has varied over the years, depending upon which agency has been responsible for governing the entry of foreigners into the nation. Nevertheless, a 1978 congressional report on immigration concluded that, "despite these long established data collection programs, immigration related data are still deficient in scope, quality, and availability."[15] As a result, the same report noted, "immigration statistics are particularly inadequate as tools for policy analysis and demographic research."[16] Reliable information on the number of legal immigrants living in the United States is scant, and for illegal immigrants it is nonexistent.[17] Likewise, data on emigration have not been collected since 1958. Hence net immigration, which is the really critical number, cannot even be approximated.

As for the data that are available, several federal agencies in the course of their activities collect information related to immigration. The two major data sources are the Bureau of the Census of the U.S. Department of Commerce and the U.S. Immigration and Naturalization Service (INS) of the U.S. Department of Justice. The Census Bureau, in its decennial headcount, asks and tabulates questions that distinguish between native and foreign-born persons. These data are used to determine the "stock" of foreign-born persons in the population. Periodically, in conjunction with its *Current Population Survey,* the Census Bureau asks a question pertaining to residential status at some previous point in time. These data, however, have never been fully developed with respect to the data on immigrants. Although various census questions are relevant to the study of immigration, none provides an accurate measure of actual immigration in any given year.[18]

An even more unfortunate development is the reduction of already limited data at the very time that immigration is becoming a key domestic and international issue. The traditional question on the place of birth of parents was deleted from the 1980 census despite its long history of inclusion in previous census counts. This key source of information on the status of second-generation immigrants was replaced by a nebulous question pertaining to the "ancestry" of the interviewees. Many demographers fear that the meaning of the word "ancestry" will be unclear. They anticipate that many interviewees will simply answer that they are "Americans." This means that the ability to analyze the second-generation effects of immigration has been greatly diminished.

In 1952 the INS required all foreigners living in the United States (including permanent-resident aliens) to file an address form once a year. Little research use was ever made of this information, however. The data were known to be incomplete since not all foreigners actually submitted the forms. There was virtually no enforcement of the statute that required that the reports be made. Moreover, illegal immigrants either ignored or were unaware of the obligation. In late 1981, the Immigration and Naturalization Efficiency Act did away with this annual reporting requirement. Today, all that is required is that aliens report their address whenever they move. The new act was passed because the data on the 5.3 million aliens who reported their addresses in 1981 had become too numerous for the INS—which was relying upon manual tabulation—to process. Elimination of the requirement was also viewed as a means of cutting government expenses—a primary objective of President Reagan during his first year in office. The potential research usefulness of these data is now lost.

Two principal sources of data on the annual flow of persons into the United States involve other administrative processes. The Visa Office of the U.S. Department of State publishes an annual report on the issuance of visas to immigrants and nonimmigrants. It also reports the number of visa refusals. Hence, in a rough sense, these data indicate the demand for legal admission. The INS, in turn, collects and publishes data on actual new admissions and on the adjustment of status of those foreign-born persons already in the United States who wish to remain. Included in the admissions data is information on immigrants admitted, the arrival and departure of nonimmigrants, and apprehended illegal immigrants. The INS data provide a very general picture of the annual supply trends in immigration, but there is absolutely no way of determining the number of illegal immigrants who are not caught.

Several other federal agencies collect statistics that are related to immigration matters, but these are peripheral to the agencies' primary missions. For instance, the U.S. Department of Health and Human Services collects information on the vital statistics of foreign-born persons through the National Center for Health Statistics. The U.S. Department of Labor collects data with regard to the labor certification of immigrants who do not have relatives in this country who are already citizens.

As mentioned earlier, the United States no longer collects data on persons who leave the country permanently—that is, who emigrate. Such information was collected between 1907 and 1958, but the effort was abandoned because the data proved to be very unreliable. Many permanent-resident aliens, for instance, were reluctant to report to the INS that they were leaving the country permanently, for fear they might later change their minds and have to re-apply through the lengthy immigrant visa route. Unlike most other nations, the United States does not have a passport control program for departing persons. Aliens who visit the United States are supposed to turn in a copy of their "arrival-departure" form when they leave the country. The matching of arrival and departure forms by INS could supposedly be used to verify actual departures, but the collection of these forms is lax, and the manual processing of those that are received lags many months behind the date on which the visas actually expire. In fact, about 10 percent of the arrival forms are never returned, which means the departure of about 700,000 persons a year cannot be verified.[19] These people may leave without turning in their forms, or they may violate the terms of their visas and simply remain in the country illegally. Appalled by this information gap, a congressional committee in 1978 called for the creation of a comprehensive passport control program that would make possible the meaningful collection of these vital data.[20]

The importance of data on emigration can be measured with hindsight, for throughout American history there have been periods—usually periods associated with economic downturns—when it is believed emigration exceeded immigration. It is estimated that the number of emigrants has averaged between 10 and 30 percent of the number of legal immigrants throughout the nation's history.[21] Measured against the total number of immigrants (i.e., if one includes some count of illegal immigrants in each year's total number of immigrants), of course, the percentage of emigrants would be much smaller. Given the problems associated with determining the total number of immigrants and emigrants, it is difficult to know exactly how much faith to put in any estimate of net immigration. All one can really do is be mindful of the emigration phenomenon when discussing gross immigration.

DATA AND ISSUE ASSESSMENT

With the exception of census data, statistics on immigration are gathered primarily as by-products of the administrative output of various government agencies. They are also subject to the internal priorities of these agencies. Because the agencies are largely concerned with providing their respective services, and because research is too often either nonexistent or assigned a low budget priority, it is unlikely that the deficiencies in immigration data will be corrected in the near future. This is especially true of one of the most critical dimensions of current immigration into the United States—illegal immigration.

The lack of reliable data has consistently been cited by persons and groups who oppose policy initiatives that would reduce the scope of illegal immigration.

In his criticism of the Carter administration's efforts to restrict illegal immigration, for example, Wayne Cornelius asserted that "no other major policy affecting the livelihood of millions of people in this country and abroad has been formulated on the basis of such inadequate supporting evidence."[22] This contention is an overstatement, however. Deficiencies in gross data are not unique to the study of illegal immigration. In truth, the lack of reliable and useful data plagues virtually every important area of public policy. Data are either nonexistent or grossly inadequate in such critical areas as unemployment in local labor markets, the health of the population, employment discrimination, mental health, the incidence of crime, the use of narcotics, the degree of environmental degradation, and the size of available energy supplies to the nation. It is an irony of the social sciences that the more important the issue is, the worse the data are. Yet the lack of good data has in no way retarded the initiation of significant policy interventions in these and other critical areas of public concern. It is only with respect to immigration reform that the lack of adequate data has been repeatedly and effectively used to forestall reform efforts.

Obviously, reliable data are needed, but policy formulation and the selection of topics for social science inquiry cannot depend on the quality of available data. As Charles Keely has testified, "As frequently happens with situations that develop into social issues, concern outruns information."[23] The importance of the subject of immigration dictates that the assessment of trends and the formulation of policy proceed despite the gross inadequacy of available data.

Despite the acknowledged limitations of existing data, a considerable amount of immigration research has been performed. In the succeeding chapters of this book, this repository of information will be tapped. Regardless of subject matter, policy is formulated on the basis of what is known rather than what it might be desirable to know.[24] To this extent, immigration policy does not differ from other vital areas of public interest.

The Absence of an Appropriate Theoretical Apparatus

In addition to the aforementioned problems, the study of immigration is hindered by the lack of agreement among academicians as to what theoretical models should be used to explain the phenomenon. In economics, in particular, the subject of immigration has long suffered from purposeful neglect.

The theoretical system that is taught most frequently in the United States is neoclassical economics, which extols the virtues of a free and competitive labor market. Government intervention that is designed to influence the forces of supply and demand is usually condemned under this logical paradigm. The foremost proponent of this perspective in contemporary times has been the "Chicago school of economics," which has long characterized itself as the advocate and perfecter of the free-market philosophy of economics. Yet proponents of Chicago-style economics have consistently and persistently excluded from their laissez-faire precepts the freedom to immigrate.[25] Indeed, Henry Simons—one of the intellectual founders of the Chicago school—took an adamant stand on the subject:

> As regards immigration policies, the less said the better. It may be hoped that world prosperity, increased political security, and ultimate leveling of birth rates may diminish immigration pressures. Wholly free immigration, however, is neither attainable politically nor desirable. To insist that a free trade program is logically or practically incomplete without free migration is either disingenuous or stupid. Free trade may and should raise living standards everywhere. . . . Free immigration would level standards, perhaps without raising them anywhere . . . not to mention the sociological and political problems of assimilation. Equal treatment in immigration policy, or abandonment of discrimination, should likewise not be held out as purpose or hope. As regards both our export of capital and import of populations, our plans and promises must be disciplined by tough-minded realism and practical sense.[26]

One would be hard-pressed to find an equivalent example of a major policy issue in which free-market supporters advocated both governmental restriction and overt discrimination as laudable policy goals. Subsequent standard-bearers for the Chicago school of thought have abandoned overt discrimination as a policy rationale. Nevertheless, they have continued to support strongly the need for government restrictions on immigration. As Melvin Reder wrote in 1982: "Free immigration would cause rapid equalization of per capita income across countries accomplished mainly by leveling downward the income of the more affluent. Like Simons and Friedman, I resist this proposal."[27] Reder frankly acknowledges that government efforts to restrict immigration will result in a loss of freedom of opportunity for the individual and that his approval represents an explicit acceptance of reduced worldwide efficiency in the use of human resources. He adds that "[the] intellectual defense of resistance to the implied redistribution of income and possibly of political power requires a quite sharp reformulation of the normative principles of traditional liberalism and the associated goal of an open society."[28]

Conversely, John Kenneth Galbraith, who has long been one of the most outspoken critics of the free-market school, has taken a completely polar stand on the issue of immigration. In 1979 he wrote: "Migration . . . is the oldest action against poverty. It selects those who most want help. It is good for the country to which they go; it helps break the equilibrium of poverty in the country from which they come. What is the perversity in the human soul that causes people to resist so obvious a good?"[29] Galbraith does not contend that immigration is a panacea for mass poverty or for the extensive variations in standard of living that separate the advanced and less economically developed nations of the world. But he does argue that it should be considered a vital factor in any global strategy to reduce extreme income inequality in the world.

Frankly stated, there is pitifully little in the economic literature that can serve as a theoretical basis for explaining the causes of immigration. The standard approach to this question among economists rests upon the neoclassical assumption that the operation of supply-and-demand forces will lead to tendencies that seek an equilibrium position. Immigration from nations with a slow rate of growth and surplus labor into nations with higher growth rates and labor shortages is viewed as a self-adjusting process in which spatial differences between the demand for and supply of labor are automatically reconciled. The efforts of a nation like the United States to protect its labor force from the adverse effects (i.e., competitive forces that depress wages and reduce living standards) of unlimited immigration are viewed as self-defeating, for in the absence of market forces to reduce wages and lower work standards, business will invest in capital-intensive rather than labor-intensive forms of technology. The resulting unemployment is attributed to the strength and selfishness of existing trade unions or the prevalence of government-imposed protective legislation that inhibits the equilibrium adjustment process. In other words, reliance upon much of this theoretical construct is tantamount to acceptance of the necessity of keeping labor costs cheap and living standards low for most workers. Small wonder, therefore, that even the "Chicago school of economics" is reluctant to embrace unlimited immigration as a desirable course for public policymakers to pursue.

Of course, numerous other theories of immigration from various social science disciplines are far more elaborate in their designs and assumptions. Many of these theories, however, contradict each other. Some stress the economic motivations of the individuals involved, but most introduce other sociopolitical factors as well. Some stress institutional practices by businesses and governments that focus on demand for labor objectives; others focus upon supply factors that propel people to leave their homelands; and obviously some emphasize both "push" and "pull" processes. Some are explicitly Marxist in their belief that capitalist economic development triggers emigration motivations within the "have not" nations of the world. Thus, the debate among academicians in search of an explanation for the causes of immigration is endless. Rather than devote attention to a fruitless review of the various theories and their respective deficiencies, or attempt to adopt any particular theoretical approach, this study will focus on immigration policy—not immigration theory—and on the evolution of its influences upon the labor force of the United States. This approach accepts the wisdom of John Dunlop, who has poignantly observed: "Theories are intellectually exciting and challenging but their relevance and application to policy making is scarcely within the reach of most researchers."[30] In fact, Dunlop asserts, the tools of analysis used by researchers and those used by policymakers are frequently separated by "millions of light years."

The Relationship of Immigration Policy to Broader Labor Force Trends

Immigration policy, of course, does not function in a vacuum. It cannot be discussed as an ideal or romanticized as a cost-free principle to be endlessly pursued for its own sake. Rather, immigration policy has economic implications for the participants in the process and for society as a whole. It can determine trends as well as respond to them. For this reason, the adequacies and inadequacies of immigration policy must be judged in part on the basis of how the policy relates to broader labor force trends at any given time. A particular policy tactic that is consistent with the needs of the economy at one point in time may be totally inappropriate at a later time. Changing economic conditions influence the demand and supply of labor and therefore dictate different policy responses.

The U.S. economy is presently in the midst of a major structural transformation.[31] Not only has the labor force been growing annually by unprecedented numbers, but new technological advances and major shifts in consumer tastes and federal government defense expenditures have radically altered the character of the demand for labor. On the supply side, major changes have occurred in the expectations of minorities and women concerning their availability and their status in the labor force. Combine these trends with greatly enhanced foreign competition, an increasingly rigid institutional structure that resists downward adjustments in wages and prices, and rapidly changing demographic and geographic employment patterns and it becomes clear that unparalleled demands are being placed upon U.S. economic policymakers to provide sufficient employment opportunities and to improve the standard of living of the nation's citizens. Because immigration has reemerged during this period as a major aspect of American life, it is essential that the nation's contemporary immigration policy be congruent with the pursuit of these goals.

Thus, the efficacy of past, present, and future immigration policy will ultimately be judged in terms of how it relates to the prevailing economic conditions of the time in which it functions. In succeeding chapters, an attempt will be made to indicate how immigration policy has related to labor force trends throughout its evolution. Chapter 2 reviews the role of immigration policy from 1788 to 1965. During America's formative years, immigration policy decisions were erratic but generally accorded with the economic needs of the nation. Unskilled workers were required, and throughout much of this era immigration policy assured their availability. Following World War I, however, the role of immigration policy shifted from meeting largely economic needs to serving essentially political and social interests. The first ceiling was imposed on the number of immigrants admitted, and overt racism became the admissions norm. The effects of these changes were not felt immediately because enforcement was weak and because the Depression in the 1930s and World War II in the 1940s interrupted the demand-and-supply forces that influence the flow of immigrants. During the 1940s, national security concerns dominated the formulation of immigration policy. Accordingly, the fateful decision was made to shift the administration of the immigration system from the U.S. Department of Labor (an employment and bureaucratically-oriented agency) to the U.S. Department of Justice (a political and judicially-oriented agency). The full implications of these fundamental changes were not immediately measurable. Immigration during the 1930s and 1940s did not even approach the authorized ceilings. But by the 1950s the rigidity and exclusionism of the system had become totally incompatible with the rise of the nation as a world power, and methods of circumventing the system's restraints proliferated.

Chapter 3 examines the nation's post-1965 efforts to establish a unitary immigration system. The system governing legal admissions was greatly liberalized both quantitatively and qualitatively. Racism was purged from the system and in its place the politically popular doctrine of family reunification was instituted. The economic ramifications of adhering to such a doctrine were ignored. Because immigration had been relatively insignificant in the preceding few decades, the adverse consequences of this policy shift did not surface immediately. In the late 1960s, however, immigration began to contribute significantly to the annual growth of the U.S. labor force and to the actual operation of a number of local labor markets in the United States. Immigration policy, however, has yet to be held accountable for its role in these developments.

Another aspect of immigration policy has long been purposely directed toward selected labor markets. This nonimmigrant policy involves programs that permit foreign workers to be employed within the United States and its territories. The nation's continuing and controversial experiences with these endeavors are the subject of Chapter 4.

In Chapter 5, attention is focused on the Achilles heel of the nation's immigration policy: illegal immigration. Although the problem has existed for as long as the nation has sought to impose restrictions on entry, all indications are that the problem has increased exponentially in the past two decades. Although it cannot be officially calculated, illegal immigration probably accounts for the entry of more immigrants each year than does the complex legal immigration system. Thus, illegal immigrants also have a significant effect on the nation's labor force. The growth of this shadow labor force implies the creation and perpetuation of a significant subclass within American society as well as the inherently dire consequences associated with such a development. Public policy measures that will affect all employers and workers are needed to make the nation's immigration system enforceable. Such reform proposals are not only controversial but their broad societal implications transcend the question of immigration itself.

One of the most difficult questions to confront policymakers since the end of World War II is the admission of refugees and the accommodation of persons seeking political asylum. Determining who is actually in fear of persecution and who is motivated by the desire simply to improve their economic lot in life has proved to be among the most difficult challenges facing policymakers. This aspect of public policy is the subject of Chapter 6. The number of refugees and asylees soared in the 1970s and early 1980s, and as a result the importance of immigration policy to the size, location, and skill composition of the nation's labor force has mounted. The judicial thicket that entraps all who attempt to address this issue logically, however, calls into question the efficacy of the entire immigration control system.

In Chapter 7 the special effects that certain aspects of immigration policy have upon the labor markets of the nation's border regions are outlined. The arrangements that permit workers to commute from their homes in Mexico (and sometimes Canada) to jobs in the United States are reviewed, as are other policy measures that impact strongly on these labor markets.

Lastly, in Chapter 8 the combined effects of all the components of U.S. immigration policy are discussed in terms of the labor market trends of the early 1980s. Despite the fact that immigration has reemerged as a significant source of labor supply, public policy has yet to recognize this development. Special political interests rather than the economic needs of the nation continue to dominate the policymaking process. As a consequence, immigration policy is often at cross-purposes with national, regional, and local economic interests. To the degree that immigration policy serves to enhance the economic well-being of the nation, it does so accidentally, and it appears to be honored more in the breach of its provisions than in the realization of its goals. In this era of renewed mass immigration, the nation needs to regain control of this key determinant of national well-being.

CHAPTER 2

The Quest for a Policy on Immigration, 1787–1965

The authority of the federal government to regulate immigration is derived from the principle of national sovereignty. It is not a power that is specifically granted by the U.S. Constitution. In fact, the authors of the Constitution mentioned the subject only tangentially. They simply declared that no state would be allowed to impose a head tax of more than $10 on any immigrant until 1808. This provision was intended to apply to the importation of slaves. Elsewhere the Constitution states that "Congress shall have power to establish uniform rule of naturalization."

The claim that immigration responsibilities belong exclusively to the federal government is derived from a decision by the U.S. Supreme Court in 1892.[1] Since that time, local and state governments have found themselves in the position of responding to the human resource consequences of federal action or inaction pertaining to immigration matters. They often express concern and sometimes try to influence the outcome of debate, but in reality they have little to do with the determination of basic immigration policy thrusts or inaction. In the past, local and state governments have occasionally tried to set or influence immigration policy with respect to specific issues. For example, in the 1970s a number of states passed laws making it illegal for an employer to hire an illegal immigrant. To the surprise of most judicial observers, in 1974 the Supreme Court upheld the right of California to do this.[2] The federal government had debated the subject of employer sanctions through the early 1970s, but it had not acted. The California case was exceptional because it proved the opposite of the general rule: the forum for immigration policy debates and action is at the federal level.

The Era of Nonintervention: 1787–1860

Prior to the Civil War, there was virtually no federal law of substance pertaining to immigration. The only Constitutional provision that impinged on the subject was the compromise on continuing the importation of slaves, an issue which endangered the possibility of unifying the former colonies. Georgia and

South Carolina threatened to withdraw from the union if the slave trade was banned. The compromise that was reached in 1787 allowed slaves to be brought into the country until 1808.[3] In 1807, legislation was enacted which prohibited the importation of slaves after January 1, 1808.[4] The slave, of course, was an exception to the normal definition of an immigrant. Unlike all others, slaves were involuntary immigrants. Blacks had arrived in Virginia in 1619 aboard a Dutch slave ship, but because slavery did not exist at that time, they were initially treated the same as many white settlers. They became indentured servants, who could eventually earn their freedom. By the late 1640s, however, the practice of treating blacks as slaves had begun. Thus, while racism cannot explain the origin of black slavery in the United States, it quickly became an excuse for it, an excuse which prevailed for the next 225 years.

Slavery grew slowly in the South until the 1690s, when the demand for slaves increased sharply with the rise of the southern plantation system. With the turn of the century, the flow of slaves became "enormous," and by 1710 it had reduced the supply of white indentured servants in the South to negligible numbers.[5] As a lasting legacy of this transformation, the white indentured servants from Europe and their successors—the European immigrants—became the backbone of the labor supply of the North and the Midwest—but not of the South. To this day, the foreign-born population of the South constitutes by far the lowest percentage of the total population of any region of the country.[6]

It is important to note that the legislation of 1807 did not end slave trading, nor was the institution of slavery affected by the attempt to restrict the importation of new slaves in 1808. In fact, the demand for slaves increased markedly in the ensuing years. During the 1820s, cotton became "king," and the modern cotton manufacturing industry began to develop.[7] As can be seen in Table 1, the number of slaves in the labor force increased sharply during subsequent decades. In short, slave trading flourished despite the ban on the practice. The agencies given responsibility for enforcing the ban (first the Department of the Treasury, then the U.S. Navy, and later the Department of the Interior) all had multiple duties to perform. In addition, the funds appropriated by Congress for patrol of the long sea border of the southeastern United States were grossly inadequate. Nationwide there was general public apathy about the importance of addressing the issue, which was seen to be regional in nature.[8] All these factors are hauntingly similar to the explanations given for the problem of illegal immigrants in contemporary times. In fact, slave trading did not end until slavery itself was terminated. This was accomplished by President Abraham Lincoln in 1862 when he issued the Proclamation of Emancipation, which freed all slaves as of January 1, 1863, and by ratification, in 1865, of the Thirteenth Amendment, which forbade the practice of slavery.

Aside from the slavery issue, the only legislation prior to 1860 on the subject of immigration dealt with the transportation of immigrants to the United States. In 1819, ship captains were required to collect and report data on immigrants. As for the naturalization of immigrants, an attempt to regulate naturalization pro-

TABLE 1. THE LABOR FORCE OF THE UNITED STATES, 1800–1860 (in thousands)

Year	Labor Force (10 years old and older)			Employment[a]							
	Total Labor Force	Free Labor	Slave Labor	Agriculture	Fishing	Mining	Construction	Manufacturing	Trade	Transport	Service
1800	1,900	1,370	530	1,400	5	10	—[b]	2	—	40	45
1810	2,330	1,590	740	1,950	6	11	—	90	—	60	82
1820	3,135	2,185	950	2,470	14	13	—	17	—	50	130
1830	4,200	3,020	1,180	2,965	15	22	—	75	—	70	190
1840	5,660	4,180	1,480	3,570	24	32	290	596	350	102	285
1850	8,250	6,280	1,970	4,520	30	102	410	1,327	530	145	430
1860	11,110	8,770	2,340	5,880	31	176	520	1,695	890	225	715

Source: Stanley Lebergott, *Manpower in Economic Growth: The American Record since 1800* (New York: McGraw-Hill, 1964), table A-1, p. 510. Copyright © 1964 by McGraw-Hill Inc. Reprinted by permission of the publisher.

Note: Because labor market data were not collected in a consistent manner during the nineteenth century, the data for separate industries do not add up to the "Total Labor Force" figures. Moreover, separate sources of information were used to compile the data. Hence, while these figures are the best historical estimates available, they should be viewed as only rough approximations of orders of magnitude.

[a] "Persons Engaged" was the classification used during the early census counts. It includes employees, the self-employed, and unpaid family workers.

[b] — = data not available.

cedures lasted from 1798 until 1802, but no further efforts of consequence were made until 1906. Essentially, the naturalization requirements that evolved called for five years of residence, good moral character, acceptance of the principles of the U.S. Constitution, a declaration of intention, and witnesses. The proceedings were formalized before a state court.

The absence of substantive federal statutory action during this long period did not mean that there was no public interest in the topic of immigration, however. On the contrary, immigration was the subject of extensive political debate at both the national and the state level. In some instances states passed laws that directly affected immigrants.

From the end of the Revolutionary War until 1819, it is estimated that 250,000 persons immigrated to the United States.[9] As indicated in Table 2, over 143,000 immigrants entered during the 1820s. Beginning in the 1830s and continuing through 1860, the first wave of immigrants landed on America's shores; they came in massive numbers. Most settled in the northeastern states, primarily in the cities of New York and Pennsylvania. These immigrants represented an infusion of new ethnic groups into the population. Over two-thirds of them came from Ireland and Germany. Many of the remaining third were of French ancestry, especially French Canadians.

The population of Ireland had increased rapidly during the early nineteenth century. The potato had become a vital component for both domestic consumption and export; in the 1840s almost half of the Irish population was tied directly to its production. In the early 1840s, the potato crop was struck by a blight that resulted from years of inadequate agricultural practices. Unemployment and famine swept the country. It is estimated that tens of thousands of persons died, while many more lingered on the verge of starvation. The famine provided the impetus for emigration. Between 1845 and 1855, almost a quarter of a million persons emigrated from Ireland to the United States.

During these same years, political upheaval swept across continental Europe. From Paris to Budapest, established governments were confronted by insurrectionists. A serious economic depression struck the confederation of German states in the 1840s. As unemployment mounted, hunger riots broke out. In February 1848, following the overthrow of the king of France, a series of sympathetic revolutions began in various regions of the German confederation. A liberal movement was launched to establish a constitutional government that would unify the various German states, but, having replaced the old order, the reform movement quickly fell into disarray over the distribution of power. By the spring of 1849 the liberal movement had collapsed and a period of political reaction set in. Supporters of the reform movement were subjected to harassment, penalties, imprisonment, and, in some instances, death. The more radical elements were forced into exile. This political upheaval encouraged many to emigrate from Germany between 1847 and 1853. The new and rapidly expanding German railroad network provided the means of exit from the hinterlands to the

TABLE 2. THE FIVE COUNTRIES WITH THE HIGHEST NUMBER OF ADMISSIONS, RANK ORDERED, AND PERCENTAGE OF TOTAL ADMISSIONS, 1821–1860

Decade	Total Legal Immigrants	Ranking of Countries and Percentage of Admissions										Percentage of Total Admissions Accounted for by Five Highest-Ranked Countries
		First	%	Second	%	Third	%	Fourth	%	Fifth	%	
1821–1830	143,439	Ireland	35.4	United Kingdom	17.5	France	5.9	Germany	4.7	Mexico	3.4	66.9
1831–1840	599,125	Ireland	34.6	Germany	24.4	United Kingdom	12.7	France	7.6	Canada	2.3	81.6
1841–1850	1,713,251	Ireland	45.6	Germany	25.4	United Kingdom	15.6	France	4.5	Canada	2.4	93.5
1851–1860	2,598,214	Germany	36.6	Ireland	35.2	United Kingdom	16.3	France	2.9	Canada	2.3	93.3

Source: Select Commission on Immigration and Refugee Policy, *U.S. Immigration Policy and the National Interest: Staff Report* (supplement to the final report) (Washington, D.C.: GPO, 1981), pp. 230–31.

seaports. Over a million Germans entered the United States during this time span.

Moreover, in the 1840s and 1850s, French Canadians began to immigrate into the New England area in large numbers. This movement actually began in 1837 and 1838 as a direct result of a rebellion that broke out in Montreal and Upper Eastern Canada, where the French Canadian population was clustered. The rebellion was the result of a severe economic depression and soon became linked to an unplanned republican uprising for political independence from Great Britain. The uprising was quickly crushed by British garrison troops and local militia. The aftermath of this fiasco, as well as the overpopulation of the region and the collapse of the timber trade due to the prolonged depression, sent thousands of French Canadians over the border in pursuit of jobs in America. It is estimated that in 1845 alone over 22,000 French Canadians moved into the rapidly developing textile towns of New England.[10] At that time the textile industry was primarily interested in hiring whole families to work as a unit in its plants. The French Canadians tended to immigrate as whole families and thus were seen as an ideal source of labor. The Irish immigrants who sought work in the textile industry were largely young, unmarried men, and they were gradually displaced by the French Canadians. The major textile employers believed that the French Canadians were "better, steadier, more industrious, and reliable than were the Irish" and that they were more willing to "accept conditions as they found them."[11] This perception was reinforced in the late 1850s when a group of Irish workers became involved in several unsuccessful efforts to establish unions for textile workers. Many employers never forgave them for this action, and by the eve of the Civil War, the French Canadians had become the dominant immigrant group in many of the New England textile mills.[12]

With them the Irish, Germans, and French Canadians brought their customs, language, and religion (predominantly Catholicism). Among the numerically dominant Anglo-Saxon and strongly Protestant citizens of the urban Northeast, a nativist reaction set in. It took the form of verbal assaults on Catholicism and political radicalism in general and on the personal characteristics of the new immigrants in particular. On several occasions, full-scale riots erupted. One of the worst of these was a three-day riot in Philadelphia in 1844. Similar anti-immigrant riots also occurred in Boston and New York. Fierce debates were conducted in various state legislatures and in Congress over the desirability of unrestricted immigration and the unregulated naturalization of such ethnic groups.

The movement hit its political zenith with the establishment of the Native American party in the early 1850s. The party was the product of years of anti-Catholic attacks by Protestant clergymen and journalists. A secret society known as the Order of the Star-Spangled Banner had been formed earlier for the express purpose of restricting immigration from non-Anglo-Saxon countries. Members were instructed to answer any inquiries about the order with the words "I know nothing about it." As a result, the order and its subsequent political manifestation were labeled "the Know Nothing Movement." The movement struck a responsive chord among workingmen who felt threatened with economic competition from the new immigrants. Other persons felt that Catholicism represented a genuine threat to American institutions. These feelings became the springboard for opportunistic politicians who were searching for a cause that would get them elected. In 1854, the "Know Nothing party" won control of the Massachusetts legislature and made substantial gains in the legislatures of a number of other northeastern states. The "Know Nothings" were especially critical of the naturalization laws, which allowed immigrants to become citizens and to become participants in the political process.

The "Know Nothing Movement" soon faltered, however. In Massachusetts, for instance, the "Know Nothings" led a statewide investigation of life inside convents. No improprieties were found, but the legislators themselves incurred the wrath of the electorate when they submitted enormous expense account charges for reimbursement. In 1855 the party split into Northern and Southern factions over the issue of slavery. In 1856, the "Know Nothing party" nominated former President Millard Fillmore of New York for President. He captured the electoral votes of only one state (Maryland, ironically a state founded by Catholics). After that election the party faded away as the nation was swept into civil war in the 1860s. The antislavery movement for a moment overwhelmed the anti-immigrant sentiment.

In the meantime, on the West Coast, another bitter anti-immigrant movement had begun to incubate. From 1820 through 1850, only 526 persons from all of Asia had officially immigrated to the United States. During the decade of the 1850s, the number of Asians jumped to 41,538.- These immigrants were primarily from China and they settled largely in California.[13] In the beginning, one of the factors contributing to the immigration of the Chinese was the Taiping Rebellion, which lasted from 1850 to 1864. It was the most important political event in the Chinese Empire in the nineteenth century. Combining politics with religion, its leaders sought to arouse the masses of impoverished workers and farmers in a vain effort to secure a more equitable society. During the rebellion, seventeen provinces were ravaged and twenty million lives were lost. Countless others were injured. Many Chinese sought to escape the turmoil, bloodshed, and massive poverty of their homeland through emigration. These "push" factors in China exactly paralleled the simultaneous need for workers in the underpopulated economy of the new state of California during the 1850s.

Originally, the Chinese were recruited to help build the western portion of the transcontinental railroad. It was not long, however, before they began to spill over into jobs in mining and into service jobs in various West Coast cities. Non-Asian workers soon felt threatened. Public pressure in the 1850s led the California legislature to enact a number of anti-Chinese laws.[14] Among these were a tax on foreign miners in 1852, a head tax on Chinese immigrants in 1855, and a resolution to enforce these statutes in 1862. These laws were struck down by both the California Supreme Court and the U.S. Supreme Court.

LABOR MARKET EFFECTS

During the pre–Civil War era, the United States was largely an under-developed and underpopulated land. The industrialization of its economy was just beginning. A review of Table 1 shows that agricultural employment dominated the nation's economy at this time, but that by the 1840s manufacturing was beginning to make substantial headway. The labor force statistics for this era are quite sparse. Even the data from the censuses prior to 1870 are fragmentary, for these counts were carried out primarily as simple measurements of the size of the population.

During this prewar period of nonintervention, the human resource implications of U.S. immigration were twofold. In the South the illegal importation of slaves was a substantial factor in the growth of the slave labor force. Slave workers, as reported in the census reports, accounted for a minimum of one out of every five workers in the nation's labor force throughout the entire period. It is likely that there was extensive statistical undercounting of the slave population and labor force in these census reports. Because of the growth in the number of slaves—through natural reproduction and illegal importation—the cotton and tobacco industries were able to expand rapidly. Statistical data on the "enormous" number of illegally imported slaves are, of course, nonexistent, for after 1808 even ship manifests were regularly altered to conceal evidence of illegal smuggling.[15]

In the North and West, the pre–Civil War immigrants were largely unskilled workers. Over half had no occupational classification when they entered the United States.[16] Granted, many of these persons were wives and children, but the lack of a clear occupation also aptly depicted the status of many adult males from China and Europe as well. It was, of course, precisely the unskilled workers who were in greatest demand after 1840 to staff the emerging factories, to work the mines, and to build the railroads and the public works infrastructure associated with a nation on the verge of entering the industrial revolution. It is also estimated that upwards of one-third of the nation's regular army in 1840 was composed of immigrants.[17] Only about 10 percent of the laborers who immigrated during this period were classified as skilled workers at the time of their entry.

The fact that the factory system was gradually but methodically taking command of the economy of the Northeast and Midwest meant that many artisans were being replaced. No doubt these skilled workers felt threatened by immigration, but it is more likely that the industrialization process represented the real threat to their job security. Productivity increased sharply. Money wages rose substantially faster than prices (i.e., real wages rose sharply from 1820 through 1850).[18] From 1850 to 1860, however, there was virtually no change in real wages, and it is likely that the effects of the unprecedentedly high rate of immigration during this decade were a critical part of the explanation of this reversal.[19]

The Beginnings of Direct Public Policy
Intervention: 1860–1890

With the advent of the Civil War came mandatory conscription of young men who could not afford the optional high fee for the buying out of one's military commitment. In addition to military demands on the labor force, the expansion of military production increased the demand for workers in manufacturing. Labor shortages developed throughout the North. With most of the Democratic congressmen gone from Congress (due to the secession of the Southern states), a Republican party dominated by business interests sought to find a way to increase the supply of workers but not of settlers per se. President Abraham Lincoln, in a message to Congress in December 1863, proposed a law that would foster immigration. Early in 1864, the Act to Encourage Immigration was adopted. Due to some of its unique procedural aspects, it was more popularly called the Contract Labor Act.

The act allowed private employers to recruit foreign workers and to pay their transportation expenses to the United States. The enlisted workers signed legally binding contracts whereby they agreed to pledge their wages for up to twelve months to the employer who paid these transportation costs. In addition, they were often induced to sign contracts for additional years of work to defray the costs of their maintenance during the initial year.

The law was designed primarily to attract unskilled workers. A number of private labor recruiting firms had earlier sought unsuccessfully to have the government subsidize their activities. Under the aegis of the new law, these private firms—especially the American Emigrant Company—entered into very lucrative business ventures. These companies were paid fees by both the employers for whom they contracted workers and the steamship lines who transported the recruits from Europe to the United States.

Opposition to the Contract Labor Act from existing worker organizations arose at once. In some instances, the new immigrants became involved in labor disputes as strikebreakers. When the war ended, the economy slipped into a serious recession that lasted from 1866 to 1868. Organized labor—especially the newly formed National Labor Union (NLU)—blamed the immigration law for the unemployment and depressed wages that existed in the postwar period.[20] The NLU sought repeal of the Contract Labor Act and was successful in 1868. Contract labor continued into the 1880s, however, because the practice itself had not been banned.

From the mid 1860s through the mid 1880s, the second wave of immigrants arrived in the United States. They settled primarily in the states of the Northeast and Midwest along the Great Lakes. As shown in Table 3, once again Germany, Great Britain, and Ireland were the primary source countries. There were as well, however, immigrants from Sweden and Norway who were fleeing religious persecution, compulsory military service, and stagnant economies. All were attracted by the job opportunities of a nation now in the throes of rapid indus-

TABLE 3. THE FIVE COUNTRIES WITH THE HIGHEST NUMBER OF ADMISSIONS, RANK ORDERED, AND PERCENTAGE OF TOTAL ADMISSIONS, 1861–1890

Decade	Total Legal Immigrants	Ranking of Countries and Percentage of Admissions										Percentage of Total Admissions Accounted for by Five Highest-Ranked Countries
		First	%	Second	%	Third	%	Fourth	%	Fifth	%	
1861–1870	2,314,824	Germany	34.0	United Kingdom	26.2	Ireland	18.8	Norway	3.1	Canada	6.6	88.7
1871–1880	2,812,191	Germany	25.5	United Kingdom	19.5	Ireland	15.5	Canada	13.6	China	4.4	78.5
1881–1890	5,246,613	Germany	27.7	United Kingdom	15.4	Ireland	12.5	Canada	7.5	Sweden	7.5	70.6

Source: Select Commission on Immigration and Refugee Policy, *U.S. Immigration Policy and the National Interest: Staff Report* (supplement to the final report) (Washington, D.C.: GPO, 1981), pp. 230–31.

trialization. Most of the newly created jobs were in unskilled occupations in manufacturing and mining. Some were in farming.

On the West Coast, the number of Chinese immigrants increased significantly during this period. The Burlingame Treaty, signed between China and the United States in 1868, guaranteed the right of Chinese immigrants to enter the United States under the same terms as all other foreigners. Although it placed restrictions on the naturalization rights of Chinese, it gave a significant boost to Chinese immigration.

With the completion of the transcontinental railroad in 1869, thousands of job-seekers, as well as cheaper manufactured goods, arrived in California from the East Coast. Concurrently, thousands of Chinese immigrants who had previously worked in railroad construction were seeking other jobs. As a result, the California economy slipped into deep recession in the late 1860s. Unemployment rose steadily. The competition for available jobs rekindled latent anti-Chinese prejudices that had first surfaced in the 1850s. Chinese workers were usually paid less by employers than other workers doing the same tasks. As a result, white workers deduced that the Chinese were willing to work for less than whites were. Hence, white workers—many of whom were immigrants themselves— held the Chinese responsible for their economic plight.

Because earlier anti-Chinese state laws had been overturned by the courts, many white workers looked to the existing National Labor Union for aid. The NLU responded with demands that the federal government abrogate the Burlingame Treaty and enact "anti-coolie" importation laws. In this context, it is interesting to note that the anti-Chinese immigration movement spawned what subsequently became an important instrument of union policy: the use of the union label on products. The union label was introduced for the first time anywhere in San Francisco in 1872. It was used by white unionized cigar makers to notify consumers that their products were manufactured by white workers and not by Chinese workers. The label itself was "white in color to indicate to the purchaser that he was buying a product manufactured by Caucasian workers."[21] It was hoped that such labeling would lead to a consumer boycott that would protect the higher wages and better working conditions of the white workers.

Employer groups in California were initially able to stem the anti-Chinese movement. A nationwide depression hit California in 1877, however, and the brutal two-day riot that broke out in San Francisco that summer was directed specifically at the Chinese population. In the aftermath of this riot, the Sand Lot party—named for the site of the original rally of discontented workers that led to the riot—was formed. Denouncing Chinese labor, the party in 1878 elected mayors in Oakland and San Francisco and filled other public positions throughout California. An amendment to the state constitution was subsequently enacted that year forbidding any corporation in California to employ "any Chinese or Mongolian" in any capacity. A federal court invalidated this law in 1880, but when Chinese immigration increased substantially in the early 1880s, the anti-Chinese movement spread beyond California to become a national issue. At its founding convention in 1881, the Federation of Organized Trades and Labor Unions (the lineal predecessor of the American Federation of Labor) passed an anti-Chinese resolution that called for laws "to get rid of this monstrous immigration."[22] By this time both national political parties had taken up the cause of restricting Chinese immigration.

As a result, the Chinese Exclusion Act was enacted in 1882.[23] It forbade the entry of any additional Chinese immigrants for the next ten years. The law was extended at succeeding ten-year intervals until it was repealed in 1943 when it became an embarrassment because China was an ally of the United States in the war with Japan.

The move to deny entry to the Chinese was part of a broader drive to exclude other groups. Prior to 1875 the only effort to exclude a specific group had been the Alien Act of 1798 and the Alien Act of 1800, which empowered the president to expel any alien deemed to be "dangerous." These acts proved to be very unpopular and were repealed in 1800. In 1875 the first statute that specifically excluded a class of immigrants was enacted. It barred the immigration of convicts and prostitutes. In 1882 idiots, lunatics, and paupers also were banned. These groups were the first of the thirty-three specific categories of exclusion that now shape the nation's immigration laws.[24]

It was also during the 1880s that the issue of importation of contract workers came to a head. Throughout the 1870s and 1880s immigration increased despite the prolonged periods of economic recession from 1873 to 1879 and from 1884 to 1886. The major labor organization of this era—the Knights of Labor—as well as a number of independent craft unions became openly hostile to the policies that favored tariff restrictions to protect industrialists while permitting new immigrants to enter and to compete freely with citizen workers for jobs. As indicated earlier, organized labor had lobbied hard for the Chinese Exclusion Act and had supported the exclusion of other groups as well. It was in this context that the Alien Contract Labor Law of 1885 and its 1887 and 1888 amendments were adopted.[25] These laws sought explicitly to prohibit any person or business enterprise from assisting financially or encouraging in any way the immigration of aliens under the terms of any contracts or agreements. A fine of $1,000 per violation was set—a considerable penalty at that time.

The significance of the alien contract laws lies in the fact that they were the first statutes designed to restrict immigration from Europe and the inflow of workers who were capable of self-support.[26] The only reason that such restrictions were politically acceptable was that they demonstrated the need for "special protection against a definite recognized evil."[27] The "evil" was that contract labor was perceived to be a form of artificial immigration used by employers primarily to undermine existing labor organizations.

Despite these laws, the practice of contracting for foreign labor continued. Courts interpreted the laws in a manner that tended to perpetuate the tradition of a generally open border policy for Europeans.[28] As a result, contract workers continued to be a factor in labor disputes. One notable example involved the hiring of sixty-two Scottish stonecutters to build the mammoth state capitol in Texas. In 1885 the stonecutters were recruited in Scotland and transported to Austin, Texas, after the members of the Granite Cutter's International boycotted the project. As one study of that dispute concluded, "It was not the scarcity of American stonemasons, however, which necessitated the importation of alien labor, but the conditions under which the Capitol Syndicate required their stonemasons to work."[29] By the time the case came to court (in 1889), the work by the contract workers had been completed and they had scattered. The contractor was found guilty, but only a pittance of a penalty was assessed.

Although no details are available on the number of persons who entered the United States under contract agreements, it is known that almost 400 suits were filed by the federal government in response to violations of the Alien Contract Act in the ten-year period following its enactment.[30]

INITIAL ENFORCEMENT EFFORTS

The federal government's move toward intervention in immigration affairs raised the simultaneous issue of enforcement. The first tentative step toward centralized control of immigration by a federal agency came with passage of the Contract Labor Act of 1864. A commissioner of immigration was appointed by the president and placed within the U.S. Department of State. The commissioner was given responsibility for opening a federal office of immigration in New York City. The act was repealed in 1868, however, and these activities ceased.

The growing significance of immigration and the mounting controversy in some parts of the country over its unregulated effects led to a series of court contests over who was responsible for immigration matters. Several states had adopted immigration-related statutes on their own initiative. These efforts came to an end in 1876 when the U.S. Supreme Court ruled that state immigration laws in California, Louisiana, and New York were unconstitutional.[31] States could no longer regulate immigration or exclude certain groups of immigrants. The Court ruled that Congress was the more appropriate body to deal with the subject of immigration. Since that decision, state and local governments have been placed largely in the position of adjusting to the actions or inaction of the federal government in this vital policy area.

When the federal government began to place restrictions on immigration in the 1870s and 1880s, it became clear that enforcement procedures would have to be devised. In 1882 Congress enacted the first law that actually provided a semblance of systematic control over immigration.[32] It established a procedure whereby the secretary of the treasury was granted general supervisory authority over enforcement. The secretary was empowered to create state offices (which were, in turn, filled by the respective state governors) to examine immigrants upon their arrival. A tax of fifty cents was to be charged each immigrant who crossed the nation's water borders, and this tax was to be paid into a fund to cover the administrative costs of enforcement. In 1887 responsibility for enforcement of the immigration laws was specifically assigned to the secretary of the treasury by law, and in 1888 he was empowered to return persons in violation of the statutes to their homelands. The actual enforcement of the federal laws, however, was delegated to state officials.

In response to complaints that the existing laws were not being adequately enforced, Congress launched an investigation into immigration matters in 1888. Indeed, the ensuing congressional report noted widespread violations and circumventions and attributed these to the fact that enforcement authority was divided between federal and state officials. From this report came the Immigration Act of 1891, which ended state involvement in the administration of immigration matters.[33] The Bureau of Immigration was established within the U.S. Department of the Treasury. All immigration duties previously performed by state agencies were transferred to this new federal office. The 1891 law also provided for regulation of overland immigration from Canada and Mexico and created several more categories of exclusion.

LABOR MARKET EFFECTS

As shown in Table 1 and Table 4, the proportion of the labor force engaged in agriculture remained relatively constant—about 50 percent—from 1850 to 1880. This percentage persisted despite the economic dislocations associated with the Civil War. Agricultural production soared because of the introduction of technological improvements. Nevertheless, during the period 1880–1890 new employment trends began to emerge that would soon dominate all employment patterns for the nation. Most notable among these was the decline in the proportion of the labor force employed in agriculture. Agricultural prices began to fall in the mid 1870s and continued to decline throughout the 1880s. As a result, agricultural employment lost its luster. Simultaneously, the nonfarm industrialization of the nation began in earnest in the north-central states. The expansion of manufacturing during this era began in long-established industries. In the steel industry, for instance, the Bessemer converter and the open-hearth furnace were introduced, and steel became the first truly large-scale American industry. Steel production and employment were centered in the area between Pittsburgh and Cleveland, in Gary, Indiana, and on the southern tip of Lake Michigan. In New England the textile and shoemaking industries also underwent a fundamental transformation in character and size as machines were introduced into all branches of these enterprises. Similar changes occurred in other basic industries as extensive infusions of capital made possible the first stage of the technological revolution in the nation: mechanization. As a result of the increase in employment opportunities, the north-central states sustained the largest absolute gains in population of any geographic region in the nation. Urban clustering had begun.

The workers who filled the country's expanding factories were predominantly unskilled. The same can be said of the growing mining industry, which provided

TABLE 4. THE LABOR FORCE OF THE UNITED STATES, 1860–1890 (in thousands)

Year	Total Labor Force (10 years of age and older)	Employment[a]							
		Agriculture	Fishing	Mining	Construction	Manufacturing	Trade	Transport	Service
1860	11,110[b]	5,880	31	176	520	1,695	890	225	715
1870	12,930	6,790	28	180	780	2,683	1,310	295	1,170
1880	17,390	8,920	41	280	900	3,595	1,930	541	1,360
1890	23,320	9,960	60	440	1,510	4,701	2,960	870	1,930

Source: Stanley Lebergott, *Manpower in Economic Growth: The American Record since 1800* (New York: McGraw-Hill, 1964), table A-1, p. 510. Copyright © 1964 by McGraw-Hill Inc. Reprinted by permission of the publisher.

Note: Because labor market data were not collected in a consistent manner during the nineteenth century, the data for separate industries do not add up to the "Total Labor Force" figures. Moreover, separate sources of information were used to compile the data. Hence, while these figures are the best historical estimates available, they should be viewed as only rough approximations of orders of magnitude.

[a] "Persons Engaged" was the classification used during the early census counts. It includes employees, the self-employed, and unpaid family workers.

[b] Includes 2,340,000 slave workers.

coal and iron ore to the burgeoning manufacturing sectors of the economy. Mining and manufacturing created the demand for workers, and unskilled immigrants supplied the labor needed to meet the requirements of the expanding economy. At the same time, signs of discontent reappeared among nonimmigrant workers. The economic rules and conditions governing the transformation of the nation from an agricultural society into an industrially based manufacturing society were being shaped in large part by the forces of uncontrolled immigration. Citizen laborers resented the fact that they could only react to these forces.

The Era of Screening without a Numerical Ceiling: 1890–1921

From 1820 through 1890, 85 percent of the immigrants to the United States came from western and northern Europe. Beginning in the late 1880s and continuing through the pre–World War I era, however, the ethnic composition of America's immigrants shifted dramatically. As indicated in Table 5, countries of southern and eastern Europe became the dominant source countries—specifically, Austria-Hungary, Bulgaria, Greece, Italy, Poland, Portugal, Rumania, and Russia. During these years the number of French Canadian immigrants increased markedly, and limited immigration from Japan and mass immigration from Mexico began. The presence of these immigrants was accentuated not only by their large number but also by the parallel decline in the absolute number of persons emigrating from northern and western Europe. Numerically speaking, the third major influx of immigrants to the United States occurred between 1900 and 1914. Approximately thirteen million persons arrived during those years, and in 1905, 1906, 1907, 1910, 1913, and 1914, the yearly total exceeded one million.

The largest source of new immigrants was Italy. Due to extreme population pressures, the Italian government had initiated a policy of encouraging people to emigrate. It was the only major government of Europe to adopt such an official policy. Most of the Italians who left were from the economically depressed and severely impoverished regions of Sicily and southern Italy. Most came from rural, peasant backgrounds. In their local communities they were confronted with landlord tyranny, compulsory military service (two years for all young men), and often the prospect of unemployment and starvation. Nudged by their government, many Italians moved en masse to Argentina, Brazil, and Uruguay as well as to the United States. From 1890 to 1914, almost four million Italians emigrated to the United States.

The Slavic-speaking nations also were a substantial source of immigrants to the United States in the years prior to World War I. Among the groups that came were Slovaks, Croatians, Rumanians, Poles, Russians, Bulgarians, Serbs, and Dalmatians. It is estimated that 95 percent of these persons were peasants. Many were only a generation removed from family ties that had endured through

TABLE 5. THE FIVE COUNTRIES WITH THE HIGHEST NUMBER OF ADMISSIONS, RANK ORDERED, AND PERCENTAGE OF TOTAL ADMISSIONS, 1891–1920

Decade	Total Legal Immigrants	Ranking of Countries and Percentage of Admissions										Percentage of Total Admissions Accounted for by Five Highest-Ranked Countries
		First	%	Second	%	Third	%	Fourth	%	Fifth	%	
1891–1900	3,687,564	Italy	17.7	Austria-Hungary	16.1	Russia	13.7	Germany	13.7	Ireland	10.5	71.7
1901–1910	8,795,386	Austria-Hungary	24.4	Italy	23.3	Russia	18.2	United Kingdom	6.0	Germany	3.9	75.8
1911–1920	5,735,811	Italy	19.3	Russia	16.1	Canada	12.9	Austria	7.9	Hungary	7.7	63.9

Source: Select Commission on Immigration and Refugee Policy, *U.S. Immigration Policy and the National Interest: Staff Report* (supplement to the final report) (Washington, D.C.: GPO, 1981), pp. 230–31.

centuries of serfdom. Most were illiterate in their own language. Many were fleeing from oppression.

Among the oppressed groups were the Jews, who constituted a large portion of the immigrants from Poland, Russia, and Rumania during this period. Since the Middle Ages, many European Jews had immigrated to Poland because its kings were—relative to the views of the leaders of other European nations—the most tolerant and liberal in Europe. During the late eighteenth century, however, Poland was partitioned by Russia, Austria, and Prussia. Poland lost about 28 percent of its land to Russia. Many Polish Jews lived in this lost region. Following the ascension of Czar Alexander III to power in Russia in 1881, a policy of deliberate persecution of Polish Jews was launched. Jews were forbidden to move between provinces; they were required to serve in the military but could not be officers; and they were required to pay taxes but were denied the right to hold public office.

While new European immigrants settled in the northeastern and midwestern areas of the United States, Japanese immigrants settled in the western states. Japan itself had for many years resisted the inflow of foreigners. A policy of national seclusion was imposed in the early seventeenth century, and with only minor exceptions, this policy held sway until the 1840s and early 1850s. By then it was simply impossible to keep foreigners out and to isolate the country from the rest of the world. With the overthrow of the last of the feudal shoguns in 1868, Japan restored imperial rule, and the building of the modern Japanese industrial state commenced. During the rule of Emperor Mutsuhito (1868–1912), Japan entered into world affairs. In the 1880s, the struggling Japanese economy slipped into a recession that caused widespread economic distress and civil unrest, and a wave of severe government repressions followed. In 1884 these events forced the Japanese government to adopt the first policies permitting Japanese citizens to work in foreign nations. In that year, diplomatic relations between the United States and Japan were established for the first time. It was also the year in which the Hawaiian Sugar Planters Association initiated informal efforts to recruit Japanese workers.

Because Chinese immigrants had officially been refused entry to the United States in 1882, an ideal opportunity to secure the admission of unskilled Japanese workers presented itself. A meeting was held in 1886 between the Japanese government and Robert W. Irwin, an American businessman who was serving as the consul to Japan for the still-independent government of the Hawaiian Islands. A formal agreement, known as the Irwin Convention, was reached. Under its terms, the Islands' sugar growers (who were mostly American citizens) were permitted to hire Japanese farm workers.[34] The rapid increase in the number of Japanese workers that ensued spurred latent efforts on the part of the United States to take possession of the Islands. The revolutionary government of Hawaii, which was dominated by Americans, triggered an international incident in March 1897 when it refused to grant entry to 1,700 Japanese immigrants. A

little over a year later, on August 12, 1898, the United States unilaterally annex-
ed the Hawaiian Islands, and in 1900 it declared them a U.S. Territory.

Japan bitterly opposed these actions. By 1900, 40 percent of the population of
the Islands was Japanese, and these Japanese Hawaiians were among the large
number of Japanese immigrants who arrived in California at the turn of the
century.[35] As opposition to Japanese immigration intensified on the U.S. mainland, the Japanese government began to deny permission for workers to immigrate directly to the mainland United States. Immigration of workers directly to
Hawaii, however, was allowed to continue until 1905. These Japanese immigrants were overwhelmingly unskilled workers—most were peasants. When
they arrived on the U.S. mainland, they tended to settle in Southern California
and to seek work in the growing agricultural sector of that region. As their
numbers mounted, prejudice against them developed among the white population. The Hearst newspaper chain spewed forth a constant flow of articles on
"the yellow peril." Following Japan's victory over the Russian navy in 1905,
many Californians feared that the steady stream of mostly unskilled Japanese
immigrants might soon develop into a massive tide. The Congress of the United
States was initially indifferent to these concerns, however, and Californians
began to take action themselves. In October 1906 the San Francisco School
Board classified Japanese children as "orientals"—an offensive term to the
Japanese in particular and to all Asians in general—and required that all such
children be placed in racially segregated schools.[36]

Meanwhile, the California legislature adopted a resolution that urged Congress to stop all immigration from Japan. Similar steps were taken in the legislatures of Idaho, Nevada, and Montana. The Japanese government interpreted
these actions as an insult and lodged an official protest with the U.S. government. Because of the distinct possibility that the incident could provoke a war,
President Theodore Roosevelt intervened directly in the matter.[37] He recognized
that the source of contention was the prospect of continued Japanese immigration
to the United States, and he determined that it must be stopped. He began secret
negotiations with the Japanese government and in February 1907 also persuaded
the San Francisco School Board to rescind its earlier actions. That same month, a
face-saving solution for the government of Japan was proposed by U.S. Secretary of State Elihu Root. Root suggested, and the Japanese government agreed,
that as of February 24, 1907, the Japanese government itself would refuse to
issue passports to peasants or to other would-be workers. Only those who were
joining families already in the United States would be allowed to immigrate to
the United States. It was understood that, in return, the United States would not
enact against the Japanese the type of overt exclusionary legislation that had
earlier been directed at the Chinese. This understanding became known as the
Gentlemen's Agreement. Although it was to take effect at once, its details were
not formalized until February 1908. The agreement was not spelled out in a
single document. Rather, its text consists of a series of letters exchanged by the
two governments over a year's time. It lasted until April 1924, when, as will be

discussed later in this chapter, further debate on the subject of Japanese immigration culminated in statutory exclusion.

STATUTORY REACTION TO THE NEW PATTERN OF IMMIGRATION

With the growth in the number and new sources of immigrants to the United States, concerns soon arose over the effects these immigrants would have on U.S. society and the ability of the new groups to assimilate. Some of the worries were spawned by citizens' groups that expressed fears of adverse economic conditions. Among these groups were labor organizations, which at that time were fighting a desperate battle of survival in their quest to organize and maintain workers in unions. The American Federation of Labor (AFL), which had been founded in 1886, began in the early 1890s to favor a policy of opposition to uncontrolled immigration. By 1896 it had adopted formal resolutions favoring restrictions on immigration. The noted labor historian Philip Taft observed that "it was the adverse influence of the immigrant upon the labor market rather than opposition based on race or religion which accounts for the attitude of organized labor."[38] Samuel Gompers, the long-time and influential president of the AFL, became a strong critic of the process whereby large numbers of immigrants were moving in uncontrolled numbers into labor markets that he felt were already overstocked and where they competed with citizen workers for jobs. Gompers, who was a Jewish immigrant from England, and many other foreign-born labor leaders saw no contradiction between their own immigrant origins in the past and their advocacy of restrictions for the future. Many socialist labor leaders who were prominent in political affairs at the turn of the century echoed Gompers' position. Socialist leaders in Milwaukee, for instance, openly stated their belief that the solidarity of all workers in the world did not mean that they all had a right to assemble in Milwaukee.[39]

Other groups, however, argued that the new character of immigration did portend assimilation problems. Sociologists, anthropologists, economists, and social workers argued that many of the immigrants were feeble-minded and "inferior," and that they were diluting the strengths of the population.[40] They expressed the fear that the religious, ethnic, and linguistic differences of the immigrants would make it very difficult for them to meld with the established citizenry. There were, of course, nativist groups that did not try to camouflage their prejudices with scholarly trappings. They simply did not want the new groups as fellow countrymen. It was not long, of course, before opportunistic politicians were ready to exploit the issue.

The initial political effort to control the character of the flow of immigrants to the United States was Congress's call for the imposition of a literacy test in the native language of each immigrant nationality. Legislation to this effect passed both houses in 1895 but was vetoed by President Grover Cleveland. In 1906 the issue was revived in the form of a bill that would require literacy in one's own language as a condition of entry as an immigrant and proficiency in English as a condition for naturalization. Supporters of the bill were unable to pass the literacy test for either entry or naturalization, but they succeeded in making proficiency in English a condition for naturalization.

There were, however, political risks in any effort to address the immigration issue directly. Archconservative Republican Joseph Cannon from rural Illinois became the powerful Speaker of the House of Representatives in 1902. He feared that the immigration issue might split the Republican party, which had dominated the American political scene since the Civil War era.[41] He was virtually in total control of the House until 1910, when his power to determine what matters would be discussed by that body was finally checked. From 1902 to 1910 Cannon kept the immigration issue from being fully debated. His assessment of the issue was shared by President Theodore Roosevelt. Roosevelt feared the possible divisive effects the immigration issue could have on his party, which drew its strength from northern and western states. In addition, he was, in 1907 and 1908, engaged in the previously mentioned secret and delicate negotiations with Japan over immigration. He believed that these talks would collapse if immigration legislation surfaced at that time for general debate.

Hence, when a proposal to enact a literacy test was reintroduced in Congress in 1906, Roosevelt joined other opponents in the drive to block the move. Instead, he supported the proposal that a full-scale investigation be made into the entire immigration issue. Many Republican leaders felt that this would be an effective means of burying the issue, as it had been in 1891 and 1892.

THE DILLINGHAM COMMISSION

President Roosevelt proposed that the normal congressional investigative procedure be set aside in this instance. He called for the appointment of a commission of experts that he would select. A compromise was eventually struck whereby the commission would be composed of nine members—three members from the Senate, three from the House of Representatives, and three experts appointed by the president. The plan immediately gained the support of many nongovernment groups and politicians who envisioned that this arrangement would ensure a scientific investigation. In February 1907, legislation establishing the Immigration Commission was enacted. Senator William Dillingham, a Republican from Vermont, was chosen to chair the commission.

The American public developed high expectations that the commission would produce a body of verifiable facts about which there could be no debate and upon which immigration reform legislation could be based. The presence of experts on the commission, the fact that it took the commission three years to complete its work, and the commitment of one million dollars and over 300 staff members to the project all served to enhance the public's belief that a thorough and impartial study was in progress. The commission added to this perception by producing forty-two volumes of reports on a wide variety of topics. Its investigation has been described as "one of the most ambitious social science research projects in the nation's history up to then, barring only the censuses."[42]

The Dillingham commission found that the new immigrants differed significantly from the nation's older immigrants. It deemed the new immigrants to be "inferior" and to possess attributes that would make it difficult for them to assimilate. It argued that a slower rate of expansion—a rate that emphasized the ability of immigrants to adapt to their new surroundings—would be preferable to a rapid and uncontrolled rate, which imperiled the prevailing wages and employment opportunities of American citizens. Laced throughout the commission's argument were pseudoscientific theories pertaining to "superior" and "inferior" persons. The mixture of economic and ethnic arguments in the commission's report has plagued all efforts to discuss and to legislate immigration reform impartially since that time.

As later reviews of the Dillingham commission's work were to show, "the Commission's report was neither impartial nor scientific."[43] The public's confidence was not justified. The commission held no public hearings; witnesses were not cross-examined; much of the original research work was not completed until after the final report was issued, which means that these findings were not available to the commissioners when they were making their recommendations; and many of the commission's key professional staff members were persons who had previously expressed support for reductions in the number of immigrants admitted and for restrictions based on race and ethnic group. In its final report the commission expressed as an initial premise the main fact that it sought to prove: that the immigrants of 1890–1911 were significantly different from those who had come before.[44] It asserted that the pre-1890 immigrants had assimilated easily and that the more recent arrivals had not. No mention was made, however, of the length of time the various immigrant groups had lived in the United States. Thus, this faulty comparison of groups that had arrived recently with groups that had come generations before indicated that the newer arrivals were having greater difficulty assimilating. The commission also claimed that the newer immigrants were less skilled than the older immigrants. Its data, however, showed that the great preponderance of the older immigrants also were unskilled workers who, like the new immigrants, had had very little previous experience in manufacturing or mining. Nonetheless, the commission blamed the new immigrants for depressing wages, causing unemployment, and hampering the development of trade unionism in America.

The Dillingham commission also compiled a "Dictionary of Races," in which it assigned various attributes to different ethnic groups. It then linked these generalizations with other data on bodily forms to suggest that the new immigrants were racially inferior to immigrants from western and northern Europe.

Thus, the opportunity to conduct an objective study of immigration was lost. The Dillingham commission began with preconceived ideas. Unable to present evidence to support its assertions, it twisted the data it did accumulate to support its original premise. As a result, Oscar Handlin has observed, its conclusions "offered an unsound basis for the legislation that followed."[45]

Following release of the report, efforts were made to implement some of its proposed restrictions. In 1912 Congress again passed a bill requiring a literacy test for immigrants but President William Taft vetoed it. A similar bill was passed in 1915 but it was vetoed by President Woodrow Wilson. Nonetheless, with the outbreak of World War I, the findings of the Dillingham commission were used to help win passage of the Immigration Act of 1917.[46] This legislation was the capstone of an "Americanization" campaign that had swept across the country in 1915 and 1916; fear of the impending war had generated a grass-roots movement to unify the country. The act, which was passed over the veto of President Wilson, required all immigrants over the age of sixteen to pass a literacy test. It also established an "Asiatic Barred Zone," which essentially banned all immigration from Asia. Technically speaking, however, the ban did not apply to immigration from Japan, which had already been covered by the Gentlemen's Agreement. The Immigration Act of 1917 codified the denial of entry to the classes of persons previously excluded and added a number of new groups. The act also provided for the admission of temporary workers who might otherwise be excluded by these restrictions if the secretary of labor deemed it to be necessary. This provision for the admission of nonimmigrant workers was used on numerous occasions over the next thirty-five years.

Thus the Immigration Act of 1917 was designed to control the type of person who immigrated to the United States. The issue of the number of immigrants to be admitted was not specifically addressed. Immigration from Europe had fallen off precipitously and the admission of immigrants from Asia had been banned. Elsewhere, however, violence precipitated events that would add to the flow of immigrants to the United States for the next sixty years. Namely, in 1911 a violent civil war broke out in Mexico, and the fighting continued for ten years. As a result, a quarter of a million Mexicans immigrated to the United States legally in that decade. Their ranks were swollen, however, by hundreds of thousands of other Mexicans who entered illegally over the largely unpatrolled southwestern U.S. border. These Mexicans fled the violence of their homeland, but they were also attracted by the expansion of job opportunities within the rapidly industrializing U.S. Southwest. They formed the numerical foundation for the present-day Mexican-American population. They also marked the beginning of the process of institutionalization of the flow of legal and illegal immigrants from Mexico that has continued to this day.

ENFORCEMENT: THE CONSOLIDATION OF RESPONSIBILITIES

From 1891 until 1903 the Bureau of Immigration of the U.S. Department of the Treasury remained in charge of enforcing the nation's immigration statutes. During these years the bureau's duties were expanded to include inspection of potential immigrants for communicable diseases at foreign ports. The bureau lacked the authority to stop persons from boarding ships, but it informed the shipping companies that certain people were not likely to be admitted and that, if refused, these persons would have to be returned to their home countries at the companies' expense. The Bureau of Immigration also found itself involved in processing the paperwork on the many immigrants who entered the country during these years. Finally, it warned of the need to encourage the dispersal of the immigrants, who had generally settled in the urban centers of the Northeast.

In 1903 the U.S. Department of Commerce and Labor was established and the Bureau of Immigration was transferred to it. The commissioner of immigration, who headed the bureau, was granted authority over all immigration matters. During the next several years, he reiterated his views that the agency lacked sufficient means to enforce the existing immigration statutes, repeated the agency's earlier recommendation concerning the need to disperse the growing concentration of immigrants in New York and Pennsylvania, and warned that illegal immigration from Mexico was becoming a serious problem.[47] He also indicated that fraud and carelessness were causing serious problems in the naturalization process. As a result, immigration and naturalization functions (which were still being handled by state courts) were consolidated by Congress at the federal level.[48] The Bureau of Immigration and Naturalization (BIN) was created in 1906. The power to grant naturalization remained with the courts, but uniform naturalization requirements were established throughout the nation, including the requirement that records of these proceedings be submitted to the bureau.

In March 1914 the BIN was shifted to the newly established U.S. Department of Labor. Here the previously combined immigration and naturalization functions were assigned to two separate sections, the Bureau of Immigration and the Bureau of Naturalization. Each bureau had its own commissioner.

During the period when the Dillingham commission's findings were being debated, the Bureau of Immigration also expressed concern in its annual reports about the origins of the new immigrants.[49] It repeatedly issued warnings about the ability of the nation to assimilate these new nationalities. The bureau argued that assimilation would be enhanced only if immigrants could be persuaded to move away from the areas of their heaviest concentration—namely the cities of the Northeast. A number of southern states, in fact, had expressed interest in finding ways to entice immigrants to settle in the South.[50] The bureau also repeatedly indicated the need for greater funding to enable it to carry out its enforcement duties adequately. The administrative demands on the agency became even more extensive following passage of the Immigration Act of 1917.

When immigration from Europe declined sharply during World War I (1915–1918), immigration enforcement procedures also changed. In response to the growing fear of spies and saboteurs, inspection of all persons entering the United States was stepped up. Beginning in 1917, a system of passport controls for all entrants was established. It was discontinued in 1919, but its feasibility had been established. The Bureau of Immigration sought unsuccessfully to continue the program.

LABOR MARKET EFFECTS

Between 1890 and 1920 the labor market of the United States was rapidly transformed. The decline in farm employment continued in both absolute and relative terms. Conversely, nonfarm employment increased dramatically in both respects. Table 6 indicates the magnitude of these aggregate changes. Table 7 summarizes the differences in the various industrial employment patterns within the nonfarm sector. Clearly, during this era manufacturing emerged as the dominant sector of the American economy. In 1920, employment in manufacturing exceeded employment in agriculture for the first time in the nation's history. This growth was spurred by the development of numerous new industries—for example, automobile manufacturing and its complementary industries, rubber and petroleum production. The growth of these new industries also placed extensive new demands on the steel and mining industries.

The overwhelming need of the manufacturing and mining industries was for unskilled blue-collar workers, and it was precisely these types of jobs that the multitudes of immigrants of this era sought.[51] The north-central states in particular became the meeting place of the job-providers and the job-seekers. Despite the fact that productivity in manufacturing and mining increased significantly, real wage improvements were not substantial. Money wages rose only slightly more rapidly than prices. According to the economist Stanley Lebergott, "The data [on employment, earnings, and productivity] do suggest that heavy increases in the flow of immigrants tended to depress wage increases despite rising real factor productivity."[52]

The effects of immigrants on wages and employment are measured in several ways. Throughout this period the foreign-born population constituted a larger portion of the labor force than of the total population.[53] This difference can be attributed to two facts: the immigrant population consisted disproportionately of working-age persons with relatively few children, and the number of men greatly exceeded that of women.[54] Moreover, immigrants were highly concentrated with respect to their occupations and their geographic location. In 1910, for instance, immigrants accounted for over half of all operatives in mining and in apparel work; over half of all laborers in steel manufacturing, bituminous coal mining, meat packing, and cotton textile milling; over half of all bakers; and about 80 percent of all tailors in the United States.[55] In such large cities as Buffalo,

TABLE 6.   CIVILIAN LABOR FORCE DATA FOR 1900, 1910, AND 1920 (in thousands)

Year	Civilian Labor Force (14 years of age and older)	Type of Employment		Unemployed
		Farm	Nonfarm	
1890[a]	23,320	—	—	—
1900	28,376	11,050	15,906	1,420
1910	36,709	11,260	23,299	2,150
1920	41,340	10,440	28,768	2,132

Source: Stanley Lebergott, *Manpower in Economic Growth: The American Record since 1800* (New York: McGraw-Hill, 1964), table A-3, p. 512. Copyright © 1964 by McGraw-Hill Inc. Reprinted by permission of the publisher.

[a]Data for 1890 are not comparable to figures for succeeding decades. The labor force figure for 1890 is presented solely for the purpose of making a rough comparison. For details for 1890, see Table 4.

TABLE 7. EMPLOYEES IN NONFARM ESTABLISHMENTS, BY INDUSTRY, 1900, 1910, AND 1920 (in thousands)

Year	Total Nonfarm Employees (14 years of age and older)[a]	Nonfarm Employees, by Industry							
		Mining	Construction	Manufacturing	Transport and Utilities	Trade	Finance	Service	Government (Civilian Employees)
1900	15,178	637	1,147	5,468	2,282	2,502	308	1,740	1,094
1910	21,697	1,068	1,342	7,828	3,366	3,570	483	2,410	1,630
1920	27,434	1,180	850	10,702	4,317	4,012	902	3,100	2,371

Source: Stanley Lebergott, *Manpower in Economic Growth: The American Record since 1800* (New York: McGraw-Hill, 1964), table A-5, p. 514. Copyright © 1964 by McGraw-Hill Inc. Reprinted by permission of the publisher.

[a]Totals for nonfarm employment differ slightly in this table from those cited in Table 6 because slightly different definitions were used in the respective data sources on which these tables are based.

Chicago, Detroit, Milwaukee, Minneapolis, New York, Portland, and San Francisco, foreign-born men constituted a majority of the male labor force throughout much of this period.[56] Thus, there can be no question that immigrants were determining conditions of supply that prevailed in these micro labor markets.

The entry of the United States into World War I in 1917 led to an unprecedented expansion of the production capabilities of the manufacturing sector of the nation's economy. Much of the military output was never actually used in the war, but the build-up served to demonstrate that high levels of production were attainable—especially when aided by extensive planning. With four million men in uniform and the supply of European immigrants cut off, the United States had to locate new sources of labor. The answers proved to be increased immigration from Canada and Mexico and the tapping of surplus labor pools within the nation.

The Era of Numerical Limits with Ethnic Screening, 1921–1965

THE IMPOSITION OF QUOTAS

The movement within the United States to impose a ceiling on immigration had begun before World War I. The sharp reductions in immigration from Europe, along with the bans on immigration from Asia, had temporarily reduced the momentum of these forces. But with the end of the fighting and amid reports from American consular offices that literally millions of persons from the war-ravaged areas of Europe were planning to immigrate to the United States, the move to restrict immigration was quickly revived. The number of immigrants admitted to the United States in 1919 was 141,132, but by 1921 it had climbed to 805,228. It appeared to many that a new wave of immigration was about to commence and that it might equal or exceed the high rates of the pre-1914 era.

As already mentioned, the initial moves to restrict immigration centered on the use of literacy tests. The incorporation of these tests into the Immigration Act of 1917, however, did not prove to be effective. In other words, they did not reduce the growth in the flow of immigrants from southern and eastern Europe in the immediate postwar years, in part because it was possible to prepare people to pass such tests. In Italy, for instance, in regions where the rate of emigration was high, special schools were established specifically to teach peasants the basic fundamentals needed to pass the tests.

Consequently, a drive was launched to restrict immigration numerically. It had broad-based support. The American Federation of Labor (AFL) concluded that immigrants impeded efforts to organize workers and that their presence tended to depress wages.[57] Many sociologists and anthropologists, whose views had earlier lent credibility to the Dillingham commission's report, argued that uncontrolled immigration would create insoluble social problems in the nation's urban centers.[58] Protestant church leaders reiterated their concern that Catholics,

Jews, and the various Eastern Orthodox churches were threatening to undermine the basic Protestant character of the nation. Even business leaders joined in the chorus, expressing the fear that the ranks of the East European immigrants had been infiltrated by Communists. For example, steel industry leaders contended that in the great steel strike of 1919, strikers had been led and influenced by radical immigrant elements.[59] In addition, a number of extremist groups such as the Ku Klux Klan campaigned against the renewal of virtually unrestricted immigration for fear it would allow more Catholics and Jews into the nation. In all fairness, however, the political tide behind immigration reform was so strong that it did not need the help of extremist groups to set the cadence.

In late 1920 the House of Representatives hastily passed a bill calling for the suspension of all immigration into the United States for one year. In an alternative move, the Senate passed a bill calling for the imposition of an annual ceiling on immigration from Europe and seeking to give preference to some ethnic groups and to discriminate against others. The Senate bill was adopted at the end of the congressional session but was given a pocket veto by President Wilson. In the meantime, a new president, Warren Harding, had been elected to take office in March 1921. He had fewer reservations about the issue. Following an emergency special session in the spring of 1921, a bill based on the earlier Senate proposals was passed and in May 1921 President Harding signed into law the Immigration Act of 1921.[60] With this legislation a new era in American immigration policy was inaugurated. It set the first immigration quotas in the nation's history. The law specified that no more than 3 percent of the foreign-born population of each nationality of the Eastern Hemisphere residing in the United States in 1910 could be admitted in any given year. Thus, an annual ceiling of about 358,000 immigrants was instituted. In addition, however, the law specified that about 200,000 of these slots were to be given to immigrants from northern and western European nations, while about 155,000 were to be assigned to southern and eastern European nations. The few thousand slots that remained were to be divided among the nations of Africa and Asia that had not previously been barred. The job of actually setting the individual country quotas was assigned to the secretaries of state, commerce, and labor. It was a very complicated task, for nine new European nations and Asiatic Turkey were created after World War I, and the prewar boundaries of thirteen other nations were changed. The act did not impose any quotas at all on immigration from nations in the Western Hemisphere. The law was viewed as a stopgap measure that would expire in June 1922. It was, however, extended by joint resolution of Congress until 1924. The historical significance of the Immigration Act of 1921 was that it marked the beginning of restrictions on immigration to the United States from Europe, Africa, and Australia.

Even though immigration from Europe dropped sharply after 1921, the political momentum for a permanent U.S. policy on immigration continued unabated. This drive culminated in passage of the Immigration Act of 1924—sometimes called the Johnson-Reed Act, but more popularly known as the National Origins Act.[61] It incorporated the principles enunciated in the Immigration Act of 1921 but was far more restrictive in its quantitative and qualitative aspects. A brief transition period, 1924–1927 (later extended to 1929), was set aside to work out all the details associated with establishing quotas. Annual quotas during this interim were set at 2 percent of each nationality that had resided in the country in 1890. Numerically, this translated into a ceiling of about 164,000 immigrants a year from the Eastern Hemisphere. Exact country quotas were to be specified by the three previously mentioned Cabinet secretaries. It is important to note that no quotas were applied to the Western Hemisphere. The shift from the 1910 census to the 1890 census as the basis for issuing visas meant, for example, that the general quota for Italy declined from 42,000 to 4,000 persons; for Poland, from 31,000 to 6,000; and for Greece from 3,000 to 100.[62]

It took five years to work out the exact methodology for setting quotas. Use of the 1890 census was roundly criticized as being blatantly discriminatory against those nationalities which had immigrated in large numbers after that date. The 1910 census, on the other hand, was criticized as being discriminatory against the nationalities from northern and western Europe, which had dominated the earlier settlement stages. Thus, the quotas that were finally put in place in 1929 represented a different methodology. They were based on the national origins of both the native-born and the foreign-born population as enumerated in the 1920 census. Each country was assigned a precise quota, and that number represented the same proportion of the total quota for all nations (set originally at 150,000 quota immigrants) as the proportion of people who, by birth or descent, represented that nationality in the total population of the United States in 1920. The only exception to this formula was that each nationality was assured a minimum quota of 100. As a result the actual ceiling on immigration became 154,277 persons.

The effect of the new system was not new, however, for the methodology favored the nations of northern and western Europe, the regions with the highest rates of emigration to the United States prior to 1890. Moreover, the calculations totally excluded the descendants of slaves, of Native Americans, and of most Asian groups (who were ineligible for citizenship at the time). In other words, the base that was used in establishing quotas was essentially the white population of European ancestry. As a result of this numerical contortion, northern and western European countries received 82 percent of the total world quota, and southern and eastern European countries received 14 percent of the quota. The small remainder (4 percent) was assigned to the rest of the world. Great Britain alone received 65,000 of the authorized quota visas. Accurate statistics as to nationality were not available from the early censuses or from colonial records, and thus the list of names that was used to set the quotas was compiled haphazardly. The entire process was scientifically "indefensible."[63] Nevertheless, with only slight modifications, these quotas served as the basis of legal immigration until 1965.

Although some critics complained that the new immigration policy should have been addressed to Western Hemisphere nations as well, it was not. In part, this decision reflected the fact that immigration from nations of the Western Hemisphere had not yet become significant. In addition, a number of procedural barriers prevented their inclusion. For example, at that time it would have been futile to try to restrict entry across the United States' extensive land borders with Canada and Mexico. Moreover, the base population that was needed to calculate the national origins and thus the quotas for Central and South American countries was inadequate. Officials also feared that the restrictive provisions of the existing statutes would damage U.S. relations with these neighboring states. Thus, no quotas were applied to the Western Hemisphere until 1965. Individual immigrants from this region were, however, subject to all the general qualifications and personal exclusions of the prevailing immigration statutes.

The Immigration Act of 1924 is also unofficially known as the Japanese Exclusion Act. Since 1907, immigration from Japan had been banned under the terms of the Gentlemen's Agreement. This diplomatic agreement had sharply reduced Japanese immigration but had not stopped it. Many persons of Japanese ancestry continued to migrate from Hawaii to the U.S. mainland. As a result, along the West Coast, agitation for total exclusion continued. During the congressional session of 1923, officials of the American Federation of Labor and the American Legion joined with a number of California groups in a drive to achieve statutory exclusion. The year before, the U.S. Supreme Court had ruled that persons of Japanese ancestry were ineligible for citizenship through naturalization.[64] Responding to warnings from the Japanese government, Secretary of State Charles Evans Hughes argued that Japan should be assigned a token quota of about 250 immigrants a year. Congress, however, responded with a bill that forbade the immigration of persons who were "ineligible for citizenship." Although not named specifically, Japan was understood to be the target of this legislation. The Gentlemen's Agreement was abrogated. When he signed the Immigration Act of 1924, President Calvin Coolidge indicated his opposition to the specific exclusion of the Japanese, stating that if the issue had been submitted to him apart from the entire act, he would have vetoed it.[65] The action was received bitterly in Japan, which felt humiliated. The day the new law took effect was declared a day of national mourning in Japan. The Japanese exclusion provisions were not repealed until 1952.

The Issue of Family Reunification. Following the imposition of immigration quotas in 1921, a new issue developed and it has continued to dominate U.S. immigration policy to this day. That issue is family reunification. The separate quotas for each country—some of which were very low—meant that close relatives could be separated for long periods of time. Long waiting lists of relatives developed. As a result, the Immigration Act of 1924 exempted wives and children (husbands were not exempted until 1952) from the numerical quotas. They became nonquota immigrants. Thus, the number of persons admitted each year from a given country was and is much higher than the quota limitation specified by law.

Subsequent immigration laws continued to give preference to would-be legal immigrants on the basis of their having close relatives who were already U.S. citizens, but the fact that the United States was "a nation of immigrants" meant that other, political, means of circumventing the quota restrictions had to be found for the relatives of those who had entered in earlier years.

The Screening Process.   The Immigration Act of 1924 introduced a screening process that has continued relatively unchanged ever since. For the first time the process of screening people before they embarked from their native land became a feature of the U.S. immigration system. The 1924 law mandated that all foreign persons planning to enter the United States for whatever reason must procure a visa in advance of their departure. Decisions concerning the issuance or denial of visas were and are made by consular officials of the U.S. Department of State who are assigned to the American embassies located in the homelands of would-be immigrants, and these consular decisions cannot be appealed.

The next step in the screening process occurs at the port of entry in the United States. Here immigration officials make a decision as to the admissibility of the visa-bearer. Only on rare occasions is a person with a legitimate visa denied admission. On the other hand, the overwhelming majority of the persons who are refused admission have previously been denied a visa.

The Immigration Act of 1924 also established three categories of foreign persons who seek to enter the United States: quota immigrants, nonquota immigrants, and nonimmigrants. These descriptive terms were altered in 1952, but the three distinctive categories they define have remained in effect ever since. Quota immigrants are those persons who are admitted as permanent residents under the terms of the prevailing immigration statutes. They may ultimately become naturalized citizens. Nonquota immigrants are the spouses and unmarried children (under the age of eighteen) of those persons who are admitted as quota immigrants. They, too, may ultimately become naturalized citizens. Nonimmigrants are persons who enter the United States temporarily—tourists, businessmen, visitors, students, crewmen, ambassadors, as well as a special group known as temporary workers. No expectation of citizenship is associated with the nonimmigrant category.

Enforcement Issues in the 1920s.   Efforts to enforce the complex restrictions of the quota statutes placed tremendous strain on the administrative capacity of the Bureau of Immigration. The bureau consistently pleaded for more staff and resources. Many of its problems pertained to the need to respond to the numerous inquiries that were made concerning individual circumstances. Because quotas applied to the national origins of people rather than to their country of birth, it was often difficult to decide which nation's quota applied in a given case. In addition, the bureau was responsible for processing the 4.1 million legal immigrants who were admitted during the decade, for keeping track of the hundreds of thousands of persons who entered the country as nonimmigrants, and for processing the mounting number of requests for unskilled temporary labor that came from would-be employers.[66]

An event of lasting consequence that occurred during this era was the establishment of the U.S. Border Patrol in 1924. A small mounted patrol had been in operation along the southwestern border since 1904, but it was hardly more than a token effort, for never had more than seventy-five men been assigned to cover the 1,945-mile border between Mexico and the United States. The original rationale for establishing the Border Patrol was not worry about illegal immigration from Mexico. Rather, it was concern for the illegal entry of Chinese workers through Mexico in defiance of the Chinese Exclusion Act.[67] The prevailing view of most employers in the Southwest at the turn of the century was that the Mexicans who entered the United States illegally usually returned home (i.e., went back to Mexico) after working for brief periods in the United States.[68] This perception was dispelled, however, by the mass migration that resulted from the Mexican Revolution (1911–1917). Chaos and virtual anarchy prevailed in Mexico in the years immediately following the end of the fighting, and the mass migration of Mexicans as both legal and illegal immigrants continued throughout most of the following decade. In addition, many Europeans who had been precluded from legal entry by the new quotas or who faced long delays before they would be admitted were entering the country illegally along the vast U.S.-Mexican and U.S.-Canadian borders. It was in this context that the need to establish more than an ad hoc patrolling arrangement was addressed.

In May 1924, in response to reports by immigration officials that border-crossing violations were mounting, Congress passed legislation authorizing creation of the U.S. Border Patrol as an operational branch of the Bureau of Immigration.[69] The bureau had requested a force of at least 500 men, but the congressional appropriation was sufficient to fund a force of only 450 officers. Most of those who were originally appointed were selected from a roster of applicants for positions as railway postal clerks.[70] By 1930, the size of the force had nearly doubled.

The duties of the Border Patrol have remained the same since its founding. They include monitoring the border areas for illegal immigrants, apprehending illegal immigrants, and escorting illegal immigrants out of the country. Most of the resources of the Border Patrol have traditionally been assigned to the nation's southwestern border, but the patrol is also responsible for the U.S.-Canadian border.

In 1929 Congress passed legislation allowing for the voluntary registration of aliens who wished to legalize their unrecorded entry.[71] In a sense, this law extended amnesty to those who had previously entered illegally. In that same year, however, Congress also passed a law that made entry without inspection an offense subject to criminal penalties.[72]

Labor Market Effects.   The imposition of immigration ceilings in the 1920s seemingly presented the nation with a new challenge: how to meet its unskilled labor force needs in the absence of large infusions of immigrant workers. This concern proved to be a nonproblem, however, for despite the fact that the 1920s were marked by substantial structural changes in the labor market, the imposition of immigration ceilings was not a key cause of these changes. Contrary to most expectations, the rate of immigration continued to be high throughout the decade. The explanation for this apparent anomaly is fairly simple. First of all, the ceiling on European immigration—154,277 persons—did not go into effect until 1929 due to difficulties in assigning the original country quotas. Secondly, the curtailment of immigration from Europe and Asia did not affect immigration from nations in the Western Hemisphere. As shown in Table 8, Canada and Mexico emerged as the major sources of legal immigrants in the 1920s. Together they accounted for one-third of the legal immigrants who entered during that period. Moreover, both nations consistently ranked among the top five sources of immigrants to the United States during every decade through the 1960s. Thirdly, illegal immigration from Canada and Mexico as well as from Europe and Asia by way of these two nations was substantial throughout the decade. The total immigrant flows, therefore, significantly exceeded the high official immigration figures. Over four million legal immigrants entered the United States, as did hundreds of thousands (perhaps millions) of illegal immigrants. These figures are among the highest in the nation's history.

With regard to the U.S. labor market in the 1920s, the most important change that occurred was the rapid urbanization of the nation's population. The mass movement of the population from rural to urban American between 1920 and 1930 was, as the historian Arthur Link observed, "the most important internal demographic change of the decade."[73] During that period, six million persons moved from the rural sector to its urban sector, and the rural population of the nation sustained a net loss over the decade—the first net decline in U.S. history—of 1.2 million persons. Link called this movement "one of the most important changes in the American social fabric."[74]

The cause of this internal population shift was the simultaneous existence of strong push and pull factors. In this case the push factor was the collapse of agricultural prices—especially for crops raised in the prairie states and in the South—throughout the 1920s. The depression that was to hit the nation in the 1930s had begun a decade earlier in these agricultural regions.[75] Most of the new migrants from the rural areas were white, but they included a substantial number of blacks as well. The pull factor that attracted the rural workers was the sharp increase in real wages that occurred in these urban industrial centers.[76] In what was described as "the largest decennial increase up to that time," the annual gain in nonagricultural real wages tripled over the decade.[77] Underlying the unparalleled prosperity of the urban industrial sector was the technological revolution, which was reshaping industrial production techniques. Assembly-line production spread, and the extensive investment in research and development that had been made for the first time by many corporations during World War I began to produce results. As a consequence of these developments, productivity in manufacturing—the nation's largest employment sector—increased by 40 percent in the 1920s.

Stanley Lebergott has suggested that the restrictions placed on immigration in

TABLE 8. THE FIVE COUNTRIES WITH THE HIGHEST NUMBER OF ADMISSIONS, RANK ORDERED, AND PERCENTAGE OF TOTAL ADMISSIONS, 1921–1970

Decade	Total Legal Immigrants	Ranking of Countries and Percentage of Admissions										Percentage of Total Admissions Accounted for by Five Highest-Ranked Countries
		First	%	Second	%	Third	%	Fourth	%	Fifth	%	
1921–1930	4,107,209	Canada	22.5	Mexico	11.2	Italy	11.1	Germany	10.0	United Kingdom	8.0	62.8
1931–1940	528,431	Germany	21.6	Canada	20.5	Italy	12.9	United Kingdom	5.6	Mexico	4.2	64.8
1941–1950	1,035,039	Germany	21.9	Canada	16.6	United Kingdom	12.7	Mexico	5.9	Italy	5.6	62.7
1951–1960	2,515,479	Germany	19.0	Canada	15.0	Mexico	11.9	United Kingdom	7.8	Italy	7.4	61.1
1961–1970	3,321,677	Mexico	13.3	Canada	8.6	Cuba	8.6*	United Kingdom	6.9	Italy	6.2	42.7

Source: Select Commission on Immigration and Refugee Policy, *U.S. Immigration Policy and the National Interest: Staff Report* (supplement to the final report) (Washington, D.C.: GPO, 1981), pp. 230–31.

the 1920s contributed significantly to the real wage improvements that occurred in that decade. As he has argued:

> It [is] most unlikely that the rate of productivity advance or the nature of the productivity advance changed so at this point [in the 1920s] as to explain this turn [the spurt in real wage increases]. Instead we find that halting the flow of millions of migrants who entered the United States labor market with low wage horizons offers a much more reasonable explanation for the speed up in real wage advance. Political changes in labor supply can be more effective in determining wages than even explicit attempts to fix wages.[78]

It is Lebergott's belief that the "shortened supply" of labor rather than autonomous changes in capital productivity led to an increase in real wages during this period. Yet the premise for his conclusion is false. As has already been shown, immigration was substantial throughout the 1920s. Moreover, Lebergott's contention that "the nature of the productivity advances" did not change significantly in this period is incorrect as well, for it was during these years that the continuous-process technique of production spread throughout the nation's manufacturing sector. As Walter Buckingham has written:

> Essential to the mass production system was implementation of the concept of continuous flow or process. Mass production technology is often referred to as a second stage in the industrial revolution. . . . The unique feature of mass production technology is that it permits an enormous increase in productivity, or output per man hour, not through the use of any new machines or the development of any new power source as did mechanization, but mainly through a new system of organizing the production process itself.[79]

Thus the technological changes that took place in the twenties were largely the products of a revolution in industrial organization which spawned its own demand for capital formation. As for the timing of these changes, it is true that the assembly line was introduced shortly before World War I, but it was "between the world wars [that] the assembly line spread to a host of industries while the automobile industry, where it was used first and most effectively, mushroomed into one of the largest industries in the world."[80] The increase in capital formation during this period enhanced not only the capacity to produce but also the capacity to consume, by disbursing income into the hands of consumers. It is for this reason that "the decade of the 1920s has become known as the 'prosperity decade.'"[81]

As a result of these technological changes, output in manufacturing soared throughout the 1920s, while employment in manufacturing remained virtually constant (see Table 9). Thus, in the nation's largest single employment sector there was no net increase in employment over the entire decade. Given the technological developments of this era, there was little need for large numbers of new workers. During the 1920s, second-generation workers from the families of the immigrants of the 1890–1914 period entered the labor force, but many did not follow their parents into the same jobs. Instead, they moved into a wider

TABLE 9. EMPLOYEES IN THE MANUFACTURING SECTOR
IN THE UNITED STATES, 1919–1929 (in thousands)

Year	Number of Employees	Year	Number of Employees
1919	10,702	1925	9,942
1920	10,702	1926	10,156
1921	8,262	1927	9,996
1922	9,129	1928	9,942
1923	10,317	1929	10,702
1924	9,675		

Source: Stanley Lebergott, *Manpower in Economic Growth: The American Record since 1800* (New York: McGraw-Hill, 1964), table A-5, p. 514. Copyright © 1964 by McGraw-Hill Inc. Reprinted by permission of the publisher.

array of industries and occupations.[82] This limited upward movement opened up some opportunitites at the bottom of the labor force for the migrants from rural America and for some of the nation's new immigrants. These workers moved into industrial jobs that became available through normal attrition and the rise and fall of selected individual manufacturers during the decade. Among the new industries that emerged in the 1920s were manufacturers of electrical appliances, electrical machinery, aviation equipment, and radios.

The most important group to respond to the relative prosperity of the Northeast and Midwest was the nation's black population. As late as 1910, over 91 percent of the black population lived below the Mason-Dixon line. This was approximately the same percentage of blacks as lived in the South on the eve of the Civil War. Moreover, of the 9.8 million blacks in the population in 1910, 6.9 million lived in rural areas (almost exclusively in the South). During the decade 1910–1920, there was a net out-migration from the South of 454,000 blacks; during the years 1920–1930, the net out-migration increased to 749,000 blacks. This mass migration of blacks was a classic example of the push-and-pull relationship. One of the push factors was the collapse of the cotton culture of the rural South following the devastation of the cotton crop by the boll weevil. The boll weevil had spread into the United States from Mexico in the 1890s, and over the next two decades conditions in the cotton industry deteriorated. In 1921 the boll weevil destroyed 30 percent of the region's cotton crop. Thus, planters were forced to diversify their crops, but the prices for these crops generally remained depressed throughout the period. As a result, many blacks were forced to leave the South and seek jobs elsewhere.

The second push factor during the years 1890–1920 was passage of the Jim Crow laws, which required segregation by race. In addition to imposing secondary status upon blacks, these laws created a climate of fear and intimidation. In 1915 the Ku Klux Klan was reorganized, and by 1919 it was flourishing throughout the South.

The primary pull factor was the aforementioned rise in real wages in the nonagricultural industries of the northeastern and midwestern regions of the country. Blacks joined in the migration of rural workers to these sectors of the economy. Many writers have pondered why the blacks waited so long after the Civil War to begin their exodus.[83] An examination of the unique confluence of push-and-pull events that occurred between 1915 and 1929, however, reveals that the mass movement could not have begun before that period. Moreover, the significance of the exodus lay not in its size (it was numerically small compared to the out-migration of rural whites) but rather in the fact that the departure of blacks from the rural South had finally begun.

Thus, in the urban areas of the Northeast and Midwest, rural migrants—black and white—competed with European and Canadian immigrants for available jobs. Table 10 indicates the nonfarm employment patterns of the 1920s and later decades.

The large number of Mexicans who immigrated to the United States during the 1920s settled largely in the border regions of the four southwestern states and sought work in the urban and rural sectors of the economy.[84] At that time, the Southwest was still in the early stages of industrial development and diversification. Thousands of Mexican agricultural workers had been displaced by the violent revolution of the previous decade and the total collapse of the hacienda agricultural system after 1917.[85] Many had migrated from the central states, where the fighting was most intense, to the northern border states. The resulting oversupply of workers in these areas further depressed existing economic conditions in Mexico. These push factors caused thousands of Mexicans to cross the U.S.-Mexican border during these years. Simultaneously, a demand for unskilled workers was created in the United States by the completion of massive irrigation projects that stretched from the lower Rio Grande Valley in Texas to the Imperial Valley in California.[86] Millions of acres of land came into production after 1910 and during the next two decades. These water projects had been made possible by the Reclamation Act of 1902, which set the course of development for the U.S. Southwest. As Carey McWilliams has noted, "Irrigation . . . had more to do with the economic growth of the Southwest than any other factor."[87] The expansion of the railroads into previously remote sections of the border region also facilitated the entry of Mexican workers and the exit of agricultural produce. As historians Arthur Corwin and Lawrence Cardoso have observed, "The economic development of the American Southwest coincided with the northward drift of Mexico's population."[88] Once again the push-and-pull relationship explains the mass immigration that occurred in this period. Not until pressure existed on both sides of the border could the immigration of Mexicans begin in earnest.

The entry of Mexican workers into the agricultural labor force of the southwestern United States provided growers in the region with an extremely cheap supply of labor by American standards. By Mexican standards, the U.S. wage rates were very high. As a result, many agricultural employers came to expect that Mexican workers could be hired for considerably less than non-Mexican workers.

TABLE 10. EMPLOYEES IN NONFARM ESTABLISHMENTS, BY INDUSTRY, 1920, 1930, 1940, AND 1950 (in thousands)

Year	Total Nonfarm Employees (14 years of age and older)	Nonfarm Employees, by Industry							
		Mining	Construction	Manufacturing	Transport and Utilities	Trade	Finance	Service	Government (Civilian Employees)
1920	27,434	1,180	850	10,702	4,317	4,012	902	3,100	2,371
1930	29,424	1,009	1,372	9,562	3,685	5,797	1,475	3,376	3,148
1940	32,377	925	1,294	10,985	3,038	6,750	1,502	3,681	4,202
1950	45,222	901	2,333	15,241	4,034	9,386	1,919	5,382	6,026

Source: Stanley Lebergott, *Manpower in Economic Growth: The American Record since 1800* (New York: McGraw-Hill, 1964), table A-5, p. 514. Copyright © 1964 by McGraw-Hill Inc. Reprinted by permission of the publisher.

Agriculture in the Southwest did not suffer the severe effects that other agricultural areas of the United States experienced during the 1920s. In part this was due to the lower costs made possible by the use of Mexican labor, but it also reflected the fact that the mix of agricultural products in the Southwest was (and is) dominated by specialty produce. These crops were less susceptible to the decline in general agricultural prices that occurred during this period.

It should also be noted that not all Mexican immigrants sought agricultural employment, nor did they all remain in the Southwest. Indeed, the urban Midwest also attracted a significant number of Mexican immigrants.[89] Industrial plants in the Chicago and Calumet areas of Illinois in particular became strong employment centers for such immigrants during the 1920s.

THE DECLINING AGGREGATE SIGNIFICANCE OF IMMIGRATION, 1930–1965

Having been a prominent feature of American economic history for over a century, immigration policy began to decline in importance in 1930—at least quantitatively—and it remained dormant until the mid-1960s. Qualitatively, however, it did on several occasions become a significant issue during this period. Understanding this era of benign neglect of the nation's immigration policy is crucial to understanding the policy crisis that developed after 1965.

During the 1930s, the United States fell prey to a worldwide economic depression. With the collapse of employment as well as wages and prices in all industrial sectors and geographic regions of the country, immigration also declined dramatically. In fact, as shown in Table 8, immigration reached its lowest levels in over a hundred years during the 1930s. In 1933, for instance, only 23,068 persons immigrated to the United States legally. The number had not been that low since 1829. Even the minimal quotas assigned to the countries of eastern and southern Europe were not met during the early 1930s. Also during 1933 more people emigrated than immigrated, and some of these were former immigrants.

The Mexican Repatriation Movement.   Of the immigrants who left the United States during the 1930s, Mexicans were the most numerous. The cause of this phenomenon lingers as one of the most controversial episodes in the history of U.S. immigration. As previously discussed, immigration from Mexico had been substantial throughout the preceding two decades. As jobs became increasingly scarce in the early 1930s, however, immigrants in some geographic areas of the United States became scapegoats. This reaction must be evaluated within the context of the fact that the initial response of the Hoover administration was to do nothing about the mass unemployment confronting the American labor force. Responsibility for providing relief for those who did not have jobs or income fell largely to the state and local governments. But rising unemployment also meant that tax revenues to support such undertakings were dwindling. Thus, many states set priorities in dispensing the limited relief funds that were available. California, for instance, raised its requirement for relief eligibility to three years of state residency.

With respect to recent immigrants to California and elsewhere, the provisions of the Immigration Act of 1917 were sometimes used to frighten recent legal immigrants from applying for assistance. Under the terms of that act, a legal immigrant who sought relief within five years of his or her admission was subject to immediate deportation as a public charge. Precedent for use of the act in this manner had been set in the Southwest during a brief recession in 1921–1922.[90]

As Abraham Hoffman has argued, most Mexican repatriation during the early years of the Depression (1929–1931) was "self-aided and self-propelled."[91] He estimates that 200,000 Mexicans left of their own volition during this period, although some were aided by various Mexican relief organizations that paid for the transportation of immigrants back to their original home communities once they actually crossed the border. Hoffman also notes, however, that a second stage of the "repatriados" movement began in mid 1931. In this phase various state and local relief agencies in the United States encouraged Mexican immigrants to return to Mexico. These agencies concluded that it was cheaper to pay the transportation costs back to Mexico than to continue to support families on relief for what appeared to be an indefinite duration. Hoffman, who has done the most intensive research available on the topic, suggests that the prodding involved in this second phase of the Mexican repatriation movement took the form of "inducements, subsidies, and persuasive techniques" that involved the cooperation of U.S. and Mexican government officials as well as railroad officials from both nations.[92] The assistance varied. Whether it consisted of cash payments, food parcels, or medical help while en route, all such aid was linked to acceptance of a one-way rail ticket back to the immigrant's home community in Mexico—not just to the border. Hoffman admits that some local officials gave Mexican immigrant families a Hobson's choice: either accept the railway tickets or be denied any further assistance. Similar efforts were also launched outside the Southwest. In Detroit, for instance, the Department of Public Welfare set up a Mexican Bureau to encourage repatriation. Chicago, St. Paul, and Gary also organized such programs.

As for illegal immigrants, as a matter of policy they were denied any assistance if they applied. Many were even threatened with being reported to immigration officials for deportation if they did not leave. These efforts were supported by parallel publicity campaigns by private groups to persuade illegal Mexican immigrants to leave the country; a notable one was led by the Los Angeles Chamber of Commerce. The Arizona legislature even went so far as to pass a law in 1930 requiring that 80 percent of the employees in all enterprises be U.S. citizens. This law proved to be unenforceable, but its message was clear.

Rodolfo Acuña has argued that during these years the pressure for persons of Mexican heritage to leave the United States was extensive.[93] He and other Chicano writers suggest that this drive caused widespread fear among immigrants from Mexico. For those who actually repatriated, the move caused hardship (i.e., the uprooting of families and the loss of possessions that could not be carried) and prolonged bitterness. Acuña and other authors also argue that more intimidation was used to persuade people to leave than Hoffman indicates in his accounts.

The momentum of the repatriation movement greatly dissipated (but did not end) in 1933 with the coming of the New Deal. The large-scale work and relief programs that President Franklin Roosevelt initiated during the early days of his administration reduced the financial pressure on some communities. Legal immigrants were eligible for these federal programs. As for the immigrants who had repatriated, many found conditions in Mexico to be as bleak as, if not worse than, those in the United States, and it was not long before some again chose to immigrate to the United States. Between 1929 and 1937, approximately 500,000 persons returned to Mexico as "repatriados," but of these about 175,000 were back in the United States by 1940.[94] The exact number of persons who left the United States and returned is, of course, unknown and can only be inferred from disparate sources.

The Emergence of the Refugee Issue.   During the 1930s, political events in Europe portended major changes in U.S. immigration policy. As political repression swept through Germany and Italy and spread into neighboring nations as well, people sought to immigrate to the United States. There were no provisions in the extant U.S. immigration laws, however, that would permit exceptions to be made for political refugees. Thus, persons who sought to enter the United States were admissible only if (1) they fit within the numerical quota for their country and if a quota opening was available, or (2) they otherwise qualified for nonquota status. Many of the people who tried to flee Europe were highly skilled, educated, and talented. Among them were noted scientists, engineers, scholars, and musicians. The United States and the world were greatly enriched by the subsequent contributions of many of the persons who were admitted. Countless others, however, were denied entry because of the inflexibility of the existing laws, and many of these persons subsequently perished in concentration and labor camps.

Due to the complexity of the topic, refugees will be the exclusive subject of Chapter 6. Here it is sufficient to note that the dislocations and devastation of World War II produced millions of refugees. In the period 1945–1953, over half a million refugees were admitted to the United States under special interpretations of the Immigration Act of 1924 or following passage of special supplemental legislation. The experience of this period, however, vividly demonstrated a major deficiency of the existing statutes.

A New Role for Enforcement.   During the 1930s and 1940s the administration of the nation's immigration laws changed extensively. In June 1933 the Bureau of Immigration and the Bureau of Naturalization were consolidated by executive order to form the Immigration and Naturalization Service (INS). The agency remained within the jurisdiction of the U.S. Department of Labor, but its staff and budget were sharply reduced.

During the Depression years, the number of legal immigrants admitted and the number of illegal immigrants apprehended declined sharply. By the late 1930s, however, events in Europe had created a new problem: how to process the applications of persons fleeing their homelands. Lacking provisions for the admission of refugees, the INS chose to act "dispassionately, in spite of the tragic circumstances of their [the refugees'] plight."[95] This decision foreshadowed major and lasting changes in the agency's organization and duties.

In June 1940 the INS was shifted from the U.S. Department of Labor to the U.S. Department of Justice as part of another reorganization of the executive branch of government. National security interests were cited as the rationale behind this shift. The government argued that rapidly changing international events dictated a more effective means of controlling the admission of immigrants and nonimmigrants. Concern over the influx of possibly "subversive elements" replaced the historic concerns of the agency. As a result, Congress more than doubled the budget and manpower of the INS between 1941 and 1943. During this period passport controls were imposed on citizens wishing to travel abroad and visas were required of all foreign visitors wishing to enter the country. Responsibility for the issuance of these documents was not given to the INS, however. Rather it was assigned to the U.S. Department of State, where it has remained ever since.

Also in 1940 the Alien Registration Act was adopted. It required that all resident aliens and nonimmigrants be fingerprinted and that they register annually at local post offices. The fingerprinting requirement remains in force, but in 1982 the annual reporting feature was abolished and a new requirement, that the INS be notified of any change in address, was substituted. In 1941 over 600,000 Italians, 300,000 Germans, and 90,000 Japanese residing in the United States were registered under this act. When the United States declared war on the Axis Powers, these persons were classified as enemy aliens whose movements were subject to government control. The INS was given responsibility for interning in detention centers those persons among these groups who were deemed to be a threat to national security. Several thousand persons were actually placed in such camps, the last of which was not closed until 1947.

During World War II the INS also became involved in administering several special nonimmigrant worker programs. These programs, which will be discussed in Chapter 4, were designed to permit specified numbers of unskilled workers from Mexico and the British West Indies to work in the United States.

Following the war, the INS returned to its more traditional responsibilities. Almost at once, the problem of illegal immigration resurfaced. Between 1946 and 1951 the number of illegal immigrants apprehended soared from 99,591 to 509,040. As a result, the INS was forced to adopt a policy that has had lasting implications. For reasons of expediency, the voluntary departure system became the dominant means of removing illegal immigrants from the country.[96] Under this system, an apprehended person is given the choice of leaving the country as soon as this can be arranged or contesting his or her apprehension by means of a lengthy and costly deportation proceeding. On the average, about 95 percent of the illegal immigrants apprehended in the United States each year avail themselves of the voluntary departure option.

A Reaffirmation of the Status Quo. The Depression and World War II brought a greater reduction in immigration than supporters of the Immigration Act of 1924 has sought to accomplish. In the twenty years following implementation of the national-origins system in 1929, only 27 percent of the existing quotas were used. Even including nonquota persons, total immigration was only about 75 percent of the anticipated quota level. Moreover, if allowance is made for emigration, net immigration during those years averaged only about 22,000 a year.[97] The most severe criticism of the system, however, was that ethnic discrimination was distorting not only the composition of the immigrant flow but also the administration of the entire system. Some nations—Great Britain in particular—had many unused quota slots each year, while other nations had massive backlogs of persons waiting to emigrate. Concern was expressed that it was time to convert the U.S. immigration system from one of ethnic selectivity to one that emphasized the potential human resource contribution of immigrants to the labor market. These considerations and others—including the fear that Communists were infiltrating the nation through the immigration system—prompted a congressional review of the immigration process. The Senate Committee on the Judiciary began its work in mid 1947 and issued a comprehensive report in April 1950.[98]

The report of the committee set the tone and established the principles that were embodied in the Immigration and Nationality Act of 1952 (also known as the McCarran-Walter Act), which was passed over President Harry Truman's veto.[99] Passage of this bill was a defeat not only for Truman but also for all others who had hoped to change the nation's immigration system from one that was racist and restrictive in character to one more in keeping with the nation's growing international leadership responsibilities. Although some modifications were made, the act of 1952 retained the basic precepts of the prevailing immigration law. It perpetuated the principles of the national-origins system for Europe and it maintained the total ceiling for the Eastern Hemisphere at 154,277 immigrants. The act did eliminate all immigration and naturalization exclusions against Asians, but the provisions for administering quotas for Asians were more restrictive than those that applied to Europeans. Thus, in essence, the act was merely a reaffirmation of the main principles that had prevailed since the 1920s.

Many of the provisions of the McCarran-Walter Act were simply codifications of previous court decisions and various ad hoc legislative enactments dating from 1924. One important provision was for the creation of a preference system by which to distribute visas within the quota allotments assigned to each country. Four categories of preference were set up. In the first category half of the visas issued under each quota allotment were to be granted to workers with a level of education, technical training, special experiences, or exceptional abilities that were deemed by the attorney general to be of benefit to the United States. By creating this category, Congress gave official recognition to the idea that immigration policy could be used as a human resource instrument to select types of workers by training and according to the needs of the nation's labor market. The other three levels of assigned priority to various categories of relatives of citizens or permanent-resident aliens.

At first glance, it might seem that the preference for workers regardless of whether they had family in the United States should have had a significant effect on the makeup of the nation's immigrant population. It did not, however. Only a small fraction—often less than one percent of all immigrants—entered the United States as first-preference workers in the ensuing thirteen years.[100] The reason for the lack of impact was that most of the immigration in this period occurred outside the quota system. The persons who were admitted came from the Western Hemisphere or were relatives accompanying quota immigrants. In addition, it was not necessary to impose the preference system on those nations of the Eastern Hemisphere which had a large number of unfilled quota slots (e.g., Great Britain). Thus, the only nations to use the first-preference slots were those Eastern Hemisphere nations that had skilled workers and that also had a backlog of applications for visas.

The McCarran-Walter Act also introduced for the first time the concept of labor certification as a prerequisite for the admission of immigrants. This certification, however, was carried out in a purely passive manner. The secretary of labor was empowered to certify that the admission of nonrelative immigrants would not adversely affect the wages and working conditions of citizen workers who were similarly employed. The Department of Labor was obligated to refuse certification if it anticipated an adverse impact. The Labor Department, however, was not staffed to carry out such a task. In practice, it acted only in response to complaints or when immigrants were used in a blatant manner to break a strike or to bring about a drastic alteration in prevailing work standards. In the ten years following its establishment, the labor certification power was exercised on only six occasions.[101] Between 1962 and 1965, when Labor Department procedures were amended slightly, use of this power increased to only about twelve times a year.

The Immigration and Nationality Act of 1952 did not alter the status of immigrants from the Western Hemisphere. They remained immune to the ceilings and the national-origin quotas for the same reasons they were omitted from the provisions of the Immigration Act of 1924.[102]

With regard to general exclusions, some of the most controversial aspects of the McCarran-Walter Act dealt with the contention that the control of communism was an immigration problem. With the onset of the cold war in the late 1940s, Congress had passed the Internal Security Act of 1950, which specifically barred Communists and Fascists from admission as to the United States as immigrants or nonimmigrants. For nonimmigrants, the provision could be waived by the attorney general. In 1952 this act was incorporated into the McCarran-Walter Act along with language that permitted the attorney general to ban anyone whose presence might be prejudicial to the public welfare. This use of immigration legislation to bolster national security interests reflected the shift in responsibility for immigration policy to the Department of Justice only a decade before. The fear of Communist infiltration dominated the debate over the terms of the Immigration and Nationality Act of 1952 to such a degree that the most pressing reform needs of the immigration system were simply ignored.

In vetoing the bill, President Truman assailed the lack of attention given in the legislation to reform of prevailing immigration procedures. As he wrote to Congress:

> The basis of this quota system was false and unworthy in 1924. It is even worse now. At the present time this quota system keeps out the very people we want to bring in. It is incredible to me that, in this year of 1952, we should again be enacting into law such a slur on the patriotism, the capacity, and the decency of a large part of our citizenry. . . .
>
> In no other realm of our national life are we so hampered and stultified by the dead hand of the past as we are in this field of immigration.[103]

Despite his urging, both houses of Congress easily mustered the two-thirds majority needed to override his veto.

In his veto message, President Truman requested that a bipartisan commission of "outstanding Americans" be set up to review the existing immigration statutes and to suggest ways in which they could be "brought into line with our national ideals and our foreign policy." After overriding the veto, Congress saw no need to establish such a commission. Consequently, in an executive order of September 4, 1952, Truman established the President's Commission on Immigration and Naturalization and appointed Philip Perlman, former solicitor general of the United States, as chairman. In its report, which was issued a few months later, the commission severely criticized the nation's existing immigration legislation and recommended that the system be "revised from beginning to end."[104] It argued that U.S. immigration laws were racially and ethnically discriminatory, ignored the needs of the nation, were based upon an attitude of hostility and distrust of foreigners, and were difficult to administer. It recommended that the national-origins system be replaced; that immigration ceilings be raised; and that responsibility for immigration matters be shifted from the Department of Justice to a new, independent, agency. The commission's report had no immediate impact on Congress, but it was to become the basis for extensive reforms in the 1960s.

★ CHAPTER 3 ★

The Legal Immigration
System, 1965–1984

The overt racism of the national-origins admission system could not be sustained in a nation that was already multiracial and multicultural in its composition and that boasted to the world of these attributes. Thus, the movement in the 1950s and early 1960s to overhaul the U.S. immigration system gradually accumulated sufficient momentum to accomplish most of its goals. The capstone of this drive occurred on October 3, 1965, when President Lyndon Johnson signed into law the Immigration and Nationality Amendments of 1965, or the Hart-Celler Act (hereafter referred to as the Immigration Act of 1965).[1] Technically speaking, the legislation was a lengthy series of amendments to the Immigration and Nationality Act of 1952, but in terms of its policy significance it has been called ''the most far-reaching revision of immigration policy'' since the imposition of the first numerical quotas in 1921.[2] Since its passage, immigration to the United States has changed dramatically both quantitatively and qualitatively. The reemergence of immigration as a significant labor market influence virtually dates from the implementation of this legislation.

By the late 1970s and early 1980s, however, the immigration system that was created in 1965 had itself become the subject of a comprehensive and controversial reform movement. (Institutional arrangements always lag behind the events they seek to govern.) Some of the provisions of the Immigration Act of 1965 had proven inadequate, others had triggered unanticipated consequences, and new issues had emerged with which the existing system proved unable to cope.

In addition, the labor market of the United States sustained a radical transformation during the 1970s and into the 1980s. In fact, unprecedented structural changes continue to occur in the demand for labor at the same time that major demographic and social changes are taking place with respect to the available supply of labor. The nature of these broad economic changes will be discussed in Chapter 8, after all aspects of contemporary U.S. immigration policy have been presented. For the purposes of this chapter, it is sufficient to say that the immigration reform movements of the 1960s and the early 1980s sought to bring about significant changes in the legal system, but they were predicated largely upon political concerns. It has yet to be fully appreciated that immigration in all its forms has emerged as a major economic force that influences the size, location, and composition of the nation's labor force. It is vital, therefore, to study the progression of immigration policy since 1965 in order to see how contemporary policy has evolved independently from responsibility for its economic consequences.

The Reform Movement of the Early 1960s

Between 1952 and 1965 the legal U.S. immigration system found itself in a paradoxical situation. During this thirteen-year period, only 61 percent of the system's quota visas were issued. Yet tens of thousands of persons sought to immigrate to the United States who were ineligible only because they were from the "wrong" country. During this interval, therefore, Congress was forced to enact a series of temporary special admission programs to circumvent the barriers imposed by the basic immigration laws. As will be discussed in Chapter 6, most of those admitted under these arrangements were refugees from Western Europe and Mainland China or escapees from various Communist-dominated nations of Eastern Europe. In sum, almost half a million persons were admitted through channels other than the immigration quotas in this thirteen-year period. Expressed differently, only about one of every three immigrants to the United States during this time span was admitted under the terms of the national-origins system.[3]

In addition to the fact that the prevailing immigration system had been rendered obsolete, it is also true that the nation's attitudes toward race and ethnic background had changed dramatically by the early 1960s. The Civil Rights movement, which had begun in earnest in 1957 with the Montgomery, Alabama, bus boycott, had culminated in passage of the Civil Rights Act of 1964 and the Voting Rights Act of 1965. Thus, it has been observed: "The 1965 immigration legislation was as much a product of the mid-sixties and the heavily Democratic 89th Congress which produced major civil rights legislation as the 1952 Act was a product of the Cold War period of the early 1950s."[4] Just as overt racism could no longer be tolerated in the way citizens treated their fellow citizens, neither could it be sanctioned in the laws that governed the way in which noncitizens were considered for immigrant status.[5]

As always, however, a political consensus had to be built, and this required that specific compromises be struck if the general objective was to be accomplished. The primary intent of the 1965 reform movement was to change the character of immigration policy—that is, to abolish the national-origins system—not to increase the level of immigration. In fact, there were fears in Congress at this time that increasing the number of immigrants would lead to adverse employment and wage effects in the labor market. Only the year before, the Mexican Labor Program (see Chapter 4) had been terminated after twenty-two years of existence largely because Congress believed it was depressing wages, retarding improvements in working conditions, and causing unemployment for a significant number of low-income citizen workers. With these concerns in mind, Congress deemed it necessary to include two critical amendments in the 1965 legislation.

One of the amendments called for the imposition of a ceiling on the number of immigrants admitted from the Western Hemisphere. Congress feared that the absence of such a limit, combined with the extraordinarily high population growth rates in Latin America, would lead to an uncontrolled influx of immigrants in the near future. Hence, "the final inclusion of the ceiling in the enacted bill was a necessary *quid pro quo* in exchange for abolishment of the national origins quota system."[6] The Johnson administration opposed this ceiling on the grounds that it would adversely affect U.S. relations with Latin America but realized that without it the bill would not pass. Thus, a ceiling of 120,000 immigrants from the Western Hemisphere was included in the final version of the bill. It would take effect on July 1, 1968, unless other legislation was enacted prior to that date to change it. A special commission—the Select Commission on Western Hemisphere Immigration—was appointed to study the issue, but it was unable to agree upon a firm recommendation to Congress concerning the efficacy of the ceiling. As a result the ceiling went into effect on the specified date.

The second major policy amendment included in the Immigration Act of 1965 dealt with a change in labor certification procedures. Under the 1952 statute, the Labor Department's ability to protect citizen workers from the adverse impact of admission of nonrelative immigrants was restricted to a purely negative role. That is to say, the secretary of labor could deny labor certification only if he felt that certain immigrants would have an adverse labor market impact. The Immigration Act of 1965 reversed this logic. Thereafter, immigrants who were entering the nation on a basis other than family reunification or refugee status had to receive certification from the U.S. Department of Labor that their presence would not adversely affect employment opportunities or the prevailing wage and working conditions of citizen workers.

With these two amendments, redesigning the immigration system to exclude the discriminatory national-origins feature became politically feasible. Under the new law, the country of origin of immigrants remained a basic policy component, but preference could not be given on the basis of race, sex, place of birth, or place of residence. Of special importance was the fact that this legislation eliminated the last vestiges of the discriminatory Asian-Pacific Triangle provisions. Until this change, any person whose ancestry was one-half or more Asian was not charged against the quota of the nation of his or her birth—as was normally the case—but rather was charged against the quota of the country in Asia or the Pacific which was designated as that person's ancestral nation. Because the quotas for these areas had generally been quite low, it had been virtually impossible for such Asians to qualify as immigrants no matter what their actual citizenship was.

Under the Immigration Act of 1965 an annual ceiling of 170,000 visas was imposed on all the nations of the Eastern Hemisphere combined. This figure was slightly higher than the limit set in the Immigration Act of 1952. The rationale for the increase was recognition that refugees from Europe and Asia were likely to be a continuing reality and not just a post–World War II phenomenon. It was hoped that this increase in the ceiling would absorb such persons. With the new Western Hemisphere ceiling of 120,000, the total number of visas to be issued in any year was 290,000. The 1965 bill also set a ceiling of 20,000 visas for any single country in the Eastern Hemisphere. No limit was applied to any Western Hemisphere nation. To determine which individuals were to be admitted within the framework of the numerical ceiling set for the Eastern Hemisphere, a seven-category preference system was created. Within the scope of these seven categories, visas were made available on a "first come, first served" basis. The preference categories and the labor certification provisions of the law did not apply to Western Hemisphere nations. Subject to the various general exclusions that apply to all immigrants (see Appendix A), persons from nations in this region had only to comply with the total hemisphere ceiling.

Table 11 outlines the preference system that was created in 1965. The new system brought a dramatic shift in emphasis away from the priority given to labor force considerations (the norm since 1952) and toward family reunification. Seventy-four percent of the persons who became immigrants had to be related to a resident of the United States. Furthermore, immediate relatives (i.e., persons defined under the act as spouses, minor children, and parents of U.S. citizens over the age of twenty-one) were not to be counted as part of either the hemispheric or the country ceiling. The number of immediate relatives who have entered the country since 1965 has ranged between 100,000 and 150,000 annually. Consequently, the number of immigrants legally admitted each year always exceeds the statutory limits by a significant margin. Since 1965, family reunification has served as the cornerstone of the nation's immigration policy.[7]

It should also be noted that the Immigration Act of 1965 changed several of the key terms used to classify immigrants. The term *quota immigrants* was replaced simply by the term *immigrant,* which is applied to an alien admitted for permanent residence. Similarly, the term *nonquota immigrant* was replaced by two terms. One was the already defined term *immediate relative.* The other was *special immigrant,* which was used for all persons who immigrated from the Western Hemisphere; these persons did not have to comply with the preference category requirements that were applied to would-be Eastern Hemisphere immigrants.

THE CREATION OF A NEW ADMISSIONS CATEGORY

In addition to seeking compromises that would make the new law politically palatable, Congress needed to address issues about which the old law had been silent. Most prominent of these concerns was the issue of refugees. The addition of a seventh preference category—for refugees—in the Immigration Act of 1965 marked the first time an explicit provision dealing with this issue had been

TABLE 11. THE PREFERENCE SYSTEM CREATED UNDER
THE IMMIGRATION ACT OF 1965 (in effect until 1980)

Preference	Category	Maximum Proportion of Total Admitted
First	Unmarried sons and daughters of U.S. citizens	20%
Second	Spouses and unmarried sons and daughters of aliens lawfully admitted for permanent residence	20% plus any not required by first preference
Third	Members of the professions, scientists, and artists of exceptional ability	10%
Fourth	Married sons and daughters of U.S. citizens	10% plus any not required by first and third preferences
Fifth	Brothers and sisters of U.S. citizens	24% plus any not required by first four preferences
Sixth	Skilled and unskilled workers in occupations for which labor is in short supply	10%
Seventh	Refugees to whom conditional entry or adjustment may be given	6%
Nonpreference	Any applicant	Numbers not used by preceding preferences

included in immigration legislation. It represented an acknowledgment that refugee accommodation had become a permanent policy issue with which the nation must grope. Six percent of the available visas (or 17,400 slots) were set aside for refugees. This figure was far below the average number of refugees admitted during the preceding thirteen years. Those refugees—largely from Eastern Europe and Cuba—had been admitted under ad hoc arrangements involving both temporary admission legislation and the use of administrative powers assigned to the attorney general. Continuation of these practices, however, was seen to be an unsatisfactory method of dealing with what had proved to be an on-going issue (see Chapter 6). For the purposes of this chapter, it is sufficient to say that the Immigration Act of 1965 was the first tentative effort by the nation to address this critical issue in a consistent manner. The act of 1965 created a "conditional entry" status for those persons who met the statutory definition of being a "refugee." After a two-year period such individuals could adjust their status to become permanent-resident aliens and, later, naturalized citizens if they wished.

REGISTRATION ADJUSTMENT

The Immigration Act of 1965 also advanced the cutoff year for making persons who had entered the country illegally, or who had entered legally but improperly overstayed their visas, or who had entered as nonimmigrants but remained in the country illegally, eligible for naturalization. This practice began in 1929, when all persons who had lived in the United States since July 1, 1924, were given a chance to legitimize their unauthorized presence. In 1958, the cutoff date was advanced to June 28, 1940—the day on which the Alien Registration Act of 1940 was signed into law. The Immigration Act of 1965 advanced this cutoff date to June 30, 1948. The year 1948 was chosen simply because it was a compromise between the Senate version of the bill that year, which specified 1958, and the House Bill, which had no such provision in it. Thus, in effect, an amnesty was given to those persons who had lived in the country for many years illegally. If they wished, they could become naturalized citizens if they met certain conditions. These requirements were and are that such persons establish that they had resided in the United States continuously since before the specified cutoff date, that they are persons of good moral character, and that they are eligible for citizenship by virtue of not belonging to an excludable class (see Appendix A). The number of persons whose status was legalized under the 1958 revision of the registration cutoff date is shown in Table 12. The registration cutoff date has not been advanced since 1958, although some forms of amnesty or forgiveness have been suggested in most of the legislative proposals made since the mid-1970s to deal with illegal immigration.

TABLE 12.   LEGALIZATION OF STATUS UNDER THE 1958 REVISION
OF THE REGISTRATION CUTOFF DATE

Year	Number of Immigrants	Year	Number of Immigrants
1959	4,321	1971	1,190
1960	4,773	1972	1,653
1961	5,037	1973	1,254
1962	3,399	1974	875
1963	2,680	1975	556
1964	2,585	1976	633
1965	2,064	1976	163[a]
1966	2,595	1977	546
1967	3,195	1978	423
1968	2,148	1979	262
1969	1,565	1980	428[b]
1970	1,520	1981	241[b]
		Total	44,106

Source: The *Annual Report*(s) of the Immigration and Naturalization Service as updated in an open letter from Congressman Hal Daub of the U.S. House of Representatives to his fellow congressmen, September 8, 1982 (photocopy).
[a]Transitional quarter.
[b]Provisional figure.

Achievement of a Worldwide Immigration System

In the 1970s two important amendments were made to the Immigration Act of 1965 that have had long-term implications for U.S. immigration policy. These amendments were dictated in part by the effects of the 1965 legislation. They were also logical policy progressions.

In 1968, imposition of the first ceiling on immigration from the Western Hemisphere created a massive backlog of applications for visas from persons living in these nations. The backlog gave credence to earlier arguments that population pressures in Latin America were so strong that if restrictions were not imposed a massive migration from these nations to the United States would eventually take place. By 1976, 300,000 visa applications were pending from persons living in the Western Hemisphere. This translated into a waiting period of more than two and a half years for many new applicants.

There was little congressional support for removing the ceiling itself. Nonetheless, because of the size of the backlog, the speed with which it developed, and the fact that it was causing hardship to families that were separated because of it, efforts were made to implement some sort of mechanism to regulate admissions under the new ceiling requirement. In 1976 an amendment was enacted to accomplish that goal. It extended a slightly modified version of the seven-category preference system, which had previously been applied only to Eastern Hemisphere nations, to all Western Hemisphere nations as well.[8] Thus the term *special immigrants,* which prior to that time had been used to describe Western Hemisphere immigrants, was no longer applicable. In addition, refugees from Cuba were permitted to adjust their status to that of permanent-resident aliens without diminishing the Western Hemisphere quota.

The 1976 amendment also imposed for the first time an annual ceiling of 20,000 immigrants from any single nation in the Western Hemisphere. Since the Immigration Act of 1965 had taken effect in mid 1968, immigration from Mexico had annually exceeded this limit by at least 20,000. In 1974, for instance, 45,364 visas out of the 120,000 available for the entire Western Hemisphere had gone to Mexican applicants. In fact, relatives of these visa-holders increased the total to 71,586.

Extension of an annual visa ceiling to all countries of the world marked the legal manifestation of an ideal: that the people of all nations—even those that were contiguous to the United States—should be treated equally in terms of their opportunity to immigrate to the United States. Mexico, however, was most affected by the implementation of this ceiling. The action has not only increased the backlog of visa requests by Mexicans but has also contributed to the multiple pressures that cause illegal immigration. To many Mexicans who have already made the personal decision to immigrate to the United States, it often seems preferable simply to enter illegally rather than wait several years for a visa to become available.

In 1978, as a result of another amendment to the Immigration Act of 1965, the United States finally achieved the unified immigration system that advocates of reform had sought for the past two decades. The two hemispheric ceilings were merged into a single worldwide quota that permitted 290,000 visas to be issued to immigrants each year.[9] With only slight modifications, the preference for admission was to be assigned on the basis of the seven-category admission system created in 1965.

Thus, the amendments of 1976 and 1978 eliminated all preferences based on the place of birth of a prospective immigrant. Persons from all countries and both hemispheres were to be subjected to the same admission requirements. All had to compete equally for the available visas. The short-term effect of the 1978 amendment was an increase in the number of admission opportunities available to applicants from the Western Hemisphere and therefore a reduction in the backlog of visa requests from the nations in this region. Supporters of this single system also hoped to free-up accrued, unused slots for refugees (the seventh preference category) from the Western Hemisphere and make them accessible to the growing number of persons seeking to be admitted as refugees from the Eastern Hemisphere.

Thus, by the end of the 1970s the legal U.S. immigration system was operating under a single policy that applies uniformly to the people of all nations. Yet the system is very complex in its requirements and highly mechanistic in its operation. It relies upon a case-by-case decisionmaking process to determine individual eligibility. It should not be surprising to learn, therefore, that those who are legally admitted—with the general exception of refugee groups—are disproportionately the better-educated and the financially well-off members of the societies they leave. They are usually better able to master the intricacies of the immigration system and to afford both the time and the costs involved in completing the process.

The Shift in Admissions Priorities

It is important at this point to elaborate briefly on the procedural shift whereby family reunification became the cornerstone of U.S. immigration policy. It should be recalled that the Immigration Act of 1952 had stipulated that 50 percent of the available visas be assigned on the basis of U.S. labor force considerations and that this group be given preference over other admission categories. In 1965 the Johnson administration's immigration proposals retained both of these features, but during the legislative process Congress rewrote the bill. As a result the Immigration Act of 1965 reduced the occupational preference category to only 20 percent of the available visas. Moreover, the previous single occupational preference grouping was split into two separate categories that were downgraded to the third and sixth levels of priority respectively. Ostensibly, the rationale for these changes was that between 1952 and 1965 the occupational preference category—for reasons cited in Chapter 2—was underutilized, while the family preference groupings were chronically backlogged. The most significant shift in priorities, however, occurred as a result of the addition of a new fifth preference group for brothers and sisters of U.S. citizens and the assignment of 24 percent of the available visas to this new family grouping. Under the Immigration Act of 1952, would-be immigrants in this category had been eligible to compete only for the system's limited number of unused visas.

These seemingly drastic changes in eligibility were made in response to the lobbying of various groups (e.g., the American Legion and the Daughters of the American Revolution) that were generally opposed to abolition of the national-origins system. Recognizing that they could not block the reform drive on this fundamental issue, they sought to make the changes in the admissions criteria more symbolic than real. These groups and their congressional sympathizers believed that by stressing family reunification it would be possible to retain the same racial and ethnic priorities that the national-origins system had fostered even if the formal mechanism itself was abolished. It seemed unlikely, for instance, that many persons from Asia or from southern or eastern Europe would be admitted in the near future, for the prohibitions imposed during the national-origins era had prevented the entry of many of their relatives. An organization of Japanese-Americans recognized the implications of this ploy and protested the change. It contended that

> inasmuch as the total Asian population of the United States is only about one-half of one percent of the total American population, this means that there are very few of Asian-Pacific origin in this country who are entitled to provide the specified preference priorities to family members and close relatives residing abroad, even if all qualified family members and close relatives desire to emigrate immediately to the United States.
>
> Thus, it would seem that, although the immigration bill eliminates race as a matter of principle, in actual operation immigration will still be controlled by the now discredited national origins system and the general patterns of immigration which exist today will continue for many years to come.[10]

Despite these real concerns, the debate on immigration reform centered on other provisions, and this change was written into the law by the Judiciary Committee of the House of Representatives.

The disproportionate stress given to family reunification in making admissions decisions is a factor that significantly distinguishes the immigration system of the United States from the systems of the other nations that are willing to admit immigrants. This shift in emphasis, however, has greatly diminished the possibility of using the U.S. immigration system as a means of labor force adjustment to supply talents and skills that are needed and to restrict the entry of those possessing skills that are in surplus. There is essentially no relationship between the operation of the nation's immigration system and the parallel public efforts in the post-1965 era to construct a coherent national human resource policy. Furthermore, the dominance of the family reunification principle has frequently been criticized for making the immigration system highly nepotistic. Aside from the special case of refugees, the only way persons can be admitted legally if they do not already have relatives in this country is to compete for the relatively few positions available under the system's occupational preference categories. For these people illegal immigration is often the only alternative if they cannot qualify as refugees.

Changes in the Labor Certification Program

It is also important to discuss briefly the reversal in labor certification procedures that was embodied in the Immigration Act of 1965. In contrast to their position earlier in the century, the nation's trade unions strongly supported repeal of the national-origins system in 1965. In the process, they pressed hard for a change in labor certification procedures. The result of their efforts was the new requirement that nonrelative immigrants can be admitted only after the secretary of labor has certified that an insufficient number of citizen workers are able, willing, and qualified to do the work at the time a visa request is made and at the intended destination of the would-be immigrant. In addition, the 1965 law requires that the labor secretary certify that the presence of the applicant will not adversely affect the wages and working conditions of citizen workers already employed in the specified occupation of the visa applicant. The law places no limits on the number of certifications that can be issued in a given year. Those persons who meet these requirements and the general eligibility standards set for all immigrants may enter the United States as the third preference category (if they are professionals, scientists, or artists of exceptional ability); or under the sixth preference category (if they do not qualify for the third); or as nonpreference immigrants (if any visas remain unused in the other preference categories).

Employers in the United States usually file applications for labor certifications on behalf of would-be immigrants. In these applications they specify the skills required for the job and the wage rates that will be offered, and they indicate the efforts they have made to find citizen workers. The applications are reviewed by the public job service (sometimes called the employment service) in each state on a case-by-case basis and are subsequently forwarded to the U.S. Department of Labor for final certification. Obviously, it is difficult for many nonprofessionals to secure job offers when they are not yet in the United States. This is even more true in the 1980s than it was in 1965, for now there are backlogs in immigrant visa requests from many countries. This means that an employer often has to wait a year or two (or more) for the worker(s) he is seeking to hire to be admitted under normal admissions procedures.

Thus, Walter Fogel contends, the labor certification system since 1965 has actually encouraged illegal immigration.[11] He indicates that some persons enter the United States without proper documents or violate the terms of visitor visas, obtain job offers, and then use these offers as levers in applying for the labor certifications that will qualify them to become immigrants. If the job certifications are granted, these persons succeed, but even if the requests are denied, because visa violators are already in the country, they are likely to remain as illegal immigrants. Indeed, it was estimated in 1978 that 45 percent of all labor certifications "simply legalize the presence of workers already here illegally."[12] This is one reason Fogel argues that the entire labor certification process should be eliminated.[13]

With the rise in the number of refugee admissions in the late 1970s, the number of immigrants admitted under the labor certification program declined to about 5–6 percent of all admissions. Indeed, the usefulness of the labor certification requirement has been questioned on a number of grounds. In addition to noting the fact that it has been used to legalize illegal immigration, Fogel argues that it should be abolished "as a condition of permanent immigration because it has no effect toward the accomplishment of its original objective—that of protecting American wages and working conditions."[14] He contends that since it applies to such a small proportion of those admitted as immigrants, it cannot really accomplish what it seeks to do and is therefore more of a nuisance than a useful regulatory device. David North, in a detailed study of the certification system, also has questioned "the overall significance of a fairly stringent procedure which covers such a tiny portion" of all immigrants.[15] On the other hand, North and LeBel have defended the concept (though not the existing system): "The labor certification program is important because it is the only part of the immigration process that deliberately seeks talent for the nation, which is not to say that the relative and refugee admission procedures do not produce talent, but simply that they do so accidently."[16] They argue that rather than abolish it, Congress should give the program a more influential role, a role whereby the number of workers admitted each year could be adjusted upward or downward depending on the vitality (i.e., the unemployment situation) of the nation. North and LeBel would prefer to see the labor certification requirement applied to a greater percentage of the immigrants admitted each year and to have the number of immigrants admitted under the family preference categories reduced accordingly. They argue that to accomplish this goal the labor certification system could be enlarged to include (1) the issuance of visas to would-be immigrants who have skills that are in demand, but without tying that provision to specific employer needs, because the system is already "a made to order system for illegal immigrants and their employers"; (2) a public-service apprenticeship program in which potential immigrants with needed skills would accept public-service jobs as nonimmigrant workers (e.g., serve as a doctor in a rural community) and then convert to permanent-resident status after two years; (3) a self-employed-craftsman program for highly skilled workers who would not work for others; or (4) perhaps a limited worldwide skills lottery program that would offer young persons with a skill or an education a chance to enter the United States as immigrants even if they did not fit into any other admission category.[17]

A Separate Admissions System for Refugees

In 1980 the immigration system of the United States was again altered by the Refugee Act of 1980.[18] Despite the fact that the Immigration Act of 1965 had created a preference category for refugees, the number of refugees admitted to the United States each year had regularly exceeded the annual quota of 17,400 refugee slots—often by several multiples of that number (see Chapter 6). Thus, the Refugee Act of 1980 removed refugees from the jurisdiction of the nation's existing immigration policy and established a separate admissions policy for them. It eliminated the seventh preference category and reduced the annual worldwide ceiling for all immigrants in the remaining six categories to 270,000 visas. The preference system that emerged as a result of these changes is described in Table 13. The Refugee Act of 1980 set a separate worldwide ceiling of 50,000 refugees a year through 1982. It also provided that the president could admit more than that number after consultation with Congress if he deemed that circumstances required such action. In fact, each year since 1980 the number of refugees admitted has exceeded 50,000, which was defined as the "normal" level. Finally, the act stipulated that beginning with fiscal year 1983 (i.e.,

TABLE 13.   THE PREFERENCE SYSTEM CREATED
UNDER THE REFUGEE ACT OF 1980

Preference	Category	Maximum Proportion of Total Admitted
First	Unmarried sons and daughters of U.S. citizens	20%
Second	Spouses and unmarried sons and daughters of aliens lawfully admitted for permanent residence	26% plus any not required by first preference
Third	Members of the professions, or persons of exceptional ability in the sciences and arts	10%
Fourth	Married sons and daughters of U.S. citizens	10% plus any not required by first and third preferences
Fifth	Brothers and sisters of U.S. citizens, 21 years of age and over	24% plus any not required by first and fourth preferences
Sixth	Skilled and unskilled workers in occupations for which labor is in short supply	10%
Nonpreference	Any applicant	Numbers not used by preceding preferences

October 1982), the exact number of refugee admissions each year would be determined in advance by the president after consultation with Congress. During an extensive debate on immigration reform in 1982, Congress tried unsuccessfully to set a specific numerical ceiling on the number of refugees that could be admitted annually. It was understood, however, that if the Simpson-Mazzoli bill passed in 1983, the issue of a legislative ceiling on refugees would have to be addressed in the next round of the immigration reform debate. Accordingly, the Refugee Act of 1980, which was due to expire on September 30, 1983, was extended just days before this date to September 30, 1984. Given the fact that action on the Simpson-Mazzoli bill was still pending in mid-1984, however, it is likely that still another extension will be required before the issue of a refugee ceiling can be addressed directly.

The Consequences of Post-1965 Immigration Legislation

Since the passage of the Immigration Act of 1965, the amendments of 1976 and 1978, and the Refugee Act of 1980, several important trends have emerged that can be traced directly to their provisions. Some of these results were anticipated; others were not. Brief mention of these trends is necessary if we are to understand the events that led to formation of the Select Commission on Immigration and Refugee Policy in 1979 and to the subsequent legislative reform drive of the early 1980s.

AN INCREASE IN THE LEVEL OF IMMIGRATION

The number of legal immigrants entering the United States—those admitted with visas, their immediate relatives (who are exempt from numerical limitations), and refugees—has increased dramatically since the Immigration Act of 1965 was signed into law. Before citing specific examples of this change, however, it is important to note that annual legal immigration totals do not reflect the true size of the gross migration flows that have occurred since 1965. They do not because they have not been adjusted for illegal immigration into or legal emigration out of the country each year. Nor do they reflect the administrative decisions that have, since the end of World War II, regularly allowed additional refugees to enter the nation in numbers that exceed the legislative limits specified for a given year. The totals for the latter admissions are not recorded as formal immigration statistics until these individuals convert to immigrant status—a process that usually starts two years after they arrive in the United States.

Nonetheless, orders of magnitude can be discerned in the difference between the average number of immigrants admitted annually from 1924 to 1965 and that number for the period 1966–1980. From 1924 until 1965 the average annual number of legal immigrants admitted to the United States was 191,000. From

1966 until 1981 the average was 435,000 immigrants. Moreover, in the years 1978–1980 the average was decidedly higher—approximately 547,000 immigrants a year (or almost three times the pre-1965 rate). Thus, immigration has once again assumed a major role in both aggregate population and labor force growth.

Indicative of the impact of the growth in the number of immigrants to the United States since 1965 is the fact that the 1980 census showed that in terms of the nation's overall population both the absolute number and the percentage of foreign-born persons (a figure which excludes children of citizens born abroad) increased for the first time since 1920. From 1920 through 1970 both figures had declined in each succeeding decennial count. In 1920 the foreign-born population numbered 13.9 million and accounted for 13.2 percent of the overall population. By 1970 the number of foreign-born persons in the population had fallen to 9.6 million, or 4.7 percent of the population. The 1980 census, however, showed that the foreign-born population had increased sharply over the decade to 13.9 million (or 6.2 percent of the population).[19] Moreover, because it is likely that illegal immigrants were severely undercounted in 1980 (due to their natural aversion to contact with federal government representatives and to the fact that the subject of illegal entry was an important subject of national debate at that time), the real numbers and percentages for the foreign-born were probably even higher. Undoubtedly the problem of undercounting had skewed earlier census data as well, but as will be discussed in Chapter 5, indications are that illegal immigration increased significantly in the 1970s, and so it is at least plausible that the undercounting of illegal immigrants was proportionately greater in 1980 than in prior population counts.

It is conservatively estimated that during the 1970s immigration (in all its forms) accounted for 40 percent of the nation's population growth. Signs in the early 1980s indicate that the trend is continuing. In fact, because of the sustained increase in the total number of immigrants throughout the 1970s and early 1980s, it is appropriate to conclude that the nation is admitting a fourth wave of immigrants. The sharp rise in the level of immigration and a parallel decrease in the nation's birth rate over the same period led Leon Bouvier to write in 1981: "Immigration to the United States has reached levels not attained since early in this century. If both legal and illegal entries are included, close to half to all [population] growth may be attributable to this demographic variable."[20] Thus, one of the clearest results of post-1965 immigration policy has been the revival of immigration as a significant quantitative factor in the nation's human resource policy.

THE GEOGRAPHIC DISTRIBUTION OF IMMIGRANTS

Reflecting a historic pattern, the geographic distribution of immigrants since 1965 has not been regionally balanced. On the basis of information gathered from arriving immigrants with regard to their intended permanent state of residence, five states have been shown to account for almost two-thirds of the nation's immigrants. The exact percentages, of course, vary slightly each year, but as shown in Table 14 the states themselves tend to remain about the same over time. Since 1976 California has emerged as the largest receiver of legal immigrants. It accounts for almost one-fourth of all immigrants each year. New York, long the leading destination, now ranks second, accounting for about 16–21 percent of the nation's immigrants each year. Thus, California and New York alone have for many years been the intended destinations of about 40–45 percent of all immigrants. Texas, Florida, Illinois, and New Jersey have consistently vied for the next highest rankings. With the exception of Florida, all the major immigrant-receiving states were also the destinations of the wave of immigrants that arrived during the first two decades of the twentieth century.

In addition to recording the immediate destination of immigrants, the 1980 census provides information that tends to confirm the short-term settlement pattern of immigrants nationwide and to suggest the long-term pattern. The percentage of immigrants within the total population of each state is shown in Table 15. The states with the highest percentage of foreign-born persons in 1980 were California (14.8 percent), Hawaii (14.0 percent), New York (13.4 percent), Florida (10.9 percent), and New Jersey (10.3 percent). Of these, only Hawaii did not rank among the top five states that were the initial destination of new immigrants.

Within the states in which they settle, legal immigrants have demonstrated a consistent preference for the nation's large central cities.[21] Although the exact percentages vary each year, a central city was the destination of about 55 percent of the immigrants admitted between 1960 and 1979. The trend was even more pronounced in the late 1970s. Suburban areas with a population of between 2,500 and 99,000 have been the clear second choices, while rural areas have ranked a distant third. These patterns of initial residence differ distinctly from the preferences of the general population, for whom suburban areas have been the overwhelming first choice since 1960 (housing almost half the nation's population), followed by an almost equal preference (about 25 percent each) for central cities and rural areas.

The 1980 census information on the foreign-born population of the United States vividly demonstrates the effect that immigration is having in a few large metropolitan areas. In 1980, for instance, the metropolitan area with the highest percentage of foreign-born residents was Miami, Florida, with a phenomenal 35.2 percent. The second highest was Los Angeles, California (21.6 percent), and the third was New York City (20.8 percent). Both Miami (40.1 percent) and Los Angeles (37.3 percent) also have a larger-than-average proportion of internal migrants (native-born residents from other states) as well as immigrants (foreign-born residents), but for New York (16.9 percent) this has not been the case. Hence, in the New York metropolitan area the influx of immigrants has tended to offset some of the population losses stemming from the fact that far fewer internal migrants have chosen to reside there than has been the pattern nationwide (29.0 percent in 1980).

Illustrative of the emerging effects of the geographic concentration of the

TABLE 14. THE FIVE STATES OF INTENDED RESIDENCE WITH THE HIGHEST NUMBER OF ADMISSIONS, RANK ORDERED, AND PERCENTAGE OF TOTAL ADMISSIONS, 1966–1979

					Ranking of States and Percentage of Total Admissions						
Year	First	%	Second	%	Third	%	Fourth	%	Fifth	%
1966	N.Y.	23.92	Calif.	22.62	Ill.	5.62	N.J.	5.47	Fla.	4.34
1967	N.Y.	23.86	Calif.	19.1	Fla.	6.28	Ill.	5.6	N.J.	5.19
1968	N.Y.	21.52	Calif.	15.92	Fla.	15.31	N.J.	6.1	Ill.	5.48
1969	N.Y.	26.33	Calif.	19.85	Ill.	5.69	Mass.	5.31	N.J.	5.28
1970	N.Y.	26.2	Calif.	19.89	N.J.	6.35	Ill.	5.6	Tex.	4.89
1971	N.Y.	24.96	Calif.	18.85	N.J.	6.37	Ill.	6.28	Tex.	5.45
1972	N.Y.	24.38	Calif.	20.83	Ill.	6.66	N.J.	6.24	Tex.	6.14
1973	N.Y.	23.4	Calif.	21.26	Tex.	6.65	Ill.	6.37	N.J.	6.31
1974	N.Y.	22.3	Calif.	22.5	Tex.	7.34	Ill.	6.28	N.J.	6.25
1975	N.Y.	22.4	Calif.	21.54	N.J.	6.73	Ill.	6.39	Tex.	6.21
1976	Calif.	22.25	N.Y.	21.5	Ill.	6.9	Fla.	6.31	N.J.	6.95
1977	Calif.	21.4	N.Y.	19.21	Fla.	12.34	N.J.	7.24	Ill.	5.4
1978	Calif.	24.28	N.Y.	16.72	Tex.	7.77	Fla.	6.55	Ill.	5.59
1979	Calif.	25.82	N.Y.	20.5	Tex.	6.63	Fla.	5.84	N.J.	5.75

Sources: U.S. Department of Justice, Immigration and Naturalization Service, *1974 Annual Report: Immigration and Naturalization Service* (Washington, D.C.: GPO, 1975), p. 50; and idem, *1979 Statistical Yearbook of the Immigration and Naturalization Service* (Washington, D.C.: GPO, 1982), p. 30.

TABLE 15. FOREIGN-BORN RESIDENTS AS PERCENTAGE OF
TOTAL POPULATION OF EACH STATE, 1980

Region and State	Percentage Born in Foreign Country	Region and State	Percentage Born in Foreign Country
New England		West South Central	
Maine	3.8	Arkansas	1.0
New Hampshire	4.2	Louisiana	2.1
Vermont	4.1	Oklahoma	1.8
Massachusetts	8.4	Texas	6.0
Rhode Island	8.8	West North Central	
Connecticut	8.5	Minnesota	2.7
Middle Atlantic		Iowa	1.7
New York	13.4	Missouri	1.8
New Jersey	10.3	North Dakota	2.3
Pennsylvania	3.6	South Dakota	1.4
South Atlantic		Nebraska	1.9
Delaware	3.4	Kansas	2.0
Maryland	4.6	Mountain	
Virginia	3.2	Montana	2.3
West Virginia	1.0	Idaho	2.3
North Carolina	1.5	Wyoming	1.9
South Carolina	1.4	Colorado	3.8
Georgia	1.7	New Mexico	4.1
Florida	10.9	Arizona	6.0
East North Central		Utah	3.5
Ohio	2.7	Nevada	6.7
Indiana	1.9	Pacific	
Illinois	7.3	Washington	5.8
Michigan	4.4	Oregon	4.2
Wisconsin	2.6	California	14.8
East South Central		Alaska	3.9
Kentucky	0.9	Hawaii	14.0
Tennessee	1.0		
Alabama	1.0	United States as a whole	6.2
Mississippi	0.9		

Source: U.S. Department of Commerce, Bureau of the Census, *1980 Census of Population and Housing: Provisional Estimates of Social, Economic, and Housing Characteristics* (Washington, D.C.: GPO, 1982), table P-2, pp. 14–19.

nation's immigrant population are the findings of Gregory DeFreitas and An-driana Marshall.[22] Their work is one of the first research studies to be based on 1980 census data pertaining to the foreign-born population of the nation. They found that one-third of all foreign-born workers were employed in manufacturing (as opposed to 23 percent of native-born workers). Of greater significance was the finding that 75 percent of all workers employed in manufacturing in Miami were immigrants, as were over 40 percent of those in Los Angeles and New York City, 25 percent in San Francisco, and 20 percent in Chicago and Boston. When DeFreitas and Marshall examined the thirty-five metropolitan areas of the nation having a population of one million or more, they found that the rate of wage growth in manufacturing was inversely related to the size of the immigrant population of these areas.

Thus, only a few states and a handful of cities have borne the brunt of the revival of immigration that has occurred since 1965. It is also important to note that the settlement patterns of illegal immigrants (to be discussed in Chapter 5) has closely resembled the geographic preferences of legal immigrants. In an effort to avoid detection, illegal immigrants often settle in communities that already have large numbers of persons with similar ethnic backgrounds. This tendency, of course, only intensifies the pressures on these few states and cities to accommodate immigrants. Indeed, a major political factor that has inhibited the willingness of the nation to address immigration policy issues is the fact that most states and localities have not been directly affected by the unique policy issues that mass immigration poses.

THE CHANGE IN COUNTRIES OF ORIGIN

The most important qualitative change in the pattern of U.S. immigration that has occurred since the national-origins system was phased out in 1965 has been the complete shift in the major regions of origin of immigrants. As shown in Table 16, by the end of the 1970s, nations in Latin America—followed closely by some in Asia—had become the primary sources of fourth wave U.S. immigrants. Beginning with the decade of the 1960s, Europe was replaced by Latin America as the leading source of immigrants to the United States. By the 1970s, Asia, against which the discriminatory features of the previous immigration system no longer applied, was challenging Latin America for that distinction.

This shift in the source of immigrants can be seen in Table 17, which lists in rank order the five countries with the highest number of admissions for the years 1969–1981. The last time a European nation appeared in this ranking was in

TABLE 16.   IMMIGRANTS ADMITTED TO THE UNITED STATES, BY REGION OF BIRTH, 1961–1979, AS PERCENTAGE OF TOTAL IMMIGRATION

Region of Birth	Percentage of Immigrants Admitted to the United States		
	1961–1970	1971–1976	1977–1979
Europe	33	20	13
Northern and Western	17	7	5
Southern	16	13	8
Latin America	39	41	42
Asia	13	32	39
North America	12	4	3
Other	3	3	3
Total	100	100	100

Source: Leon F. Bouvier, *Immigration and Its Impact on U.S. Society,* Population Trends and Public Policy no. 2 (Washington, D.C.: Population Reference Bureau, Inc., Sept. 1981), p. 2.

1973, when Italy placed fifth. Mexico has clearly become the country that supplies the most U.S. immigrants, and the Philippine Islands have tended to be the runner-up. The other source nations vary from year to year, but since 1974 they have all been located in either Southeast Asia or the Caribbean Basin.

Because of the magnitude of this shift in the countries of origin of U.S. immigrants, it is necessary to comment briefly on how it happened. The increase in Western Hemisphere immigration is self-explanatory. Prior to 1968, immigration from this region was unrestricted, and from 1968 to 1976 it was subject to a ceiling but not to preference categories. Hence, there was ample opportunity for a broad range of individuals from the Western Hemisphere to immigrate to the United States and subsequently to use their presence as a lever to reunify families both through the admission of immediate relatives and through preference categories for other relatives. Some immigrants from the Western Hemisphere of course used the occupational preference category. The result was a sharp increase in total immigration from the Western Hemisphere. This process obviously cannot explain why Southeast Asian immigration has become so prominent, however. In fact, as indicated earlier, the various restrictions on Asian immigration that applied throughout most of this century, as well as the priority assigned to family reunification under the Immigration Act of 1965, would seem to have worked against their immigrating in significant numbers. The expectations of both Congress and the Johnson administration in 1965 were that Asian immigration would increase only slightly. Moreover, illegal immigration from Asia has not been a major issue relative to the inflows of such persons from Mexico and the Caribbean area since 1965.

The answer to this seeming paradox lies in the way in which Asians have used the U.S. immigration system to their collective advantage. One of the obvious means has been the system's refugee provisions. From 1975 through 1981, over half a million refugees were admitted from Southeast Asia as a direct result of the end of the war in Vietnam. These refugees came from Vietnam (including ethnic Chinese from that country who were expelled by its new Communist government in the south), Kampuchea (formerly Cambodia), and Laos. In addition, legal immigrants came from the Philippines, China-Taiwan, Korea, India, and Hong Kong. Because immigrants had previously come from the Philippines and China-Taiwan, family reunification could be allowed to some extent in these cases (especially as defined in the second and fifth preference categories). But immigrants from these two countries have also made significant use of the occupational preference categories, for these groups were dominated by doctors, nurses, engineers, and scientists.

During this period the occupational preference category was also used by Koreans and Indians, who through opportunities to study in the United States gained professional training that in turn qualified them for the occupational preferences given to doctors, engineers, and scientists. (Once admitted, of course, a new immigrant can use his or her status to gain admission for all immediate relatives and more distant ones under the family preference catego-

TABLE 17. THE FIVE COUNTRIES WITH THE HIGHEST NUMBER OF ADMISSIONS, RANK ORDERED, AND PERCENTAGE OF TOTAL ADMISSIONS, 1969–1981

Year	Total Legal Immigrants		Rank Order of Immigrant Source Countries					Percentage of Total Admissions Accounted for by Five Highest-Ranked Countries
			First	Second	Third	Fourth	Fifth	
1969	358,579	Country: Total No.: Percent:	Mexico 44,623 12.4	Italy 23,617 6.6	Philippines 20,744 5.8	Canada 18,582 5.2	Greece 17,724 4.9	34.9
1970	373,326	Country: Total No.: Percent:	Mexico 44,469 11.9	Philippines 31,203 8.4	Italy 24,973 6.7	Greece 16,464 4.4	Cuba 16,334 4.4	35.7
1971	370,478	Country: Total No.: Percent:	Mexico 50,103 13.5	Philippines 28,471 7.7	Italy 22,137 6.0	Cuba 21,611 5.8	Greece 15,939 4.3	37.3
1972	384,685	Country: Total No.: Percent:	Mexico 64,040 16.7	Philippines 29,376 7.6	Italy 21,427 5.6	Cuba 20,045 5.2	Korea 18,876 4.9	35.8
1973	400,063	Country: Total No.: Percent:	Mexico 70,141 17.5	Philippines 30,799 7.7	Cuba 24,147 6.0	Korea 22,930 5.7	Italy 22,151 5.5	44.2
1974	394,861	Country: Total No.: Percent:	Mexico 71,586 18.1	Philippines 32,857 8.3	Korea 28,028 7.1	Cuba 18,929 4.8	China-Taiwan 18,056 4.6	42.9
1975	386,194	Country: Total No.: Percent:	Mexico 62,205 16.1	Philippines 32,857 8.5	Korea 28,362 7.3	Cuba 25,955 6.7	China-Taiwan 18,536 4.8	43.4

Year	Total	Country	No.	%	Country	No.	%	Country	No.	%	Country	No.	%	Country	No.	%	Other %
1976	398,615	Mexico	57,863	14.5	Philippines	37,281	9.4	Korea	30,803	7.7	Cuba	29,233	7.3	China-Taiwan	18,823	4.7	43.6
1976[a]	103,676	Mexico	16,001	15.4	Philippines	9,738	9.4	Korea	6,887	6.6	Cuba	6,763	6.5	China-Taiwan	5,034	4.9	42.8
1977	462,315	Cuba	69,708	15.1	Mexico	44,079	9.5	Philippines	39,111	8.5	Korea	30,917	6.7	China-Taiwan	19,764	4.3	44.0
1978	601,442	Mexico	92,367	15.4	Vietnam	88,543	14.7	Philippines	37,216	6.2	Cuba	29,754	4.9	Korea	29,288	4.9	46.0
1979	460,348	Mexico	52,096	11.3	Philippines	41,300	9.0	China-Taiwan	29,264	6.4	Korea	24,248	5.3	Vietnam	22,546	4.9	36.8
1980	530,639	Mexico	56,680	10.7	Vietnam	43,483	8.2	Philippines	42,483	8.0	Korea	32,320	6.1	China-Taiwan	27,651	5.2	38.2
1981	596,600	N.A.[b]	N.A.	N.A.	N.A.	N.A.	N.A.	N.A.	N.A.	N.A.	N.A.	N.A.	N.A.	N.A.	N.A.	N.A.	N.A.

Sources: For 1969–1980, Select Commission on Immigration and Refugee Policy, *U.S. Immigration Policy and the National Interest: Staff Report* (supplement to the final report) (Washington, D.C.: GPO, 1981), pp. 230–31. For 1981, *1980 Statistical Yearbook of the Immigration and Naturalization Service* (Washington, D.C.: GPO, undated but made available in 1984), table 6, pp. 15–17.

[a]Transitional quarter.
[b]Not available.

ries.) In 1979, for instance, 14,728 foreign students adjusted their status to remain in the United States as permanent-resident aliens. Of that total, 8,945 (or 61 percent) were from Asia: 1,501 from China-Taiwan, 577 from Hong Kong, 1,045 from India, 328 from Korea, and 133 from the Philippines.[23] The reverse side of this picture, of course, is the issue that the immigration system of the United States is causing a "brain drain" from these less developed nations. In 1982, for instance, the Deputy minister of Education for Taiwan complained: "We have given America the cream of our youth, not our problem people; it improves your work force but is our brain drain problem."[24]

It is clear that Asian immigration is increasing dramatically, but it is also clear that it is dual in nature. On the one hand, the legal U.S. immigration system is admitting Asians who are the educational and (in relative terms) the wealthy elite of the sending nations. On the other hand, since 1978, most Southeast Asian refugees have been unskilled, poorly educated, and generally poorly prepared for work in a complex industrial society (see Chapter 6).

Finally, it is important to note that although the leading sources of U.S. immigrants have changed since 1965, the percentage of total legal immigration that the top five source countries account for has dropped substantially from the rates of all decades prior to 1960. A comparison of the data in Table 17 with similar data in Chapter 2 (Tables 2, 3, 5, and 8) shows that at no time prior to 1960 did the top five source countries account for less than 60 percent of total legal immigration. Since 1969, the comparable percentages have ranged from 34 to 46 percent of total immigration. Thus, it would certainly seem that one effect of the post-1965 legislation has been to increase the number of nations that supply immigrants. To this end, the act would appear to be contributing to an ethnic pluralism of the population to a degree that has never truly existed before.

LABOR MARKET EFFECTS

Because of the paucity of credible research on the precise employment and earnings experiences of post-1965 immigrants, there is no statistical data base for immigrants that is comparable to the information compiled in the monthly Current Population Survey (CPS) by the U.S. Census Bureau for all workers. In fact, only a few ad hoc studies on the employment, unemployment, and labor force participation of immigrants have been conducted over the past decade, and it is to these that we must turn for admittedly limited findings on the labor market effects of immigration since 1965.

Legal immigrants are asked at the time they apply for an immigrant visa to specify an "occupation." The answers to this question have traditionally been the source for the scant occupational information that exists on immigrants. In the early 1970s David North and William Weissert found in a small sample survey that those immigrants who at the time of entry specified an "occupation" did in fact turn out to be in the labor force.[25] In other words, the answer to the question tended to be a rough basis for a labor force participation rate. Using this data, they determined that the labor force participation rate for adult immigrants who entered the United States in the 1960s was 59.3 percent (only fractionally higher than the rate for the general population, 59.0 percent).[26] They then compared this rate with the "thunderous 83.2 percent" they calculated for adult immigrants who entered during the first decade (a 1910 cohort) of the twentieth century (i.e., those who entered during the third wave of immigration).[27]

More importantly, when North and Weissert compared the original data supplied by immigrants at the time of entry with registration cards completed by immigrants two years later, they found a 20 percent increase in the number of persons who indicated they had an occupation. The additional workers were largely adult women who had previously listed themselves as "housewives" and men and women who had initially listed themselves as "students." Thus, North and Weissert contended, studies that relied only on labor force information at the time of entry seriously "understated" the real impact of legal immigrants on the labor market because they failed to allow for subsequent labor force entry decisions.[28] As a result, the actual labor force participation rate for legal immigrants is likely to be considerably—not marginally—higher than that of the general population.

With regard to occupational distribution, North and Weissert examined the pattern for a 1970 cohort of immigrants. They found that the distribution of jobs (as declared at entry) did not resemble the occupational distribution of the overall labor force. Instead, the pattern for the immigrants was decidedly skewed toward the professional, technical, skilled craftsman, and semiskilled operative occupations. Such was especially the pattern among immigrants from the Eastern Hemisphere. In review of this cohort two years later, the authors sought to ascertain what jobs these immigrants actually held. They found that although the general occupational pattern was the same, to the extent there was change from the original distribution, it was downward.[29] Proportionately fewer changes had occurred in the professional and technical categories than in all the other occupations.

In a follow-up study completed in 1979, David North conducted a more detailed examination of the 1970 cohort of immigrants.[30] This time he used social security earnings data as well as personal interviews to obtain a longitudinal perspective in describing the labor market experiences of these immigrants. Mindful of the fact that the immigrants in the cohort were admitted primarily for familial and not societal (i.e., labor market) considerations and that this particular cohort represented a transition between the ethnocentrism of the 1924–1965 era and the newly emerging nondiscriminatory basis for admission after 1965, North concluded that the labor force participation rates, unemployment rates, and educational attainment rates (with age held constant) within the cohort were "very much like those of the population as a whole."[31] He also found that although the earnings of legal immigrants initially tended to be lower than those of U.S. citizens with comparable backgrounds, the two tended to move toward equal levels over time.[32] It should be noted, however, that North's cohort had been in the United States for only five years at the time it was studied.

Barry Chiswick also has studied the earnings of immigrants. Drawn from 1970 census data on the foreign-born population of the nation, his sample was composed of persons who had lived in the United States for varying lengths of time—some since the 1920s.[33] Moreover, the persons he labeled as immigrants may have been legal immigrants or may have been illegal immigrants—there is no way to distinguish between them in the census data. Nevertheless, he too found that immigrants initially earned lower wages than native-born workers, but that, *ceteris paribus,* the earnings differential narrowed over time. With regard to male immigrants, he found that after eleven to fifteen years they actually reached parity with native-born male workers and that after twenty years their earnings were actually 6.4 percent higher than those of native-born men. He attributed this difference to the fact that immigrants were likely to be more highly motivated than native-born workers. With regard to male refugees, however, he found that it took some longer to achieve parity, while many others never did. He also noted that initial wage differences were smaller, and the time needed to reach parity was shorter, among whites than among nonwhites. Moreover, of all the immigrants he studied, he found that those from Mexico and the Philippines were "the least successful" in achieving these goals. As noted in Table 17, these two countries have been the leading sources of immigrants to the United States since 1970. The data Chiswick gathered on female immigrants is less clear, partly because the labor force participation rates for all women departed from past patterns radically in the 1970s. Women who immigrated with their husbands— especially Asian "war brides"—tended to earn less than women who immigrated alone. Chiswick also found that although the sons and daughters of first-generation immigrants earned 5–10 percent more than those with native-born parents, by the third generation the differential had disappeared. He attributed this change to the fact that initially higher motivations and abilities dissipate over time and, as a result, earnings regress toward the mean as successive generations are born in the United States. In subsequent research on employment and unemployment, Chiswick also found that after initial adjustment difficulties, it took immigrant men about five years to achieve the same employment and unemployment experiences as native-born men.[34] As in his earlier study, he noted that the experiences of female immigrants were less clear. He also found that immigrants from Mexico, Cuba, and China had the greatest difficulty achieving these results. They were consistently employed fewer weeks a year than other immigrant groups and the labor force as a whole.

In reviewing Chiswick's ambitious research on this subject, it is vital to keep in mind that his analysis is of foreign-born persons who entered the United States prior to 1970. Since 1970, the full effects of the Immigration Act of 1965 and its amendments and the Refugee Act of 1980 have come to bear on the nation's immigrants and labor force. As North has noted, 1970 census data on the foreign-born describe "persons of above average age, most of whom came to the U.S. many years earlier and under provisions of earlier legislation."[35] Consequently, he warns, "one must not assume that the profile of the foreign-born which emerged from the 1970 Census will be similar to that emerging from the 1980 or 1990 censuses."[36] Another factor to consider is that Chiswick's work dealt primarily with the experience of prime-working-age males (twenty-five to sixty-five years old). Females, who have constituted the majority of immigrants since 1970, as well as young and older workers, either were not the major focus of his study or were omitted. Likewise, minorities, which since 1970 have come to dominate immigration to the United States, were given scant attention by Chiswick. Moreover, in order to conduct his work, Chiswick had to use proxy groups for various immigrant categories (e.g., he used the experiences of immigrants from China prior to 1970 as the basis for his conclusions regarding the adjustment of refugees to the U.S. labor force). Since his data did not come from INS sources, his definitions of all the key terms—*immigrants, resident aliens, illegal immigrants,* and *refugees*—were not the same as those used by the federal government or as those used throughout this volume. Hence, one must be very careful how one interprets his findings.

The critical question in the present context, therefore, is, What has happened since 1970? Changes in the countries of origin of immigrants and in the conditions of entry have occurred since that year. It will take examinations of a 1980 cohort of immigrants as well as data for all the foreign-born as of 1980 to determine if Chiswick's conclusions are still valid. As indicated earlier, North believes it is very doubtful they will be. Legal immigrants from the Western Hemisphere have consistently had lower incomes and human capital endowments than those from the Eastern Hemisphere.[37] Indications are that the proportion of the total legal immigrant population coming from the Western Hemisphere has increased significantly since 1970 relative to that from the Eastern Hemisphere. Likewise, the proportion of Eastern Hemisphere immigrants who have come from Europe (and who have had higher earnings and levels of education) has declined sharply relative to the number coming from Asia (who have had lower levels of both). In addition, the number of refugees admitted to the United States from less economically developed nations during the mid-1970s and early 1980s has increased dramatically. Although at this point in time the statement is necessarily conjectural, it seems logical to expect that a downward shift in the occupational structure of the immigrant population has taken place— a shift from the professional, technical, managerial, and craftsman groupings toward the semiskilled, unskilled, and service occupations. It also seems very unlikely that the high level of human capital endowments of the pre-1970 immigrants remains characteristic of the post-1970 immigrant population. The dramatic increase in the number of semi- and unskilled illegal immigrants—especially from Mexico and the Caribbean Basin—also challenges the conclusions offered in the existing literature. Research on the employment patterns and human capital endowments of contemporary immigrants (legal and illegal) should be assigned the highest priority by the nation's policymaking and social science research bodies. Too many changes have occurred in the past decade to justify support of the earlier findings today.

The study by DeFreitas and Marshall mentioned earlier in this chapter was based on 1980 data on the foreign-born population of the United States, and it revealed a statistically significant negative relationship between the size of the foreign-born population in the nation's largest metropolitan areas and wage growth in the manufacturing sector during the 1970s.[38] The DeFreitas and Marshall study does suffer from some of the same data problems that confronted Chiswick (i.e., all categories of immigrants are lumped together, the data are cumulative in that they include all immigrants regardless of how many years they have been in the country, and illegal immigrants are most likely undercounted), but its findings underscore the importance of looking at data that reflect the impact of the resurgence of immigration that has occurred since 1970.

The Demand for Visas, 1982

One of the most troubling aspects of a system in which demand exceeds available supply is that backlogs develop. In this instance, the ceiling on the number of visas that can be issued (270,000), as well as the ceiling on the number of visas that can be issued to people from any one nation (20,000), means that people must wait varying lengths of time after they apply and are found eligible before being admitted. In a real sense, visa slots are economic "goods" that bring the opportunity for economic gain to most of the people who secure them. In the absence of a price-setting mechanism for these goods, the only way to overcome the backlog is to raise the ceilings or, in the case of the immigrants, to wait until one's turn comes. As of January 1, 1982, the backlog of visa applications registered at consular offices around the world totaled 1,176,983.[39] This number, however, does not include the immediate relatives who would be admitted with each visa applicant. Hence, the backlog is substantially greater than the number of visa applications indicates.

Of the visa requests pending in January 1982, 59 percent (or 698,498) were for the fifth preference category (brothers or sisters of adult U.S. citizens). The second highest number of requests—for the second preference category (spouses and unmarried sons and daughters who had already been admitted as permanent-resident aliens)—accounted for 18 percent of the applications. The third highest number of requests were for the catch-all nonpreference category (13 percent of the applications). Because of the existence of a backlog in all the preference groups, however, there have been no admissions of persons in the nonpreference category since 1978. Thus, the chances that applicants in this last category will be admitted in the near future are dim, if not nonexistent, unless the present system is changed.

It is also useful to note that the backlogs are extremely unequal in terms of the countries of origin represented by the visa applicants. Not surprisingly, the countries that became the largest sources of legal immigrants in the 1970s have accumulated the largest backlogs. Mexico has by far the largest number of pending visa applications. As of January 1, 1982, it had a backlog of 271,582 visa applications (or 23 percent of the total). Of these, the largest number (113,546) were for nonpreference admission. On January 1, 1982, the Philippines had the second largest backlog (269,094 visa applications, or 22.8 percent of the total). Of these, the largest single group (171,108 applicants) sought the fifth preference category. The nation with the third largest backlog was Korea, China-Taiwan ranked fourth, and India was fifth.

In light of the massive backlog of Mexican visa applications pending at the end of 1981, it is interesting to note that officials of the U.S. Embassy in Mexico estimated that as of 1981 "from 65 to 70 percent of these applicants are already in the United States."[40] They had, of course, simply immigrated illegally.

Efforts to Achieve Comprehensive Reform of the Legal Immigration System

Throughout the 1970s, concern over various immigration issues led to a movement to reform the entire U.S. immigration system. The dominant issue of this period was illegal immigration, but refugee accommodation and the status of temporary foreign workers also became subjects of extensive debate. As these separate issues arose, it became apparent that they were in fact interrelated and that a study of the entire system was needed.

Thus, in 1978, responding to a series of legislative proposals introduced the year before by President Jimmy Carter to deal with the problem of illegal immigration,[41] Congress elected to establish the Select Commission on Immigration and Refugee Policy rather than debate the single issue of illegal immigration. It charged the commission with the task of studying and evaluating "existing laws, policies, and procedures governing the admission of immigrants and refugees to the United States" and making "appropriate legislative recommendations."[42] The commission began its work in 1979.

The Select Commission was composed of sixteen persons. Four members were appointed by the president from the general public. Among these was the chairman, Reubin Askew, former governor of Florida. When Askew resigned in October 1979, he was replaced by the Reverend Theodore Hesburgh, president of Notre Dame University and a former chairman of the U.S. Civil Rights Commission. Also appointed were four members of the Cabinet whose departments traditionally impinge upon the subject of immigration (the attorney general, the secretary of health and human services, the secretary of labor, and the secretary of state); four members from the Senate; and four members from the House of Representatives.

During its deliberations the Select Commission had access to the work of its own staff as well as that of the staffs of several congressional committees; the advice of "dozens of consultants who participated in 21 special consultations"; and the opinions of "over 700 witnesses who testified at 12 regional public hearings." The commission funded a limited amount of research on a few specialized subjects, but because the original deadline for its report was October 1, 1980 (later extended to March 1, 1981), it did not undertake any ambitious research projects that would add to the meager store of knowledge that was available. For most of its inputs, therefore, it drew upon the existing literature on the subject. Unlike the Dillingham commission, which did initiate massive research projects (but, as discussed in Chapter 2, largely ignored the results of this research when preparing its final report), the Select Commission on Immigration and Refugee Policy did not even pretend to follow such a course. In all fairness it should be noted that at the time the Dillingham commission was appointed very little relevant information was available. By the late 1970s, however, the nation had amassed volumes of wisdom on the topic. Unfortunately, this store of knowledge was (and still is) limited and often contradictory. The Select Commission therefore based its findings largely upon what was known. It added very little that was new.

It is important to mention here only those conclusions of the commission which pertain to legal immigration. The other issues to which the commission addressed its attention will be discussed in the chapters on illegal immigration, refugees, and nonimmigrant workers.

The overriding theme of the commission's final report was that the United States should continue to accept large numbers of immigrants, but that it must confront "the reality of limitations." The commission concluded that the nation needed to adopt "a cautious approach" with respect to its immigration policy. It therefore recommended that a modest increase be made in the number of immigrants admitted annually (from 270,000 to 350,000); that a special effort be made to eliminate the massive backlog of visa requests that had resulted primarily from the effort to reunify families (it was proposed that an additional 100,000 visas be issued each year for five years without regard to any single country ceiling); and that a new immigration system—one designed to be "more equitable" and more in keeping with "our interests as a nation"—be set up.

According to the commission's recommendations, the new system would separate immigrants into two categories. One category would consist of immigrants who were in the process of being reunited with family members already in the United States. The other would consist of nonrelatives and would encompass the former occupational preference groups as well as provide opportunities for "new seed immigrants." Currently, the familial and nonfamilial categories are mixed together, and the result of this mixing has been confusion and hardship. The Select Commission correctly noted that the only way to assure that "new seed immigrants'' are admitted is to establish a separate channel of entry for them.

Under the existing system, only the third and sixth preference categories and any unused visas that remain for the nonpreference category are available to persons who are not relatives of citizens. The third and sixth preference categories, it should be recalled, require labor certifications, which means they are usually reserved for more skilled and highly educated persons. Moreover, since 1978 there have not been any visas that remained unused by the preference categories, and given the existing backlogs, it is unlikely that any nonpreference visas will be available in the foreseeable future. Hence, nonrelatives have had very little chance to enter the United States legally unless they could qualify for a labor certification or be ''fortunate enough'' to be admitted as a refugee. The Select Commission expressed the belief that the regulated entry of nonrelatives, or ''independent immigrants,'' would be consistent with the nation's historic interest in attaining cultural diversity. In particular, the commission noted that such a new channel would allow persons from countries that in the past had not had the opportunity to establish an immigration base—for example, ''many African nations''—to qualify as immigrants. The commission did not specify how many visas should be set aside for ''independent immigrants''; it recommended that this decision be made by Congress.

By the time the Select Commission on Immigration and Refugee Policy released its final report (on March 1, 1981), a new president had been sworn in. The incoming Reagan administration had not made immigration reform a key issue in its campaign and consequently took a cautious approach to the report. It established a special task force, chaired by Attorney General William French Smith, to review the commission's findings. This task force ultimately issued its own report citing a number of policy options on July 30, 1981. The preferred option of the task force was to retain the ceiling of 270,000 annual immigrant admissions, but to add 100,000 additional visas for five years in order to relieve existing backlogs. The Reagan administration subsequently submitted to Congress the Omnibus Immigration and Control Act of 1981, which contained all its proposals on immigration matters. This bill was never reported out of committee in either house, however. Instead, the immigration reform drive in Congress coalesced around a bipartisan bill drafted by Senator Allan K. Simpson (R., Wy.) and Congressman Romano L. Mazzoli (D., Ky.), the respective chairmen of the Senate and House subcommittees on immigration. Both men had served as members of the Select Commission on Immigration and Refugee Policy, and together they drafted the comprehensive Immigration Reform and Control Act of 1982 (popularly called the Simpson-Mazzoli bill). The bill, in amended form, passed the U.S. Senate on August 1982 by an overwhelming vote of 80 to 19. It then went to the House of Representatives, where after further refinements it cleared the Committee on the Judiciary on September 27, 1982. Due to other pressing matters, however, the final debate in the House was deferred until the special session of Congress that was held in December 1982. When this ''lame-duck'' session was convened, opponents of the bill were able to stall it by adding 300 amendments for discussion. As a result, the bill died on the floor of the House on December 18, 1982.[43]

In February 1983 the bill was reintroduced in each house of Congress in exactly the form that had passed the respective judiciary committees the previous year. In May 1983 the bill again passed the Senate by an overwhelming margin (76 to 18) and was sent to the House, where it was reported out of the Judiciary Committee that same month (by a vote of 20 to 9) and was voted on favorably by the three committees that considered subsections of the bill in June. Throughout the summer and early fall, sponsors of the bill awaited a rule that would place it on the floor for final debate and vote. Suddenly, without warning, Speaker of the House Thomas P. O'Neill announced in early October that the House would not consider the bill in that session.[44] He claimed that the bill had no real constituency and he expressed the fear that President Reagan would veto the bill if Congress passed it, in a play for political support from the nation's Hispanic community. Spokesmen for the White House immediately denied the charge of political trickery. The attorney general declared that the president would sign the Senate-passed version of the bill if it were sent to him (he could not make a similar statement about the House version because final action on its content had not yet been taken).[45] Indeed, at a news conference on October 19, 1983, President Reagan expressed his support for immigration reform, his willingness to sign the Senate version of the Simpson-Mazzoli bill, and the strong likelihood that he would sign the revised version of the bill (assuming the House acted) that would result from the normal Senate-House conference committee resolution of congressional differences.[46] In the wake of these developments, the arbitrary actions of Speaker O'Neill were condemned and a petition of discharge was filed in the House in an attempt to force a vote on the issue. In a complete reversal, Speaker O'Neill announced in late November 1983 that he had changed his mind and would now press for passage of the bill in early 1984.[47] He indicated that he had been assured that President Reagan would now sign such a measure. Soon thereafter, however, the administration raised a possible red flag: Budget Director David A. Stockman issued a report warning that the financial costs of implementing the bill might prove to be too high.[48]

In early May 1984, Speaker O'Neill announced that he would delay debate on the bill until after the Democratic presidential and congressional primary in California was held on June 6, 1984.[49] The Speaker made this decision in response to pleas by the Democratic congressional delegation from California and by the three Democratic presidential candidates (Walter Mondale, Gary Hart, and Jesse Jackson) to postpone consideration of the bill. During the campaign, all three of these candidates openly stated their opposition to the pending Simpson-Mazzoli bill. Then, true to his word, the Speaker announced the day after the California primary that the bill would be given a rule that would allow debate to commence the following week.[50] On June 8, 1984, the Rules Committee of the House unanimously approved a rule to debate the House version of the bill as well as discussion of sixty-nine separate amendments to the legislation. On June 11, 1984, the House of Representatives voted in favor of the terms of the rule, 291 to 111.[51] Accordingly, the debate commenced. After seven sessions that involved over fifty hours of floor debate, an amended form of the bill passed on June 20, 1984, by a narrow margin of 216 to 211. The amended bill differs in a number of significant ways from the Senate version, and it remains to be seen if the conference committee version will be acceptable to both houses of Congress and to the president. In any event, as noted in the preface to this book, the Simpson-Mazzoli bill—regardless of its fate—marks only the opening chapter in what promises to be a lengthy struggle to reform the entire immigration system of the United States.

According to the provisions of the Senate version of the Simpson-Mazzoli bill that passed in both 1982 and 1983, the number of immigrants admitted each year would be increased to 425,000 and would include both immigrants and their immediate relatives. Thus, a cap on total immigration (those with visas plus immediate family members) would be set. Of the available visas, 350,000 would be set aside for family reunification cases and 75,000 would be reserved for "independent immigrants." Refugee admissions, however, would continue to be excluded from specific limitations (despite an effort on the floor of the Senate in 1982 to include a refugee ceiling in the bill). The 1982 version of the Senate bill also called for the abolishment of the fifth preference category (a special category added in 1965 that established preference for brothers and sisters of adult U.S. citizens), but this provision was dropped from the 1983 Senate version of the bill. Labor certification requirements remained unchanged.

The Senate version of the bill (1982 and 1983) also included an important provision pertaining to immigration from Mexico. Namely, it sought to modify the effect of the 1976 amendment that placed immigration from Mexico on a par with that from all other countries. Many observers in Mexico and the United States believe that the imposition of the same 20,000-visa ceiling on Mexico as applied to all other nations has proven to be counterproductive. Enacted in the name of equity to all nations, it ignores the reality that Mexico is the single largest source of actual and would-be immigrants to the United States. Enforcement of the ceiling has resulted in a massive backlog of visa applications from Mexico and thus has indirectly enhanced the problem of illegal immigration. Thus, the 1982 and 1983 Senate versions of the Simpson-Mazzoli bill have proposed raising the ceiling on immigration from Mexico and Canada to 40,000 visas for each country. Moreover, the bill calls for the establishment of a special reciprocity procedure whereby each of these nations could claim the unused visas of the other. Canada in recent years has not used more than half of its allowable visas. Given the continued imposition of a ceiling on the total number of immigrants admitted to the United States, the special treatment of Canada and Mexico would result in a small reduction in the number of legal immigrants admitted from all other nations. Although it is common throughout the world for neighboring nations to make special exceptions in many of their laws for the countries with which they share a border, in the House version of the Simpson-Mazzoli bill, the reciprocity arrangement was deleted. In short, Mexico would not be allowed to use any extra Canadian visas.

Lessons from Other Nations

In the realm of economic policymaking, it is often useful to study how other nations respond to similar problems and dilemmas. Due to the existence of differing institutional structures, however, it is seldom possible to transfer solutions in their entirety from one nation to another. Nonetheless, comparative policy studies can sometimes provide useful insights with respect to both what might be done and what probably should not be done. In this and in subsequent chapters, a brief review of some of the pertinent experiences of other nations will be presented.

As a generalization, it can safely be said that few of the industrialized nations of the world permit significant numbers of immigrants to be admitted. From the 1950s through the early 1970s, however, many nations of Western Europe were confronted with serious labor shortages. Rather than encourage permanent immigration, they embarked upon a course that entailed recruitment of foreign workers primarily from the less developed nations of the Mediterranean Basin.[52] The idea was to create a temporary-worker program. On a regular, short-term basis individual workers would be rotated back to their homelands and replaced by other workers. This form of nonimmigrant labor policy will be examined closely in Chapter 4. It is sufficient to say here that the rotation principle did not work out as planned. Consequently, when Western Europe experienced its first postwar recession in 1973–1974, most of the nations of this region quickly ceased the practice of actively recruiting new foreign workers. The major quandary, however, was what to do with the large numbers of foreign workers who had not been rotated over the years. Many had settled in these countries and did not wish to return to their homelands. Opting not to try forcibly to expel the several million foreigners involved, most of these "host" nations grudgingly decided to integrate them into their societies. Due to natural population growth and the rising number of illegal immigrants, most of these nations now have rapidly growing foreign populations in their midst. Thus, although permanent immigration was not the intended goal of the temporary-worker programs, it has been the result in many West European nations.

In the less developed nations of the world, there is little or no interest in immigration policy. Most are already struggling under immense problems of population and labor force growth. The only exceptions that some are willing to make involve the admission of foreign persons with special skills or talents that are chronically in short supply. Work by foreigners within these nations is often severely regulated or even prohibited. Some of these nations—for example, Thailand, Pakistan, Somalia, Rwanda, and Lebanon—have had large numbers of refugees foisted upon them.[53] It is a cruel irony that the burden of refugee accommodation is presently borne in large part by many of the world's poorest nations.

One of the world's most prominent noncommunist industrial powers has traditionally held to a strict policy of not permitting immigration. That country, of course, is Japan. With only a few exceptions, it has determined that it has an ample supply of citizen workers relative to its size, population, and resources. Most of the Communist bloc nations have also adhered to a policy that prohibits permanent immigration and in addition have greatly restricted emigration.

Thus, in the early 1980s only a handful of countries are allowing immigration of any numerical consequence to take place. Most of these countries can be characterized as having large land masses relative to their existing populations. They are Argentina, Australia, Brazil, Canada, New Zealand, South Africa, and the United States. Other nations, though smaller in size, have sought immigrants because of national security conditions. Israel is the prime example of this rationale. Australia and New Zealand, which are geographically distant from their traditional allies, also view immigration in terms of national security. All these nations are relatively advanced industrial economies that have determined that they have the capacity to absorb a regulated flow of immigrants. They expect those persons who are admitted to become permanent settlers, and thus it is usually easy for immigrants to become citizens soon after they arrive.

Of the few industrial nations that are admitting legal immigrants on a regular basis, Australia and Canada are most similar to the United States in their settlement histories and institutional structures. As a result, they are usually cited as the two nations whose immigration policies would most likely provide useful lessons for the United States. Yet both of these countries have developed immigration policies that are entirely different from U.S. immigration policy in terms of priorities and operational procedures.[54]

In the United States the Immigration and Naturalization Service (INS) is buried within the structure of the multipurpose Department of Justice. In both Australia and Canada a separate government ministry performs the functions associated with implementing immigration policies. By U.S. standards, the Australian and Canadian agencies are permitted an immense latitude of discretion in determining both the level of immigration that will occur in a given year and the composition of the immigrant flows. These agencies station a substantial staff in their consulates around the world. U.S. immigration officials do not have contact with immigrants until they arrive. As indicated earlier, the U.S. Department of State reviews visa requests and issues visas to potential immigrants as a part of its consular functions in foreign nations. Immigration is only one of many tasks that State Department officials perform abroad. In the case of Canada and Australia, the work done by immigration officials abroad has an impact on the career advancement of these officials within their respective agencies. In the United States, the career advancement of State Department officials has little to do with the manner in which they perform immigration assessment tasks. In fact, many

State Department employees view immigration duties as a drudgery, as only a phase in the process by which one is eventually promoted to a more rewarding position in the Foreign Service. Few, if any, persons join the Foreign Service of the United States because they want to process immigration applications.

The major reason that the administration of U.S. immigration policy differs so much from that of Australia and Canada is that the duties assigned to the respective agencies are so different. In the latter two nations, immigration officers interview prospective immigrants and assess their desirability in largely qualitative terms. These standards vary depending on the state of the receiving country's economy. In 1982, for instance, Canada announced that because it had an unemployment rate of over 12 percent, for the fiscal year 1983 it would sharply reduce the number of immigrants admitted on the basis of their labor market skills (a category called "selected workers") from a target range of 20,000–25,000 to a range of 8,000–10,000.[55] (In fact, the number actually admitted in this category in fiscal 1983 was less than 7,000).[56] Those workers who were admitted in this category were restricted to occupations in which a labor shortage had developed.

Both Canada and Australia make some exceptions in enforcing their qualitative admission standards—in order to admit the close relatives of immigrants, for example—but in most cases their standards prevail. Canada has long used a point system to evaluate and rank prospective immigrants, and under that system a minimum score determines one's qualification for actual admission. Australia for many years relied upon positive recommendations from its overseas immigration officers, but in 1979 it, too, converted to a point system. In assigning points, both nations give high priority to the ability of applicants to meet defined labor market needs in their countries. Thus, their immigration officials are endowed with immense power. Most of Australia's and Canada's assessment criteria call for highly subjective evaluations. Among these criteria are the would-be immigrant's educational background and occupational training; occupational demand in the receiving country; the applicant's ability to speak English (or French, in the case of Canada), and the immigrant's intended destination in the receiving country (e.g., remote areas are given more points than labor surplus regions). Other factors pertain to health, character, and the likelihood that adjustment to life in the new country will be easy.

In contrast, the U.S. system is highly mechanistic in its application of specified preference categories. There is little room for personal judgments, and hence the role of U.S. immigration officials is essentially indirect. State Department officials review visa applications, and Labor Department officials review labor certification requests in the relatively few circumstances in which this is required. INS officials are left with little to do but verify that all the applicant's documents are in order.

In terms of outcome, the differences between the systems are stark. The U.S. system relies essentially upon family reunification principles and refugee accommodation goals; virtually no labor market factors are involved in the decisionmaking process. As North and LeBel have concluded, "Policy making in the manpower field and policy making in immigration are only distantly connected [in the United States]."[57] In contrast to the U.S. pattern, immigrants to Australia and Canada are typically younger, predominantly male, more likely to be in the prime working-age cohort (eighteen to thirty-five), more likely to settle in regions that need workers than in those that do not, and more likely to have occupational skills that are in short supply in the economy they are about to enter.

Precisely because Australia and Canada view labor market needs as the primary goal of their immigration systems, both countries couple their immigration policies with extensive postarrival assistance programs to ease the settlement process for both the immigrants and their communities. In the United States, with the exception of some refugee groups, the adjustment process is largely left to the individual, to relatives, and to local communities to carry out. The difference in treatment, of course, is based on the fact that Australia and Canada are motived to facilitate the entry of immigrants into their economies because that was the primary rationale for admitting them. In the United States the legal system is predicated largely upon family reunification objectives, and how immigrants adapt to the labor market is left largely to chance.[58] Obviously, given the number of persons involved and the high concentration of new immigrants in a few selected labor markets of the nation, labor market consequences do flow from the operation of the immigration system. So far, however, responsibility for the specific labor market consequences of that policy have largely been ignored by the federal government.

If family reunification remains the primary goal of the legal U.S. immigration process, a federally financed categorical assistance program will be needed to cushion the economic hardships imposed on communities that receive large numbers of legal immigrants, and especially on those receiving large infusions of refugees. National policymakers should not be permitted to impose hardship on local communities without also providing some form of compensatory aid. It is the present author's belief that such an aid program should be based on the principles of the "impacted areas" program created under the Impacted Areas Act of 1950, which was used to assist local communities in adjusting to the presence of new or expanded federal government installations. Federal immigration policy raises similar concerns. An ideal immigration assistance package would include more than job training and language instruction. It would provide funding to local public agencies to defer the costs of education, health, and perhaps housing—in short, the local social costs of national policy.

CHAPTER 4

Nonimmigrant
Labor Policy

The employment of foreign workers as a supplement to the available domestic labor force has been a recurrent public policy issue throughout the history of the United States. Under specified circumstances, nonimmigrant workers have been allowed access to the nation's labor market. They should not be confused with illegal immigrants, who do not legally have this privilege. Every person who enters the nation legally is classified as an immigrant or a nonimmigrant. Nonimmigrants are essentially those members of all categories of visa applicants who are not granted immigrant status. Among the small number of applicants who are classified as nonimmigrants, a considerably smaller proportion are given permission to work.

Several features of the nonimmigrant labor policies of the United States are both logical and beneficial to the economy and quality of life of the nation. Foreign students sometimes need jobs to supplement inadequate stipends provided by their own governments or families; sports fans wish to see a higher grade of competition, and thus some foreign players are allowed to play for American hockey and soccer teams; opera stars and rock bands from abroad perform before American audiences in the name of cultural diversity; visiting professors from abroad add to the quality of many university programs; and with the growth of multinational corporations, foreign executives have been stationed in the United States to administer such enterprises. These examples, as well as numerous others, suggest that nonimmigrant labor policies have the potential of creating a realistic and desirable flexibility in what must otherwise be termed a rigid immigration system.

Yet within the broad dimensions of nonimmigrant labor policy a programmatic history has evolved that is not easy to rationalize. Within the various nonimmigrant programs, provision has been made for the employment of workers who are less skilled and less talented than the workers who are generally available within the American labor force, but who are otherwise similar in their employment capabilities to large segments of the American labor force. Because of this pattern, the sanguine attitude surrounding nonimmigrant labor policy must be challenged. These programs have in fact been persistently misused and abused. Consequently, the legislative and the administrative actions involved in establishing such programs have generally been controversial. Concern has centered on the effect nonimmigrant laborers would have on the working conditions of some citizen workers and on the special restrictions that are often imposed on nonimmigrants—restrictions that would be considered unfair and illegal if applied to citizen workers.

Traditionally, nonimmigrant labor policy has been viewed as a means of overcoming labor shortages. In the late 1970s, however, some analysts began suggesting that nonimmigrant labor policy might also provide a means of reducing illegal immigration. In order to understand this largely unpublicized yet persistent dimension of U.S. immigration policy, it is essential that we place nonimmigrant labor policy in its evolutionary perspective. Examined as isolated decisions made at different points in history, the policy seems to consist of ad hoc reactions to events of a particular time. A long-term perspective, however, reveals developmental patterns. Recognition of these themes and characteristics is essential to any effort to evaluate the efficacy of contemporary nonimmigrant labor policy and to proposals that call for an expansion of that policy.

Antecedent Programs: The Pre-1952 Experience

As mentioned in Chapter 2, the right of American employers to recruit and hire foreign laborers to work in the United States was established in the Contract Labor Act of 1864. This legislation was enacted as a wartime measure and was repealed in 1868. The practice, however, continued with little interruption until 1885, when such activities were specifically banned by the Alien Contract Labor Act. During these years, the nation had an essentially open immigration policy, turning away only the Chinese. Thus, technically speaking, contract labor was not a nonimmigrant labor program. Those who were recruited were encouraged to stay as permanent immigrants. Moreover, contract labor was practiced prior to the establishment of immigration ceilings and country quotas. Nevertheless, it laid the conceptual foundation for subsequent nonimmigrant labor programs.

THE FIRST BRACERO PROGRAM, 1917–1922

Only months after the U.S. Congress enacted the most restrictive immigration legislation in its history—the Immigration Act of 1917—the first publicly sanctioned foreign-worker program for nonimmigrants was initiated.[1] Responding to strong pressure from the leading agricultural employers of the Southwest, Congress included in the Immigration Act of 1917 a provision granting entry to "temporary" workers from Western Hemisphere nations who would otherwise be considered inadmissible. The statute authorized the secretary of labor to exempt such persons (in this instance, Mexicans) from the head tax required of each immigrant and from the ban on immigrants over the age of sixteen who could not read. In May 1917, with the nation officially at war with Germany, a temporary farmworker program for nonimmigrant Mexicans was created, and later it was expanded to permit the employment of some of these laborers in nonfarm work. When the program was announced, a number of rules and regulations for governing it also were set forth. Ostensibly, these rules were designed to protect both citizen workers and Mexican workers and to ensure that the Mexicans returned to their country when their work was completed. As soon became apparent, however, "these elaborate rules were unenforced."[2]

The temporary-worker program that was established in the United States during World War I was defended, in part, as a step taken in the national interest, but it was subsequently extended until 1922—well after the war had ended. In later years the program came to be referred to as "the first bracero program."[3] The term *bracero* is a corruption of the Spanish word *abrazo,* which means "arm." (Literally, the term means "one who works with his arms.") The program was terminated in 1922 because it could no longer be justified as a national defense policy. Organized labor contended that the program had undermined the economic welfare of citizen workers. Other critics argued that labor shortages no longer existed in the United States and that greedy employers wanted the program to continue so that they could go on tapping a secure and cheap source of docile workers. It is interesting to note that during the life span of the program, 76,862 Mexican workers were admitted to the United States. Of this number only 34,922 returned to Mexico.[4]

THE MEXICAN LABOR PROGRAM, 1942–1964

With the advent of World War II, the military manpower requirements of the United States and the related need for laborers in manufacturing led to assertions that another labor shortage existed in the nation's agricultural sector. Growers in the southwestern United States had foreseen these developments before the attack on Pearl Harbor in 1941, and on this basis they made two fateful decisions: first, to again tap the pool of cheap labor in Mexico in order to fill the alleged manpower deficit; and second, to ask the federal government to again serve as the vehicle of deliverance.[5]

The requests made by southwestern growers in 1941 for the establishment of a new contract labor program were denied by the federal government, but by mid-1942 the U.S. government had come to favor the program. The government of Mexico, however, balked at the prospect of a formal intergovernmental agreement. According to Article 123 of the Mexican Constitution of 1917, the unregulated hiring of Mexican citizens by foreign nationals is prohibited.[6] Moreover, in the 1940s the Mexican economy was flourishing. Mexican workers feared that they might be drafted if they went to the United States; they had bitter memories of the efforts to "repatriate" Mexicans in the 1930s; and they were aware of the discriminatory treatment accorded people of Mexican ancestry throughout much of the southwestern United States.

Negotiations between the two governments ultimately resulted in a formal agreement, however, and in August 1942 the Mexican Labor Program—more popularly known as the "bracero program"—was created by the U.S. Congress. Under the terms of the agreement, Mexican workers were to be afforded protection with respect to housing, transportation, food, medical needs, and wage rates. Originally included within an omnibus appropriations bill known as Public Law 45 (P.L. 45), this bracero program was extended by subsequent enactments until 1947.

According to P.L. 45, braceros were permitted to work only in the agricultural sector. If they were found working in any other industry, they were subject to immediate deportation. Although the U.S.-Mexican agreement that had led to the creation of the Mexican Labor Program expired on December 31, 1947, the program continued informally and without regulation until 1951. In that year, under the guise of a labor shortage caused by the Korean War, the bracero concept was officially revived by Public Law 78 (P.L. 78). This legislation was extended on three separate occasions until the program was unilaterally terminated by the United States on December 31, 1964. It is important to note that the authority to establish the bracero programs was not included in the nation's immigration statutes, but was created by separate congressional enactments.

Under P.L. 78, only Mexican workers could be hired to work in the United States. The scale of the program can be seen in Table 18. Employers were required to pay the prevailing agricultural wage, provide free housing, provide adequate meals at a reasonable charge, and pay all transportation costs from government reception centers near the border to the work site. As in earlier bracero programs, however, these requirements often were not met.[7] Braceros were exempt from U.S. social security and income taxes, which meant that they received more income than a citizen worker employed at the identical wage rate.

In Mexico, the federal government determined the actual allocation process by which workers would be selected from the various states. The state governments in turn made similar decisions for their cities and other political subdivisions. Understandably, the Mexican government sought to spread out the job opportunities geographically rather than select workers from the available labor surpluses in the border towns. It was feared that recruiting only in border towns would set off a mass internal migration to the border region. Nevertheless, there were many more applicants than job openings in every designated labor market where recruitment occurred. Corruption in the allocation process soon became widespread at the local level, however. Potential workers often were forced to pay a *mordida* (a bribe; literally, "a bite") if they wished to be chosen.

The bracero program of 1951 demonstrated precisely how border labor policies can adversely affect citizen workers in the United States—especially, in this case, Mexican Americans, who at that time comprised the bulk of the nation's southwestern agricultural labor force. Agricultural employment in the Southwest was virtually removed from competition with the nonagricultural sector. At the program's peak, almost half a million braceros were working in the

TABLE 18. FOREIGN WORKERS ADMITTED FOR TEMPORARY EMPLOYMENT IN U.S. AGRICULTURE, BY YEAR AND NATIONALITY, 1942–1980

			Number Admitted, by Nationality			
Year	Total Admitted	Mexican[a]	British West Indian (including Bahamans)	Canadian	Japanese and Filipino	Spanish
1942	4,203	4,203	—[b]	—	—	—
1943	65,624	52,098	13,526	—	—	—
1944	83,206	62,170	19,622	1,414	—	—
1945	72,900	49,454	19,391	4,055	—	—
1946	51,347	32,043	13,771	5,533	—	—
1947	30,775	19,632	3,722	7,421	—	—
1948	44,916	35,345	3,671	5,900	—	—
1949	112,765	107,000	2,765	3,000	—	—
1950	76,525	67,500	6,225	2,800	—	—
1951	203,640	192,000	9,040	2,600	—	—
1952	210,210	197,100	7,910	5,200	—	—
1953	215,321	201,380	7,741	6,200	—	—
1954	320,737	309,033	4,704	7,000	—	—
1955	411,966	398,650	6,616	6,700	—	—
1956	459,850	445,197	7,563	6,700	390	—
1957	452,205	436,049	8,171	7,300	685	—
1958	447,513	432,857	7,441	6,900	315	—
1959	455,420	437,643	8,772	8,600	405	—
1960	334,729	315,846	9,820	8,200	863	—
1961	310,375	291,420	10,315	8,600	40	—
1962	217,010	194,978	12,928	8,700	404	—
1963	209,218	186,865	12,930	8,500	923	—
1964	200,022	177,736	14,361	7,900	25	—
1965	35,871	20,284	10,917	4,670	0	—
1966	24,080	8,647	11,194	3,683	0	477
1967	23,959	6,125	13,578	3,900	0	356
1968	13,704	0	10,723	2,600	0	381
1969	16,221	0	13,530	2,300	0	391
1970	17,937	0	15,470	2,004	0	463
1971	14,235	0	12,143	1,541	0	551
1972	12,847	0	11,419	1,107	0	321
1973	13,551	0	11,712	1,458	0	381
1974	14,197	0	11,625	1,250	0	322
1975	12,426	0	11,245	970	0	211
1976	12,325	0	11,568	572	0	185
1977	12,266	0	11,661	399	0	206
1978	11,581	0	10,955	312	0	274
1979	12,791	0	12,246	287	0	258
1980	11,544	0	11,004	391	0	149

Sources: For 1942–1972, U.S. Senate, Committee on the Judiciary, *The West Indies (BWI) Temporary Alien Worker Program, 1943–1977* (Washington, D.C.: GPO, 1978), table 2, p. 27. For 1973–1980 U.S. Department of Justice, *Immigration and Naturalization Service, 1980 Statistical Yearbook of the Immigration and Naturalization Service* (Washington, D.C.: GPO, 1984), table 18, p. 113.

Note: Due to the carry-over of workers from one year to the next, the number of workers admitted each year is generally lower than the actual number of persons employed during peak harvest seasons.

[a]Data for the years 1951–1964 are for workers admitted under P.L. 78.

[b]— = data not available.

agricultural labor market of the Southwest. The availability of Mexican workers significantly depressed existing wage levels in some regions, moderated wage increases that would have occurred in their absence, and sharply compressed the duration of employment for many citizen farmworkers.[8] In its thorough report on the bracero program in 1952, President Truman's Commission on Migratory Labor found that "wages by States [for agricultural workers] were inversely related to the supply of alien labor."[9] Citizen farmworkers in the Southwest simply could not compete with braceros. The fact that braceros were captive workers who were totally subject to the unilateral demands of employers made them especially appealing to many employers. It also led to extensive charges of abuse of workers by employers as most of the provisions for the protection of braceros' wage rates and working conditions were either ignored or circumvented.[10] Moreover, the bracero program was a significant factor in the rapid exodus of rural Mexican Americans between 1950 and 1970 to urban labor markets, where employment and housing often were difficult to find.[11]

The drive to repeal Public Law 78 was led by the AFL-CIO, various Mexican American groups, and an array of other community organizations generally concerned with the welfare of low-income workers. The Kennedy administration, which came into office in 1961, did not initially support repeal of the program. Instead, it sought significant amendments to the law which were designed to strengthen the protection of domestic workers from the adverse effects of competition with the braceros. Believing that in southwestern agriculture the prevailing wage was in fact set by the braceros themselves rather than by domestic labor market factors, the Kennedy administration agreed in 1961 to extend the program, but promised that much tighter administrative regulations would be imposed.[12] In mid-1962 the Department of Labor began setting an "adverse-effect wage rate" for each state. These were minimum wage rates that the department determined had to be paid to prevent braceros from undercutting the wages of citizen agricultural workers. In most cases, the adverse-effect wage rates were actually higher than the prevailing wages. They had to be offered to citizen workers if the agricultural employer also intended to hire foreign workers. Under these terms, the bracero program became much less attractive to employers. The bitter political struggle ended in 1963 when the program was extended by compromise for one more year with the understanding that it would not be renewed after December 31, 1964. Within the Kennedy administration the only strong support for the program came from the Department of State. A spokesman for the department noted that "the program has been beneficial to Mexico and, therefore, from our point of view the continuation is desirable."[13] He also warned that if the bracero program was terminated, the Mexican workers would likely continue to come anyhow—albeit illegally. This same appraisal was made by the Mexican government in an official note to the United States in June 1963:

> It is not to be expected that the termination of an international agreement governing and regulating the rendering of service by Mexican workers in the

United States will put an end to that type of seasonal migration. The aforesaid agreement is not the cause of that migration; it is the effect or the result of the migratory phenomenon. Therefore, the absence of an agreement would not end the problem but rather would give rise to a de facto situation: the illegal introduction of Mexican workers in the United States which would be extremely prejudicial to the illegal workers and, as experience has shown would also unfavorably affect American workers.[14]

It was primarily the request by Mexico for a gradual phasing out of the bracero program—if in fact it had to end—that caused the United States to extend the program from 1963 to 1964.[15] As will be seen later, illegal immigration from Mexico began to accelerate when the bracero program was terminated at the end of 1964.

THE BRITISH WEST INDIES LABOR PROGRAM

Following the precedent set by creation of the Mexican Labor Program in 1942, the U.S. government established a similar nonimmigrant program to recruit workers from the British West Indies. Several governments of the British West Indies (Jamaica, the Bahamas, St. Lucia, St. Vincent, Dominica, and Barbados) entered into an intergovernmental agreement with the U.S. government in April 1943 pertaining to the supply of agricultural workers. This agreement served as the foundation for the British West Indies (BWI) Program. The BWI program was established in response to concerns voiced by employers along the U.S. East Coast that they, too, were experiencing wartime manpower shortages. Because many of the potential BWI workers spoke English, they offered an advantage to employers over the Mexican workers recruited for the bracero program. The scale of the BWI program can be seen in Table 18.

The original BWI program was established largely by informal memoranda, or "understandings." Like the bracero program, it was formalized on the basis of P.L. 45 and was to be operative from 1943 through 1947. In terms of aggregate numbers—about 24,000 workers a year—the BWI program was small compared to the bracero program, but its impact was substantial in the particular agricultural labor markets where these workers were employed.[16] Of the eleven East Coast states that participated in the program, Florida was by far the largest recipient. In one respect the BWI program differed substantially from the Mexican program. During the actual war years BWI recruits were also permitted to work in the nonagricultural sector. In 1945, for instance, close to 16,000 BWI workers were employed in foundries, food processing plants, and logging camps.[17]

During the years 1947–1952 the BWI program was converted into a temporary-worker program, as allowed under the provisions of the Immigration Act of 1917. Tripartite contracts were drawn up between U.S. employers, the foreign workers, and the governments of the participating nations of the West Indies. The U.S. government was not a direct participant. Travel and recruitment expenses were paid entirely by U.S. employers, and the workers who were recruited were employed only in agriculture.

A review of the BWI program by the President's Commission on Migratory Labor in 1951 led to condemnation of the administration of the program. In its report the following year, the commission attacked the lack of "vigilance for the protection of [the] living and working standards" of these workers.[18] Whereas the same commission was critical of the adverse effects of the Mexican program on the wages of citizen workers in the Southwest, it did not make a parallel argument about the wage effects of the BWI program—probably because the BWI program was considerably smaller in scale.

During the legislative debate over the continuation of the Mexican Labor Program in 1951, the BWI program was specifically included in the original draft of what was to become P.L. 78. But because East Coast employers—especially those in Florida—specifically requested that the BWI workers not be included in the legislation, the language of the bill was changed and only "agricultural workers from the Republic of Mexico" were included in its provisions. The East Coast employers preferred to keep the BWI program as it was, and hence the program continued to function according to the provisions of the Immigration Act of 1917.

Policy Development: The Post-1952 Experience

As discussed in Chapter 2, U.S. immigration policy was revised significantly by the Immigration and Nationality Act of 1952. This statute, which remains in effect today, maintains the principle that all persons entering the United States must be classified either as immigrants or as nonimmigrants. Its definition of *nonimmigrants,* however, is infinitely more complex. Twelve classes of nonimmigrants are specified, and these classes, in turn, are divided into a number of subclasses. Several classes of nonimmigrants are not permitted to work in the United States (e.g., visitors for pleasure and aliens in transit). Others are allowed to work in the United States, but their work has little or no impact on the U.S. labor market (e.g., foreign ambassadors, officials of international organizations, or representatives of foreign news media). Still others are permitted to work and their employment has a direct impact on the American labor force.[19] It is this last group, of course, that is relevant to the present discussion. In passing, it should be noted that the Immigration and Nationality Act of 1952 specifically repealed the ban on contract labor that had been imposed by the Alien Contract Labor Act of 1885 and by the 1887 and 1888 amendments to that law.

Since 1952 an unofficial convention has evolved whereby the individual classes and subclasses of nonimmigrants are identified by the letters and numbers of the sections of the act under which they were defined. Table 19 indicates all the categories that permit nonimmigrants to work in the United States and the corresponding number of nonimmigrants who were admitted in fiscal year 1978

TABLE 19. NONIMMIGRANTS ADMITTED TO THE UNITED STATES
UNDER IMMIGRATION CATEGORIES THAT PERMIT NONIMMIGRANTS TO WORK,
FISCAL YEAR 1978

Category	Classification	Number Admitted
Treaty trader or investor	E	50,431
Student	F-1	187,030
Temporary worker of distinguished ability or merit	H-1	16,838
Other temporary worker	H-2	22,832
Industrial trainee	H-3	3,309
Exchange visitor	J-1	53,319
Fiancé (fiancée) of U.S. citizen	K-1	5,730
Intracompany transferee	L-1	21,495
Total		360,984

Source: U.S. Department of Justice, Immigration and Naturalization Service, 1978 Annual Report of the Immigration and Naturalization Service (Washington, D.C.: GPO, 1979), tables 16 and 16B.

under each of these classifications. Not all of the 360,984 persons who are so listed actually secured jobs, but it is likely that many did. Unfortunately there is no way to determine the precise number of nonimmigrants who become gainfully employed.

Among the nonimmigrants who enter the nation's labor market, several classes are free to change jobs at will. They are not contractually linked to employers. Among these, for instance, are foreign students (F-1 workers), who may legally work in any occupation if they receive permission from the INS. Most other nonimmigrants are under some binding contractual obligation to their employers. Among these are H-1 workers (people of distinguished merits and ability, such as opera singers, actors, and various other professionals); J-1 workers (persons who are visitors by virtue of various international exchange programs); and L-1 workers (people who are intracompany transferees of multinational corporations). Most of these nonimmigrants work in white-collar occupations or secure other highly skilled jobs.

The H-2 classification ("other temporary workers"), however, has generated the most controversy over the years. In quantitative terms, the largest number of H-2 visas (69,288) were issued in 1969, but by the end of the 1970s that number had declined to about 23,000 a year. Table 20 indicates the occupational distribution of all H-2 workers during fiscal year 1978. Within the H-2 classification, the largest single occupational grouping has generally been farmworkers.[20] Moreover, as the size of the overall program has declined, the proportion of the total

TABLE 20. OCCUPATIONS OF NONIMMIGRANT H-2 WORKERS ADMITTED TO THE UNITED STATES DURING FISCAL YEAR 1978

Occupation	Number Admitted
Professional and technical	8,406
Managers and administrators	170
Sales workers	103
Clerical workers	135
Craft workers	2,845
Operatives (except in transportation)	298
Transportation operatives	97
Nonfarm laborers	1,585
Farmers and farm managers	0
Farm laborers and foremen	8,306
Service workers (except in private households)	511
Private household workers	376
Total	22,832

Source: U.S. Department of Justice, Immigration and Naturalization Service, *1978 Annual Report of the Immigration and Naturalization Service* (Washington, D.C.: GPO, 1979), table 16B.

who are agricultural workers has risen to over one-third of the annual number of H-2 admissions.

Nonagricultural H-2 workers represent a wide variety of occupations. Most, however, are professional and technical workers, who are generally "of lower status than those entering on H-1 visas, or as exchange visitors."[21] The largest subgroupings within this category are writers, artists, and entertainers, followed by athletes and musicians. The remainder of the nonagricultural H-2 workers are employed largely in white-collar and skilled jobs.

Theoretically, H-2 workers can be admitted "[only] if unemployed persons capable of performing such service or labor cannot be found in this country."[22] It is up to the Department of Labor to determine whether citizen workers are actually available. To help it make that determination, the department has devised guidelines pertaining to minimum citizen wage rates and working conditions. These wage rates and working conditions are defined in regulations issued by the Department of Labor, and the regulations must be followed by employers who wish to hire foreign workers under the H-2 program. The purpose of the requirements is to prevent the nonimmigrant program from depressing existing work standards. The number of job certifications granted by the department for H-2 workers in agriculture and logging in the years 1971–1981 is shown in Table 21. The number of certifications recorded each year always exceeds the number of H-2 admissions for agricultural work (shown in Table 18) because some of those who are admitted work at different times for different employers. It is

TABLE 21. JOB CERTIFICATIONS GRANTED FOR TEMPORARY FOREIGN WORKERS
(H-2s) IN AGRICULTURE, 1971–1981

Year	Number of Certifications Granted	Year	Number of Certifications Granted
1971	21,893	1977	15,281
1972	21,423	1978	15,441
1973	20,138	1979	18,282
1974	20,634	1980	18,371
1975	16,499	1981	17,953
1976	15,231		

Source: Mimeographed material from the U.S. Department of Labor, Division of Labor Certifications, January 29, 1982, p. 1.

interesting to note that the final admission decision in H-2 cases comes not from the Department of Labor but from the Department of Justice. Frequently, negative admission decisions made by the former are overruled by the latter.

It is also interesting to note that H-2 workers do not pay social security taxes. This means that the employer does not deduct the tax from the employee's wage, nor does he have to match the tax, as is the case with citizen workers. H-2 workers are also exempt from unemployment compensation taxes on employer payrolls. Hence, an employer may secure H-2 workers at wages that are lower than those paid to citizen workers even though the nominal wage rates are the same for both.

During the late 1970s and early 1980s, four rural industries in the continental United States became primary users of H-2 workers: the sugar cane industry in Florida (using BWI workers); the apple industry in New York, Virginia, and a few other eastern states (using BWI workers); the woodcutting industry in Maine (using Canadians); and the sheepherding industry in the Northwest (using Spaniards). On the surface, these major users of H-2 workers seem to be rather incidental industries, but in fact each has a very powerful political lobby, as the Department of Labor has regularly found out to its chagrin when it has tried to tighten the regulations governing H-2 admissions.[23]

Although many nonagricultural H-2 workers enter the United States under contractual terms that tie them to specific employers, their wages and working conditions are not controversial, nor are they seen as a threat to citizen workers. They tend to reflect rather than to influence their respective labor markets. The same cannot be said of agricultural H-2 workers or of the entire H-2 worker program in the U.S. territories of Guam and the Virgin Islands. Each of these cases requires special elaboration, for as one study of nonimmigrant labor programs concluded, even though the total number of H-2 workers in the American labor force is small, H-2 workers have at times had "severe impacts on micro labor markets."[24] In this context it has been observed that "[the] H-2s play their most important roles on the fringes of the United States," and that these programs "make good social science laboratories" for the study of the general efficacy of the temporary-worker concept.[25]

AGRICULTURAL H-2 WORKERS

The agricultural H-2 program inherited all the undesirable features of its predecessor, the bracero program. Its workers are totally dependent upon their employers. Eligibility for the program often depends upon a worker's contacts with certain officials of his government. It is often considered a privilege to be selected, and corruption in the selection process is rampant in most source countries. If chosen, the worker will have the opportunity to return again only if his work and attitude please his American employer—this because the employer may "request by name" a set proportion (usually 60 percent of those who successfully completed their work in the prior harvest season) of one year's H-2 workers for employment the next year. In effect, this means that the workers must compete with one another on terms that are very favorable to the employer. If any aspect of a worker's demeanor is deemed unsatisfactory by his employer, the worker may be expelled at once—that is, sent back to his homeland without an appeal. Moreover, any worker who is expelled during the harvest season must pay for his passage back home and will be barred from future participation in H-2 programs.[26] The agricultural H-2 program has another feature that is highly prized by employers. Namely, it guarantees employers a work force. If a worker is expelled or if he becomes sick, is injured, or has to return home because of a family crisis, he will quickly be replaced by another grateful worker selected by the government of the sending nation. Given this system, it is not surprising that H-2 aliens are generally characterized as "hard working and diligent."[27]

Although several different countries send agricultural H-2 workers to the United States, about 90 percent of the number admitted annually are from the British West Indies (predominately from Jamaica). These H-2 workers represent a continuation of the aforementioned BWI labor program. As noted earlier, the employers of BWI workers resisted the move in 1951 to include their workers under P.L. 78, which extended the Mexican Labor Program until 1964. As a result, the BWI workers were subsumed under the H-2 program that began in 1952. Throughout the 1950s the use of BWI workers increased, but the overall program was dwarfed by the coexisting bracero program. Hence, the BWI program escaped close scrutiny. In addition, during the early years of the BWI program the U.S. government had virtually no role in its administration. Only when the bracero program was phased out in the early 1960s did the government begin to take notice of the BWI program. Despite differences in legislative authorization, the programs were in fact very similar, and the arguments that had led to termination of the bracero program seemed to apply to the BWI program as well. Thus, in the early 1960s the Department of Labor began to issue more restrictive regulations for all H-2 workers. Responding to this change, in 1965 a group of congressmen introduced legislation that would have shifted the labor certification and wage-setting authority for the H-2 program from the Department of Labor to the Department of Agriculture. The bill was narrowly defeated, however.[28]

In 1977, "major and controversial revisions in the regulations" for H-2 workers were proposed by the Department of Labor.[29] If enacted, these regulations would have restricted the use of H-2 workers. In August 1977, however, despite opposition from the Labor Department, a district court judge ordered the department to admit 5,000 applepickers—mostly Jamaicans.[30] The secretary of labor responded to the ruling by stating that it "undermines my fundamental responsibility to approve the importation of temporary foreign workers only when domestic workers are unavailable."[31]

Employers of H-2 agricultural workers contend that the major alternative to H-2 workers is illegal immigrants. They claim that although illegal immigrants have been involved in East Coast agriculture, the incidence of illegal immigration has been much higher in the agricultural enterprises of the Southwest. The East Coast employers argue that termination of the bracero program in 1964 led to the widespread use of illegal immigrants in the Southwest.[32] They also contend that

> in a land that encourages education, that emphasizes working with brains rather
> than with backs, that is steadily going from an agricultural to an industrial
> society, where agricultural operations have become mechanized to the point that
> there is a greatly lessened incentive to pursue a livelihood as an agricultural
> worker, and where Federal policy is directed toward removing U.S. workers
> from agricultural migrancy, it seems quite apparent that the need for seasonal
> foreign workers will increase and that the use of such workers must be
> permitted if the abundance of agriculture is to continue for this country and the
> other countries around the world.[33]

Yet in Florida, where the number of Haitian refugees continues to grow, Florida Rural Legal Services, Inc., argues that an effort should be made to recruit Haitian refugees to replace the Jamaican H-2 workers who are presently being brought into the country to cut sugar cane.[34] Many of the Haitian refugees have had extensive experience as agricultural workers in Haiti and as sugar-cane cutters in the Dominican Republic. They have also had great difficulty finding jobs in Florida's primarily urban job market. A spokesman for the sugar-cane growers has responded, however, that "neither the Americans nor the refugees can keep pace with the West Indian workers."[35] Thus the growers continue to employ these foreign workers.

Thus, the H-2 program in agriculture remains highly controversial because the policy seeks to reconcile two sharply conflicting goals. On the one hand, there is the need to protect citizen workers from the competition of foreign workers who are willing to work at wages and under conditions that few citizen workers would tolerate. On the other hand, there is also the need of agricultural employers who still rely upon labor-intensive production techniques to secure a plentiful supply of low-cost laborers.

THE VIRGIN ISLANDS H-2 PROGRAM

The fifty islands and keys that comprise the Virgin Islands have belonged to the United States since 1917, when they were purchased from Denmark. They are an unincorporated U.S. territory, and native-born islanders are U.S. citizens. The affairs of the islands are supervised by the U.S. Department of the Interior.

Prior to 1917, free travel to find employment was permitted among the Caribbean islands controlled by Denmark and Britain. This practice continued for some years after the United States purchased the islands, but in 1938 the U.S. government ruled that the Immigration Acts of 1917 and 1924 applied to the islands. All aliens who resided in the islands as of 1938 were deemed to be legal resident aliens. During World War II, however, unskilled workers were needed to build up the defense forces on the island of St. Thomas, which was viewed as an important part of the defense fortifications for the Panama Canal. Word of the need for workers spread throughout the nearby French and British islands, and large numbers of people sailed to St. Thomas in an illegal search for jobs. For various reasons of expediency, they were permitted to stay, and efforts to force them to leave were largely unsuccessful.

In 1952 the H-2 provisions of the Immigration and Nationality Act laid the groundwork for ratification of the process that had already begun. In 1956 a temporary-worker agreement was signed by the United States and representatives of the government of the nearby British Virgin Islands, and in 1959 the agreement was expanded to include the many islands of the British, French, and Dutch West Indies.[36] The agreement stipulated that workers were to be employed only in the agricultural and tourist industries.

Nominal efforts were made to determine if citizen workers were available to fill these jobs, but in fact, by the early 1960s, admission of H-2 workers was permitted "for any job."[37] There were no effective occupational restrictions. More and more jobs ceased to be temporary in nature and by the end of the 1960s "alien labor constituted roughly half of the Virgin Islands labor force."[38] There were 13,288 aliens in a total labor force of about 27,000 persons. One explanation for the increasing dependence on H-2 workers was that the wage rates in many of the occupations in which they were employed were too low relative to the islands' extremely high cost of living to attract citizen workers. By the late 1960s the housing, education, and social conditions for H-2 workers had become "terrible," and the H-2 workers were described as "the biggest single problem" on the islands.[39] Some observers expressed the fear that if the H-2 workers were allowed to become resident aliens (which would entitle them to become naturalized citizens five years later), the native-born population might lose political control of the islands.

In 1970 the U.S. immigration statutes were amended to permit the entry of H-4s (the spouses and children of nonimmigrants). The effect of this seemingly humane gesture to allow family reunification was unforeseen, however. The number of H-4 persons in the Virgin Islands reached 30,000 by the mid-1970s, and the aforementioned housing and social problems worsened. Local government officials sought to prevent the children of H-2 workers from attending the islands' public schools, but a federal court intervened to stop the practice.[40]

By this time it was obvious to the Department of Labor that "the non-immigrant aliens virtually determined the prevailing wage in many occupations," and it therefore decided to issue indefinite labor certifications to the H-2 workers and to allow them to change jobs freely.[41] In effect, it would no longer first try to locate available citizen workers. Moreover, procedures were established whereby the nonimmigrants could become resident aliens and eventually citizens if they wished. In short, the temporary-worker program was abandoned. H-2 workers were permitted to perform year-round work and to remain indefinitely. The resulting resentment of the H-2 workers by the citizen population and the discrimination these workers experienced were inevitable given the fact that the program had "fostered the development of a two-tiered labor market" that made the islands' "economy dependent upon foreign labor in spite of relatively high unemployment."[42]

By 1975 the admission of new H-2 workers had virtually stopped, but in that year the program's regulations were changed to permit the children of H-2 workers (originally classified as H-4s) to seek to adjust their status to that of H-2 workers when they reached the age of twenty-one. Moreover, responding to the realization that the H-2 workers and their families had for all intents and purposes become permanent settlers in the islands, Congress attempted to secure for them the opportunity to become permanent-resident aliens. These efforts paid off in 1982 when the Virgin Islands Nonimmigrant Alien Adjustment Act was passed.[43] Under its terms, all persons who had been admitted to the Virgin Islands as H-2s or H-4s prior to June 30, 1975, were eligible to become permanent-resident aliens if they had lived in the islands continuously since that date and if they were present in the islands at the time of their application. Applications were accepted for a one-year period ending September 30, 1983. By implication, therefore, all persons who were eligible for adjustment but who failed to apply during this period would lose their legal status. The law also contained a unique feature that was designed to prevent the adjustment process from creating a chain migration process. Namely, persons who availed themselves of the opportunity to adjust their status under this act were prohibited from using their citizenship as a means to secure the admission of additional relatives. David North has suggested that this provision is "vulnerable to challenge" because it creates a "second class legal alien category." Such persons have fewer rights than aliens who are admitted under other immigration statutes.[44] It was originally estimated that about 5,600 persons would adjust their status under the act. By February 1983, halfway through the grace period, 1,879 persons had actually done so.[45] It should be noted that the act officially terminated the Virgin Islands H-2 program (except for brief visits by athletes and entertainers).

THE GUAM LABOR PROGRAM

The island of Guam was ceded to the United States in 1898 as part of the treaty ending the Spanish-American War, but U.S. citizenship was not extended to its residents until 1950. Because of the island's strategic location in the mid-Pacific, it is a key military installation for the United States, and as a result, its economy and labor force have been strongly influenced by U.S. military and other government activities. The Immigration and Nationality Act of 1952 was the first U.S. immigration statute applied to Guam.

When the island was recaptured from the Japanese in 1944, it became the major American military center that it remains today. During its recapture, however, its private economy was devastated. Thus, when the rebuilding process began, many residents sought jobs with the U.S. government. It was against this backdrop that nonimmigrant laborers began to be imported to fill a wide variety of jobs. The largest number of these foreign workers were employed in construction. In May 1947, workers from the Philippines and other Pacific islands were hired on a voluntary basis under short-term contracts. Authorization for the "program" consisted of an exchange of intergovernmental notes, and no attempt was made to reconcile the program with existing U.S. immigration laws until 1952. At that time, the status of the contract workers on Guam came into immediate conflict with the H-2 provisions of the newly enacted Immigration and Nationality Act. Not only were these workers employed in a variety of occupations but many had been on Guam for a number of years. Clearly they were not "temporary workers." Nonetheless, in 1953 the INS accepted the U.S. Navy's contention that the workers were needed for defense purposes and it approved the granting of blanket H-2 status to all of them. In March 1957, limitations on the length of time an H-2 worker could initially be employed on Guam was set at six months and the maximum extension was set at three years.

In the island's labor market a "triple wage system" soon developed: a high wage for "statesiders"; a medium wage for native-born residents; and a low wage for H-2 workers.[46] Criticism mounted that the H-2 workers were receiving "slave wages." In addition, some observers charged that racketeering—involving wage kickbacks and bribery in the selection process—was rampant among labor recruiters in the Philippines. Consequently, in 1958 the INS announced that it would phase out the H-2 program for nondefense employers. This decision affected 971 workers, including doctors, accountants, cooks, and mechanics. Despite protests from many business groups, a three-year phase-out of the non-defense H-2 worker program began in March 1959.

In 1960 the INS decided that the H-2 defense worker program also should be phased out. Noting that few efforts were being made to train citizen workers for the jobs that H-2 workers held, it expressed the fear that the H-2 program would become a permanent part of Guam's economy. After the phase-out, however, nonimmigrant workers continued to be admitted under the separate parole authority given to the attorney general under the Immigration and Nationality Act of 1952 to admit persons temporarily for "emergent reasons" or to serve the public interest.[47] Thus, nonimmigrants from the Philippines were again admitted to meet the requests of defense contractors and the U.S. military. This practice continued until 1975. A second parole program was instituted in 1962 for temporary workers to do reconstruction work after the island was hit by a severe typhoon in 1962. This program was terminated in May 1970 when the INS decided that it was more appropriate to admit construction workers under the H-2 program than via parole procedures.[48]

Revival of the H-2 program came in response to employer claims of labor shortages caused by the island's expanding tourist industry in particular and by the growth of the island's population in general. The government of Guam also began to seek H-2 workers as a means of developing new industries, especially in agriculture and fishing, but many fewer H-2 workers were admitted than were requested in the early 1970s. Then, during the mid-1970s, U.S. Labor Department officials recognized a long-prevalent problem: Many of these H-2 workers had not complied with the terms of their admission and as a result the problem of illegal immigration had become serious.[49]

In 1977 a Labor Department report described labor market conditions on Guam as "abysmal."[50] The report noted that in 1976 there were 4,293 H-2 workers in a civilian labor force of 26,910. Of greater significance was the fact that 82 percent of the persons employed in construction, 47 percent of those in agriculture, and 15 percent of those in manufacturing were H-2 workers.[51] With reference to working conditions, the report was resplendent with examples of worker abuse by employers and labor recruiters. It also detailed the inability of the department to enforce existing labor standards in an environment in which many workers were completely beholden to their employers. In these circumstances, the H-2 workers had become preferred workers for employers. Citizen workers could not compete with them and often became unemployed or underemployed. As the report noted, "Alien workers constitute such a large proportion of the work force that the wages at which they are certified are the prevailing wage rates."[52] It also noted that the wages and working conditions were not set by a free market but rather were the result of government policies.

Nonimmigrant Policy and Illegal Immigration

In addition to the various categories of nonimmigrants, there are millions of illegal immigrants who have simply by-passed the complexities of the existing immigration system. They will be discussed in detail in the next chapter. It is necessary to mention illegal immigration during a discussion of nonimmigrant labor policy for two reasons. First, illegal immigrants themselves constitute a nonimmigrant labor program, albeit totally unregulated. Officially, of course, illegal immigrants are unsanctioned, but because the immigration policy of the United States has been so blatantly tolerant of their presence, it can be argued that they are unofficially both condoned by the government and welcomed by many employers. Second, a number of proposals that address the problem of illegal immigration have included various nonimmigrant programs among the array of possible policy solutions. Hence, the questions of illegal immigration and nonimmigrant policy have been intertwined in the past and many suggestions are being made that would increase the relationship in the future. Three of these proposals will be discussed here.

PROPOSALS FOR NEW NONIMMIGRANT PROGRAMS

One proposal draws from the years of experience of Western European nations with foreign-worker programs. Suggested by W. R. Böhning, this plan addresses only illegal immigrants from Mexico.[53] Böhning says that there is a demand for unskilled workers in the United States because these workers are "cheap and industrious."[54] He argues that illegal immigrants "are necessary for the smooth functioning of the economy as it exists today."[55]

Under the Böhning plan, a Mexican worker—called an "undocumentado"— could get a visa to cross the border and look for a job anywhere. The worker would have three months to find a seasonal or nonseasonal job. If a nonseasonal job was found, the worker would request a contract for up to twelve months. At the end of that period, the contract could be renewed "on the spot." If the "undocumentado" found only seasonal contract work, he or she would have to return to Mexico but could be requested by name the following year. If these Mexicans could not find work after three months or for a full season, they would be required to return to Mexico or be subject to deportation. When they returned to Mexico, they would have to compete with all other Mexican workers to get back on the list of visa eligibles. No indication is given in the plan as to how a person would be selected to become an "undocumentado."

While in the United States, the "undocumentados" would be accorded the same economic and social rights as citizen workers. Nonseasonal workers could be joined by their families at the moment of renewal of their first contracts. For seasonal workers, family reunification would be possible after two consecutive seasons in the United States. After five years of continuous residence, the "undocumentado" could apply for permanent-resident-alien status. If apprehended, employers of illegal immigrants as well as the immigrants themselves would be subject to stiff penalties, but no further changes would be made in the existing immigration system.

Another proposal, for "a temporary labor program," has been made by Charles Keely.[56] His program would permit foreign workers to be employed "in regions and sections" identified by the U.S. Department of Labor "as in need of labor."[57] The decision would be made after consultation with employers and labor unions. Temporary workers could be granted immigrant status (i.e., become a resident alien) if they could find work for a set period of time (Keely suggests fifteen to twenty-five consecutive months). The theoretical basis of the plan is that "if a worker worked here, he could build up some rights to settle."[58] Family members would be allowed to accompany the temporary immigrants and would be eligible for the same social programs that were available to citizen workers. Keely's proposal includes additional recommendations for the enforcement of existing labor laws and sanctions against employers of illegal immigrants.

A third proposal, by Edwin Reubens, pertains to the existing H-2 program.[59] Reubens sets forth two variants of an expanded foreign-worker program: "a new H-2 program" and "an improved H-2 program." With regard to the "new" H-2 program, he suggests enlarging the existing program "in certain jobs" for periods of one year with renewals for up to three years. After this period the H-2 permit-holder would have to leave the United States and join the pool of job-seekers back in his or her country. The next cohort of job-seekers would not be admitted until the preceding group had departed as scheduled.

Reubens also suggests that application of the new H-2 program be limited to "those jobs of low skill, low paid work, which currently are often filled by undocumented aliens and are not very attractive to American unemployed workers."[60] He notes that this has been the focus of guestworker programs in Western Europe and claims that complaints about European guestworker programs have been related more "to local social pressures and disparities than to any undercutting of wages or working conditions."[61] One way to avoid such social pressures, he reasons, would be to exclude all dependents of foreign workers. This requirement would have to be made clear to all applicants for H-2 permits, and those who were unwilling to accept the deprivation would be advised not to enter the program.[62] Reubens also expresses the belief that the U.S. Department of Labor should "conduct an outreach program in the source countries [to] ensure that appropriate types and numbers of persons are recruited [to] meet the actual needs of U.S. labor markets."[63] Wage rates would be set by the U.S. Department of Labor and they would be minimum wages comparable to those paid to domestic workers. As such, these established rates could be used to "sustain present labor standards" and could gradually be raised in order to attract more citizen workers.

Reubens admits, however, that in order to absorb the jobs currently held by illegal aliens, the program would have to enroll "hundreds of thousands" of H-2 permit-holders a year.[64] This, he notes, could easily disrupt the existing administrative functions of the government agencies involved in the program. For example, a sizable number of persons could elect not to leave on schedule. Reubens' first proposal is designed for workers from Mexico, although he does not explicitly restrict it to them.

Reubens' second proposal is simply to improve the existing H-2 program. According to this plan, the program would remain at its present small level of magnitude but an effort would be made to improve existing procedures for recruiting citizen workers before relying upon H-2 workers (by establishing better job information channels, upgrading existing jobs, enhancing mobility, and providing more training) and to tighten the existing certification regulations for occupations and industries in need of H-2 workers.

Reubens prepared his study for the National Commission for Manpower Policy, which in August 1977 had been asked by President Jimmy Carter to study the H-2 program as part of the Carter administration's comprehensive review of the problem of illegal immigration.[65] Although President Carter explicitly denied any interest in establishing a bracero program, the implication of the review was that an expanded temporary-worker program might meet the needs of some employers while not adversely affecting citizen workers. At the end of its review, however, the Commission for Manpower Policy advised the president that it was "strongly against" any expansion of the H-2 program.[66]

As discussed in Chapter 3, Congress did not respond directly to the Carter administration's proposals. Instead, it established the Select Commission on Immigration and Refugee Policy to study all dimensions of the nation's immigration policy. In its report, the Select Commission acknowledged that the H-2 program had been the source of criticism. Nevertheless, it concluded, "continuation of the program is necessary and preferable to the institution of a new one."[67] Several suggestions were made to "streamline" the administration of the program. In an effort to remove "inducements to hire H-2 workers over U.S. workers," the commission recommended that employers be required to pay both social security and unemployment compensation payroll taxes for all H-2 workers.[68] It also advised that no new temporary-worker program be established as part of any strategy to combat illegal immigration.[69]

It should be recalled that by the time the Select Commission issued its report—1981—the Carter administration was no longer in office. The Task Force on Immigration and Refugee Policy, which was created by President Ronald Reagan to review the Select Commission's report, released its own recommendations on July 30, 1981.[70] It did not mention the H-2 program, but it did propose that an "experimental temporary worker program for Mexican nationals" be established.[71] The "pilot program" would operate for a two-year trial period and would be limited to 50,000 workers each year. The workers would be allowed to stay in the United States for from nine to twelve months. Geographic and occupational restrictions could be imposed on them if particular labor market conditions warranted them. In all other instances, however, the temporary workers would be free to change employers at will. In an effort to prevent the abuse that had characterized the H-2 program and the earlier bracero programs, these workers would not be bound to one employer. Moreover, employers would be required to pay the same payroll taxes that were applicable to citizen workers. The workers could not bring their families with them and they would be ineligible for most social programs (i.e., food stamps, unemployment compensation, or welfare assistance). It was understood at the time the pilot program was set up that the Reagan administration hoped the program would prove the viability of the temporary-worker concept and could be expanded to a million or so workers in subsequent years.[72]

During the congressional debates over the Simpson-Mazzoli bill in 1982, the Reagan administration's proposal for a new temporary-worker program was dropped. The bill did not mention any new temporary-worker program, but it did contain a series of proposals that were ostensibly designed to enhance the administrative efficiency of the existing H-2 program. Because there is still no ceiling on the number of H-2 workers that can be admitted, because the proposed changes in the H-2 program would have allowed the Department of Agriculture to share responsibility with the Department of Labor for the operation of the program, and because the Simpson-Mazzoli bill would have permitted the attorney general to overrule negative decisions made by these agencies, organized labor and many Hispanic organizations opposed the legislation. They feared that the changes would culminate in a major expansion in the size and scope of the H-2 program. For instance, the Mexican American Legal Defense and Education Fund charged in October 1982 that "the Simpson-Mazzoli H-2 program is really just a replay of the bracero program" and that its provisions would actually "foster" illegal immigration, just as the old program had.[73] The divisive debates over the H-2 provisions of the bill in the House of Representatives in December 1982 were partly responsible for the decision to let the bill die on the House floor.

In the 1983 Senate debates and the 1984 House debates over the bill, these earlier concerns were again raised. In the Senate version of the bill, the regulations pertaining to H-2 temporary workers were liberalized but no new temporary-worker program was authorized. The House version also eased the restrictions on the process by which H-2 temporary workers could be admitted to the United States and it went much further. It approved a provision calling for a three-year transition program that would permit agricultural employers to adjust to the terms of the proposed law. During the first year, all the workers hired by an agricultural employer could be illegal immigrants; in the second year, 67 percent could be; and in the third year, 33 percent could be. After this period, the program would be terminated. The requirements of the program were minimal. The grower would have to notify the Department of Labor of the number of such workers hired each year and would be required to secure a work permit for each designated foreign worker. There is no way to know in advance what the actual size of such a nonimmigrant labor program might be. The League of United Latin American Citizens (LULAC) has bitterly attacked this amendment, just as most Hispanic organizations have fought against the adoption of similar foreign-worker programs. LULAC has charged that the proposal program "reflects a contradiction" of the goal of immigration reform. Its members believe that a "transitional guestworker program," like its predecessors, would only encourage more Mexican workers to come to the United States. LULAC has also opposed the amendment because it contains no worker safeguards, provides no penalties for employer abuses, and establishes no monitoring mechanism for supervision of the program.[74] During the floor debate on the bill, the House also approved a provision to create an entirely new foreign-worker program for the agricultural industry. It was proposed by Congressmen Leon E. Panetta (D., Cal.) and Sid Morrison (R., Wash.). Under its terms temporary farmworkers could be admitted to the United States to harvest fruits and vegetables for up to eleven months a year. The temporary workers could move freely from one employer to another within a specified region. No specific limit was placed on the life of this expanded foreign-worker program. The scope of the program would be determined by the attorney general after consultation with the secretary of labor and the secretary of agriculture. The attorney general would be required to rule on petitions from agricultural workers within 72 hours in the case of urgent requests. As the Department of Justice has no particular expertise in labor market analysis, it is feared that the administration of such a program would be dominated by political considerations rather than demonstrated economic factors. It is estimated that the number of foreign workers participating in the program could be anywhere from 200,000 to 500,000 a year.[75] The adopted amendment immediately drew the wrath of Hispanic leaders and of the AFL–CIO. Congressman Henry B. Gonzalez (D., Tex.) charged that

> the farm worker program created in the bill is odious, but this amendment would even offend a slave driver. People who wanted slaves would at least buy them; this amendment is a "rent-a-slave" device. The amendment does not even provide the skeletal labor protections that existed under the infamous bracero program which Congress terminated 20 years ago.[76]

Likewise, because of the addition of this amendment (as well as several other deletions from the overall bill) during the House floor debate, the AFL–CIO suddenly withdrew its support for the entire Simpson-Mazzoli bill and called for its defeat.[77]

It is doubtful that the amendment calling for the creation of this open-ended program will be approved in the conference to reconcile differences between the Senate and the House versions of the bill. It has been suggested as a compromise that the aforementioned transitional farmworker program be extended from a three-year to a five-year phase-out in lieu of adding another program.[78]

An Assessment of the "New" Role of Nonimmigrant Labor Programs

It should be apparent from the preceding review of the evolution of nonimmigrant labor policy that use of this policy to combat illegal immigration is a departure from the historical pattern. Interest in temporary-worker programs is not based on a demonstrated need for such workers in the labor market. All the proposals for new or expanded nonimmigrant labor programs are designed exclusively to recruit more workers for unskilled and semiskilled occupations in primarily low-wage industries. These are precisely the same labor markets in which those subgroups of the American labor force with the highest unemployment rates are already disproportionately represented. No one has suggested that a foreign-worker program be established to supply more workers for white-collar occupations. Not only would such proposals lead to charges of a "brain drain" from source nations, but the opposition of the privileged and protected workers in these domestic labor markets could be counted on to kill any such idea at the moment of its conception.

As is the case with the job-holding patterns of illegal immigrants, there is not a modicum of empirical evidence that citizen workers will not do the work that nonimmigrants do. Nevertheless, this fundamental assertion continues to be made by the advocates of new or expanded nonimmigrant work programs.[79] In order to substantiate their claim, these lobbyists would have to prove that too few citizen workers are available to work for the wages and benefits associated with certain occupations in the American economy. Certainly no one can seriously support this contention, for it is refuted every day by millions of low-wage citizen workers who are already employed in all the industries for which nonimmigrant workers are sought.

Nonimmigrant workers not only compete with citizen workers for job opportunities but they also affect wage levels in any given labor market. These wage effects make both nonimmigrant workers and illegal immigrants attractive to American employers. Employers are able to pay such workers in selected labor markets lower wages than would be possible in their absence. Moreover, foreign workers in low-wage American industries are less likely than citizen workers to make demands for job rights or to join unions.

One major flaw in the proposals outlined earlier is their intended magnitude. A foreign-worker program cannot do anything to reduce illegal immigration unless the program is significant in size (at least in the range of 500,000–750,000 persons each year). But the larger the program, the greater the certainty it will have an adverse impact on citizen workers in selected labor markets. On the other hand, if the scale of the program is small, what will deter people from entering illegally? Politically, if not economically, speaking, some limitations on the size of the program must be set, but what will stop those who are not selected from coming, or those whose period of work has expired but who wish to remain from staying? A new or expanded nonimmigrant labor program would not solve any of the nation's major problems with its immigration policies, but it would add a host of new ones.

Moreover, most of the proponents of a new nonimmigrant labor program assume implicitly—or explicitly in the case of the Reagan plan—that the program would be a bilateral arrangement with Mexico. This was feasible during the years when the bracero programs were operating, but times have changed in both Mexico and the United States. Illegal immigrants are streaming into the United States from many countries other than Mexico. If a nonimmigrant program were open only to Mexicans, it would do nothing to reduce the problems associated with these other nations, which collectively represent about one-half of all illegal immigrants. Because many illegal immigrants are blacks and Asians, it is very unlikely that any foreign-worker program could be restricted to workers from Mexico. Such a program would appear to be racist and designed to favor the people of only one nation.

In a study conducted in San Diego, California, in 1981, Joseph Nalvern and Craig Frederickson sought to examine the alleged need for foreign workers from the viewpoint of U.S. employers. In particular they sought to discover if, in fact, employers could not pay competitive wages for citizen workers in several industries in which illegal immigrants were already widely used. Or did employers actually prefer foreign workers—illegal immigrants if need be, but guestworkers if possible—over citizen workers. If employers could "afford to hire domestic workers, but chose not to do so, then the claim of a labor shortage or 'need' must be considered to be devoid of empirical support."[80] In this context, Nalvern and Frederickson argued that employers who hire foreign workers contribute to the unemployment of citizen workers who would otherwise be hired to do the work. To support this contention, they interviewed employers in agriculture, restaurants, and electronic manufacturing in San Diego. Consistently these employers expressed greater admiration for the work of illegal immigrants than for that of citizen workers. Many agricultural employers lauded the braceros they had once been able to employ. But rather than rely only on the attitudes of these employers, Nalvern and Frederickson decided to determine whether it was true that employers would be forced to go out of business (or, in the case of electronic manufacturing, would be forced to relocate south of the border) if they had to compete actively for citizen workers. Hence, they did not ask the employers if they were willing to pay the prevailing wage. Instead they asked them this: "At what wage would you go out of business if you had to raise wages in order to attract U.S. workers?" The employers' answers led Nalvern and Frederickson to conclude that the maximum wage the employers were willing to pay was high enough to attract citizen workers but that the employers preferred foreign workers. Thus, labor displacement was indeed occurring in the San Diego labor market.[81] With regard to the desirability of establishing a formal foreign-worker program, these researchers added:

> The preceding discussion indicates that some employers play a very active role in the displacement of domestic workers—more so in some industries than in others. By examining the employer's view towards the labor market, we find that there is a definite strategy for pulling in illegal labor from across the border and that this strategy is an excellent way to avoid more expensive American labor. A foreign-worker program would simply legitimize this strategy.[82]

Nonimmigrant labor programs have other pernicious long-term effects on low-wage industries. Namely, when workers come from economically less developed countries to the United States, they discover opportunities that for many are beyond imagining. The relatively higher wages and the broader array of job opportunities cause many to seek ways to remain. Thus, rather than being an alternative to illegal immigration, nonimmigrant labor programs sometimes actually foster the phenomenon. Moreover, it is generally the citizen workers who are least able to defend themselves in the ensuing competition for jobs who are hurt.

It is not surprising, therefore, that some of the strongest opposition to proposals to expand temporary-worker programs has been voiced by groups that are most closely associated with protecting the opportunities of low-wage workers. For example, at a 1979 conference entitled "Jobs for Hispanics" (sponsored by the Labor Council for Latin American Advancement), Hispanic trade unionists and Hispanic community groups from across the country took a unanimous stand against foreign-worker programs. In their conference manifesto, called the "Declaration of Albuquerque," they proclaimed: "The federal government should *not* include any type of 'Bracero' program or foreign labor importation, as a solution to the current problem of undocumented workers."[83] Similar statements of opposition were made to the Select Commission during its deliberations by the National Hispanic Task Force (a group representing eight of the nation's largest Hispanic organizations) and by such groups as California Rural Legal Assistance, Texas Rural Legal Aid, Inc., and the National Center for Immigrants' Rights.[84] All these organizations have long supported low-income citizen workers in their efforts to compete with foreign temporary workers for jobs in America's labor markets.

In 1981, when the Reagan administration announced its support for a new foreign-worker program, it was met by a chorus of opposition. It had probably anticipated an attack by the AFL-CIO, which called the proposal a mechanism for employers to find "a docile and controllable work force."[85] It was perhaps surprised, however, when the Mexican labor movement, the Confederación de Trabajadores de México (CTM), also strongly condemned the idea. In a "Manifesto to the People," the president of CTM, Fidel Velásquez, said that the Reagan proposal would convert Mexican workers into "the biggest strategic labor reserve in contemporary history, subject to super-exploitation and servitude."[86] Velásquez argued that the proposal would relegate Mexican workers to a second-class status since they would be required to pay taxes but would be specifically denied benefits such as food stamps, unemployment compensation, and other forms of public assistance. The fact that CTM is an integral part of the Party of Revolutionary Institutions (PRI), which has controlled Mexican political affairs since its founding in 1929, meant that it was speaking for the Mexican government. Officially, the Mexican government did not comment on the Reagan proposal, but it is inconceivable that CTM would have expressed opposition to the plan publicly if it did not represent the consensus view of the PRI.

Foreign-Worker Programs: The European Experience

The United States is not unique in its interest in foreign-worker programs. Since the end of World War II, the hiring of workers from one nation to work under contract in another has become a feature on almost every continent.[87] Western Europe, in particular, has made extensive use of foreign workers during this period, and it is to that experience that the United States might turn in seeking new ideas and guidance.

In the years following World War II, many of the nations of Western Europe were confronted with war-torn economies. The infrastructure of their national economies (bridges, roads, schools, dams, transportation systems, etc.) as well as their factories and distribution facilities had to be rebuilt. As these were repaired or replaced, the demands of consumers for various durable goods developed. All the nations of Western Europe sought to find ways to meet these pent-up demands. The available work force in the countries that had participated in the war, however, had been seriously depleted by the deaths and injuries associated with the fighting and its related hardships. For these reasons, the labor markets of most Western European nations were extremely tight throughout most of the 1950s, 1960s, and early 1970s. The unemployment rate in many of these nations was frequently below 2 percent. (Such a rate could only be imagined in the United States, where the unemployment rate over the same time span was considerably higher and, with the exception of the Vietnam interregnum, has continued to creep upward.) It was in the context of a tight labor market that various Western European nations developed programs to import workers from various labor surplus nations.

The foreign-worker programs of Western Europe—also called guestworker programs—were created through bilateral government agreements that resembled those of the bracero era in the United States. France and Germany became the major recruiters of foreign workers. Together, they employed about 70 percent of all foreign workers in Western Europe prior to 1973. Switzerland, however, became the most dependent on foreign workers. These temporary workers comprised about 35 percent of its labor force in 1970. Austria, Belgium, Luxemburg, the Netherlands, Sweden, and the United Kingdom also have participated in such programs extensively.

The source countries varied, but they tended to be the less economically developed nations around the Mediterranean Basin. They included primarily Turkey, Greece, Yugoslavia, Algeria, Morocco, Spain, Portugal, and Tunisia. Foreign workers also came from Ireland, Finland, Austria, and Italy. As nations such as Greece, Spain, and Italy sent their own nationals abroad, they began to receive workers from other nations (often illegally) to take their places.

Obviously, there has been an extreme diversity of experience among the sending and receiving nations. Some general patterns, however, are easily discernible. Spanish workers tended to concentrate in France and Germany; Irish workers, in the United Kingdom; Finnish workers, in Sweden; Algerian and

Portuguese workers, in France; and Turkish and Greek workers, in Germany. Italian workers tended to emigrate to Germany, Switzerland, and France.

The labor flows between some nations have reflected former colonial relationships. Such was the case of persons emigrating from Indonesia and Surinam to the Netherlands and from Algeria to France. Likewise, the United Kingdom received many workers from former British Commonwealth nations—for example, Pakistan, the British West Indies, and various East African nations.

In 1957 the European Economic Community (EEC) was founded. Among the requirements for membership is the guarantee of free labor mobility among the nations. Of the six original members, only Italy proved to be a sending nation. The other five were nations of destination for foreign workers. In 1972 Denmark, Ireland, and the United Kingdom joined the EEC. In 1981 Greece became a member. Ireland and Greece have continued to be sending nations, while the United Kingdom has been a receiver of foreign workers. Other European receiving nations—Sweden and Switzerland—are not members of the EEC. Still other nations—Portugal and Spain—are senders and are expected to join the EEC in the mid-1980s. Tentative talks concerning the possible entry of Turkey into the EEC have been held, but such a step does not seem likely in the near future.

Initially, participation in the foreign-worker programs was restricted to adult males, who were to be regularly rotated back to their homelands and replaced by a fresh supply of workers. Thus the temporary nature of these arrangements was emphasized. Rotation was to be accomplished through the issuance of one-year work permits that had to be renewed for longer stays. Also implicit in the arrangements was the expectation that the social costs associated with the presence of foreign workers would be minimized. Male workers could live in dormitory-type housing, and little demand would be placed on such social services as medical care, education, or recreation. In the prosperity climate of the 1960s, however, administration of the programs tended to become lax. Rotation was useful to employers as a means of "weeding out" persons who did not prove capable or desirable. But why repeatedly change good workers—and incur the associated readjustment costs—just for the sake of changing them? Hence, the principle of rotation was never really institutionalized.[88] As the workers began to stay longer, families began to reunify or, in some instances, to be started within the native populations. Slowly, as the broader social and political aspects of the programs emerged, ugly incidents began to occur that reflected the citizen populace's racial prejudices and fear of the presence of foreign workers and their families. Most of these incidents were isolated, but their frequency began to raise questions concerning the noneconomic aspects of the foreign-worker programs. The subject became a topic of contention within and among political parties as well as within the labor movement and other social institutions. By 1973 the number of foreign workers employed in the major Western European countries (excluding the United Kingdom) totaled 6.7 million and the total foreign population was much larger.[89] Collectively, foreign workers that year accounted for about one-seventh of the employed labor force in the continental European nations that were importing laborers.

Before considering the general experience of continental Europe, however, we should make brief mention of the British case, for although the end result was the same in that instance, the course of developments was sufficiently distinctive to warrant separate discussion. Prior to the United Kingdom's admission to the EEC in 1972, its foreign workers came from countries that were distinctly different from those that supplied workers to the countries of continental Europe. Britain relied heavily upon workers from its Commonwealth members. Its non-native-born workers came primarily from the British West Indies (Jamaica in particular), India, and Pakistan. But Britain also began to experience a negative reaction to these workers among its citizens. These concerns were reflected in citizen workers' fears of adverse economic effects and in overt acts of racial discrimination against the newcomers. As a result, the Commonwealth Immigration Act of 1962 was passed. It sharply reduced the flow of additional immigrant workers from these nations. This law reversed the traditional principle that members of the British Commonwealth were free at all times to enter the mother country and to enjoy all the prerogatives of citizenship—including the right to work. The act established a voucher system that was ostensibly tied to worker qualifications but was "in fact designed to slow non-white immigration."[90]

The new policy set the annual number of available vouchers at 8,500—a fraction of the number that had been available in the years prior to its enactment. The immigration of unskilled laborers was banned entirely. Exceptions were made, however, to permit families to reunify, and thus the population of workers from the former colonies continued to grow in Britain. It was in response to this growth that the even more restrictive Immigration Act of 1971 was adopted. The law created eight separate admission categories for immigrants. Only persons whose parent or grandparent had actually been born in the United Kingdom were allowed free entry. This meant that virtually all nonwhite citizens of the Commonwealth nations were excluded while most whites in Commonwealth nations could continue to enter at will. Temporary-contract workers from these nations could be admitted if they were needed, but they could not automatically qualify for citizenship. In practice, Britain's temporary workers have tended to be white workers from Ireland. Gary Freeman argues that it was "the reality of mass resistance to immigration that led the British to move from a generous policy . . . to a racially exclusive, temporary contract system."[91] In other words, he concludes, the restrictive policy was adopted because "the social costs of migration were very much more salient in Britain than economic disadvantages."[92]

On January 1, 1983, a new nationality act went into effect that made it even more difficult for nonwhite British subjects to immigrate to the United Kingdom.[93] The Nationality Act of 1983 ended the 700-year policy in Great Britain of *ius soli,* or "right of soil," whereby any child born in Britain is automatically eligible for citizenship (this principle is still recognized in the United States). The act created three categories of British subjects: (1) all citizens of the United Kingdom, the Channel Islands, and the Isle of Man; (2) 3 million citizens of dependent territories (e.g., Hong Kong, Bermuda, and the British Virgin Islands); and (3) about 1.5 million overseas British citizens who opted for British citizenship when independence was given to Britain's East African colonies and Malaysia. Only the people in the first category have the automatic right to live in Great Britain and to pass that right on to their children. In criticizing the discriminatory implications of the legislation, the Archbishop of Canterbury noted: "This Act will result in injustice, greatly increase the number of stateless men, women, and children, create uncertainties and feelings of insecurity and exacerbate racial tensions."[94]

To return to the continental European experience, all the nations of Western Europe were hit in 1973–1974 by the first major economic recession since the end of World War II. It was prompted by the Arab oil boycott, but the sluggish recovery from it served to teach the policymakers of these nations that full employment could no longer be assured. Thus the recession also provided the labor-importing nations with "a welcome pretext"—"an opportunity to rethink their immigration policies and address the serious socio-economic and political implications of labor importation."[95] Germany halted the admission of new foreign workers in November 1973; France and Switzerland followed suit in July 1974. The immediate policy question for these nations was, What was to be done with those foreign workers and their families who were already within their boundaries at the time the ban was placed on new admissions?

Two changes were subsequently initiated by policymakers in the labor-importing nations. In the first, strong efforts were made to encourage the foreign workers to return to their homelands. Financial incentives were provided for those who agreed to turn in their work permits and leave. Most of the foreign workers and their dependents did not respond to these enticements, however. Hence, the alternatives for European policymakers were mass deportations or initiation of efforts to integrate these foreign workers and their families into the host societies. Reluctantly in most cases, the integration route was selected. By the early 1980s the number of foreign workers seemed to have stabilized at about 5 million, but the foreign-born population had mushroomed to about 12 million. The growth of the foreign-born population in spite of the termination of the foreign-worker programs has been due to family reunification, natural family reproduction, and the mounting problem of illegal immigration. As always, it is impossible to measure the number of illegal immigrants with any degree of precision. The EEC estimates that there were over one million illegal immigrants in France, Germany, and Switzerland as of the early 1980s and that the problem is increasing.[96] As Martin and Miller have observed, "The labor recruiting countries have learned that guestworker programs are far easier to start than to stop."[97]

For our purposes a complete review of the foreign-worker experience in Western Europe is not appropriate. It is instructive, however, to take into account the general employment patterns that did develop. In Germany over one-third of the foreign laborers were employed in metal-working jobs in the manufacturing sector. The steel and automobile industries were especially prominent employers of foreign workers. In Switzerland and France, construction work was the primary employing sector, accounting for almost one-third of all foreign workers in both countries. Together, construction and manufacturing accounted for the employment of over three-quarters of all foreign workers in Germany and almost two-thirds of all such workers in France, Sweden, and Switzerland.[98] Only in France did a sizable proportion of the workers (8–9 percent) find employment in the agricultural sector. In none of the countries did mining provide significant employment opportunities for foreign workers.

Foreign-worker employment patterns have been entirely different in the United States, where braceros and mainland H-2 workers have for the most part been restricted to agricultural work. In fact, the automobile, steel, and building industries are usually considered to be the primary U.S. labor markets, and jobs there are highly prized by American workers.

W. R. Böhning has described the European experience with foreign-worker programs as follows:

> If one looks in ideal-typical terms at how labor migration began, one finds that it originated in the shift of national workers away from what has been termed "socially undesirable jobs." This shift, in turn, was induced by the labor shortage of the sustained postwar boom which seemed to occur at first in more highly skilled and higher status jobs in both industry and services. It was not directly followed by the import of foreign labor into these jobs because, with very few exceptions, the labor potential abroad did not come up to the skill and language requirements of the jobs or was scarce in these categories; and secondly, because it was relatively easy for national workers to advance into these jobs. This, then, tore gaps in the labor market, directly or via a chain reaction, which finally left a great number of workplaces vacated where wages were low and/or working conditions bad. As such jobs generally required few skills [and not] necessarily a sufficient knowledge of [the] local tongue, the foreign labor supply could be tapped.[99]

His thesis, therefore, is that European employment patterns can best be explained as the expression of a feeling of relative deprivation in a labor shortage environment. Jobs that had once been attractive to citizen workers were no longer desirable because opportunities for better jobs had become plentiful. Gradually the labor market was divided between preferred and nonpreferred jobs. As the labor market became segmented, foreign workers were able to move into the void. As the foreign workers filled the less desirable jobs, the jobs became even more stigmatized. Thus, when the 1973–1974 recession hit, the citizen workers did not immediately seek to reclaim their old jobs, and unemployment rates for foreign workers did not exceed those for citizen workers. The explanation seems to be that the unemployed citizen workers took advantage of the extensive and liberal unemployment compensation schemes their governments introduced. Thus, the foreign workers were spared displacement as long as the unemployment compensation schemes were available to the citizen workers and the foreign workers were content to keep the types of jobs that the citizens rejected as being unfit. The situation, Böhning notes, was one in which "institutional factors prevent an effective play of the market forces which could theoretically rectify the demand/supply situation."[100]

Yet even with the extensive employment of foreign workers, Böhning concedes, "there are still large numbers of national workers who man undesirable jobs," although "these numbers are decreasing faster [than]—or [are] not growing as fast [as]—the number of undesirable jobs."[101] It would seem that by describing occupations in the manufacturing and construction industries as "undesirable" the citizen workers of Europe have themselves contributed to the transformation. The gradual labeling of such jobs as "occupations for foreigners" undoubtedly contributed to the market forces that made these jobs less economically competitive over time with other occupations. Since 1974, when restrictions began to be imposed on the admission of new foreign workers, efforts have been made to "restructure" some of these occupations in order that they might again be attractive to citizen workers. One such effort has been to make the jobs more financially attractive. At the same time, as unemployment levels continue to rise and as eligibility for unemployment benefits begins to expire, jobs that were once labeled "undesirable" will again become more attractive to citizen workers.

As far as the sending nations are concerned, they originally touted the foreign-worker programs as a means of providing their economies with substantial benefits. Not only would these programs reduce unemployment by opening up more opportunities at home but in addition, as the rotation process became operative, foreign workers would return home with enhanced skills, better knowledge, and sufficient earnings to contribute to the modernization of their economies. In other words, as Ray Rist has noted, the foreign-worker concept was envisioned by many as a process in which "there were to be no losers."[102] Unfortunately this did not prove to be the case. Aside from the fact that the rotation concept never really developed, studies made in the labor-exporting nations show convincingly that "the long term disadvantages" of the programs "override some of the short term benefits."[103] S. Sussen-Koob notes that the selectivity of labor importers led to the recruitment of "the younger, healthier, best educated segment of the labor force" of the more developed regions of the sending nations.[104] As a result, all the labor-exporting nations experienced a significant depletion in the supply of their skilled workers. Moreover, the importing nations were able to cull from the ranks of these workers those who did not exhibit "at least the rudiments of a capacity for social and occupational adjustment—as well as lower levels of labor union and political activism."[105] They accomplished this by simply not renewing such workers' contracts. As a result of this negative selection process, only the "cream of the crop" were retained, while the less skilled and less adaptable were returned to their homelands.

Another negative outcome for the sending nations was the failure of the exported workers to provide the capital that was so desperately needed back home in these less developed nations. Because the workers' remittances went directly to family members who had been left behind, they were usually spent on consumer goods. These expenditures tended to aggravate already serious inflationary tendencies and to contribute to balance-of-payments difficulties by stimulating a demand for imported consumer goods.

The Western European foreign-worker programs were established on one major premise: they were to be temporary programs. No plans were made for the long-term economic, political, and social problems that inevitably developed. With the growth in the number of foreign-born persons residing in the receiving nations have come unanticipated problems pertaining to housing, education for children, political participation, and mounting concerns with prejudicial attitudes and discriminatory practices. As the Swiss dramatist Max Frisch so poignantly expressed the contemporary European dilemma, "We asked for workers, but they sent us human beings."[106] Resolving these broader issues will pose challenges that far exceed the concerns that led to creation of the foreign-worker programs. For these programs have become institutionalized phenomena that exert a narcotic influence on all who become involved in the process—employers, foreign workers, and source governments.

CHAPTER 5

Illegal Immigration

Over the years, as the United States has struggled to establish viable immigrant and nonimmigrant policies, large numbers of persons have managed to circumvent whatever regulations were put into place. Thus, illegal immigration is not a new policy issue. Rather, it is a persistent problem that has generally been ignored or considered to have only regional consequences. It is important to note, however, that the scale of illegal immigration has increased considerably over time, as have the adverse consequences of the phenomenon. Hence, the fact that the problem has been around for a long time is not a sufficient reason to adopt a benign attitude toward its present importance or to express resignation that it is futile to try to control it.

In many ways illegal immigration is a dilemma that is inherent in a free society. It is unlikely that the United States will ever be able to stop completely the flow of persons who enter the country illegally. Yet the problem is not one that can be ignored simply because of the difficulties that may be encountered in designing appropriate policy responses. The policy objective, therefore, is not to stop illegal immigration but rather to bring the flow under control by significantly reducing both its scale and its adverse effects. Laws against speeding on the nation's highways have not stopped all speeders, but they have probably reduced the incidence of speeding from what it would be in their absence. Moreover, laws against speeding have enabled law enforcement officials to focus attention upon the most serious offenders. The same expectations can be expressed in policy measures aimed at controlling illegal immigration. The fact that there are presently no meaningful deterrents to illegal immigration at least implicitly signals to people of other countries that the United States is not really committed to enforcing its immigration statutes. Until this incongruity is rectified, it will be impossible to say that the nation has a coherent immigration policy.

The Subtleties of Terminology

One of the minor features of a discussion of illegal immigration that distinguishes it from other controversial public policy issues is the debate that continues to take place over the descriptive terms one should use when describing the phenomenon. This terminological quandary is an example of a process that has been associated with discussions of other subgroups of the population for some time. Since the 1960s public policymakers have moved away from broad, aggregate policies and have tended to favor tailor-made remedies for labor market difficulties. In the process, many of them have become sensitive to the fact that some of the nation's population subgroups wish to be known by descriptive terms other than the phrases the dominant culture has imposed on them over the years. Hence the term *Negroes* has given way to *blacks; Mexican Americans* to *Chicanos; Indians* to *Native Americans;* and *orientals* to *Asian Americans.* Often spurred by activist leaders, these subgroups have sought to escape the labels that they feel reflect past periods of discrimination and subjugation. At times, the willingness of non–group members to use the new phrases has been considered a litmus test of their sensitivity to the aspirations of the various subgroups. In point of fact, the preferences of the subgroups have usually been adopted by policymakers.

Much the same can be said with respect to the phrases that are used to describe persons who have violated the immigration laws of the United States. In the past, terms such as *wetbacks* (or its literal Spanish translation, *los mojados*) were used in the Southwest. But most of the persons who enter the United States illegally do not swim across the border. Moreover, the term *wetback* has both a slang and a derisive connotation that many Chicanos find offensive. Gradually, as illegal immigration came to be recognized as a national issue involving persons from countries other than Mexico, the terms *illegal entrants, illegal aliens, illegal immigrants, deportable aliens,* and *undocumented workers* gained coinage. None of these phrases is entirely acceptable to everyone, and none adequately describes all the forms of unauthorized immigration. There are, for example, persons who entered the United States legally, with the proper documents, but who overstayed their visas. Technically they did not enter illegally and they were not originally undocumented. Also, while all undocumented entrants come illegally, they may not all be workers. Some are spouses, children, or aged relatives, and a few are criminals and vagrants. Likewise, the term *immigrant* is not always appropriate. When used accurately, it means that a person is seeking to settle permanently. Some portion of these persons—at least some of those from Mexico—have no such intention. For them the term *migrant* would seem to be more appropriate. In Europe, in fact, the foreign workers who were imported legally from abroad in the 1960s and early 1970s were called migrants because they were viewed as temporary workers, or "guestworkers." In the United States, however, the term *migrant* is used by professional demographers to describe a native person who makes permanent change of residence. That is to say, the term is generally used to describe citizens who move from one part of the United States to another. Someone who moves from New York to Arizona to work or to retire is said to be a migrant, as is one who moves from Puerto Rico to New York City. In addition, in the United States the term *migrant* is often used to describe itinerant workers who move from place to place to find employment (e.g., to harvest seasonal crops). Another term that is considered by some to be offensive is *alien,* for it conjures up an image of a thing from outer space. In a few instances, even the terms *illegal* and *deportable* are inappropriate. Due to subsequent statutory registry revisions or judicial interventions, some persons who entered the country illegally in the past are now entitled to regularization of their status if they seek it.

Thus, no phrase has yet been found that encompasses all the above categories of noncitizens. For a discussion to take place, however, a term must be chosen. Not wishing to add a new term to the already overcrowded lexicon, I have opted for *illegal immigrant,* despite the acknowledged limitations of that phrase.

The Classification of Illegal Immigrants

There are essentially two types of illegal immigrants. One type enters the United States in a surreptitious manner—by swimming, sailing, rowing, driving, climbing, or walking across some portion of the nation's land or sea border. Sometimes these immigrants come individually; sometimes they come in groups. Many are guided or transported by smugglers for a fee. In the Southwest, such smugglers are often called "coyotes." The conditions of entry are often hazardous and dangerous.[1] The unifying characteristic of these immigrants is the fact that they enter the United States without appropriate documents. In the parlance of the INS, they are persons who have "entered without inspection" (EWIs). Typically, EWIs come from Mexico and Canada, but the term may also be applied to persons from nonneighboring nations who use Canada or Mexico as a waystation for eventual illegal entry into the United States. It is the act of entering without inspection that is illegal.

The second type enters the United States legally by passing through an established port of entry. These persons originally present authentic documents but subsequently violate the terms of their visa. Some stay beyond its expiration date; others seek to work during this period despite the fact that, except in prescribed circumstances, nonimmigrants are prohibited from doing so. Some present false documents when they enter or illegally use someone else's documents as a means of entry. Still others unlawfully pose as American citizens when crossing a border. All these persons are called "visa abusers." They come from virtually every country in the world. They are tourists, students, businessmen, crewmen, and a host of other categories of persons who have already entered the country. The fact that they overstay their visa or that they seek employment during their legal stay places them in violation of U.S. immigration statutes.

Thus, the entry process is distinctly different for EWIs and visa abusers even though both groups are collectively referred to as illegal immigrants. Testifying before a congressional subcommittee, David North noted a distinction between the two groups which is vital to the formulation of appropriate policy remedies:

In a very real sense, the presence of EWIs in the nation is a reflection of border patrol failures and the presence of visa abusers is a reflection of State Department failures. In other words, consular officials have granted a non-immigrant visa to a tourist or student in the belief the applicant will not violate the terms of the visa. That is the only reason they gave the visa in the first place.[2]

Frequently, illegal immigrants use their time in the United States to establish the conditions they will depend on later in their efforts to become legal immigrants. Indeed, the practice of adjusting one's status after the fact of one's entry—for example, as a refugee, a nonimmigrant, or an illegal immigrant—often accounts for as many as one-third of the legal immigrants "admitted" in any given year. It is more difficult for an illegal immigrant to adjust his or her status to that of a legal resident alien than for other groups to do so, but all groups succeed. The fact that it is possible for illegal immigrants to move into the legal immigrant category in relatively substantial numbers only adds to the immense difficulty of studying illegal immigrants as a discrete grouping.

The Statistics on Illegal Immigration

The problems of defining and classifying illegal immigrants are complex, to be sure, but the problems of determining their number are monumental. Because of the nature of their entry, illegal immigrants seek to avoid contact with U.S. government agencies. If they admitted they were EWIs or visa abusers, they would be subject to deportation. Hence, no effort has been made to collect data through self-identification. The only available government data, therefore, pertain to the number of apprehensions of deportable aliens and the number of persons required to depart each year by the INS in the performance of its enforcement duties.

The total number of reported illegal immigrants actually apprehended by the INS during the years 1925–1983 is shown in Table 22. As can be seen there, prior to 1983 the largest number of apprehensions occurred in the early 1950s. During 1953 and 1954, the Eisenhower administration directed the INS to launch an aggressive sweep of the southwestern border region. The INS campaign, called "Operation Wetback," was led by a former military officer, General Joseph Swing, who was the INS commissioner at the time. Given the enhanced sensitivity of policymakers to the feelings of racial and ethnic subgroups of the population and the subsequent development of a number of strong Hispanic community organizations, it is unlikely that any such indiscriminate and massive roundup will ever occur again. It is to be hoped that it will not.

While the apprehensions that were made during 1953 and 1954 were considered to be a tactical aberration, the data in Table 22 indicate that by the end of the bracero program in 1964 the number of apprehensions had begun to increase significantly, and they continued to increase steadily until 1980. From 1980

TABLE 22. ILLEGAL IMMIGRANTS APPREHENDED, 1925–1983

Period	Number of Illegal Immigrants Apprehended	Period	Number of Illegal Immigrants Apprehended
1925–1930	128,484	1957	59,918
1931	22,276	1958	53,474
1932	22,735	1959	45,336
1933	20,949	1960	70,684
1934	10,319	1961	88,823
1935	11,016	1962	92,758
1936	11,728	1963	88,712
1937	13,054	1964	86,597
1938	12,851	1965	110,371
1939	12,037	1966	138,520
1940	10,492	1967	161,608
1941	11,294	1968	212,057
1942	11,784	1969	283,557
1943	11,175	1970	345,353
1944	31,174	1971	420,126
1945	69,164	1972	505,949
1946	99,591	1973	655,968
1947	193,657	1974	788,145
1948	192,779	1975	756,819
1949	288,253	1976	866,433
1950	468,339	1977	1,033,427
1951	509,040	1978	1,047,687
1952	528,815	1979	1,069,400
1953	885,587	1980	910,361
1954	1,089,583	1981	975,780
1955	254,096	1982	962,687
1956	87,696	1983	1,248,000[a]

Source: U.S. Department of Justice, *Annual Reports* of the Immigration and Naturalization Service.

[a]Provisional figure.

through 1982, the number of apprehensions fell off slightly, but it is unlikely that the actual number of illegal immigrants seeking to enter declined during this period. Indeed, the apprehensions in 1983 totaled 1,248,000—the highest number ever recorded. It is interesting to note that the number of apprehensions has increased since 1964 despite the fact that there has been very little appreciable increase in the real budget of the INS (adjusting for inflationary increases) or in the number of its personnel.

There are severe problems associated with using the number of illegal immigrants apprehended as an indicator of the magnitude of illegal immigration. To begin with, the data reflect multiple counting. Some persons—especially in the Southwest—are caught more than once in a given year. About 95 percent of the persons who are apprehended each year are given the choice of departing voluntarily or being subjected to lengthy and costly deportation proceedings, and most choose the former. As a result, there is virtually no legal deterrent to keep them from again trying to enter the United States. Presumably, however, the problem of repeat captures has always been reflected in the data on apprehensions. There is no reason to believe that this problem is proportionately more severe now than it has been in the past. Hence, the increase in the number of apprehensions can be used in a general way to infer an increase in the number of illegal immigrants entering the United States, but it cannot be used as a precise indicator of the number of individuals involved.

It is also important to note that the INS and its predecessor agencies have at times changed the definitions used to classify apprehended aliens. Hence it is difficult to draw long-term comparisons from the data.[3] Moreover, the number of apprehensions made in any one year to some degree reflects the staffing patterns of the INS.[4] The slight drop in apprehensions in 1980, for instance, reflects budget cutbacks that year and the moratorium on raids that was imposed by the INS during the several months the 1980 census count was in progress. The moratorium was deemed necessary to assuage fears that as a result of participating in the census illegal immigrants might be turned into the INS. In 1981 and 1982 further budgetary restrictions limited the ability of the INS to perform its duties. It is unlikely, therefore, that the slight decline in apprehensions between 1980 and 1982 represents a slackening of illegal immigration (those apprehended plus those not apprehended).

Another serious bias in the apprehension data derives from the fact that the INS concentrates most of its border patrol activities in the southwestern United States. Hence it is not surprising that over 90 percent of the illegal immigrants apprehended each year are from Mexico. The INS long ago recognized that it is much easier and cheaper to apprehend EWIs along the southwestern border than to ferret out visa abusers, who could be living and working almost anywhere in the United States. Because most EWIs are Mexican, it is Mexicans who usually get caught. Illegal immigrants from nations other than Mexico tend to be visa abusers and are least likely to be apprehended. The apprehension data have therefore created the false impression that illegal immigration is exclusively a Mexican problem. It is not. It is generally believed that Mexico accounts for 60 percent of the annual inflow of illegal immigrants, the Caribbean countries account for 20 percent, and other nations in both the Eastern and the Western Hemisphere account for the remaining 20 percent.[5] There is, of course, no way to confirm the actual distribution since the total number is unknown. The U.S. Department of Justice reports that "at least 60 countries are significant regular 'source' countries."[6] Aside from Mexico, which the department acknowledges is the primary source country, fourteen other nations are considered to be prominent sources. They are the Dominican Republic, Haiti, Jamaica, Guatemala, Colombia, Peru, Ecuador, the Philippines, Korea, Thailand, Greece, India, Iran, and Nigeria.

The most serious problem with INS apprehension data, however, is the fact that apprehensions are only the tip of the iceberg. Most illegal immigrants— especially most visa abusers—are never caught. For instance, the only serious study involving exclusively illegal immigrants who had not been apprehended as of the time of their interviews was prepared for the U.S. Department of Labor and released in 1979. According to that study, 69.6 percent of 1,970 illegal immigrants interviewed in Los Angeles who were or had been employed had never been apprehended.[7] Most of the people in this sample were Mexicans (92.6 percent of the total) and EWIs. The study thus lends credence to the theory that the actual number of illegal immigrants entering the United States each year is several multiples of the number apprehended.

Despite the gross deficiencies of the data that exist on the apprehension of illegal immigrants, the U.S. General Accounting Office (GAO) was forced to conclude in its 1982 survey of the literature on illegal immigrants that the apprehension statistics constitute "the most comprehensive data on illegal aliens" that are presently available.[8] The GAO also observed that despite their limitations, these statistics played important roles in a variety of policy decisions.

Most persons who had studied this issue had expressed dissatisfaction with the use of apprehension data as an indicator of the magnitude and character of illegal immigration flows, however, and in the mid-1970s the INS had undertaken the mission of trying to determine the total number of illegal aliens living in the United States (i.e., those apprehended plus those not apprehended). Such a figure was not available from any regular data series. The INS estimate was later used during congressional hearings, in news releases, and in public speeches by officials of the INS. Exactly how this estimate of total illegal immigration was computed is something of a mystery. Even high officials in the INS were uncertain as to precisely where the figure came from. For instance, the commissioner of the INS—at that time General Leonard F. Chapman, Jr.—told an inquiring reporter from the *Washington Post* in early 1975 that the overall estimate of the number of illegal aliens was a composite of separate estimates provided by thirty-two district offices of the INS. The local estimates, he stated, were made by the district directors, each of whom used "a formula" as the basis for his or her estimate. But when the *Post* reporter called several of the INS district directors to learn the nature of the formula, he was told that none existed. Upon further investigation, the reporter learned that the estimates were based on a composite of information sources. Among these were "leads" (which the INS investigators were unable to follow up); the monitoring of electronic sensors planted in the desert and border areas of the Southwest; estimates made by local police; an appraisal of the economic conditions existing in the home countries of the immigrants; and "street wisdom."[9]

Thus it should not surprise us to learn that when Commissioner Chapman was asked by a congressional committee how the INS in 1973 had estimated the magnitude of illegal immigration to be 4 or 5 million, he testified: "It is just a mid-point between the two extremes. I have heard one or two million at one end of the scale and eight or 10 million at the other. So, I am selecting a mid-point— just a guess, that is all. Nobody knows."[10] Nor should we be shocked to read in the INS *Annual Report* for 1974 this statement by Commissioner Chapman: "It is estimated that the number illegally in the United States totals 6 to 8 million persons and is possibly as great as 10 or 12 million."[11]

Obviously, these estimation techniques did not inspire public confidence. The INS then sought credibility by turning to outside consultants. In one contract with Lesko Associates, a Delphi sampling technique was used whereby a number of nongovernmental "experts" who had studied the issue were asked to submit independent estimates of the number of illegal immigrants residing in the United States in 1975. After these estimates were compiled, the panel members were asked if they wished to revise their individual projections on the basis of the initial average of all the panel members' estimates. The revised figures were then given to the INS. The average figure set by this procedure was 8.1 million illegal immigrants as of 1975; the individual estimates ranged from 4.2 to 11 million.[12] This procedure was roundly criticized by scholars who claimed that there was no scientific basis at all for averaging the guesses made by the "experts."[13]

In 1977 the INS funded an expensive private consulting contract with Reyes Associates which promised to do a house-to-house survey of the foreign-born population in selected neighborhoods in the twelve states that had the highest number of foreign-born persons in their population. The design of the survey was subsequently modified to focus on specific areas in these twelve states that had large pockets of permanent-resident aliens. Reyes Associates believed that it would be possible to deduce from the answers to its questions whether an interviewee was an illegal immigrant. This study design was widely criticized, however, for it seemed inconceivable that respondees would answer such questions or, if they did, that they would answer truthfully. It is not surprising that the study was never completed.

The crudeness of the INS's efforts to determine the number of illegal immigrants in the nation at any one time led to extensive criticism—even ridicule—of the agency. Many academicians felt that they could hardly do worse than the INS in their selection of methodologies. Hence, they too made estimates. Even the Mexican government supported efforts to calculate a number. All these intellectual exercises have been severely limited methodologically and they have produced a wide range of partial estimates. None has yet attempted to estimate the total number of illegal immigrants. An overview of the studies made by U.S. scholars is presented in Appendix B of this volume; studies undertaken by scholars in Mexico are discussed briefly in Appendix C.

In 1979 the National Commission on Employment and Unemployment Statistics completed its study of the adequacy of the nation's labor force indicators. With regard to illegal immigrants, the commission concluded: "No single area in labor statistics is as undeveloped, incomplete, and imprecise as is our data on undocumented workers. Estimates of the illegal alien population, the labor market situation of undocumented workers, and the effects of their presence on the supply and the demand for resident workers vary widely."[14] The commission strongly recommended that "the scope and frequency" of studies that would estimate the number and impact of illegal immigrants "should be increased." The frustration expressed by the commission and by Congress over the inability to determine the number of illegal immigrants residing in the United States can be seen in the following exchange, which took place in 1979 between the chairman of the commission, Sar Levitan, and Congressman Jake Pickle, a member of the Oversight Subcommittee of the Ways and Means Committee of the U.S. House of Representatives:

> *Congressman Pickle:* . . . How many do you think there are?
> *Mr. Levitan:* I really don't know, Mr. Pickle. I would be guessing. It may be between 3 and 12 million but nobody knows for sure. In the National Commission on Employment and Unemployment Statistics we talked to the best authorities in and out of the government. We asked them, "Can we get a reliable number?" The answer was, "No." So we threw up our hands and said, given the present survey instruments—which are voluntary—we cannot hope to obtain a reasonably precise number. The Immigration and Naturalization Service does not have it; the Bureau of Labor Statistics does not; and the Census does not have it. . . .
> *Congressman Pickle:* I know nobody knows exactly. We accept that but somebody ought to give us a very good guess or estimate of it.[15]

Given its mandate in 1978, the Select Commission on Immigration and Refugee Policy also felt obliged to secure some count of the nation's illegal immigrants. Wisely, however, the commission elected not to make an independent study. Instead, it requested a report by the Bureau of the Census. In its subsequent review the bureau estimated that the number of illegal immigrants ranged from 3.5 million to 6 million.[16] These figures, however, were derived exclusively from a staff review of the aforementioned reports by the INS, consultants, and academicians. These earlier reports had employed various methodologies and all were based on data for various years in the early and mid-1970s—*not for 1981,* the year the Select Commission's report was released. The point that needs to be emphasized here is that the Bureau of the Census did not make any *new* estimates for the Select Commission. The range that it supplied to the commission and that the commission then published in its final report was derived by averaging the noncomparable "guestimates" from the previously mentioned studies, many of which were of dubious statistical validity. Unfortunately, none of these limitations will be apparent to many of the people who read the report of the commission. Nor will readers find the following qualification made by the Census Bureau in its review:

We have, unfortunately, been unable to arrive at definitive estimates of the number of illegal residents in the United States or the magnitude of the illegal migration flow. The phenomenon we have sought to measure, by its nature, is not an easy one to deal with. Researchers and policymakers will have to live with the fact that that number of illegal residents in the United States cannot be closely quantified. Therefore, policy options dependent on the size of this group must be evaluated in terms which recognize this uncertainty.[17]

Because this warning was not included in the commission's report, the quoted range has subsequently been widely cited as a maximum range for 1981 when in fact it is, if anything, a minimum estimate of the illegal immigrant population of the United States in the early 1970s.

There will, however, never be any better data available on this question. The character of the entire process precludes the possibility that an actual tabulation of persons who immigrate illegally will ever be made. But before despairing that little can be learned because the data are so poor, we should realize that this is also the case with most of the major social problems of the day. And in all these other vital areas of public concern the lack of data has not precluded the adoption of major policy initiatives to meet perceived needs. Furthermore, it makes little conceptual difference whether the number of illegal immigrants in the nation is 3 million, 6 million, 9 million, or 12 million. The precise number is irrelevant if we concede that the number of persons involved is substantial and is increasing annually.

Illegal Immigration from Mexico

Mexico is the primary source of illegal immigrants to the United States. To understand this phenomenon it is important to discuss briefly the nature of the historical relationship between the two nations and to assess the political and socioeconomic factors in Mexico that impinge upon the immigration process.

THE HISTORICAL LEGACY

Many people in the United States are either unaware of the fact, or do not think it consequential to remember, that the southwestern part of their country once belonged to Mexico. Few wish to be reminded that this land was acquired as a result of the nation's "first successful offensive war."[18] For many Mexicans, however, this event remains a vivid reminder of past national humiliation. The memory is partly responsible for the climate of suspicion that has since haunted Mexico's relations with the United States. As Alan Riding, *New York Times* specialist on Mexico, has observed:

> For the United States, then, Mexico is a new issue. But for Mexico, the United States is an old problem. Washington is, therefore, looking to the future, while Mexico is remembering the past. And more even than language, race, religion, culture and politics, the two countries are separated by history. It is not that Mexico cannot "forgive" the past; it is that for Mexicans, the past is still present.[19]

Thus, to truly understand the roots of the illegal immigration issue as it pertains to Mexico, it is necessary to understand the key events that preceded and followed the Mexican War of 1846–1848.

The war with Mexico was the culmination of events that began when settlers from the United States were given permission by the Mexican government to settle in the Province of Texas during the early 1820s. Before the decade was over, these settlers outnumbered the Mexican population. Conflicts between the settlers and the Mexican government soon developed over such issues as slavery (which Mexico opposed), decentralized rule versus central rule from Mexico City, required allegiance to the Catholic Church, as well as Mexico's unsuccessful efforts to stop further settlement by immigrants from the United States. Consequently, in late 1835 the Texans revolted against the central government of Mexico. Mexico responded by sending federal troops to squelch the uprising and recapture the territory in early 1836. In the ensuing battles both sides employed barbarous tactics. At the siege of the Alamo in San Antonio in March 1836 the Mexican army was victorious, but it was subsequently defeated at the Battle of San Jacinto (an area northeast of present-day Houston, Texas) on April 21, 1836. The victorious Texans sought immediate annexation by the United States, but in pre–Civil War America, Northerners opposed this move, for fear it would increase the number of states that permitted slavery. Consequently, Texas became an independent republic. Mexico, however, refused to sign a peace treaty recognizing an independent Texas, and its leaders pledged revenge. In the early 1840s, the economy of the Republic of Texas began to falter and overtures were made for assistance from various European nations. The United States, which since the promulgation of the Monroe Doctrine had opposed the intervention of European nations in the Caribbean area, began to reconsider the annexation issue. A treaty that called for such action, however, was defeated in the Senate in 1844. The topic subsequently became an issue in the presidential campaign of that year. The Democratic party, recognizing that expansionism was popular in the Mississippi valley, voted at its convention to support the annexation of Texas if it was combined with the acquisition of the Oregon Territory. The party platform actually called for the ''re-annexation'' of Texas, alleging that the territory had really been part of the Louisiana Purchase of 1803. The Whig party opposed the annexation. When its presidential candidate softened his opposition, however, many Northern Whigs bolted the party and voted for a third-party candidate. As a result, the Democratic candidate, James K. Polk, was elected and the statehood of Texas was assured.

Although Polk is one of the lesser-known American presidents, few others have accomplished more. The Oregon question was settled easily. In a treaty with Great Britain in 1846 the 49th parallel was established as the United States' northern boundary with Canada and thereby added to its territory the area that would later become the states of Washington, Oregon, and Idaho. The dispute with Mexico, however, proved to be infinitely more complex.

While the admission of Texas was being discussed in Congress in early 1845, Mexico reversed its position, announcing that it would recognize the independence of Texas if it remained a separate republic. This offer came too late, however. Four days before Polk was inaugurated, the outgoing president, John Tyler, finally persuaded Congress to pass a joint resolution extending an offer of annexation to Texas. The overture was subsequently accepted and Texas was admitted to the Union on December 29, 1845. Mexico had threatened that such action would lead to war. It did break diplomatic relations with the United States, but it did not immediately take any steps that indicated it intended to actually fight.

The most pressing problem that arose as a result of the admission of Texas was a dispute over the location of the precise boundary between Texas and Mexico. The Texans claimed that the boundary was the Rio Grande (which would also have given the United States a large part of what is today the state of New Mexico); Mexico claimed that it was the Nueces River, which was about 200 miles north of the Rio Grande. Skillful negotiations probably could have prevented a military confrontation over the issue, but President Polk was more interested in securing California than in settling the Texas boundary dispute. He wanted to purchase the entire land area that today comprises most of the southwestern United States, and he mistakenly feared Mexico was going to sell that land to Britain. When Mexico refused to consider Polk's offer, he resurrected another issue. He called for Mexico to pay off debts that had been owed to U.S. business investors since the time of earlier political upheavals in Mexico. In 1839 Mexico had promised to make these payments but later defaulted because of a genuine inability to pay. Thus, when the negotiations concerning the border and Mexico's debt failed in the spring of 1846, Polk sent U.S. army troops to occupy the area between the Nueces and Rio Grande rivers. Mexico did likewise and fighting ensued. Only a few days after a message was received in Washington that the Mexicans had "shed American blood on American soil" Congress declared war.

The United States won all the major battles of the war and ultimately the war itself. Mexico City became the first foreign capital ever to be occupied by U.S. troops. Polk had earlier ordered a State Department official, Nicholas Trist, to accompany the army in its assault on the city, instructing him to see if a peace agreement could be arranged in advance of the attack that would settle the boundary dispute and permit the United States to buy the remaining territory it desired. When these efforts failed and after Mexico City was captured, Trist was ordered to return to Washington, but he ignored these orders and with the approval of the leaders of the U.S. military forces proceeded to carry out his original orders.

On February 2, 1848, the Treaty of Guadalupe Hidalgo was signed in a suburb of Mexico City. Under its terms Mexico ceded to the United States not only Texas with its Rio Grande boundary but also the entire land area of present-day California, Nevada, and Utah, most of Arizona and New Mexico, and parts of Colorado and Wyoming. In exchange, Mexico received $15 million and an agreement that the U.S. government would assume the aforementioned debts owed to American business investors. Polk resisted the political pressure from some congressional quarters to annex all of Mexico. Although he was indignant with Trist for ignoring his recall orders, he submitted the treaty for ratification in the form in which it had been negotiated, and it was ratified by the Senate in March 1848.

Under the terms of this treaty, Mexico lost about 1,000,000 square miles of territory, or almost half of its land mass. By the same token, the United States acquired a region approximately the size of present-day India. Of even greater consequence was the fact that this new territory proved to be extraordinarily rich in oil, gas, minerals, timber, and fertile soil. Only nine days before the treaty was signed, gold was discovered at Sutter's Mill in California.

Soon after surveyors began marking the western land border from El Paso, Texas, to California, U.S. railroad owners realized that the new boundary line did not follow the best route to California. The preferred route lay south of the Gila River (in present-day Arizona and New Mexico), which still belonged to Mexico. In 1853, as tensions mounted over the ownership of this land and as the threat of warfare again surfaced, the United States sent James Gadsden to Mexico to negotiate the purchase of the additional land. Essentially, Mexico was given an offer it could not refuse: sell it or we will take it.[20] Mexico elected to sell the contested territory (about 45,532 square miles) for the sum of $10 million. Shortly afterward, earlier reports were confirmed: one of the world's richest copper deposits was located about a mile inside the new U.S. border in the southeastern corner of present-day Arizona.

Thus, with the Gadsden Purchase, the southern border of the continental United States and the northern border of Mexico were set. According to Carey McWilliams, however, the boundary is "a border of the borderlands rather than a national boundary based on economic or ethnic factors."[21] McWilliams contends that it is "unreal in every sense" because it is an imaginary line. There are no natural geographical barriers or ethnic differences between the populations that live on either side of it.

With the land, of course, came the people who lived on it. It is estimated that 75,000 Mexican citizens lived in the regions that were ceded to and purchased by the United States during this period. About two-thirds of these people lived in the Taos–Santa Fe area of what is today the state of New Mexico. The remainder were scattered from Texas to California. The Treaty of Guadalupe Hidalgo specified that the landholdings and other rights of these people would be protected. The people would be given the choice of becoming U.S. citizens or returning to Mexico. Most remained where they were, for very few had real ties with Mexico. As of 1848 the actual cultural border of Mexico was still hundreds of miles south of even the newly established political border.[22]

It was not until the first three decades of the twentieth century that Mexican immigration to the United States began in earnest and the border communities began to assume real prominence. In fact, these cities and towns exist primarily because the border exists. U.S. efforts to control illegal immigration across the U.S.-Mexican border began in the 1920s. Since that time, Mexican border cities have been depicted as serving "a kind of 'Ellis Island' function, with people waiting to enter the United States."[23] This description is particularly apt for those who seek to enter illegally. Typically, Mexican border communities are far larger than their U.S. counterparts.

In 1848, at the end of Mexico's disastrous war with the United States, the Mexican economy lay in ruins. Virtual anarchy prevailed, and most of the population existed in total impoverishment while various political factions wrestled over who should take nominal control of the country. Then, from 1861 to 1867, Mexico was occupied by the French, and following this invasion the country was again torn by internal strife. Ultimately, in 1876, the dictator Porfirio Díaz gained control of the government and except for a brief period remained in power until 1910. During these years the political stability that was needed to develop a favorable climate for business and investment was achieved, but the price for this stability was a massive denial of human rights and the widespread use of physical terror.[24]

In 1911 Mexico was swept by a revolution that would continue off and on throughout most of the next decade. Virtually no opportunities had been provided for the education of the general population, however, and thus there was no intellectual foundation for the establishment of an effective new order. Díaz fled into exile. In October 1910 Francisco Madero was elected president in what has been described as "probably the freest election in the nation's history."[25] Basing its platform essentially upon the call for a decentralized political system and civil liberties for individuals, the new regime directed little attention to the basic economic problems of the nation. Although the United States initially supported the new Mexican government, President William Howard Taft soon found that Madero was not about to continue to grant special concessions to U.S. business investors as had been the case under the Díaz dictatorship. Madero's quest to establish a government that would abolish the special privileges of the upper classes led to counterrevolution. In 1912 U.S. Ambassador Henry L. Wilson, who was described as "an unrelenting foe" of the new Mexican leader, became actively involved in a plot to overthrow the Madero government.[26] This support of dissident leaders forced Madero to resign as president in February 1913 and he was killed a few days later by a group of army officers.

In the struggle for power that ensued, Mexico suffered the most extensive human carnage in its history. It is estimated that a million people were killed during the revolutionary fighting from 1911 to 1917—or about one of every fifteen people in the population. Many more were injured and left homeless. President Woodrow Wilson, who had assumed office in March 1913, opposed the military junta that had ousted Madero, and he sought assurances that a free election would take place. In 1914, when these efforts appeared to stall, he found a pretext—the fact that Mexico refused to apologize for the inadvertent arrest of crew members of a U.S. naval vessel who had gone ashore in a restricted military zone near Tampico—to seize the port city of Veracruz. Two hundred Mexicans were killed trying to defend the city. Even more serious was the fact that the leader of one of the revolutionary factions in northern Mexico, Francisco ("Pancho") Villa, turned against the United States after President Wilson reluctantly extended diplomatic relations in late 1915 to another faction that appeared to have secured control of the government. In retaliation, Villa sought to provoke the United States into a war. In January 1916 a Mexican train was stopped by Villa near the city of Chihuahua and sixteen U.S. citizens who were on board were killed. On March 19, 1916, in a raid conducted by Villa on the border town of Columbus, New Mexico, nineteen people were killed and the city was burned. President Wilson responded by sending a military force led by General John Pershing across the border into Mexico. Mexicans from all the warring factions resented the attack on their sovereignty. A crisis could perhaps have been averted if Villa and his men had been caught quickly, but they eluded the Pershing search party. A month later U.S. troops were more than 300 miles inside Mexico and they had taken on the character of an army of occupation. The Mexican government demanded that they withdraw, but President Wilson refused. It appeared that the two nations might actually go to war again. Despite repeated efforts, Wilson failed to gain concessions from Mexico that would guarantee the safety of U.S. border communities as a condition for withdrawal of General Pershing's forces. When events in Europe led to U.S. involvement in World War I, however, Wilson had no choice but to order the unilateral withdrawal of Pershing's forces, and in January 1917 this "nearly tragic chapter in the history of American foreign relations" was closed.[27]

Meanwhile, the lasting legacy of Mexico's revolution—that nation's Constitution—was adopted in 1917. The Constitution ended the era in which principles of natural law held sway over the destiny of the Mexican people. The basis for creation of a strong, centralized government was established. A parliamentary system was adopted, but the government was given the power to change the Constitution if it wished—something it has subsequently done on many occasions. The Constitution was strongly anticlerical. Moreover, it called for comprehensive agrarian reform, nationalization of the country's natural resources, and legalization of trade unions. The actual laws that would implement these concepts had to be enacted by Parliament. As originally defined, the office of president was not very powerful, but extensive changes were soon made that permitted the president to exercise immense powers if he wished. Groups that felt adversely affected by the terms of the new document reacted bitterly, and scattered fighting continued. When Mexico's newly elected president was assassinated in 1920, President Wilson refused to recognize his successor. By 1920 the Mexican government was again on the verge of collapse. Economic conditions continued to deteriorate throughout the 1920s, and intermittent fighting broke out as the central government sought to consolidate its hold over the countryside.

It is important to note here that it was during this period that a mass exodus of Mexicans to the United States began. A quarter of a million Mexicans legally immigrated to the United States between 1910 and 1920, and another half-million came between 1920 and 1929. Many more, it is believed, entered the United States illegally.

Unfortunately, the revolutionary reform movement in Mexico did not change the conditions of poverty under which most of its people lived. The United States did not reestablish diplomatic relations with Mexico until 1923. The major delay was caused by President Warren Harding, who feared that Mexico might actually try to carry out its constitutional mandate and nationalize the extensive oil and natural gas holdings of private U.S. and British businesses in Mexico. When Mexico agreed not to nationalize any enterprises retroactively, President Calvin Coolidge finally extended formal recognition to the Mexican government.

Throughout the 1920s the government of Mexico was preoccupied with the issue of nationalizing its resources and with efforts to purge the influence of the Catholic Church from Mexican society. Both of these moves were strongly resisted. Moreover, widespread corruption among government officials prevented the achievement of the ideals of the revolution. In the late 1920s political turmoil and the continued disintegration of the economy led to a grand coalition of divergent interest groups to form a single political party. Established in 1929, the coalition originally called itself the National Revolutionary party. It has since gone through two name changes and reorganizations, but it has maintained total political control of Mexico. Today it is known as the Party of Revolutionary Institutions (PRI).

In 1934 Lázaro Cárdenas, the last of the leaders of Mexico to pledge to honor the goals of the revolution, was elected president. During his administration some large landholdings were broken up and distributed to peasants as communal holdings; a federation of labor unions, the Confederación de Trabajadores de México (CTM), was created; and railways and foreign oil holdings were nationalized. Nationalization of the railway and oil industries in the late 1930s laid the foundation for the industrialization of Mexico that occurred in subsequent years.

According to the Mexican Constitution, the president can serve only one six-year term, but according to custom, the outgoing president essentially hand-picks his successor. Thus, in 1940, Cárdenas chose a conservative general, Manuel Camacho. With Camacho's subsequent election, the era of radical enthusiasm came to an abrupt end and the revolution "veered to the right."[28] The rhetoric of Mexican leaders since 1940 has often been leftist, and as the nationalization of the banking industry in 1982 by the lame-duck president López Portillo showed, the revolutionary spirit can be rekindled at times. Nonetheless, the fact is that since 1940 all Mexican presidents have sought to place Mexico on a capital-intensive course of economic development. Partly out of fear that the nation would be dominated by the United States and relegated to a de facto form of colonial dependence, these leaders have sought to develop Mexico's economy as rapidly as possible. The implications of this strategy for a labor surplus nation that has paid scant attention to human resource development are cruelly obvious.

One result has been that the out-migration from rural to urban areas involves the very persons who have the least prospect of finding employment in Mexico's already overcrowded cities. Mexico City, for instance, had a population of 5.6 million in 1960, 8.6 million in 1970, and close to 15 million in 1980. Some analysts project that it may reach 30 million by the year 2000. If that happens, Mexico City will be the world's largest population center. Even though unemployment and underemployment (due largely to the irregularity of opportunities to work) are estimated to be 30–40 percent, rural people continue to migrate to urban areas—especially to Mexico City and the border cities. In these urban centers, they enter a kind of lottery for the scarce jobs that sometimes become available. Many are frustrated in their quest and turn to the United States as the one remaining alternative.

Tragically, Mexico's political leaders have come to regard emigration to the United States as a "safety valve," for it allows some of the workers who would otherwise be searching for jobs in labor-surplus Mexico to flee to the United States. Moreover, in 1982, during the period when the initial Simpson-Mazzoli bill was pending in the U.S. Congress, the Mexican Senate unanimously adopted a resolution questioning the basic right of the United States to control immigration and expressing "alarm and concern for the repercussions" that would occur "if the Simpson-Mazzoli legislation . . . passed."[29] By encouraging emigration, Mexico's leaders have been able to avoid making the internal changes that are needed to eliminate political corruption, to improve the distribution of the nation's income, and to develop a comprehensive job creation strategy.

THE LONG-TERM "PUSH" FACTORS

Having looked briefly at the quarrelsome relations that have existed between the United States and Mexico as well as Mexico's tumultuous political evolution, let us now consider how these key factors, among others, relate to the issue of illegal immigration. An understanding of these historical relationships and institutional developments is necessary if we are to place the immigration process in a proper context.

Mexico is one of the world's largest nations geographically; it ranks thirteenth. As of 1980, it was the tenth largest in terms of its population and the seventeenth largest in terms of the size of its gross national product. As indicated earlier, Mexico embarked on a course of rapid economic development when it nationalized its oil industry in 1938. Since that time the central government has played a prominent role in the shift from an agricultural and small-enterprise economy to a large-scale and diversified production-oriented economy. It has sought to accomplish this transformation through a variety of policy endeavors, including, of course, the nationalization of key industries, but it has also undertaken joint public-private ventures and has supported an independent private-business sector. The government has not seriously engaged in any form of national planning and it has generally been sympathetic to the needs of the private sector. It has actively sought foreign private investment. U.S. businesses in particular have been involved in the industrialization process.

In the early 1970s, massive oil reserves were discovered in southern Mexico. By the middle of that decade the oil was actually available for sale and Mexico began to use the reserves to finance further capital investments. By 1981 Mexico was the world's fifth largest oil producer and in 1982 it became for the first time the largest foreign supplier of oil and natural gas to the United States.

During this period of rapid growth, the Mexican government decided to follow the so-called Cambridge (England) approach to economic development. The Cambridge strategy advocates the use of expansionist fiscal and monetary policies to stimulate domestic economic growth coupled with extensive protectionist policies against foreign imports.[30] Mexico has refused to become a signatory to the General Agreement on Tariffs and Trade, which would commit the nation to a policy of relatively open markets to world trade. Instead, it has chosen to try to shelter its domestic industries against foreign competition during their infant years. It claims that both the United States (during the nineteenth century) and Japan (in the 1950s) followed just such a course during the early stages of industrialization. The acceptance of protectionism, of course, neatly dovetails with the strong sense of nationalism that has historically characterized Mexico's political leadership. In short, Mexico's economic development has been based on a policy of strong governmental intervention.

From 1962 through 1981 the policy seemed to work; the annual economic growth rate averaged close to 6 percent. Mexico was heralded as "one of the world's successful developing countries."[31] Unfortunately, however, the benefits of the growth of the economy were not evenly distributed. In a 1980 report, the World Bank showed that while some redistribution of income took place in Mexico during the revolution and during the Cárdenas administration, the trend toward greater equality of income ceased in the era of development that began in the 1940s.[32] The report also noted that there was "little or no change in distribution" during the 1960s and 1970s, when the transformation of the Mexican economy was at its zenith. During the growth phase, the report claimed, Mexico consciously adopted a policy that "exploited agriculture to finance industrialization, by lowering the price of agriculture's produce relative to the price of manufactures."[33] Thus poverty, which was already a severe problem in rural areas, continued and the income differentials between rural and urban areas widened significantly. The income differences, along with the introduction of more capital-intensive agricultural production techniques, served to accelerate the rural-to-urban migration of the Mexican population. In the urban areas, however, the stress placed on capital-intensive production, together with the gross neglect of the education and training of workers, reduced the opportunity for a large part of the Mexican labor force to participate in any of the real benefits of economic growth. As a result, the World Bank study concluded, in terms of the distribution of its income, Mexico ranked ninth among sixteen "middle-income" nations of the world. Its income distribution was significantly worse than that of such countries as South Korea, India, Taiwan, Sri Lanka, and the Philippines. Thus it is not surprising that a sizable portion of the 45 percent of the population that was regarded as poor (having a dollar-equivalent family income of $1,315 in 1977) decided to emigrate.[34] Conditions would no doubt have been worse had they chosen to remain.

How could things be so bad for so many people in Mexico when things were so good for the Mexican economy? Part of the paradox can be attributed to the seemingly endemic corruption in the Mexican government and to the unwillingness of the essentially one-party political elite to address the issue of reform. Wholesale corruption in government was a major issue in the Mexican elections of 1976 and 1982, but the issue tended to languish after the balloting was completed. So widespread is the problem that just prior to assuming the presidency in 1976, López Portillo proclaimed that "corruption is the cancer of this country" and "Mexico runs the risk of devouring itself unless we control corruption."[35] At the time, an aide to outgoing president Luis Echeverría exclaimed: "The public morals have been steadily worsening and the loss of the people's faith in the government comes partly from the corruption."[36] Yet in the campaign of 1982 the topic was still a paramount issue. Upon taking office that year, President Miguel de la Madrid spoke in his inaugural address of the necessity for "a moral regeneration of society" to combat corruption and the cynicism it generates among the population. Indeed, one of his first actions was to abolish the infamous secret police force in Mexico City known as the Department of Investigation to Prevent Delinquency. For over forty years this government agency had used extortion, robbery, and even rape and murder to terrorize citizens largely for the personal gain of its members. Whether this step represents a real change in the administration of Mexican justice or whether the agency will simply reconstitute itself elsewhere in another format remains to be seen. What is significant is that this secret police force went unchallenged for many years, and it is only one of many sources of widespread and condoned corruption.

The line between corruption and privilege is thinly drawn in Mexican society. The small upper class that has dominated the Mexican government since the 1940s has benefited immensely from the toleration of corrupt and unethical practices in government and in society in general. The greed of the upper class has made a shambles of the idealism of the Mexican Constitution. As one writer has caustically observed:

> Mexico is changing rapidly but too much of her past remains to haunt her.
> Quite aside from the population growth rate, there is another dimension: Too
> many upper and middle-class Mexicans lack a sense of national responsibility;
> too many adhere to the tradition of caring only for themselves and their
> immediate families and not about where their country is going; too many
> continue through tax loopholes and flagrant violations of Mexican law, to live
> with privilege that undercuts any destiny of equalitarianism, a notion as alien to

many rich Mexicans as it was a century ago to the robber barons of the United States.[37]

It is believed, for instance, that millions of dollars in oil revenues could have been used in the 1970s to provide jobs and to improve the nation's standard of living. Instead, they were siphoned off into Swiss bank accounts or squandered by officials of both the state-owned oil monopoly, Petróleos Méxicanos, and the oil workers unions.[38] In this context it is possible to understand the congressional testimony of General Paul F. Gorman, Chief of the Southern Command of the United States Army, in February 1984 that Mexico "is the most corrupt Government and society in Central America."[39]

Part of the difficulty involved in creating—or in wishing to create—a more equitable society in Mexico stems from the nature of that country's political system. Although at least five other parties exist, the PRI has completely dominated the politics of Mexico since its founding in the late 1920s. It has won every presidential election, every state governorship, and control of both houses of its Congress since its formation. The political system of Mexico and the basis for its operation are completely alien to the people and leaders of the United States. Failure to recognize these differences has repeatedly led to breakdowns in official understandings reached by the leaders of the two nations. The Mexican government functions on the basis of subtleness rather than confrontation. As the Mexican philosopher and poet Octavio Paz has pointed out, Mexico's politicians operate behind a mask of rhetoric.[40] The mask consists of the outward illusion of a one-party system, but in reality the PRI is a massive juggernaut of diverse interest groups that are constantly jockeying for prominence. The presidency of Mexico appears to be a position of immense power; its occupant, seemingly free to lead the nation at will. At times, in fact, the government is referred to as a presidential regime, not a parliamentary system. There are no apparent checks and balances similar to those that frequently lead to political stalemate in the United States. As Paz notes, however, this presidential power is also an illusion, for while it is true that the incumbent has the power to choose his successor (who will then go through the motions of campaigning even though the outcome of the election is foreknown), no individual ever arrives at the position of being considered a presidential contender unless he has already made numerous concessions to all the competing factions of the party. It takes a political life of "silence and subservience" to become a presidential contender in Mexico. It is understood that upon being elected to that mythically all-powerful position, the president will not use all his power. As Riding has observed, "Other groups accept the myth because they know the president will not test it; his role is to conciliate, not to confront."[41]

The Party of Revolutionary Institutions is not ideological in what it stands for or against. Instead, it reflects its historic postrevolutionary beginnings. It is a grand alliance supported by large and small businesses, trade unions, landless peasants, land owners, and intellectuals. Thus it incorporates almost all the extremes of the normal political spectrum that characterizes other noncommunist nations. The unifying link that holds the party together is the opportunistic objective of survival. As long as the leaders of these diverse groups can get along, the system will persevere. The requisites for political survival are "loyalty, dedication, and above all, discretion."[42] The established system therefore subordinates the special interests of the component groups to the welfare of the party. It is a system that "makes anguished fatalists of most of its earnest citizens, victims of most of its people, and opportunists out of others."[43] As Paz has lamented: "Liberal democratic ideology, far from expressing our concrete historical situation, disguised it and the political lie established itself constitutionally. The moral damage it has caused is incalculable. . . . For over a hundred years we have suffered under regimes that have been at the service of feudal oligarchies but have used the language of freedom."[44] Throughout Mexican life, Paz argues, form masquerades as substance: the legislature only mirrors what the president wants to do, the unions do not represent the interests of the workers, and the newspapers do not criticize the government. In this context, it is easy to understand why many Mexican citizens hold out very little hope that their political institutions will ever respond to the fundamental economic problems that confront the nation. Many assume that life can be changed only if they leave their homeland.

The problems that face Mexico are easy to describe. From 1950 to 1980 Mexico had one of the highest population growth rates in the world—a rate that persistently exceeded even that of India. Because the median age of the population is believed to be only fifteen years and the nation's death rate is declining, the population of Mexico will continue to skyrocket. In 1960 the population was 34 million, in 1970 it was 48 million, in 1980 it was 70 million, and by the year 2000 it is expected to reach 120 million. The labor force has been expanding rapidly, but job creation has not kept pace. It is estimated that just to keep unemployment from getting worse it will be necessary for the Mexican economy to generate a net increase of 850,000 jobs a year in the mid-1980s and even more in the future. With unemployment and underemployment conservatively estimated to be in the neighborhood of 30–40 percent, however, the employment prospects for many Mexicans are bleak. Moreover, in the absence of a social insurance system analogous to the unemployment benefits, food stamps, and aid for families with dependent children provided in the United States, many Mexicans are condemned to live a marginal existence.

SHORT-TERM "PUSH" FACTORS IN THE 1980s

As bad as domestic conditions had been during the preceding decades, they took a sudden nose dive in the early 1980s. The López Portillo administration had counted on rising oil revenues to accelerate Mexico's rate of economic development. As the oil became available and as world prices rose in the mid-1970s, Mexico made large purchases—often on credit—of the capital goods needed to finance its growing oil industry and other long-term development projects. When oil prices slumped in 1981, however, Mexico tried to defy the market trend by keeping its prices high. As a consequence, it suddenly lost some of its biggest customers. Belatedly, it too reduced its prices, but the damage had been done. By the end of 1982 it has accumulated the world's largest external debt—$82 billion. (It owed more than $30 billion to U.S. banks alone.) It had borrowed at a time when interest rates were at near-record highs. With oil revenues down and with its debt mounting, Mexico found itself in the unenviable position of having to pledge all its excess (over costs) oil revenues merely to pay the $12 billion in interest that was due on its international debt. During 1982, the government formally devalued the peso to lower exchange rates on three occasions before finally freeing it to find its own market rate. The rate of exchange fell from 26 pesos to the U.S. dollar in February to 150 pesos to the dollar in December.[45] As Mexico's external debt increased to $89 billion in 1983, the peso continued to decline at a gradual rate as the result of its ability to float freely in response to negative market pressures. One of the inevitable side effects of devaluation is that it triggers inflationary pressures. In this case, businesses raised prices and workers sought higher wages in order to recoup part of their perceived loss in purchasing power. The situation worsened when the government (as part of an austerity program imposed by the International Monetary Fund as a condition for eligibility for further credit) terminated subsidies on gasoline, food, and electricity. The prices on these basic items doubled literally overnight. As a result the inflation rate was over 100 percent in 1982 and 90 percent in 1983. Collectively, the sharp escalation in the value of the U.S. dollar (relative to the peso), skyrocketing inflation, and the rise in unemployment contributed new pressures for illegal immigration to the United States.[46]

THE "PULL" FACTORS

The political border between the United States and Mexico separates more than two different nations. It divides two entirely different levels of living. As Gene Lyons has poignantly described the contrast:

> There is no frontier anywhere in the world quite like it. It is as if Algeria were to border directly upon the South of France or West Germany upon Zaire. To enter Mexico overland from the United States is to travel in a matter of a few miles, the vast differences between those who have and those who have not, to be stunned into recognizing what most Americans, in our enormous self-absorption forget: the first couple of thousand dollars make the greatest difference; virtually all of us live closer to the Rockefellers than we do to the overwhelming majority of the world's people.[47]

In 1980 the average per capita income in the United States was $9,511 while that in Mexico was $2,130. It is unlikely that any other contiguous border in the world separates two nations with a greater disparity in annual income. This higher per capita income as well as higher wages and a wider array of job opportunities makes the United States a natural magnet for many Mexican immigrants.

Another "pull" factor is the strong cultural affinity that links the people of Mexico with many U.S. citizens of similar ethnic ancestry. Persons of Spanish heritage lived in the region that became the southwestern United States long before the first English colonies were established along the East Coast.[48] As a result, the influence of Spanish culture on the development of the region has been significant. Manifestations of that culture can be seen in the region's architecture, in the water law of the southwestern states, and in the concept of community property in marriages, which to this day distinguishes life in the Southwest from that of the rest of the nation.

Most important of all, of course, are the origins of the people themselves. In the sixteenth century Spain had tried to settle the region by establishing a series of loosely connected mission settlements, but this strategy did not work. The attempt failed in part because many of the conquistadors were more interested in exploration and conquest than in settlement. Few brought their families with them. More important, however, was the fact that some of the native Indian tribes were exceptionally warlike (toward the Spaniards and toward most of the other indigenous Indian tribes). The nomadic Apaches, Comanches, and Lipans were unrelenting in their attacks on the Spanish settlements. As a result, the mission settlements could not be linked and many did not survive. Those that did survive existed as islands of Spanish culture. In 1821 Mexico revolted against Spanish rule and laid claim to this vast region. As discussed earlier, however, Mexico itself had little opportunity to populate or develop the region. It was forced to cede this land to the United States following the Mexican War of 1846–1848, and few Mexicans emigrated to the region during the remainder of the nineteenth century. The Mexican revolution of 1911–1917 and the turmoil of its aftermath marked the beginning of the mass movement of Mexicans to the United States, and it was during this period that the full-scale development of the agriculture and the manufacturing industries of the Southwest got under way. The Mexican immigrants set the numerical base for what has subsequently become the Mexican-American (Chicano) population of the United States. By 1980 the population of Spanish origin in the four states that geographically dominate the Southwest (Arizona, California, New Mexico, and Texas) was 8.2 million. The overwhelming majority of these persons (at least 85 percent) are of Mexican ancestry. Some can trace their roots back to the time that Mexico or Spain controlled the region. Most, however, are either legal immigrants (or their descendants) or illegal immigrants (or their descendants) who have come in the twentieth century.

Thus, a substantial number of persons with cultural ties to Mexico live in the Southwest as well as in several other population pockets (e.g., in the Chicago area). Illegal immigrants from Mexico therefore settle in these areas. Such clustering not only facilitates their adjustment to the new society but also makes it difficult for authorities to detect their presence.

CATALYTIC AND REINFORCEMENT FACTORS

The standard criticism of reliance upon "push" and "pull" factors to explain the mass movement of people from one country to another is that no explanation can be given for what triggers the phenomenon at one time as opposed to another. In the case of Mexico, however, the explanation is simple. As opposed to the individual or pioneer movements of the late nineteenth century, the massive inflow of Mexicans to the United States in the 1920s resulted from th. violence of the Mexican revolution and the parallel expansion of the economy of the southwestern United States. The legal and illegal immigration of Mexicans came to a halt in the depression years of the 1930s, but then resumed in the 1940s with the re-creation of the bracero program. As detailed in Chapter 4, the nonimmigrant bracero program was originally established as a temporary war emergency program to provide agricultural workers to southwestern growers. It was extended, however, until December 31, 1964, at which time it was unilaterally terminated by the United States. In the process, close to half a million workers from rural Mexico were exposed to the wages, job opportunities, and life style of the United States each year. When the program ended in 1964, many of these individuals continued to immigrate illegally on either a temporary or a permanent basis. In fact, the upsurge in illegal immigration from Mexico dates from the termination of the bracero program.

By the early 1960s Mexico had become the largest source of legal immigrants to the United States, and it has maintained that distinction ever since. As discussed in Chapter 3, no quotas were placed on the number of immigrants from any Western Hemisphere nation until 1965. Even after the imposition of quotas, it was not until 1976 that Mexico was included under the same ceiling as applies to all other nations of the world (i.e., 20,000 immigrants a year plus immediate family members, who are not counted). The result of this seemingly equitable policy was that the demand for visas in Mexico quickly exceeded the available supply and a massive backlog of applications developed. Thus, the termination of the bracero program in 1964 and the first efforts in 1965 to place some limitations on immigration from Mexico gave impetus to the illegal immigration that has plagued the United States ever since.

The main force behind Mexican immigration—especially the illegal inflows—has always been the lure of the United States as "a promised land."[49] Acting as a network of information, "word of mouth" accounts of better job opportunities, high wages, and improved living conditions circulate from returnees and from letters that often contain remittances (which in the aggregate total in the tens of millions of dollars each year) to family members who remain behind. These tales are often exaggerated or at least tend to minimize negative aspects of the experience. The verbal and written accounts, the reality of the remittances, and the immigrants' visits home add to the desires of others to emigrate. It does not take much information for many Mexicans in the northern and central sections of the country to realize that in purely economic terms life in the United States is likely to offer far more options than the arduous and stifling life of perpetual poverty that faces most who choose to remain in Mexico.

Illegal Immigration from the Island Nations of the Caribbean

No other single country furnishes anywhere near as many illegal immigrants to the United States as Mexico does, but collectively a number of island nations in the Caribbean constitute the second largest source. This area therefore deserves brief mention.

Because most of the indigenous Indians of the Caribbean islands were killed off during the era of European colonialism, the vast majority of the current inhabitants of these islands are immigrants themselves. Many are ancestors of slaves or indentured servants who were uprooted and transplanted to the islands as laborers. As Virginia Dominguez has stated, "The history of the modern Caribbean is rooted in labor migration itself."[50] After slavery was abolished in the region, labor migration continued between the islands and the countries of Central and North America. About 100,000 workers from the British West Indies, for instance, were employed in the construction of the Panama Canal. When the canal was completed, these workers and others were employed to build the railroads and to work the plantations of the United Fruit Company in Central America.[51]

Immigration to the United States from the Caribbean began in the 1920s. At that time most of the immigrants were pioneers, and the movement came to a halt when the Depression of the 1930s set in. In the 1940s immigration links with the British West Indies (BWI) were reestablished through the BWI program (see Chapter 4), which permitted nonimmigrant workers to be employed in the United States under specified conditions. The program continued and presently operates as an H-2 worker program. Although its scale has never approached that of the bracero programs involving Mexicans, it has served as an information link between the United States and the island nations (especially Jamaica) that have provided workers. Prior to the early 1960s, however, emigration from many of these islands was primarily to the European nations that had once controlled them. During the late 1940s, throughout the 1950s, and into the early 1960s, many of the nations of Europe—most notably Britain, France, and the Netherlands—experienced worker shortages because of the losses they had sustained in World War II. In 1962, however, Britain passed the Commonwealth Immigration Act, which imposed restrictions on further immigration from present and former Commonwealth nations, and these restrictions were tightened in

1971 and 1983.[52] As a result, the flow of BWI workers shifted to Canada and the United States. Immigration to the United States, whether it be the migration of U.S. citizens from Puerto Rico to the mainland, the massive inflows of Cuban refugees to the United States from 1959 to 1980, or the admission of temporary workers under H-2 programs, has been institutionalized throughout the Caribbean area.[53] It has become part of a process that is seen by many people as the normal way to take advantage of economic opportunities. Some of the Caribbean islands have essentially become emigrant-oriented societies.

Without examining each of the island republics separately, it is fair to conclude that the same "push" and "pull" factors that have affected emigration from Mexico are also operative in the Caribbean area. Most of the Caribbean nations are overpopulated; have limited natural resources; suffer from high unemployment, pervasive underemployment, mass poverty, a high rate of illiteracy, an extremely unequal income distribution, and poor educational and job-training systems; and lack the means to achieve upward social mobility. The most fundamental problem is the population density of the islands. On many it approaches or exceeds that of such highly publicized nations as Bangladesh, India, and Japan. All the Caribbean immigrants are attracted by the better standard of living, the relatively higher wages, and the numerous job opportunities that are available in the United States.

Economic growth throughout the Caribbean region has long been a problem. For some of these island nations economic growth during the 1970s was negative (e.g., Jamaica), for others it was barely positive (e.g., Barbados), and the highest average positive rate was only 3.7 percent (in the Dominican Republic). Hence, population increases often exceed the number of jobs these economies are able to provide. Immigration has therefore become the alternative means of reducing the population overflow. Unlike the case of Mexico, however, it is not clear that the immigration process performs purely a "safety valve" function in the Caribbean. In contrast to Mexico, where most illegal immigrants simply cross the border without inspection, the persons who eventually become illegal immigrants from the Caribbean usually qualify for visas. Those who actually enter surreptitiously—for example, those who come by boat from Haiti—are the clear exception. Most illegal immigrants from the Caribbean are "visa abusers." This means they are often admitted as students, tourists, or businessmen. They must convince a U.S. consular official that they actually intend to return home after their visit to the United States. Despite the fact that these persons might be considered unskilled by U.S. standards, they are often above average in their education and skills relative to most others in their homelands. Thus, rather than serving as a "safety valve," the immigration process constitutes a serious drain of brain power and skills from these nations.[54] The Caribbean nations are losing their more productive workers, the ones they need most for their own economic development. The persons who stay behind are often the dependents of those who leave (wives, children, elderly parents, and the infirm). Moreover, as in Mexico, the remittances these dependents receive are used to buy consumer items (e.g., radios, TVs, and other appliances) that are imported into these nations. Thus, such funds often contribute both to the already serious unfavorable balance of trade confronting these nations and to inflationary pressures as the prices of these scarce items are bid up.

Caribbean immigrants are stimulated by word-of-mouth accounts, contact with tourists in the islands, and other cultural (e.g., TV programming and music) and sometimes military links to the United States. Moreover, their numbers have increased dramatically since 1962, when Britain halted immigration from that region. It is estimated that 500,000 legal immigrants entered the United States from these islands between 1900 and 1960, while 900,000 immigrated legally between 1960 and 1977 (excluding Puerto Ricans and Cubans).[55] Because legal immigration from Western Hemisphere nations has been numerically restricted since 1965, however, illegal immigration from these nations has since become the second-best route. So extensive has the mass migration become that in 1978 Dominguez testified: "Given the ratio of the number of Caribbean people already in the United States to the number of Caribbean people living in the Caribbean, I do not think it would be exaggerating to say that everyone in the Caribbean has at least one relative or friend now living, legally or illegally, in this country."[56]

In contrast to Mexico, the number of illegal immigrants to the United States from the Caribbean is small—perhaps totaling about one million. The largest single source country appears to be the Dominican Republic. Most Dominicans enter the United States through San Juan, Puerto Rico. Because they are Spanish-speaking, it is easy for them to pass as Puerto Ricans. Furthermore, there is no visa checkpoint for passengers flying to the mainland United States from Puerto Rico. Once on the mainland, Dominicans often live in or near Puerto Rican enclaves, where it "is easy for a Dominican national to pretend that he is really a Puerto Rican, hence, an American citizen."[57] For obvious reasons, other illegal immigrants from the Caribbean—for instance, English-speaking blacks from the British West Indies and French-Creole-speaking blacks from Haiti—do not use Puerto Rico as their port of entry.

Another factor distinguishes illegal entry from the Caribbean islands and Mexico. Namely, Mexico is a single nation, whereas there are at least thirty different Caribbean nations. The latter are divided by more than jurisdictional boundaries. They are often separated by race, language, culture, history, and political ideology. Bitter animosities also divide them; the Dominican Republic and Haiti are a case in point. Sometimes this fragmentation causes extreme tensions among the immigrants from these different countries when they arrive in various communities in the United States and begin to compete for jobs, housing, and political influence.

Illegal Immigration from Other Countries

Other prominent sources of illegal immigrants include Colombia and Guatemala. Still others are scattered around the globe. In most instances these other nations have established some sort of cultural or historical link with the United States, and immigrants have been a by-product of that connection. A prime example is U.S. military involvement, as in the case of Korea, the Philippines, and Thailand (which was a major military center during the Vietnam War). Other ties have been political or commercial in nature, as in the case of Iran, Nigeria, and Colombia. In most instances these countries have experienced major improvements in their economic growth rates since the 1950s. Again, however, expectations and populations have frequently grown more rapidly than the opportunities provided by these economies. As immigration to the United States from these countries has developed, more people have tried to immigrate than are legally permitted to enter. Hence, pressures to immigrate illegally have been spawned—especially among persons who do not have a relative who is already a U.S. citizen or permanent-resident alien.

The Interrelatedness of Legal and Illegal Immigration

Among the underlying "push" and "pull" forces that are operative whenever mass movements of people take place, several seem to perpetuate the immigration process. Understanding these influences can help explain how illegal immigration to the United States from some nations has become an institutionalized phenomenon.

Immigration to the United States from a given source country soon develops into predictable patterns. People from certain countries (sometimes certain areas) immigrate to certain cities (or parts of cities) or regions of the United States. Because the United States is a multicultural and multiracial society to begin with, it is likely that some communities will have people who are ethnically similar to the immigrant group. Some of the immigrants who come to the United States do not stay. They decide to return to their homelands either because they had originally intended to stay only temporarily or because they experienced difficulties in the resettlement process. In general, however, more immigrants from any particular country remain in the United States than return to their homelands. The fewer the obstacles to immigration (distance, natural barriers, or expense), the greater the number of immigrants who remain. Given its proximity, Mexico is the major source of immigrants to the United States, followed by the Caribbean island nations, other countries of the Caribbean Basin, and then countries that rank further behind because of the magnitude of the barriers that must be overcome. It does seem that the more extensive the obstacles to immigration are, the more skilled and educated and therefore more motivated the immigrants are. Most illegal immigrants from Mexico are unskilled and poorly educated. Illegal immigrants from Korea, India, Nigeria, and Iran, however, are likely to be just the opposite in their human capital endowments. In the absence of any serious deterrents to illegal immigration, it can be expected that both the absolute number of illegal immigrants who come and the net rate of illegal immigration (those who remain minus those who return to their homelands) will continue to mount.

For Western Hemisphere nations there were no limitations on the number of immigrants that could be admitted (and for all intents and purposes few qualitative restrictions other than the standard thirty-three exclusions that apply to all immigrants) until 1965. Thus, it is only since the Immigration Act of 1965 (which imposed a ceiling on immigration from the Western Hemisphere for the first time) and the 1976 amendments (which extended the preference system and a ceiling of 20,000 visas per country per year from any one nation) that illegal immigrants have surfaced as a major component of the immigration flows from the same Western Hemisphere nations that are the primary sources of legal immigrants. The same pattern holds for the Eastern Hemisphere, where the less economically developed nations—especially those with which the United States has developed strong military or commercial ties—have become the major sources of legal immigrants. Because would-be immigrants from these countries also confront the limitations imposed by the U.S. system, however, they too have turned in increasing numbers to illegal entry. Thus it appears that the United States' legal immigration system does contribute to the problem of illegal immigration. Moreover, what makes illegal immigration such a serious problem for the United States—compared to the experience of other nations—is the fact that the United States has yet to initiate any meaningful deterrents to illegal entry across its borders. In the absence of any attempt to enforce the existing immigration statutes, there is absolutely no reason why anyone who wants to immigrate to the United States illegally should not try to, for in most cases those who try will succeed. It is, of course, the purpose of the proposed Simpson-Mazzoli bill to begin to fill this void.

The Permissiveness of the Existing Immigration System

One factor—the gross permissiveness of the immigration system—is a significant part of the reason why illegal immigration has become a major problem in the United States. Despite the fact that the nation has gradually constructed a unitary immigration policy that is comprehensive in its coverage and complex in its administration, it has failed to make that policy enforceable. Illegal immigration has been allowed to make a mockery of the theory that the flow of immigrants into the population and the labor force can be regulated.

No matter what factors prompt people to leave their homelands and attract them to the United States, and no matter how frequently a review is made of the changes that occur in these conditions, the fact remains that the absence of any serious effort to enforce the existing immigration statutes is in itself a signal to many persons that the United States really welcomes illegal immigrants, despite the legal pretense that it does not. In fact, some scholars have examined this issue and are convinced that the lack of credible deterrence is no accident. They argue that the United States actually wants to have illegal immigrants on hand to keep the labor market for unskilled workers in constant surplus.[58] In 1982, while the

Simpson-Mazzoli bill was pending before Congress, for instance, one observer reported that many Mexicans "commonly assume that the U.S. economy's demand for foreign labor is ineradicable, even in a recession; and many maintain a Marxist world-view leading them to believe business interests dominate Congress and, thus, would never allow Congress to pass or to enforce stiff employer sanctions."[59]

Specifically, there is an anomaly in the laws of the United States concerning the employment of illegal immigrants. While it is against the law for nonresident immigrants to seek employment, it is *not* against the law for an employer to hire an illegal alien. The Immigration and Nationality Act of 1952 made the importation and harboring of illegal aliens a felony. As a concession to Texas agricultural interests, however, the act states that employment and the related services provided by employers to employees (e.g., transportation and room and board) do not constitute illegal harboring. The effect of this proviso is to make employers immune from prosecution if they hire such workers. Thus, one of the most effective barriers to control of illegal immigration is the fact that employing an illegal immigrant is not an illegal act.

As for the illegal immigrants themselves, it is an unimportant technicality that the law makes it a punishable offense for them to seek employment in the United States. Over 95 percent of those who are apprehended by the INS (and most, it should be recalled, are Mexicans) are simply granted a "voluntary departure" and are returned to their homelands by the most expedient form of transportation. The scant remainder, who are often multiple offenders or persons who have committed a crime in the United States, are subject to formal deportation proceedings that render any subsequent entry a felony.[60] More prosecutions could serve as a deterrent. To date, however, the U.S. government has not determined that the issue warrants an increase in the number of hearing officers sufficient to raise the level of prosecutions significantly. As a result, illegal aliens who are allowed to depart voluntarily are in no way deterred from returning.

Thus, a realistic appraisal of the current situation is that if an illegal alien is caught, he is simply returned to his native land; if he is not apprehended, he works at a job that affords him a higher income than he could earn in his homeland. For the businessman, there is no risk of loss; there are only gains from tapping a cheap source of labor—workers who are completely bound by arbitrary terms of employment.

Although the Immigration and Nationality Act of 1952 expressly states that except for immigrants who are admitted on the basis of family ties it is national policy that all other immigrants must not adversely affect the employment opportunities and working conditions of domestic laborers, paradoxically there are no corollary laws to make this objective meaningful. The California Court of Appeals commented in 1970 that the presence of illegal aliens in the Southwest "represent[s] an abject failure of national policy" and observed that the lack of meaningful corrective action "must be ascribed to [the] self-imposed impotence of our national government."[61]

The policy charade is carried one step further by the ready admission that the Immigration and Naturalization Service has been chronically underfunded and understaffed since its inception. This understaffing was mentioned repeatedly in Chapter 2 during the general discussion of the enforcement aspect of U.S. immigration policy and it continues to be a major factor in the discussion of many violations of the immigration statutes. As of 1981, for instance, the U.S. Border Patrol had an on-duty corps of only 2,093 officers.[62] Breaking this number down into eight-hour shifts and five-day work weeks, it becomes apparent that no more than 400 officers were on duty at any given time. Most of these officers were assigned to the 1,945-mile border with Mexico, but some were assigned to the Canadian border and to other duties. In addition, for inland duty (duty away from the nation's borders) the INS had only 1,489 immigration inspectors to cover the entire nation.[63] Thus, in 1981 the total enforcement apparatus of the INS was actually smaller than the police force of the District of Columbia. Given the small number of enforcement officers relative to the magnitude of the responsibilities they are assigned, it is amazing that they apprehend as many illegal immigrants as they do. Still, the level of resources assigned to this task only contributes to the cynicism of those who do not really believe that the nation is serious when it says it wishes to exclude illegal immigrants.

Thus, if it were not for the human tragedy associated with the phenomenon of illegal immigration, the nation's deterrence policy could be described as reading like a Mack Sennett comedy script. Employers who hire illegal immigrants commit no crime; most of the illegals who are caught are given no penalty; and hardly any manpower and resources are devoted to the management of entry. There is really little need to ponder or debate the complex causes of illegal immigration given the paltry state of enforcement activities and the reluctance of Congress to give the subject any serious attention prior to the mid-1980s. Stronger deterrents by themselves will not stop illegal immigration, but without them nothing else makes any sense or has any chance of stemming the tide.

The Effects of Illegal Immigration on the U.S. Labor Market

The primary reason for illegal immigrants to come to the United States is to search for jobs, and studies show that by and large they are successful. Other motivations, such as criminal activity or income maintenance support from available income transfer programs, appear to be relatively inconsequential. Thus, the impact of illegal immigrants on the U.S. labor market has repeatedly surfaced as one of the most critical and controversial issues surrounding the whole subject.

As noted earlier in this chapter, there are no established data series on illegal immigrants. Because the makeup of the illegal immigrant population is unknown, it is impossible to select a random sample that would be scientifically reliable. Hence, efforts to verify the occupational and settlement patterns of illegal immigrants have been few in number. Even the studies that are available have been conducted under extremely restricted circumstances, and only two have seriously attempted to capture some measure of these patterns. One of these was a nationwide study of apprehended illegal immigrants made by David North and Marion Houstoun in 1976.[64] The second, a study of unapprehended illegal immigrants in Los Angeles, was completed in 1979 by a research team from the University of California at Los Angeles (UCLA).[65] Both studies were funded by the U.S. Department of Labor. Both are limited in scope, but their conceptual weaknesses tend to be offsetting. The North-Houstoun cohort was composed entirely of apprehended illegal immigrants. Because a disproportionate number of apprehended Mexican illegal immigrants are employed in agriculture, the North-Houstoun study is biased in favor of farmworkers. Conversely, the UCLA study was carried out entirely within the urban center of Los Angeles. As a result, it disproportionately underestimates the employment of Mexican illegal immigrants in agriculture. In the North-Houstoun study the respondents had been in the United States for an average of 2.5 years; in the UCLA study the mean was 4.0 years. In the North-Houstoun study 48.6 percent of the 793 respondents were from Mexico; in the UCLA study 92.5 percent of the 2,792 respondents were Mexican. Neither study pretended to represent a random sample.

The occupational patterns for the respondents in the two studies are shown in Table 23. Clearly, the illegal immigrants were concentrated in unskilled occupations (farm workers, service workers, nonfarm laborers) and in semiskilled occupations (operatives). A significant number were employed in the skilled blue-collar category of craft workers. Very few were found in white-collar occupations.

In comparison, Table 24 shows the 1977 distribution of the occupational patterns for all workers in the United States; for all Hispanic workers (i.e., those of Mexican ancestry, Cubans, Puerto Ricans, and others of Spanish origin); for all workers of Mexican origin; and for all black workers. (The year 1977 was chosen because it was closest to the date of the two studies on illegal immigrants.) The data in Table 23 closely resemble the data on these racial and ethnic subgroups in Table 24. With respect to Chicanos (i.e., those workers of Mexican origin who are U.S. citizens), they were found to be employed disproportionately in exactly the same occupations as were most of the illegal immigrants in the cited studies. The employment pattern for Chicanos, in fact, better resembled the pattern for illegal immigrants than it did the distribution pattern for all U.S. workers. The fact that both the Chicano workers and the illegal immigrants were concentrated in the same selected urban and rural labor markets of the five states of the Southwest makes it clear that the two groups are competitors in the same labor markets. In fact, in 1982 a public opinion poll designed by the University of Texas to identify the most important problems facing Texas, more Mexican Americans cited the problem of illegal immigrants as the state's most pressing problem than did any other racial grouping.[66] The data on blacks given in Table 23 serve only to emphasize the fact that millions of citizen workers are employed

TABLE 23.   EMPLOYMENT PATTERNS OF ILLEGAL IMMIGRANTS, 1976 AND 1979

| | Percentage of Illegal Immigrants in Two Study Populations | | | |
| | Detention-Site Study, 1974–1975[a] | Los Angeles Community Study 1972–1975[b] | | |
Occupation	All Apprehended Aliens	Total	Previously Apprehended	Never Apprehended
White-collar	5.4	10.5	6.6	12.1
Professional				
and technical	1.6	4.3	2.7	5.0
Managers and				
administrators	1.3	0.7	0.8	0.7
Sales workers	1.1	1.9	0.8	2.3
Clerical	1.4	3.6	2.3	4.1
Blue-collar	55.2	73.0	79.0	70.4
Craft workers	15.3	28.8	32.8	27.1
Operatives	25.1	31.8	31.1	32.1
Nonfarm				
laborers	14.8	12.4	15.1	11.2
Service workers	20.6	16.1	14.2	16.9
Farmworkers	18.8	0.4	0.2	0.5
Total	100.0	100.0	100.0	99.9

[a]Data from David S. North and Marion F. Houstoun, *The Characteristics and Role of Illegal Aliens in the U.S. Labor Market: An Exploratory Study* (Washington, D.C.: Linton and Co., 1976), p. 104.

[b]Data from Maurice D. Van Arsdol, Jr., Joan Moore, David Heer, and Susan P. Haynie, *Non-Apprehended and Apprehended Undocumented Residents in the Los Angeles Labor Market,* prepared for the U.S. Department of Labor (Washington, D.C.: GPO, May 1979), p. 69.

in the same occupations as are illegal immigrants. Black workers, of course, are not concentrated in the same labor markets as are Chicanos or Mexican illegal immigrants, but in a number of specific labor markets (e.g., Los Angeles, Chicago, San Antonio, Miami, and Houston) they do compete. Likewise, it is increasingly the case that black workers in urban labor markets in the eastern and north central states are feeling the adverse effects of job competition from illegal immigrants from nations other than Mexico.[67]

The data supplied by the North-Houstoun and UCLA studies as well as numerous anecdotal accounts from other sources strongly suggest that the impact of illegal immigrants is selective. Thus it is not at the aggregate or macro level of the economy but rather in selective or micro–labor markets that their influence is manifested. At least three separate circumstances would seem to merit discussion: the substandard labor market (where illegal wages and working conditions exist despite laws that ban such practices); the secondary labor market (where wages are low but are at least in compliance with federal minimums, while working conditions and benefits are minimal or nonexistent); and the primary

TABLE 24. PERCENTAGE DISTRIBUTION OF ALL EMPLOYED PERSONS
IN THE UNITED STATES, BY OCCUPATION, 1977

Occupation	All U.S. Workers	All Hispanics	Persons of Mexican Origin	Black Workers
White-collar	49.9	31.7	27.2	35.3
Professional and technical	15.1	7.4	5.6	11.8
Managers and administrators	10.7	5.6	4.9	4.8
Sales workers	6.3	3.7	3.0	2.6
Clerical	17.8	15.0	13.7	16.1
Blue-collar	33.3	46.6	49.3	37.6
Craft workers	13.1	13.7	15.0	9.0
Operatives	11.4	20.9	20.4	15.1
Transport operatives	3.8	4.1	4.6	5.2
Nonfarm laborers	5.0	7.9	9.3	8.3
Service workers	13.7	17.1	16.5	25.0
Farmworkers	3.0	4.4	6.9	2.2
Total	99.9	99.8	99.9	100.1
Total Employed	90,546,000	3,938,000	2,335,000	9,812,000

Sources: Morris Newman, "A Profile of Hispanics in the U.S. Work Force," *Monthly Labor Review,* December 1978, pp. 3–13; and *Employment and Training Report of the President, 1979* (Washington, D.C.: GPO, 1979), pp. 262–63.

labor market (where high-paying jobs with substantial fringe benefits and desirable working conditions exist).

THE SUBSTANDARD LABOR MARKET

Some illegal immigrant workers are no doubt sought out primarily because they can be exploited. This, however, appears to be the exception rather than the rule. North and Houstoun, for instance, found that 76 percent of the respondents in their study had earned the federal minimum wage or better in the job they held at the time of their apprehension.[68] Even this percentage seems quite low, but it reflects the fact that a disproportionate number of these immigrants were last employed in agriculture. The UCLA study of urban illegal immigrants did not include wage data. It did, however, compute "income" data, which show that on the average its respondents earned about $1,000 a year more than the North-Houstoun interviewees.[69]

In the substandard labor market it is unlikely that illegal immigrants take a significant number of jobs that would otherwise be held by citizens. Yet this is certainly no excuse for the perpetuation of the exploitation. If it is wrong for citizens to labor under unfair working conditions, it is equally wrong for illegal aliens to do so. Job protection laws exist to safeguard all who work in the United States irrespective of their immigration status or their desire to be protected.

THE SECONDARY LABOR MARKET

Most illegal immigrant workers are employed in the secondary labor market of the U.S. economy.[70] It seems that as industrial societies develop, the structure of their labor markets changes. Coexistent with these nations' high-paying, stable, and rewarding jobs are jobs that lack all these features, and comparatively speaking the latter are far less attractive to would-be workers. The quandary for the industrialized nations, therefore, is how to fill the jobs that seem undesirable but that are nonetheless essential to the operation of their economies.

Michael Piore has argued that, in the past, industrialized societies looked toward the margins of the labor force to find workers to fill these jobs, and there they found youths, housewives, and farm-workers as well as the minority groups that for years were denied access to better jobs. Given the developments of the 1970s and early 1980s, however, some of these traditional sources can no longer be depended upon. Many youths, for example, have proven to be undependable because they do not act like permanent workers. Frequently they are "target earners," workers whose income is used to buy a particular object (a car or a stereo) or serves as pocket money, but rarely is needed for room and board (which is often provided by parents). With the rise of the feminist movement and the trend toward smaller families, housewives are increasingly inclined toward career development rather than toward marginal work attachments. Likewise, the dramatic decline in agricultural employment due to extensive mechanization means that there are fewer farmers who can be attracted to work second or off-season jobs in the nonagricultural sector. Finally, of course, the progression of the civil rights movement since the 1960s has been increasingly in the direction of improving the preparation of minority workers for better jobs and opening up access to a wider range of jobs. It is alleged, therefore, that the above members of the labor force are no longer available or are unwilling to work in the second-ary labor market.

Hence, many employers in Western Europe and the United States have chosen to rely on temporary workers to fill in the gaps in the secondary labor market.[71] In Europe, as discussed in Chapter 4, "temporary" foreign-worker programs were created in the post–World War II era and lasted through the early 1970s. In the United States some temporary-worker programs have been established, but illegal immigrants have come to be relied upon to fill the job voids in some industries and occupational categories. Moreover, in Europe, illegal immigration since the termination of the foreign-worker programs has become an increasingly important source of workers for certain types of jobs.

According to Piore, therefore, it is fruitless to try to restrict illegal immigration so long as the secondary labor market exists. Other scholars have echoed this belief and some have drawn the similar conclusion that illegal immigrants take only the jobs that citizens shun and thus cause a minimum of worker displacement.[72] Consequently, if the United States really wants to reduce the flow of illegal immigrants, Piore argues, it will have to eliminate the labor demand that presently exists in the secondary labor market. He suggests that this could be accomplished by raising the federal minimum wage substantially, by improving the enforcement of job protection laws, and by encouraging through legislation the unionization of many low-wage industries. He is not optimistic, however, that the nation's policymakers will take any of these steps. Thus he believes that as long as it is useful to employers, illegal immigration will continue.

It should be noted here that there are some deficiencies in Piore's thesis. To begin with, Piore does not give credence to the role of "push" factors in illegal immigration. His analysis is conducted solely in terms of an alleged demand for unskilled workers that cannot or will not be met by U.S. citizens. As contended earlier in this chapter, the economic, political, and social conditions in many of the immigrant source countries as well as the permissiveness of the existing U.S. immigration system have contributed as much or more to the inflow of illegal immigrants than any such demand conditions.

It is also important to realize that Piore and the other social scientists who have adopted his assertions of a minimal worker displacement effect in the secondary labor market do not provide any direct evidence to support their hypothesis. In fact, it would be very difficult to name a specific occupation in the U.S. economy in which the vast preponderance of workers are *not* citizen workers. Indeed, Undersecretary of Labor Malcolm Lovell, testifying in support of immigration reform, has stated that "in 1981, close to 30 percent of all workers employed in this country, some 29 million people, were holding down the same kind of low-skilled industrial, service, and farm jobs in which illegals typically find employment."[73] Moreover, according to Lovell, "the available data also does not support the claim that Americans will not take low wage jobs. In 1981, an estimated 10.5 million were employed in jobs at or below the minimum wage and 10 million more were earning within about 35 cents of that level."[74] Hence it seems absurd to contend that illegal immigrants do work that citizens will not do when in fact millions of citizen workers are employed in these occupations. Lovell has also pointed out that the unemployment rates for the segments of the labor force that compete most directly with illegal immigrants are consistently higher than the national average—a fact which challenges the notion that citizen workers are not available for secondary-labor-market jobs.

Another point that must be addressed is the fact that when a shift in the supply of labor takes place, simultaneous wage effects occur. These wage effects are typically overlooked by those who simplistically support only the employment argument—that illegal immigrants for the most part fill jobs that citizens will not take. The presence of a significant number of illegal immigrants in selected labor markets reduces the absolute wage rates below what the market would otherwise have set. It also opens up relative wage gaps between occupations and industries, depending on the degree of participation by illegal immigrants. It is in this context—the artificial suppression of wages due to the presence of illegal immigrants—that the argument that citizen workers are unavailable needs to be reappraised. The argument is, after all, a self-fulfilling prophecy. It is based on induced economic influences rather than the dubious sociological contention that U.S. workers will not do certain types of work. In a normal labor market—one in which an additional, shadow labor force of illegal immigrants is not operative—the supply of labor is generally ample when employers pay competitive wages. Indeed, in a survey taken in San Diego, employers admitted that they could afford to pay the competitive wages needed to attract citizen workers (and could stay in business after doing so), but they indicated that they preferred not to because they could hire illegal immigrants at lower wages. As the authors of the survey concluded, "There is a definite strategy for pulling-in illegal labor from across the border and . . . this strategy is an excellent way to avoid more expensive American labor."[75] Consequently, a significant displacement of workers does occur as a result of the wage effect.

As for the question, which citizen workers compete most directly with illegal immigrants, all studies and reports unanimously answer, the young and the less skilled (i.e., young people in general, women, and minorities). According to the theory of welfare economics, the government could compensate persons who are hurt by a particular policy (i.e., the toleration of illegal immigrants in the labor market) by taxing those who stand to benefit from it (i.e., those who could buy items or services for less or could hire workers at lower wages), and society as a whole would not suffer. *Only when these transfer payments are actually made, however*—and no policy proposal to this effect has been even remotely suggested—will we have a chance to test this benign hypothesis.

In the United States a substantial number of citizen workers face employment and earnings disadvantages. According to one comprehensive study, this number was 40 percent of the people who participated in the labor force in 1980.[76] Not all of these people, of course, compete with illegal immigrants for jobs. It is only in the areas where illegal immigrants are concentrated—and thus essentially only in the secondary labor markets of selected localities (as mentioned earlier, the areas that also receive the largest number of *legal* immigrants) that citizen workers must compete directly.[77] But Los Angeles, San Francisco, Houston, New York City, Chicago, and San Antonio, to name a few of these areas of concentration, are among the largest and most influential labor markets in the United States. Hence, the number of citizen workers who are adversely affected by the presence of illegal immigrants is believed to be substantial.

One of the major ways to increase the number of job opportunities for low-income citizen workers and the rewards that come with earned income, and thus to enhance labor force participation by potential workers in these highly competitive labor markets, is to reduce the uncontrolled inflow of illegal aliens into the existing low-wage sector of the economy. Many of the jobs held by low-wage workers are essential to the operation of our economy. Farmworkers, dishwashers, laborers, garbage collectors, building cleaners, restaurant employees, gardeners, maintenance workers, to name a few occupations, perform useful and often indispensable work. Most of these tasks are not going to go away even if wages do increase. The tragedy is that the remuneration these workers receive is often so poor, and one reason they are underpaid is that an abnormally large pool of would-be workers is available. It is not ordained that workers who do useful things must be paid poorly. In the normal operation of the labor market, wages increase in response to the demand for essential services. This does not happen, however, when the supply of such workers is excessive. If illegal aliens were flooding the legal, medical, educational, and business executive labor markets of this country, the problem would receive immediate national attention and would be solved. Because it is the nation's blue-collar, agricultural, and service workers who bear most of the burden of the competition with illegal immigrants, however, the issue remains largely unaddressed. Granted, illegal immigrants are not the only cause of unemployment and persistent low-income patterns among certain subgroups of the American labor force, but they certainly are a factor. Any serious full employment strategy for the United States in the 1980s, therefore, will have to include measures to curtail illegal immigration.

THE PRIMARY LABOR MARKET

In the case of the nation's primary labor market (e.g., jobs in construction and manufacturing), there is no debate that the illegal aliens employed in these positions cause worker displacement. Even though citizen workers are readily available, illegal aliens are sometimes regarded as "preferred workers." They are less likely to join unions; to complain about the denial of equal employment opportunities, safety violations, or sex discrimination; or to make other entitlement demands upon employers. In a 1982 study, which disclosed that illegal immigrants were widely employed in the high-paying construction industry of Houston, Texas, researchers found that foremen and supervisors preferred to hire illegal immigrants over citizen workers because they could easily "extract bribes" in the form of wage kickbacks from them.[78]

Because there has been little debate about the labor displacement effects of illegal immigration in the primary labor market, it is in this sector that the U.S. government has been most vigilant in its limited enforcement activities. Helping the most privileged members of our society has always been a popular role for government agencies.

FULL EMPLOYMENT

In the case of full employment it is conceivable that the presence of illegal immigrant workers could provide some aggregate economic benefits to society in the form of higher production due to an additional supply of labor. Under such special circumstances aggregate production costs might even be lower because the increased competition of citizen and alien workers for jobs could reduce overall wage pressures. But all these conceivable benefits would be very limited because most illegal immigrants—especially those from Mexico—are unskilled and poorly educated. There are technological limits to the degree of productivity a society can obtain as a result of simply increasing the supply of workers who have limited human capital endowments. Given the nation's minimum wage laws, there are also limits below which nominal wages cannot legally be reduced even if the supply of labor is artificially increased. Moreover, even under conditions of full employment, the population subgroups that would compete directly with illegal immigrants—youths, women, and minorities—would have to pay a severe price: lower wages and declining labor force participation.[79] These specific costs would have to be balanced against any possible societal benefits.

Talk of the benefits that might accrue to the nation from illegal immigrants in the context of full employment is for the time being purely theoretical. Throughout the 1970s and early 1980s, unemployment rates were consistently high. Moreover, many economists believe that it may not be possible to reduce this rate below 6.0–6.5 percent without triggering unacceptable inflation.[80] In this context a benign attitude toward any factor that contributes to unemployment among citizen workers cannot be justified.

Noneconomic Issues

In addition to the direct employment and wage effects that illegal immigration has had on the U.S. economy, there are noneconomic factors that may yet have a far greater impact on the welfare of the nation. Primary among these factors are (1) the human rights violations that derive from illegal immigration and (2) the long-term political consequences of institutionalizing the existence of a subclass within the nation's population.

HUMAN RIGHTS ISSUES

For persons who "enter without inspection," the entire entry process is dangerous. It often involves the use of professional smugglers, or "coyotes," who extract exorbitant fees for the transportation and false documents they provide.[81] Often their fees consume the life savings of the individuals they transport. Many of these individuals do not have sufficient funds and are forced to borrow the additional money from loan sharks, who charge outrageous interest rates and often use brutal methods to enforce repayment. Some "coyotes" rob and otherwise abuse illegal immigrants.[82] In many cases they use life-threatening means of transportation. In July 1980, for instance, in the desert of Arizona, thirteen illegal immigrants were found dead and thirteen more were on the verge of dying. All were citizens of El Salvador and all had Mexican passports. They had paid Mexican "coyotes" to lead them through the desert, but after they crossed the border they were deserted.[83] In October 1982 a van containing sixteen illegal immigrants was abandoned along a roadside near Edinburg,

Texas. By the time the doors were opened, four persons had died of asphyxiation and most of the remainder were near death.[84] Even illegal immigrants who do not use smugglers often encounter tragedy. In October 1981, for instance, thirty-three would-be illegal immigrants from Haiti drowned off the coast of southern Florida when their small boat broke up.[85] These stories are only a sampling of the most publicized incidents that have occurred in recent years.

Once in the United States, illegal immigrants live under constant fear of detection by authorities or of being taken advantage of by opportunists. As one illegal Mexican immigrant explained, "Being here is like a prison, a golden prison; you have everything but you have nothing."[86] Nominally, illegal immigrants are entitled to the protection of the nation's laws, but in fact their illegal status often deters them from seeking that protection.

In sum, there is nothing romantic about the process of immigrating illegally. Illegal aliens are often placed at the mercy of the most undesirable elements of both the sending and the receiving nation. In the United States the indifference of society and of policymakers to the plight of illegal immigrants is one of the most reprehensible aspects of contemporary American life. One congressional staff member has observed that "nobody gives a damn" about illegal immigrants because they are "nobody's constituents."[87] In truth, however, toleration of the abuse of illegal immigrants seems to be more deeply ingrained in the institutions and moral structure of some communities than in others. For example, one of the most controversial incidents that illustrates the cruel human dimensions of illegal immigration occurred in southeastern Arizona in August 1976. It is known as "the Hanigan affair," for it involved a wealthy rancher, George Hanigan, and his two sons. While "wetback hunting," the Hanigans came upon three illegal immigrants crossing their property. They seized and beat the immigrants, tortured them for several hours with a hot poker, robbed them, and ultimately peppered them with shotgun pellets before releasing them. When the illegal immigrants reported the incident to Mexican officials, the Hanigans were arrested and subsequently indicted on twenty-two criminal counts. When the Hanigan brothers were brought to trial in Cochise County, Arizona, in 1977, however, they were found innocent of all charges by a local jury. (The father had died a week before the trial began.) The case quickly became a cause célèbre among Chicano and other civil rights groups throughout the Southwest. Ultimately, the U.S. Department of Justice became involved in the case and secured an indictment against the brothers under an obscure interpretation of the Hobbs Act, which makes it a crime to obstruct interstate commerce by means of robbery. The second trial was held in Tucson, Arizona, in 1980 and resulted in a hung jury. The Justice Department then decided to retry the case in February 1981 in Phoenix, Arizona. In that trial one brother was acquitted and the other was found guilty and sentenced to three years in prison.[88] The verdict was appealed and as of mid-1983 a final decision was still pending.[89]

In another well-publicized case in 1983 involving abuse of illegal immigrants, two men from East Texas "bought" nineteen Mexican men from a coyote for $50 apiece.[90] The Mexicans were forced to work at gunpoint for long hours on a tree farm during the day and were held in a windowless shack without toilet facilities at night. They were barely fed any food. When some tried to escape, they were recaptured and forcibly returned. When they eventually escaped and reported their treatment to local authorities, the two Texans were charged with slavery, and were found guilty on twelve counts by a jury in a federal district court in Tyler, Texas, on June 23, 1983. The maximum sentence for their crime was ninety-five years in prison and a fine of $70,000, but in December 1983 the federal judge imposed on each only a $1,000 fine and five years' probation. The judge contended that the fault in this case rested with the INS—not the farmers—because the agency had failed to keep the Mexicans from entering the country illegally. The extraordinarily light sentence caused widespread consternation among civil rights groups and their sympathizers. As a consequence, the Department of Justice announced in March 1984 that it intended to appeal the lenient sentences, but the legal basis for such an action is apparently questionable.[91]

The treatment afforded illegal immigrants from Mexico has also become a topic of deep concern to the Mexican government. During his term as president, Luis Echeverría declared: "We insist upon the defense of the human and labor rights of those who work in foreign countries. . . . Even though they carry on an illegal activity in the territory of another state, they should nevertheless be protected by law as 'migratory workers without papers.' "[92] His successor, President López Portillo, was equally adamant in his demands for the protection of these aliens. But any demand that the United States protect the rights of people who clandestinely cross its borders in violation of its laws and who accordingly are forced into a sub rosa life style of constant fear of detection can hardly be taken seriously. Realistically, there is very little that can be done to protect the rights of these helpless people. In fact, the government of Mexico cannot even protect illegal immigrants from mistreatment by the Mexican citizens who often serve as "coyotes," or who sell counterfeit documents at exorbitant prices, or who are the Mexican border officials who sometimes arrange the immigrants' exodus and prey upon them when they return by demanding a *mordida* (a bribe or extortion payment). Once in the United States, illegal immigrants are vulnerable to other opportunists (who often are Chicanos) as well as to employers who wish to exploit the immigrants' total dependence for their own economic gain. Sometimes, as the "Hanigan affair" demonstrates, illegal aliens fall victim to violence both in the border towns and in inland areas. Of course, U.S. law enforcement officials should try to stop these inhuman and illegal acts, but in reality it is virtually impossible for them to prevent them from occurring. At best, all the U.S. government can do is react to the exploitation and the abuses. It can and should seek punishment where civil and criminal violations can be documented. But even in these circumstances it is difficult to take action if the illegal immigrants themselves do not report offenses or are unwilling or unavailable to press charges, or if local district attorneys will not prosecute, local juries refuse to convict offenders, and local judges will not impose strong sentences. The fact is that illegal immigration brings to the surface of society the worst human elements in both Mexico and the United States. Only one real human rights policy can be advocated: stop illegal entry before it takes place. Any other plea to protect human rights would be either patently naïve or purely an expression of political rhetoric.

LONG-TERM POLITICAL CONSEQUENCES

The illegal immigrant population of the United States constitutes a subclass of persons whose rights are circumscribed. Although technically entitled to avail themselves of many legal rights and protections, few illegal aliens do so. To make matters worse, they and their families are increasingly being excluded from the benefits of much of the nation's basic social legislation. These exclusions vary. At the federal level, illegal aliens are denied eligibility for such programs as Supplemental Security Income, Medicaid, and Aid to Families with Dependent Children; at the state level they are excluded from unemployment compensation and general assistance programs.[93] These actions constitute embarrassing efforts by our society to avoid the legitimate costs of our own policy inadequacies. Illegal immigrants are also denied the right to vote or to hold elective office.

In Texas an attempt was even made to forbid children of illegal immigrants from attending public schools unless their parents paid a tuition fee. In a 5 to 4 vote, the U.S. Supreme Court in June 1982 struck down the Texas statute. In its majority opinion the Court held that education is of unique importance to both individuals and society and that it would be unfair to force innocent children to bear the burden of their parents' illegal status.[94]

In addition, although most illegal immigrant workers pay social security taxes, many contribute to fictitious accounts from which they will never receive any benefits. Moreover, during the debates over social security reform measures in 1983, an effort was made to prohibit even illegal immigrants with legitimate account numbers from collecting social security benefits. This measure cleared the Senate but was deleted in the subsequent conference report that led to the final bill. The reform legislation did, however, provide for the elimination of social security payments to nonworking spouses and children of illegal immigrants who have lived in the United States for five years or less.

Certainly the growth of a subclass of rightless illegal aliens is not in the nation's long-term interest. Once before the nation tried to function with a subclass in its midst. Then the institution was slavery, and the nation is still trying to overcome the legacy of that episode. It is an experience that should not be repeated.

Policy Reform to Combat Illegal Immigration

In the myriad of studies, reports, and legislative proposals that have addressed the issue of illegal immigration, a variety of policy changes have been mentioned. Not surprisingly, there is more agreement about the need for change than there is about the precise means of achieving it. The most prominent of the reform proposals are discussed below.

EMPLOYER SANCTIONS

Any strategy to combat illegal immigration must address the need to curtail the demand for illegal immigrant workers. Thus, repeal of the "Texas proviso" and the adoption of a law to make the employment of illegal immigrants an illegal act have served as the natural starting points of all reform movements. An employer sanctions law would set the moral tone. It would define precisely who is in compliance with the laws of the land and who is not. Presently, all employers who hire illegal immigrants are fully within their rights when they do so. An employer sanctions law would clearly indicate that illegal immigrants are not wanted as workers in the United States.

It is debatable, of course, how effective such a law would be. Most proposals state that an employer would be guilty of violating the law only if he or she "knowingly" hired an illegal immigrant. Proving that such "knowledge" was operative is extremely difficult, however. Moreover, it is doubtful that many district attorneys would press for enforcement or that many juries would convict an employer for the offense of providing jobs to anyone. With court dockets already backlogged with serious criminal cases, it is hard to imagine that many employers would ever be brought to trial. Still, the possibility of prosecution would exist. Moreover, there would be some voluntary compliance, and at least the moral weight of the law would be against the employment of illegal aliens. As meaningless as this ban might prove to be, no other reforms will make sense until such a law is on the books.

Indeed, tentative steps toward the enactment of a national employer sanctions bill have already been taken. In 1974, the Farm Labor Contractor Registration Act of 1963 was amended to prohibit employers of migrant farmworkers in the United States as of 1976 from "recruiting, employing, or utilizing, with knowledge," any illegal immigrants.[95] The act also introduced numerous other requirements that were designed to protect migrant farmworkers from the unscrupulous practices of labor contractors (for whom the migrant laborers technically work, as opposed to the agricultural growers, who contract with the contractors). Like all the provisions of this act, the employer sanctions clause does not appear to have been well enforced by the U.S. Department of Labor.[96] In 1983 the 1974 act was replaced by the Migrant and Seasonal Agricultural Worker Protection Act, which also contains a ban on the employment of illegal immigrants.

Twice during the early 1970s the U.S. House of Representatives passed legislation that would have prohibited employers from hiring illegal immigrants, but both bills died in committee in the Senate.[97] During the same period several states adopted employer sanctions laws. At that time it was widely believed that these laws would be judged unconstitutional since immigration matters were considered to be the sole prerogative of the federal government. To the surprise of most legal scholars, however, the U.S. Supreme Court upheld the constitutionality of a California employer sanction law in 1976.[98] Since then, similar laws have been passed by at least eleven states, but as of 1980 only one employer had been convicted and fined (a pittance) for the offense.[99] The problem appears to be that states do not have sufficient expertise to deal with the enforcement of immigration laws and they have generally been reluctant to set up the legal apparatus that would be needed to enforce an employer sanctions law. In addition, state laws vary immensely in their provisions and penalties. The laws passed by these states should therefore be interpreted as acts of desperation designed to prod the federal government into assuming responsibility for the enforcement process, and not as genuine efforts to shift that responsibility to the states.

In 1981 the Select Commission on Immigration and Refugee Policy adopted a recommendation (by a 14-to-2 vote) urging Congress to pass a law that would make it "illegal for an employer to hire undocumented workers."[100] The Simpson-Mazzoli bill expressed the Senate's response to that recommendation. The sponsors of the bill envisioned a prohibition on the employment of illegal immigrants that would be backed up by civil penalties ranging from warnings to fines for first- and second-time offenders and criminal penalties (including higher fines and prison terms) for chronic offenders. Employers of fewer than three persons would be exempt from the prohibition. In the amended House version of the bill, there is also a graduated series of penalties ranging from a warning for first-time offenders to fines of $1,000 per illegal immigrant for second-time offenders to $2,000 for third-time and subsequent offenders. There are no criminal penalties, however, in the House bill.

This proposal proved to be one of the most controversial aspects of the bill during the floor debates that ultimately resulted in the House of Representatives' decision not to vote on the bill in 1982 and that has delayed action on the bill by the House in 1983 and 1984.[101] The employer sanctions provisions were strongly supported by the AFL-CIO and by such influential business groups as the National Association of Manufacturers, the Business Roundtable, and the National Federation of Independent Business, but they were opposed by the National Chamber of Commerce (which supported the remainder of the bill). It should be noted, however, that the National Chamber of Commerce's position was opposed by its San Diego and Houston membership as well as by the California Chamber of Commerce.[102] The strongest opposition to employer sanctions, however, has consistently come from Hispanic organizations and from other groups that have traditionally expressed concern over the plight of illegal immigrants. In general, these groups fear that employers will use such sanctions as an excuse to discriminate against persons who speak with a Spanish accent, have Spanish surnames, or otherwise exhibit "Spanish" attributes. The U.S. Civil Rights Commission, reflecting the views of a number of other civil liberties organizations, voted 3 to 2 against the concept of employer sanctions in 1980. It contended that

> an employer sanctions law would be an unjustifiable imposition of law enforcement duties upon private persons and corporations with undesirable consequences not only for the employer but for the due process of job applicants. Moreover, increased employment discrimination against United States citizens and legal residents who are racially and culturally identifiable with major immigrant groups could be the unintended result of an employer sanctions law.[103]

In another 3-to-2 vote it explicitly stated that "Congress should not enact an employer sanctions law."[104]

A NATIONAL IDENTIFICATION SYSTEM

Obviously, in order for an employer sanctions law to be enacted it will be necessary to specify exactly what an employer must do to be in compliance. A mere query will not suffice. Because fraudulent documents are readily available both inside and outside the country, traditional forms of identification (i.e., birth certificates, social security cards, drivers' licenses, etc.) are absolutely insufficient.[105] In the absence of some sort of universal identification system, a strong employer sanctions law could lead employers to act in a discriminatory manner toward citizens from the same ethnic groups that comprise the majority of the nation's illegal immigrant population. This concern is real. Hence, if a new form of identification is to be required, it must be required of all work-seekers.

One suggestion is that a new form of social security card be issued.[106] Since January 1, 1973, citizenship or resident-alien status has been a requirement for eligibility to receive a social security card.[107] The existing card can easily be counterfeited, however. Thus, any new card would have to be unalterable. Special codes have already been developed by cryptographers and computer experts, and it should be easy to use these to verify the citizenship status of any would-be employee. The coded card could be designed like the one that has been issued to resident aliens by the Immigration and Naturalization Service since 1977 (i.e., the ADIT—or Alien Documentation, Identification, and Telecommunications system—card), which includes a photograph, signature, fingerprint, and several rows of coded numbers. A social security card—or more specifically a social security number—is already required of virtually everyone as a condition of employment in the private sector. The same is true for most public employees. Thus, the argument against requiring citizens to have identification numbers has already been settled. Like it or not, the social security number has become a national identifier. It serves as a student's ID number on many campuses; it is an individual's driver's license number in eight states; most private health insurance companies use it as a policy number; the Internal Revenue Service uses it to identify taxpayers; and it is the serial number assigned to all persons in the military. The point is that it is absurd to worry about whether something will happen if it has already happened. The only questions that remain are, should social security cards be made noncounterfeitable and should checks be made of these cards to ensure that those who are using them to seek employment are legally entitled to have them.

David North and Marion Houstoun have studied the identification issue as it relates to the problem of illegal immigration and have recommended a work permit system similar to that used in many other industrialized nations.[108] In another study, however, North developed a unique way to create an identification system that would not require citizenship decisions to be made by employers.[109] Essentially the system would involve the establishment of a nationwide data base. Workers entering the labor force or changing jobs would be required to obtain a work authorization number that would be kept on file at a federal data bank. The number would be issued only after an individual offered some proof that he or she was a citizen or a resident alien. To verify the citizenship eligibility of the newly hired person, employers would only have to call a toll-free data bank number. In return they would receive a transaction number from the data bank that would indicate their compliance with the employer sanctions provision. The advantage of this system would be that it would not involve any type of card and would not require employers to make a judgment about the eligibility of a job applicant. A would-be worker would have to apply for a work permit at the nearest office of the public employment service. Several types of historical data could be used by the applicant to prove his or her eligibility (e.g., proof of payment of income taxes for a number of past years; proof of payment of social security taxes for a set number of past years; proof of service in the military, government employment, or naturalized citizenship status). An applicant would have to provide at least two types of proof. Only information provided by the applicant would be kept on file. A check of the information provided could be made by comparing it to data already on file in various government data banks. If the computers confirmed the individual's legal presence in the nation, a work permit would be issued. This system was specifically endorsed by Ray Marshall, the secretary of labor during the Carter administration and a member of the Select Commission on Immigration and Refugee Policy.[110] As will be discussed shortly, the version of the Simpson-Mazzoli bill that passed the House in June 1984 calls for the establishment of a modified version of this call-in identification system.

Other types of worker identification exist,[111] but the point that needs to be made here is that a new identification system must be included in any employer sanctions program if that program is to have a chance to succeed. Yet the members of the Select Commission on Immigration and Refugee Policy—who overwhelmingly endorsed an employer sanctions law—voted only 8 to 7 (one member absent) in favor of coupling the proposed sanctions measure with some form of secure employee identification system. Moreover, this meager majority "was unable to reach a consensus as to the specific type of identification that should be required for verification."[112] Of the ideas that were considered, a counterfeit-proof social security card received the strongest support.

When the Reagan administration offered its proposals on this issue, it recommended employer sanctions, but it, too, was reluctant to face the identification issue head on. As Attorney General William French Smith stated, "The Administration is opposed to the creation of a national identity card . . . [but it] does recognize the need for a means of compliance with the law that would provide an employer with a good faith defense if he examines documentary proof of eligibility to work."[113] Accordingly, the administration recommended two categories of acceptable proof of eligibility to work. For noncitizens, the necessary document would be the permanent-resident-alien card issued by the INS or a temporary-worker visa. For citizens, any two of the following documents would suffice: birth certificate, driver's license, social security card, or the registration certification issued by the Selective Service System. An additional administration proposal was that at the time of hiring, the employer and the new employee would sign a form certifying that the newly hired employee was eligible to work in the United States and that the employer had inspected the specified documents offered by the new employee. The employer would be required to retain this form for possible inspection by the INS.

Despite the attorney general's assurances that this approach was sufficient, the drafters of the Simpson-Mazzoli bill were not satisfied. They believed, as did many others, that all the documents mentioned in the administration's proposal were easily counterfeitable. In their view, adoption of this identification system would effectively negate an employer sanctions law. Hence, the bill's drafters rejected the Reagan proposals. In the original 1982 version of the bill, it was mandated that the president design and implement a fraud-resistant system for determining the eligibility of applicants for employment. Under the provisions of the bill, the president would have three years in which to establish such a system. The system could be used only for the purpose of verifying that employees had the right to work in the United States. Wisely, from a political standpoint, the bill's sponsors did not endorse any specific ID system. Such specificity, it was felt, would divert attention away from the principal issue—the need to establish a mechanism for creating a fraud-resistant identification system. In the 1984 Senate version of the Simpson-Mazzoli bill, the requirement that the president establish a counterproof system within three years, if it proved to be necessary, was retained, but this was not part of the House version of the bill.

In the congressional debates over the Simpson-Mazzoli bill—especially those in the House of Representatives—this issue proved to be especially worrisome. Many congressmen noted that the U.S. Civil Rights Commission had specifically rejected the idea of establishing any type of national identification system. It had contended that "such a national identity card would provide a tool that could be used to violate the right to privacy of the individual."[114] Responding to this and a similar concern expressed by others, the Reverend Theodore Hesburgh, who had served as chairman of the Select Commission on Immigration and Refugee Policy and was also a former chairman of the U.S. Civil Rights Commission, dismissed these fears, however. In 1982 he wrote:

Identification systems to be used upon application for a job and for work purposes are no different from other forms of identification required by our society today and readily accepted by millions of Americans: credit cards which must be checked by merchants; identification cards other than driver's licenses used for cashing checks; social security numbers to open bank accounts, register for school or obtain employment.

. . . Raising the specter of "Big Brotherdom," calling a worker identification system totalitarian or labelling it "the computer taboo" does not further the debate on U.S. immigration policy; it only poisons it.[115]

In its debates on immigration reform in June 1984, the House did away entirely with the idea of having the president set up a counterproof identification system. Instead, its version of the Simpson-Mazzoli bill called for the creation of the aforementioned telephone call-in system. Under this proposal, the attorney general would be required to set up a toll-free telephone number that employers could call to validate the social security numbers that employees are already required to give when they are hired. If the number was verified as being a legitimate number and if it could be ascertained that the number was not presently being used by another worker (the exact details of this process would have to be developed later), the employer would be given a confirmation number (similar to the number given by hotel chains to confirm that guaranteed reservations have been made). The confirmation number would constitute a "complete defense" for any employer against any subsequent charge that he or she had employed an illegal immigrant. The merit of this system is that the verification process—which would be required of all persons employed anywhere in the United States—would be carried out only after the hiring decision had been made. Hence, employers would not be required to make judgments about the citizenship of prospective employees before they hired anyone.

INCREASED FUNDING FOR THE INS

The need to significantly enlarge the enforcement activities of the INS is too obvious to belabor. It is the one reform issue about which there has been no debate. After initially calling for a reduction in "funds for enforcement," the Reagan administration later reversed itself and exempted the INS from its general nonmilitary budget reduction efforts in 1982. It subsequently went so far as to actually seek an increase in INS appropriations. The Simpson-Mazzoli bill contained a "sense of Congress" provision stating that funding for this purpose should be increased significantly.

LESS RELIANCE ON THE VOLUNTARY DEPARTURE SYSTEM

Unfortunately, in neither the work of the Select Commission on Immigration and Refugee Policy nor the debates on the Simpson-Mazzoli bill was any attention given to the voluntary departure system as a factor that contributes to illegal immigration. It is doubtful, however, that any policy to stop illegal immigration will ever be taken seriously so long as there is virtually no chance that a penalty will be imposed on offenders. Until all illegal immigrants are identified, records are kept, and repeat offenders are subjected to formal deportation hearings (which would permanently preclude them from legal immigrant status), aliens will have no reason even to ponder the risks of immigrating illegally. Relying more heavily on legal procedures, however, will be costly and time-consuming and will necessitate an increase in the INS budget. Nevertheless, these costs, as well as the expense of acquiring more detection hardware, must be weighed against the costs of allowing the growth of the nation's illegal immigrant population to continue unabated. It is the present author's view that it would be far less costly to assume a strong posture of prevention than to respond to the social costs of illegal immigration after they accumulate.

It should be noted, however, that both the Senate and the House versions of the Simpson-Mazzoli bill make it a felony offense with a substantial fine (up to $5,000) and possible imprisonment (up to 2 years) for anyone to use fraudulent documents (e.g., someone else's social security number or a counterfeit social security number) to secure employment in the United States.

ENHANCED TRADE AND DEVELOPMENT ASSISTANCE

International policies must be included in any effort to reduce the flow of illegal immigrants to the United States. They are needed to address the "push" factors. They are primarily needed to assist in the economic development of Mexico and the Caribbean Basin. These measures should include extensive offers of technical and financial assistance. Such efforts may have to be made through established multinational agencies—for example, the World Bank, the International Monetary Fund, or the United Nations—rather than unilaterally. Mexico, in particular, is a proud nation; its leaders have traditionally abhorred the concept of direct foreign aid from the United States.

It must be realized that to some degree the problem of illegal aliens from Mexico is a by-product of past actions by the United States. For too many years, U.S. employers in the Southwest viewed Mexico as a source of cheap labor that could be tapped at will. U.S. policymakers must not ignore this legacy and its role in creating the problems that exist today. Because of its past role, the United States is obligated to assist the Mexican government in reducing the economic forces that continue to "push" many Mexican citizens to immigrate illegally. To be sure, the population explosion, increased rural-to-urban migration, and the structural labor market changes that have resulted from the introduction of capital-intensive technologies in Mexico would have caused illegal immigration to occur regardless of any past actions by the United States. But that contention is really moot. The fact is that the United States did contribute to some of the forces that have institutionalized the illegal migration of Mexicans to this country. Thus the United States cannot place upon Mexico the full responsibility for stopping the flow.

The United States should carefully reassess its trade and tariff policies that pertain to Mexico and the entire Caribbean Basin. Efforts to lower the restrictive trade barriers that presently apply to agricultural and manufacturing imports from these countries are essential. Such actions would enhance the opportunities for the export industries of these nations to expand and would reduce some of the pressures that presently lead to illegal immigration. They would also serve to acknowledge the fact that Mexico in particular, and many other nations of this region in general, are already major importers of U.S.-made goods.

In fact, in 1983 the Reagan administration won congressional approval of a Caribbean Basin program that seeks to accomplish most of these objectives. This initiative was not specifically linked to immigration reform legislation, but the legislation certainly contains implications to that effect. The explicit rationale for the program was that it would improve U.S. foreign-policy relations in the region. The program's benefits are restricted to noncommunist nations. Among the provisions of the enacting legislation is a twelve-year moratorium on duties on certain imports into the United States. The twenty-nine eligible countries do not have to reciprocate with respect to U.S. exports to their countries. Moreover, the act provides for financial aid to these nations to help stimulate economic development, and it offers incentives to U.S. firms to invest in the region.

INCREASING THE NUMBER OF LEGAL IMMIGRANTS ADMITTED FROM MEXICO

As discussed in Chapter 3, the Simpson-Mazzoli bill sought to exempt Mexico and Canada from the ceiling that in 1976 had been placed on the number of legal immigrants that could be admitted from any one nation each year. The bill proposed maintaining the 20,000-visa ceiling for all other nations, but increasing the limit for Mexico and Canada to 40,000. The Senate bill also outlined a reciprocity agreement whereby Mexico and Canada would be allowed to use each other's unused visas. Since Canada has not in recent years used all 20,000 of its visas, Mexico would stand to gain a significant number of additional visas as a result of this agreement. The increase in available visas would then be used to reduce the massive backlog of Mexican visa requests that currently exists and, it is believed, would help reduce some of the pressures that lead Mexicans to immigrate illegally or that force them to remain illegal if they have already immigrated while waiting for their visa requests to be acted upon. The House version of the bill deleted the reciprocity feature.

This change would help reduce the number of illegal immigrants in the U.S. labor market. In the present author's opinion it was a mistake in 1976 to put legal immigration from Mexico on the same footing as that from other nations. As equitable as it might have seemed at the time, the provision ignored the reality of immigration pressures in Mexico. Similar proposals to increase the number of legal immigrants admitted from Mexico were also made by the Carter administration and by the Select Commission on Immigration and Refugee Policy. It remains to be seen whether the Simpson-Mazzoli bill will pass, and if it does, whether this change will be included.

ENFORCEMENT OF LABOR STANDARDS

Although the available data show that the overwhelming majority of illegal immigrants are not legally "exploited" (i.e., they are not paid less than the federal minimum wage and do not work under conditions that are inferior to those that citizen workers encounter), some are. Hence, all the various studies and legislative proposals that have addressed the problem of illegal immigration have included homilies about the need to enforce existing fair labor standards. Presumably, if these laws were adequately enforced, the need to hire illegal immigrants would recede and illegal immigrants would stop coming. Michael Piore has even gone so far as to make enforcement the centerpiece of his policy recommendations.[116] Such a policy tack was also the mainstay of the alternative proposal to the Simpson-Mazzoli bill that was offered in 1984 by the congressional Hispanic caucus and drafted by Congressman Edward R. Roybal (D., Cal.). Roybal's bill, however, was not given a committee hearing nor did it ever reach the floor of the House for debate.

Certainly no one can argue against the need for more effective enforcement of prevailing labor standards for all workers—citizens or not. But this, it seems, is a weak reed upon which to place the weight of an attack on illegal immigration. To begin with, it is doubtful that most illegal immigrants are legally exploited in the workplace. Some are, but so are some citizens. Greater enforcement efforts might lead to less abuse of the nation's labor laws, but it is doubtful that they would stop the employment of illegal immigrants. After all, these laws are intended to assure that minimum labor standards prevail; that is all that can be enforced. North and Houstoun, for instance, found that 76 percent of the illegal immigrants in their study were paid the minimum wage or more.[117] Most of those who did not receive an equivalent wage were employed in agriculture, which at that time was not covered by minimum-wage legislation. Not surprisingly, North and Houstoun also found that Mexican illegal immigrants are more likely than non-Mexicans to be paid at a rate below the minimum wage. Moreover, while it is true that some labor standard enforcement activities are initiated by government agencies, most of the violations that are reported stem from employee complaints. This is the way it has always been and probably always will be. Nevertheless, illegal immigrants are less likely to know how to make such complaints, and even if they do know, they are—given their precarious status in the country—quite unlikely to file complaints.

AMNESTY FOR ILLEGAL ALIENS ALREADY HERE

By all estimates, the number of illegal immigrants residing in the United States is high. If immigration reforms eventually outlaw the employment of illegal immigrants, the immediate question will be, what is to be done about all those who are already in the country? U.S. immigration policy to date has unofficially condoned the influx of illegal immigrants, and it would be totally unrealistic to expect that any roundup of aliens—who in most cases have established themselves in jobs and often have families with them—could be accomplished without immense personal and financial hardship and extensive litigation. Hence, it is essential that some form of amnesty be granted to those who immigrated prior to a specified date. The date, of course, would have to be set in the past in order to preclude any mass flood of new immigrants seeking to beat a future amnesty deadline.

All the proposals for immigration reform have contained some form of forgiveness that would cover what is believed to be the vast majority of illegal immigrants. In general, the proposals would offer these aliens the opportunity to become citizens if they (1) registered within a set grace period; (2) could prove that they have lived in the United States continuously since and prior to some specified date; and (3) were not members of any of the groups that are automatically denied admission (see Appendix A). It should not be very difficult to process the change in status that would be offered to those who have been in the country for many years. In fact, as discussed in Chapter 3, on three past occasions congressional actions have allowed illegal aliens to register to become eligible for citizenship if they have lived in the country continuously since a set date (as of early 1984, that date was June 30, 1948). These registration programs have set precedents that could be used again for a certain portion of the illegal immigrant population. Indeed, the version of the Simpson-Mazzoli bill that passed the House of Representatives contained, as part of its amnesty plan, a proposal to advance the registry date to January 1, 1973. Any illegal immigrant who had lived continuously in the United States since before that date could adjust his or her status to become a citizen automatically under procedures that are already in place and that have been used satisfactorily before. There was no such proposal, however, in the Senate bill.

In the Senate version of the Simpson-Mazzoli bill as well as in the program endorsed by President Reagan, a two-tiered legalization program was adopted. Illegal immigrants who had entered the United States before January 1, 1977, would be immediately eligible to become permanent-resident aliens, who, after five years, could apply to become naturalized citizens. Those who had entered after January 1, 1977, but before December 31, 1979, could obtain legal status as "temporary residents" (a new immigration category). After three years they could apply to become permanent-resident aliens, and after five more years could apply to become naturalized citizens. Any illegal immigrant who had entered the United States after January 1, 1980, would be subject to deportation as under present law. In the House of Representatives, however, an entirely different amnesty program was adopted. The House program would grant "temporary resident status" to all illegal immigrants who had lived continuously in the United States since before January 1, 1982. (It is to be recalled that the House bill also allowed registry adjustment to all persons who have lived continuously in the United States since January 1, 1973). After two years as temporary residents, such persons could become permanent-resident aliens if they could prove that they were studying English and U.S. history and government. After five years, they could apply to become naturalized citizens. All temporary residents would also have to enroll their minor children in school. Any person convicted of a felony or of three misdemeanors would be ineligible to adjust his status and presumably could be deported. Any person who had entered after January 1, 1982, would be subject to deportation. Obviously, there are vast differences between the two bills on this key feature of the immigration reform drive. How these differences are reconciled may well determine the ultimate fate of the Simpson-Mazzoli bill.

The amnesty issue has always been one of the most controversial features of all the immigration reform packages. Many people feel that extending amnesty to people who have violated the laws of the nation serves to reward wrongdoers. Would-be immigrants are supposed to wait to be admitted. Many applicants for immigration are found to be ineligible—especially those who do not have relatives who are already citizens or permanent-resident aliens. Others are found to be members of an excludable class. Most of these individuals must resign themselves to staying where they are. As the argument goes, however, those who are ineligible or who, by virtue of immigrating illegally, show no respect for the laws of the United States are the ones who, through amnesty, achieve exactly what they seek. Those who adhere to the law by either waiting for their visas or accepting the fact that they are not eligible to immigrate are essentially punished. To many people amnesty seems entirely unjustified. They feel that it will set a bad precedent. Given the immense "push" factors that are involved in the illegal immigration process, they fear that having once granted amnesty it will be necessary to do so again and again in the future.

Another factor that has added to the fears of those who are opposed to amnesty is the potential cost of such a program. Given the disproportionate number of illegal immigrants who are unskilled and poorly educated, it is possible that many among the illegal immigrant population will suddenly become eligible for the broad array of social services that are available to similarly situated citizens. Among these are food stamps, Medicaid, aid for families with dependent children, unemployment compensation, and housing subsidies, to name some of the more prominent entitlement programs. There is already some evidence that there is "substantial use or attempted use" of the existing federal and state income transfer systems by illegal immigrants despite the fact that they are specifically excluded from eligibility for these programs.[118]

Under the Senate bill, all persons covered by the amnesty program would be ineligible for most federal financial assistance programs during the time that they are temporary residents and for the first three years that they are permanent resident aliens. Under the House approved bill, temporary residents would be ineligible for most federal assistance programs for five years, starting with the date they become temporary residents. The bill, however, does make exceptions for child nutrition programs, assistance to the aged and disabled, services to pregnant women, and certain emergency health services. These restrictions in both bills, of course, do not apply to assistance programs provided by some states, counties, and municipalities. Some of these local and state government entities may also seek to deny assistance to those persons granted amnesty for some set period. But, some localities and states are required by their own laws to provide benefits to all persons who need them regardless of citizenship status.

In 1982 the National Association of Counties (NACO) stated that its support for amnesty as described in the Simpson-Mazzoli bill was contingent upon two conditions: "that strong enforcement measures, including employer sanctions, be implemented to control future illegal immigration; and that the federal government reimburse state and local governments for additional costs resulting from a legalization program."[119] NACO estimated that the total cost of government cash and medical assistance to the illegal immigrants who would be granted amnesty under the Simpson-Mazzoli bill (i.e., using January 1, 1980, as an eligibility cutoff date) would be $1.1 billion. It also estimated that over half of this sum—$546.8 million—would be paid by state and local governments.[120] Given the geographical concentration of illegal immigrants, it is likely that this financial burden would be carried by only a few states and local governments. For them, of course, the burden—if it materialized—could be substantial. Local costs could be higher than those estimated by NACO, however, for not only do some states and localities have many more illegal immigrants than others but some have more liberal coverage provisions and more types of social programs than others. In California, for instance, it has been estimated that an amnesty program would cost the state $1.3 billion.[121] In New York City no specific dollar cost has been computed, but officials believe that the city's total welfare budget could increase by "5 to 10 percent" and that "with legalization, New York City can expect a significant rise in utilization of municipal hospitals and out-patient clinics, which are 100 percent city-funded, as well as a substantial increase in the state and local shares of total Medicaid, public assistance, and social service expenditures."[122]

In response to these concerns, proponents of an amnesty program have argued that such cost estimates may be too high. Theoretically, illegal aliens would not be eligible to adjust their status if there was any likelihood of their becoming public charges (in which case they would belong to an excludable class). Also, as Senator Allan Simpson has argued, "These people are not refugees; these people came to the United States for one reason: to work."[123] Hence, Simpson believes, as long as illegal immigrants seek and find work, concerns about the cost of a dependent population will prove to be unfounded.

Ironically, however, in January 1984 the cost of an amnesty program was cited by David Stockman, the nation's federal budget director, as a reason not to enact the entire bill. This announcement, which came a little over a month after Speaker of the House Thomas P. O'Neill had reversed his opposition to the bill and had promised to allow the House to vote on it, revived the fears that O'Neill had initially expressed—namely, that President Reagan would veto the bill if it was passed. Stockman estimated that the cost of the Senate-passed and House versions of the Simpson-Mazzoli bill would be $10.1 billion and $13.3 billion, respectively, over the period 1984–1989. These costs would accrue primarily as a result of the fact that in time many of the legalized aliens would become eligible for the nation's various social programs. Stockman warned that ''both bills create a large new entitlement group of legalized aliens contrary to Administration efforts to control entitlement spending.''[124]

Policies That Combat Illegal Immigration in Other Nations

Following the efforts by Western European nations to curtail recruitment of foreign workers (see Chapter 4), it became obvious to the receiving governments that many workers had entered illegally and that many others had overstayed their visas. In Western Europe, as in the United States, there are no official figures on the actual size of the illegal immigrant population. Nonetheless, according to the Council of Europe, ''by the Summer of 1973 it was estimated that there were more than a half a million foreigners illegally working or living in Europe.''[125] Summarizing specific reports from individual countries, the council estimated that about 10 percent of all foreign workers in West Germany were illegal workers; about 50 percent of all foreign workers in France were illegal workers; and that in the Dutch cities of Amsterdam and Rotterdam ''the illegal workers are as numerous as the legal foreign workers.''[126] What is perhaps even more important is the fact that the Western European nations have found that it is far easier to start the flow of nonimmigrant foreign workers than it is to stop it. In 1982 it was estimated that the number of illegal immigrants in the region exceeded one million.[127]

In response to this rapid growth of the illegal immigrant population, the major countries of Western Europe have initiated a series of immigration reforms. Most countries of continental Europe have long relied on the use of work permits. Moreover, Europeans are accustomed to the requirement that they carry identification cards at all times, and they expect to be asked to identify themselves to authorities both on and off the job. Hence, the identification issue has not been a point of contention in Europe. The need for workers to establish their eligibility to work was met in these countries many decades ago. The exception is Great Britain, which, like the United States, does not have a work permit system.

The focus of the effort to reduce illegal immigration in most Western European nations has been upon employer sanctions and penalties assessed against persons who facilitate the importation of illegal immigrants. In France, persons who help bring illegal immigrants into the country are subject to fines of up to $50,000 and two years in prison. French employers are subject to a $600 fine for each illegal immigrant they hire. Within 24 hours of hiring a worker, French employers are required to record in a special register kept in their office the name of the person they have hired and his or her work permit information. This register is subject to review by government labor inspectors. Similarly, in West Germany it is the employers' responsibility to see that the work permits of their employees are in order. West German employers are also required to keep detailed information on their employees, including copies of work permits for all foreign workers as well as tax cards. Tax cards, which employees must secure from the government, must be given to employers at the time workers are hired.

In West Germany, however, employer sanctions have not worked as anticipated. Some employers have sought to circumvent these sanctions by "leasing" workers instead of hiring them, and the courts have tended to reduce employers' fines upon appeal. Such actions have negated the deterrent effect of the penalties.[128] Likewise, in France the courts have given light penalties to employers convicted of hiring illegal immigrants. To counter this trend, the government strengthened the nation's employer sanctions law in 1982 to allow the Ministry of Labor to confiscate tools and equipment used by illegal immigrants at job sites.[129]

Responding to an estimate that there are between 500,000 and 1,000,000 illegal immigrants in the nation and that "most of them work," Canada also has adopted an employer sanctions law.[130] Canada does not have a work permit system, but all workers must have a social insurance card, which employers are expected to examine. Foreign workers (i.e., nonimmigrant workers) are given a special number that indicates to employers that they must also have an additional work authorization permit issued by immigration officials. Apparently, however, the system is widely abused. Illegal immigrants obtain fraudulent documents or use legal documents that belong to someone else.[131] Employers are quite aware that some workers enter the country illegally, and some use the fear of being reported as a lever that permits them to pay lower wages and benefits to these persons.[132]

Amnesty has also been introduced in several foreign countries. After adopting its stringent Immigration Act of 1971, the United Kingdom decided that "the only decent thing to do was to allow those who entered illegally prior to the effective date of the legislation to have their presence legalized."[133] The offer applied only to citizens of Pakistan and nations that belonged to the British Commonwealth who had immigrated prior to January 1, 1973, and had lived in Britain continuously ever since. The amnesty offer was announced in April 1974. Only 4,094 persons subsequently applied, and of these, 2,409 were granted amnesty; 1,685 were found to be ineligible and some of these persons were actually deported. In Britain there is little reason for illegal immigrants to report themselves, for the nation does not have a work permit system and there is virtually no inland enforcement of its immigration laws. That is to say, little attention is given to the problem of visa-abusers because the focus has always been on illegal entrants at coastal ports. Why should visa-abusers apply for amnesty when there is virtually no chance they will otherwise be detected?

In Belgium and the Netherlands, in contrast to Britain, "amnesty was the objective, not a by-product."[134] In 1975, 14,000 persons in the Netherlands took advantage of the offer, as did 7,000 in Belgium. In these two countries, illegal immigrants had nothing to lose. If those who applied for amnesty were found to be eligible, their status was legalized; if not, their applications were destroyed and they were on their own again. David North argues that the lessons for the United States are that an amnesty arrangement should include both stepped-up inland enforcement of existing immigration laws and a no-risk registration system.

When Canada adopted a general amnesty scheme in 1973, a balanced program of incentives and penalties was introduced. The program was announced as a one-time-only undertaking. All persons were eligible, but if they did not come forward and have their status adjusted legally, they would be given no further chance to do so. All illegal immigrants who were subsequently apprehended would be deported and all nonimmigrants would be ineligible to become landed immigrants in the future. Approximately 36,000 persons took advantage of the offer. About 20,000 other illegal immigrants who would have been eligible for amnesty left the country; it is believed they illegally immigrated to the United States.[135]

In January 1982 France completed a general amnesty program for illegal immigrants that had gone into effect the year before. A total of 80,000 persons applied, but of these, 30,000 could not produce evidence that they had a job, which was a condition of eligibility, and legalization of their status is still pending.

In all these countries, therefore, there were fewer applicants for amnesty than had been anticipated. The precise reasons for this are of course unknown. Admittedly, it is very difficult to inform some illegal immigrants of these opportunities. It is also likely that many illegal immigrants are both fearful and distrustful of such offers. Given the experiences of these other nations, it is likely that a sizable number of illegal immigrants in the United States who are eligible for amnesty would not apply for it. Many would, however, and since the main objective of such programs is to reduce the size of the illegal immigrant population of a nation, amnesty could play an important role in the accomplishment of that goal in the United States.

The serious conceptual flaw in the idea of granting amnesty, however, is the inability to prevent the expectation that once it is given, it will be offered again in the future. The Netherlands has reported that the subject of additional amnesty offers has become a difficult political issue. So far it has refrained from making any new proposals, as have the other nations that provided a one-time amnesty. Admittedly, however, it is a troublesome political concern to refrain from granting it again.

CHAPTER 6

Refugee and
Asylee Policy

The accommodation of refugees and persons seeking political asylum often accounts for a significant portion of the overall flow of immigrants into the United States. The American public, however, tends to view these admissions as humanitarian gestures involving only a few individuals or groups in isolated circumstances. As events since the end of World War II have vividly demonstrated, that perception does not match reality. At times, refugees and asylees have approximated or exceeded the number of persons admitted under the legal immigration system in a given year. Consequently it is necessary to understand that as their numbers have accelerated, so has their influence upon selected U.S. labor markets. It is also widely believed that these admissions provisions are being increasingly abused by people who do not really fear persecution but rather are primarily interested in improving their economic status. To the extent that these provisions are being abused, they serve as a loophole that circumvents the entire U.S. legal immigration system and further undermines the effectiveness of the nation's immigration policy.

Since the time of the Pilgrim Fathers, some immigration to the United States has been motivated by reasons other than the desire for economic improvement. Among the immigrants admitted to the United States there have often been individuals and groups who were seeking to escape persecution in their homelands. Thus the subject of refugee accommodation is not a new one for the nation. Having paid homage to tradition, however, it is necessary to indicate that the issue of accepting refugees at a time when the nation's immigration policy was essentially to open its doors to virtually all who sought entry is entirely different from the issue of refugee accommodation today, for now there is a complex regulatory system in place to determine eligibility for admission within the scope of an overall annual admissions ceiling as well as individual country ceilings. In terms of U.S. history, then, refugee policy was of no real consequence in the policy formulation process prior to the 1920s, but since the mid-1930s it has become one of the most perplexing issues ever to confront policymakers.

As the number of refugees in the world has continued to grow, the United States has found itself under pressure to share the accommodation burden. In the

1980s it has also been increasingly the case that large numbers of persons have entered the country illegally or as nonimmigrants and have subsequently sought political asylum in lieu of deportation. The handling of these issues raises unique institutional challenges within the overall process of formulating immigration policy. As a State Department official observed in 1982:

> Asylum in the United States is intended to provide a sanctuary for persons fleeing persecution. It is not intended to be a substitute for or an alternative to the immigration laws of this country and should not become a vehicle of convenience for applicants who may wish to circumvent our immigration law.[1]

In practice it has been far easier to assert this policy distinction than to administer the policy. As a consequence of these developments, a number of local labor markets in the United States have found that they now have substantial refugee and asylee populations. In the past two decades the vast majority of these persons have come from the less economically developed nations of the world. They have often required special educational, housing, income, and job assistance, which local governments are frequently unable and sometimes unwilling to provide. As in the case of other aspects of immigration policy, local and state officials have asserted that refugee assistance should be a federal responsibility. Yet in the late 1970s, when the federal government sought to enrich the services both to individuals and to communities in an effort to complete the refugee adaptation process, representatives of various citizen groups frequently raised objections, claiming that it was unfair to provide such extensive assistance to refugees when the government was unwilling to provide comparable aid for its economically disadvantaged citizens. In the early 1980s the Reagan administration concluded that the assistance was too costly for the federal government to continue to support at previous levels and it shortened the eligibility period substantially. This step placed responsibility for any further assistance at the state and local levels if it was going to be provided at all.

Because of the unique aspects of refugee policy, this complex topic requires separate discussion. Policy development in this area is a classic example of pragmatic experimentation designed to balance the humanitarian desire to relieve human suffering with the need to maintain a semblance of control over the number of immigrants who enter the population and the labor force at any given time.

The World Perspective

Before examining the refugee issue in the United States, it is important to place the issue in an international perspective. Although refugees have existed for perhaps as long as mankind has sought to group itself into various territorial enclaves, the rise of nation-states no doubt exacerbated the issue of what to do about those persons who, for various noneconomic reasons, flee or are forced to leave their native lands. History is resplendent with ad hoc examples of refugee accommodation by individual nations. It was not until the twentieth century, however, that circumstances mandated that serious attempts be made at the international level to address refugee issues and to coordinate appropriate responses.

At the end of World War I there were several million persons who had been displaced by the fighting and the subsequent border realignments that changed the territorial makeup of many nations. Most of these persons were white and came from relatively industrialized societies. Many were skilled and well educated. Frequently the policy problems that emerged involved the issue of resettlement in the refugees' homelands rather than permanent relocation in other nations. In 1921 the League of Nations appointed the first High Commissioner for Refugees to coordinate the effort to solve what was viewed as essentially a temporary European problem.

In the early 1930s, however, the issue of refugees again surfaced in Europe as large numbers of persons sought to escape from the emerging threats of Nazism and Fascism. The League of Nations and the International Labour Organisation tried to deal with the problem, but opposition to their efforts by the governments of Germany and the Soviet Union served to demonstrate that there was no effective mechanism by which to handle the issue. As a result, millions of persons perished in the genocide of World War II. At the end of World War II, millions more refugees were thrust upon the world scene. In this period the United States made its first efforts to specifically admit some of these displaced persons through channels other than the nation's strictly enforced national-origins admission system. The post–World War II refugee problem in Europe was made worse by the fact that many refugees from Eastern Europe did not wish to resettle in their prewar homelands because the Soviet Union was extending its sphere of influence to include these countries. Many feared that if they returned they would again be subjected to persecution and regimentation. These refugees were predominately whites whose roots were in advanced industrialized societies. Relocation of these refugees to countries such as Australia, Canada, and the United States, as well as some nations in Western Europe and South America, was ultimately accomplished. Throughout this period the issue of refugees was perceived as being essentially a temporary phenomenon.

Unfortunately, since the end of World War II, events in the Middle East, Central and East Africa, Central America, and Southeast Asia in particular have demonstrated that the events that spawn refugees do not occur irregularly or confine themselves to Europe. Both the frequency of the events that produced refugees as well as the number of human beings involved took a quantum leap in the years following World War II. In 1967 the United Nations adopted a protocol on refugees that was subsequently to exert significant influence on refugee policy in the United States. It was based on the language of a U.N. convention on refugees that had been adopted in 1951. The 1951 convention, however, referred only to European refugees who had been the victims of events occurring before

January 1, 1951. The protocol of 1967 eliminated both the time and the geographic restrictions. A refugee was defined as "every person who, owing to well founded fear of being persecuted for reasons of race, religion, nationality, membership of a particular social group or political opinion, is outside the country of his nationality and is unable or, owing to such fear, is unwilling to avail himself of the protection of that country."[2] The United States became a signatory to the protocol on November 11, 1968, although it did not accept this definition of refugees until 1980. The 1951 convention and the 1967 protocol did not require that signatory nations accept refugees. They did, however, seek to ensure that the refugees received by signatory nations would be granted certain legal and political rights and that the receiving nations would provide a safe haven until, if necessary, the refugees could be relocated elsewhere.

The U.N. definition, of course, was arrived at through a consensus-seeking process in a highly political forum. It does not adequately reflect the true dimensions of the global refugee phenomenon. The critical concepts in the U.N. definition are that the person seeking refugee status must be both persecuted and outside his or her country of citizenship. As Charles Keely has noted, this definition does not include persons who flee from either a civil war or a war between nations, for such persons would not necessarily be leaving their homelands for fear of persecution.[3] Many nations, as well as some regional groups of nations—the Organization of African Unity for example—feel that persons who flee from wars of any kind are in fact refugees and thus they treat them as such.

There are other reasons to regard the U.N. definition as too narrow. Some persecuted persons are prevented from leaving their countries by their own governments (as is the case in many Eastern European nations). At the opposite extreme is the phenomenon of massive expulsions of groups of persons by some governments, which results in an arbitrary revocation of citizenship (e.g., the ethnic Chinese who were expelled by the government of Vietnam in the late 1970s and who became known as "the boat people"). In both instances, according to the U.N. definition, the people involved did not technically qualify as refugees. Thus, at any given moment the size of the world's refugee population is subject to extensive variation depending upon what definition of *refugee* is used. Regardless of definition, however, there is no doubt that the number of human beings involved is quite large and that in all probability the ranks of refugees will continue to swell.

Using its own definition, the U.S. Committee for Refugees placed the number of refugees in 1981 at 12.6 million.[4] Of these, 8 million lived outside their countries of nationality and 4.6 million were internal refugees. While it is important to determine the aggregate size of the world's refugee population (which, like other immigration data, is subject to criticism concerning its derivation and accuracy), the composition of this population is of even greater consequence. In 1981 it was estimated that over half the world's refugees resided in Africa. Ethiopians constituted the largest group of refugees living outside their country, but the numbers of refugees from Chad, Rwanda, and Zaire also were substantial. Internal refugees were largely found in Ethiopia, Zimbabwe, and Uganda. In 1981 the Middle East (with not only Palestinians but also refugees from Lebanon, Iraq, and Cyprus) and Asia (with refugees from Afghanistan, Kampuchea, and Laos) were the locations of most of the remainder of the world's refugee population. The significant point here is that in 1981 approximately 97 percent of the world's refugees lived in the less developed nations whether one counted them on the basis of where they came from or where they resided.[5] In 1981 most of the world's refugees were not white and few had ever been exposed to an industrialized society. They were typically unskilled and poorly educated; many were even illiterate in their own language. Clearly these characteristics are a marked departure from the definition of refugees that was operative following World Wars I and II. It is a tragic irony that the nations that are least able to accommodate refugees are the ones that are saddled with most of the burden. Even though the United States has become deeply involved in efforts to address the global refugee dilemma, its role to date (like that of all of the world's industrialized nations) has been minor relative to the burdens borne by many Third World nations.

Incremental Steps toward a National Refugee Policy

Prior to World War I, there was no need for a specific refugee policy in the United States. Immigration, regardless of the causative circumstances, was essentially unimpeded. With the imposition of the strict national-origins system in 1924, however, the situation changed drastically. As discussed in Chapter 2, the admission of persons from Asia was essentially prohibited and, practically speaking, the low quotas assigned to most Eastern European nations had the same effect. The Immigration Act of 1924 made no provision for special admissions. Persons were admitted only if quota slots were available or if they could qualify for nonquota status as a spouse or child of a quota immigrant, and only if they were not members of an excludable class of persons (see Appendix A). Thus, in the 1930s and early 1940s, the large numbers of Europeans who sought to flee Nazism were denied admission to the United States unless quota openings were available. Given the fact that the nation was in the throes of a major economic depression during most of these years, it would not have been politically expedient to alter the restrictive immigration laws and allow perhaps hundreds of thousands of persons to enter the United States and seek work. The strength of the opposition to making any exceptions to the nation's extant immigration policy is best illustrated by the fact that in 1939 Congress defeated a bill that would have admitted 20,000 children from Nazi Germany—all of whom had U.S. families as sponsors—on the grounds that the children would have exceeded the existing quota for Germany. This action has been called "the cruelest single action in U.S. immigration history."[6] Some special efforts were made by the U.S. Department of State in 1940 to allow consular offices outside Germany to issue visas to some German refugees to fill unused German quota slots that year, but obviously the number of these openings was trivial relative to the number of persons seeking to flee.

Following the surrender of Germany in 1945, the clash between the inflexible immigration laws of the United States and the reality of millions of refugees and displaced persons resurfaced. On December 22, 1945, President Harry Truman ordered that admission be expedited for 80,000 persons (40,000 of whom were specifically classified as refugees) from Poland and various other war-torn countries of the Baltic Sea area and southern Europe. These admissions were granted with the explanation that these countries had not used all the quota slots they were entitled to during the preceding war years. Then, on June 25, 1948, the Displaced Persons Act was signed into law.[7] This legislation was prompted by the need to relocate one million refugees from Eastern European countries who refused to be resettled in their homelands for fear of persecution by the newly installed Communist governments there. Under the auspices of the Displaced Persons Act, 205,000 European immigrants were admitted to the United States during the next two years. These admissions were made possible by stretching the meaning of the national-origins law to allow the nations involved in the war to mortgage up to one-half of each future year's quota allotments. The nations that had small quotas to begin with mortgaged their allotments far into the future. The Baltic nations of Estonia, Latvia, and Lithuania, for instance, obligated half of their visas for sixty-seven years, seventy-six years, and sixty-five years respectively.[8] Thus, in the long run, the Displaced Persons Act would not challenge the ethnic composition of the U.S. population, the constant ratio that the national-origins system had sought to protect. It was expected that a temporary increase in the number of persons admitted from low-quota nations between 1948 and 1950 would be offset by reductions in the number of admissions from these same nations in later years. The Displaced Persons Act of 1948 was amended in 1950 and 1951 to allow the admission of an additional 188,542 European refugees under essentially the same terms.

Enactment of the Immigration and Nationality Act of 1952 did not make any special allowances for refugee admissions. It should be recalled that this act maintained national origins as the basis of the U.S. immigration system. Yet the refugee problems of Europe and, by this time China, were tragic realities. Finally, in 1953, legislation was passed that permitted refugees to be admitted through channels outside the prevailing immigration system. The Refugee Relief Act of 1953 authorized the issuance of 215,000 visas for refugees from Europe and China on a nonquota basis.[9] By the time the authorization expired (at the end of 1956), 189,000 of these visas had been used. Each refugee who was admitted under this act was required to have a citizen sponsor who would be responsible for seeing that he or she got a job, found adequate housing, and did not become a public charge.

In October 1956, troops from the Soviet Union entered Hungary to suppress an extensive civilian uprising against the Soviet-supported Hungarian government. Responding to that invasion, over 200,000 Hungarians fled to nearby Austria. In November 1956, President Dwight Eisenhower announced that the United States would admit 21,500 of these refugees. He stated that 6,150 of these persons would be issued unused visas that were still available under the aforementioned Refugee Relief Act of 1953. The remainder were to be admitted under the parole authority granted to the U.S. attorney general by the Immigration and Nationality Act of 1952 to admit persons outside the national-origins quota system for "emergent reasons" that were in the "public interest."[10] By 1958 this parole authority had been used to admit an additional 10,000 Hungarian refugees. Also in that year special legislation was passed to allow these persons to adjust their status to that of permanent-resident aliens.

President Eisenhower's use of the parole authority to admit refugees set a precedent. Ostensibly, the parole authority had been established as a means of admitting individuals on a temporary basis. There was no mention in the Immigration and Nationality Act of 1952 of any conceivable use of this authority to admit groups of persons on a permanent basis. In particular, there was no mention of the use of this authority to admit refugees. Clearly President Eisenhower significantly stretched the intentions of the act and the power of his office. Relying on this precedent, subsequent administrations used the parole authority to admit large numbers of refugees. In fact, this interpretation of the law remained a controversial feature of immigration policy until 1980. In the case of the Hungarian uprising, however, the circumstances of the refugees dictated a U.S. policy response. Despite the fact that the prevailing laws of the land were silent on the entire subject of refugee accommodation, there was a will to act, and a way was found.

In September 1957 a compromise immigration law was adopted that was designed primarily to minimize some of the personal hardship that had resulted from strict enforcement of the national-origins system.[11] Among its provisions, however, was a section that permitted 18,656 visas that had not been used under the Refugee Relief Act of 1953 to be issued to "refugee-escapees": persons who were fleeing persecution in Communist nations or in countries of the Middle East. (As will be seen, in 1965 this definition was used as the basis for adding the first specific refugee provisions to the nation's immigration laws.) The 1957 legislation came to be known as the Refugee-Escapee Act of 1957, even though that provision was only one feature of the statute.

In a similar vein, the Fair Share Refugee Act was passed in 1960 in response to the fact that as late as that year refugees from the World War II period were still living in "temporary" camps in Europe.[12] These persons were under the jurisdiction of the U.N. High Commissioner for Refugees. As part of a concerted effort by a number of nations, and under the banner of "World Refugee Year," a drive was initiated to close these camps by resettling all the persons who remained in them. According to the provisions of the Fair Share Refugee Act, the United States agreed to accept its "fair share" of these persons. In addition, one quarter of the visas that were authorized by this bill were set aside for escapees from Eastern European countries who also were confined in such camps. The act established a temporary program whereby the attorney general was given specific authority to use his parole authority to admit the agreed-upon share of eligible refugees. The Fair Share Refugee Act was extended in 1962. As a result of this legislation, 19,700 "refugee-escapees" were admitted to the United States between 1960 and 1965. Provision was also made under the act to allow these persons to adjust their status to that of permanent-resident aliens after a two-year waiting period.

A SPECIAL CASE: THE CUBAN REFUGEES, 1959–1962

The incremental movement toward adoption of a national refugee policy was significantly boosted by events in Cuba in the late 1950s. These events, in fact, continue to exert an influence on U.S. policy today. On December 31, 1958, Cuban Director Fulgencio Batista fled his country in the wake of the revolution that was led by Fidel Castro. Immigration from Cuba—especially the influx of refugees—did not begin in 1959, but over the ensuing twenty-three years Cuba became the single largest source of political refugees fleeing to the United States.

Due to the geographic proximity of Cuba and the United States (a distance of about 90 miles at the closest points), as well as the significant involvement of the U.S. government and U.S. business interests on the island prior to 1959, political events in Cuba have frequently led Cuban refugees to seek asylum in the United States. Various unsuccessful insurrections against Spain during the nineteenth century marked the beginning of these refugee flows. In fact, it was a committee of Cuban exiles headquartered in New York City in 1895 whose efforts, coordinated with the work of indigenous groups in Cuba, culminated in the Spanish-American War of 1898. In 1902, following three years of U.S. military occupation, Cuba became an independent nation. Every group that has come to power in Cuba since that time has caused members of the losing groups in these political struggles to seek asylum in the United States. It is interesting to note that prior to launching his revolutionary movement in 1956, Fidel Castro was an exilee in the United States. The difference between the pre-1959 and the post-1959 flow of Cuban refugees has been one of scale. In the earlier era, Cuban refugees came individually or in selected groups; during the later period they have come in massive numbers.

When Castro assumed political control of Cuba in January 1959, the refugees who fled the island were mostly persons who had been closely associated with the Batista regime. In the spring of 1959, as land seizures under the newly implemented agrarian reform law began—as did mass political trials and summary executions of hundreds of persons charged with offenses during the Batista years—a second wave of refugees fled Cuba. In most instances, the United States was their destination.

By the end of 1960, upwards of 70,000 Cuban exiles were in the Miami metropolitan area alone, while 50,000 more had settled elsewhere in Florida and the nation. During this period the majority of the Cubans who entered the United

States did so with visas through the regular immigration channels. Those who came without visas, and those who were already in the United States with nonimmigrant visas but who did not wish to return to Cuba, were granted paroles by the U.S. attorney general as provided under the Immigration and Nationality Act of 1952.

The concentration of Cuban refugees in the Miami area led to immediate concerns over the ability of the local community to accommodate so many persons in such a short period of time. President Eisenhower sought to relieve some of the temporary pressures by authorizing the expenditure of $1 million from the President's Contingency Fund, which was created under the Mutual Security Act of 1954. These Funds were used to establish a Cuban Refugee Emergency Center in Miami in December 1960.

Immediately upon assuming office on January 20, 1961, President John Kennedy was confronted with the refugee issue. Diplomatic relations with Cuba had been severed only three weeks before. With official visas no longer obtainable from Cuba, legal immigration per se was no longer possible. The Kennedy administration therefore "adopted wholesale a practice of paroling the refugees [from Cuba] into the country."[13] Whereas 4,000 Cubans were paroled into the United States between July 1960 and June 1961, the number jumped to 58,630 between July 1961 and June 1962. To aid in the settlement process, the Kennedy administration launched the Cuban Refugee Program in 1961. This program marked "the first deliberate and substantial involvement of the Federal Government in a major refugee resettlement activity."[14] The omnibus program involved an immediate infusion of $4 million in federal assistance. In addition, it initiated a concerted effort to link available public and private programs and organizations with resettlement activities.

In 1962 Cuba was excluded from participation in the Organization of American States and the United States imposed a trade embargo that has been in effect ever since. In October of that year an international confrontation occurred between the United States and the Soviet Union over the issue of Soviet missiles in Cuba. Commercial air traffic between the two countries ceased. As a consequence of these events, Cuban refugee flows were reduced to a trickle of dangerous and unsanctioned escapes by small boatloads of persons.

Similar to the aid given to Cuban refugees was the U.S. agreement in May 1962 to admit through its parole procedures a total of 15,000 Chinese refugees who had fled to Hong Kong as the result of widespread famine in the People's Republic of China.

Statutory Recognition of the Permanence of Refugees as Immigrants

The ad hoc refugee policy responses of the 1950s and early 1960s made sense only if refugee flows were relatively random occurrences. To the contrary, the series of events that had dictated separate policy interventions clearly showed that a trend was developing. Although the precise number of refugees who were admitted to the United States fluctuated from year to year, they represented a flow whose pressure was likely to be continuous. For this reason, a political consensus gradually emerged that refugee policy needed to be integrated into the nation's overall immigration scheme.

It was in this context that the Kennedy administration proposed and Congress subsequently passed with minor amendments the Migration and Refugee Assistance Act of 1962.[15] It served as the basic refugee statute of the nation until 1980. It enunciated the principle that the United States should continue to accept persons who had been uprooted due to internal political unrest or military action within their homelands, as well as individuals fleeing from persecution because of their personal beliefs. The bill also mandated that the United States participate in international efforts to relieve the burden imposed on the nations that were the destinations of "first instance" of refugees from other countries. It indicated that the United States would contribute to efforts to reduce refugee migration and settlement costs by helping persons in labor surplus nations move to other less developed nations that were in need of additional human resources. Under the provisions of this law, refugee assistance would be separately funded rather than included in the nation's omnibus foreign-aid legislation as had been the practice in the past. Thereafter, refugee affairs would become a permanent feature of U.S. public policy.

As indicated in Chapter 3, the Kennedy administration set in motion in mid-1963 the process of overhauling the entire U.S. immigration system. These efforts culminated in the Immigration Act of 1965. Among other things, it should be recalled, this act provided for the creation of a seven-category preference system to govern the legal immigration system. The seventh preference category pertained specifically to refugees. Unlike other immigrants to the United States, refugees were to be granted "conditional entry." As the term implies, this meant that the individual would not automatically be granted permanent-resident status. To be eligible for refugee admission, the would-be entrant had to be interviewed abroad. The interviews were conducted by an INS official in a noncommunist country to see if the person met the eligibility criteria. The individual had to be admissible as an immigrant except that the usual documentary evidence required of all others seeking admission was not required of refugees. Those who were granted permission to enter would have to reside in the United States for at least two years before requesting adjustment to permanent-resident status. The definition of *refugee* in this act was essentially the one first outlined in the Refugee-Escapee Act of 1957. Refugees were either persecuted persons who had escaped from a Communist country or Communist-dominated area, or persons who had fled the persistent turmoil of the entire Middle East region. The Immigration Act of 1965 expanded this definition to include persons in Eastern Hemisphere nations who had been uprooted "by catastrophic natural calamity" and could not return to their homes, but this last admissions category was never used, for it was later realized that such persons would be leaving their homeland for economic, not political, reasons.

Obviously, the definition of *refugee* that was adopted by the United States was far narrower than the then-prevailing U.N. definition. The U.S. definition reflected the cold-war atmosphere of the 1950s rather than the contemporary or emerging exigencies of the nation or the world. It entitled refugees to 6 percent (i.e., 17,400 persons) of the worldwide quota slots (290,000) authorized by the Immigration Act of 1965. This number was far below the number of refugees that had been admitted under the parole provision during the preceding fourteen years. Because the Immigration Act of 1965 was technically only a series of amendments to the Immigration and Nationality Act of 1952, the parole option was retained, but by adding the "conditional entry" provision, Congress "intended that thereafter the parole provision would be administered solely on a case by case basis."[16] As was clearly stated in the congressional reports that accompanied the 1965 legislation, "The parole provisions were designed to authorize the Attorney General to act only in emergency, individual, and isolated situations, such as the case of an alien who requires immediate medical attention, and not for the immigration of classes or groups outside the limit of the law."[17] Clearly Congress wished to break with past practices and it believed that the addition of the seventh preference group to the basic immigration statute of the nation would accomplish this change.

A Return to the Parole Admission System

No sooner had the new immigration law been signed on October 3, 1965, however, than events once more swamped the terms of the written word. Developments in Cuba initiated the process by which Congress's attempt to limit the use of the parole authority as a means to achieve mass immigration was literally nullified. Because of the economic and political turmoil that prevailed in Cuba, Premier Fidel Castro unilaterally announced on September 28, 1965, that any Cubans wishing to leave—except young men of military age—could do so. On October 3, 1965, President Lyndon Johnson announced that any of these Cubans who desired to come to the United States could do so. He directed that several agencies of the federal government establish an orderly entry procedure. Cuba, in the meantime, announced that the port of Camarioca would be open for Cuban exiles to come by boat to pick up their relatives. The ensuing flotilla of boats was the precursor of the Mariel boatlift of 1980. About 5,000 persons were transported by private boats to the United States in the next month. This procedure was deemed to be unsafe, however, and a better means was quickly sought. In November 1965 it was announced that the U.S. and Cuban governments—acting through the government of Switzerland, which served as an intermediary—had reached a mutual accord by which an "air bridge" would be established to transport Cuban refugees to the United States. Two chartered flights a day would be permitted to land in Cuba and carry the refugees back to the United States. From the time these "freedom flights" began until they were unilaterally stopped in Cuba in 1973, about 270,000 Cuban refugees were admitted to the

United States under this arrangement. Many of these persons were relatives of Cubans who had earlier sought refuge. At the time the flights were stopped, 135,000 persons who had applied to exit were stranded. As for the characteristics of the refugees of the 1959–1973 era, they have been described as members of "the upper socioeconomic class of pre-revolutionary Cuba," persons who, because they were "the able, the educated, and the successful," represented "the biggest brain drain the Western Hemisphere has ever known."[18] These persons have sometimes been referred to as the "golden exiles" because of their extensive human capital endowments and because many of them knew the English language well.

The legal authority that was used to admit the Cuban airlift refugees was once again the parole authority of the U.S. attorney general. In 1966 a special law, the Cuban Refugee Adjustment Act, was passed to enable these refugees to become permanent-resident aliens without first leaving the country and applying for the

TABLE 25.   CUBANS WHO ARRIVED IN THE UNITED STATES,
BY CLASS OF ADMISSION, JANUARY 1, 1959–SEPTEMBER 30, 1979

Period	Total	Immigrants	Nonimmigrants	Parolees
January–June 1959	26,527	2,832	23,695	—a
Year ending June 30,				
1960	60,224	8,126	52,098	—
1961	49,961	11,239	34,822	3,900
1962	78,611	6,534	13,447	58,630
1963	42,929	5,073	1,082	36,774
1964	15,616	9,561	665	5,390
1965	16,447	13,160	965	2,322
1966	46,688	13,319	827	32,542
1967	52,147	5,464	754	45,929
1968	55,945	9,618	1,191	45,136
1969	52,625	7,408	982	44,235
1970	49,545	2,331	1,358	45,856
1971	50,001	1,889	2,042	46,070
1972	23,977	1,192	1,845	20,940
1973	12,579	1,151	2,027	9,401
1974	13,670	711	1,382	11,577
1975	8,488	361	1,187	6,940
1976	4,515	859	1,315	2,341
1976b	1,439	381	645	413
1977	3,109	900	1,655	554
1978	4,108	1,178	2,727	203
1979	8,007	3,064	2,298	2,644
Total admitted, January 1, 1959–				
September 30, 1979	677,158	106,351	149,009	421,797

Source: Undated mimeographed material from the U.S. Department of Justice, Immigration and Naturalization Service.

Note: Parole figures were not reported for Cubans prior to October 1, 1960.

a— = data not available.

bTransitional quarter.

appropriate visa. Cuban refugees who entered the United States were allowed to adjust their status after they had been in the United States for two years. These persons were originally counted as part of the annual ceiling of 120,000 quota immigrants from the entire Western Hemisphere that was set by the Immigration Act of 1965, but this practice was subsequently declared illegal.[19] As a result, 145,000 additional visas above the established numerical ceiling were issued to other persons from the Western Hemisphere who had sought entry to the United States but had been denied entry because over several years these visas had been diverted for use by Cuban refugees.

By the time the Cuban airlift ended in 1973, 677,158 Cuban refugees had entered the United States since 1959. The magnitude of the flow of Cubans to the United States from 1959 to 1979 and of the use of the parole power to accommodate their admission can be seen in Table 25. A disproportionately high number of these persons remained in the Miami–Dade County area of Florida. As for the impact of the airlift on that community, by 1980 the population of Spanish origin in the Miami Standard Metropolitan Statistical Area (SMSA) was 35.7 percent of the total population, and perhaps of even greater consequence, the foreign-born population accounted for 35.3 percent of the total Miami population—the highest percentage recorded by any large SMSA (i.e., any SMSA with a population of one million or more) in the nation.[20]

INDOCHINESE REFUGEES

Hardly had the Cuban "air bridge" ceased than events in Southeast Asia set in motion a new refugee stream that would have long-term implications for U.S. immigration policy. In April 1975 the government of South Vietnam collapsed. With the withdrawal of U.S. military forces from South Vietnam in the spring of 1975, "the largest emerging mass immigration of refugees to the United States" yet known commenced.[21] Many of the initial refugees were persons who had been closely associated with the war effort. In fact, the transportation of these persons out of South Vietnam had begun before the government fell. As of April 27, 1975 (the day before the final evacuation of Saigon), 20,221 refugees had been transported by military aircraft and commercial planes to Guam. Between April and December 1975 a total of 130,000 Indochinese refugees were admitted to the United States under the parole provisions of the Immigration and Nationality Act of 1952. Most of these persons were either related to U.S. citizens or had been closely allied with the war effort itself. The refugees in these initial selection categories were soon outnumbered, however, by the refugees from throughout Indochina who were also seeking to be admitted to the United States. As a result, three separate parole programs were authorized in 1975. In 1976, a fourth parole program was undertaken to admit 11,000 refugees who had escaped from South Vietnam, Kampuchea, or Laos and who had relatives living in the United States. Also included in that fourth grouping were some of the first "boat people" who were expelled from Vietnam and who were having extreme difficulty finding countries that would allow them to land. President Gerald Ford decided at this point that "relying upon the parole provision was not a desirable means of formulating U.S. refugee policy."[22] He announced in 1976 that he would no longer use this authority and called for new legislation to establish a systematic admissions procedure. His administration, however, was voted out of office in November of that year. When President Jimmy Carter assumed office in early 1977, he made it known that he did not feel compelled to refrain from using the parole authority but he did express a preference for new refugee legislation.[23]

Events in Southeast Asia forced upon the United States the initiation of policy measures that could only respond to what was already happening. As Communist governments took complete control of Vietnam, Laos, and Kampuchea, a massive number of refugees fled or were forced out of these countries. It is estimated that between 1975 and 1979 a total of 1.2 million persons from these three nations became refugees. The largest number fled in early 1979. The reasons for this human outflow varied—fear of political persecution, the ongoing warfare between different Communist factions, massive human rights abuses, famine, and even the forced expulsion of hundreds of thousands of ethnic Chinese from Vietnam on makeshift boats and decrepit ships. At its height in mid-1979, the mass migration out of these countries of origin averaged 58,000 persons a month.

The principal countries of first asylum for these refugees were Thailand, Malaysia, Indonesia, and Hong Kong. None of these nations had a policy that permitted refugees to immigrate on any basis other than individual circumstance. All four—as well as other nations throughout Asia—expressed great distaste when the suggestion was made that they provide settlement opportunities for significant numbers of the Indochinese refugees. On numerous occasions boatloads of persons were pushed off shore or towed back out to sea by countries that feared that if they allowed the refugees to disembark, they would not be able to get rid of them. Between January and October 1979 the United Nations estimated that 17,000 refugees on boats had been denied entry by at least one nation. Because most of the boats were only marginally seaworthy to begin with and all were dangerously overcrowded, it is likely that some boats sank at sea, taking their human cargoes down with them. Other boats were viciously attacked and plundered by pirates on the open sea. The willingness of some countries—especially Thailand—to continue to be nations of "first instance" was predicated upon the willingness of other countries to become nations of ultimate destination in subsequent relocation efforts.

In this context President Jimmy Carter announced that he would use the parole authority to accommodate a substantial portion of the flow in excess of those permitted to enter under the nation's existing refugee preference category. On April 13, 1979, the U.S. attorney general authorized the parole admission of 40,000 Indochinese refugees over the next six months. In July 1979, it was announced that an additional 14,000 Indochinese refugees a month—or a total of 210,000 such refugees—would be admitted under the parole authority between July 1, 1979, and September 30, 1980.

Besides the massive refugee flows from Cuba and Indochina in the 1970s, events elsewhere in the world resulted in the creation of either new or expanded flows of refugees. It was clear by this time that the prevailing immigration laws of the United States "were totally inadequate as the basis for a fair and coherent refugee policy."[24] The apparent aimlessness of the nation's refugee policy, together with the growing problem of illegal immigration, gave the impression that other countries had more to say about the immigration policy of the nation than did the United States itself. In this context both the president and Congress finally agreed that a new refugee policy had to be formulated.

ADJUSTMENT OF STATUS

Because only those refugees who were admitted to the United States under the preference system were automatically eligible to become immigrants after a two-year residency period, special legislation was required to grant immigrant status to all those persons who were admitted under the parole authority. The parole authority had originally been intended to apply only to individuals. With the extension of this authority to massive number of refugees, however, individual admission requirements would have caused lengthy waiting periods during which the persons involved would have been in limbo while waiting for a visa slot to open. During such an interval, they could not have worked, and they would not have been eligible for most assistance services. Hence, special legislation was separately enacted for the Hungarians, the Cubans, and the Indochinese, as well as for smaller groups that have not been discussed here. These enactments permitted these groups of refugees to become permanent-resident aliens outside the normal immigration channels.

The Refugee Act of 1980

By the end of the 1970s, "a general consensus had developed" that the prevailing provisions of the Immigration Act of 1965 "were totally inadequate as the basis for a fair and coherent refugee policy."[25] Thus, a new bill was drafted in Congress in 1979 that sought to rectify the situation. Testifying in favor of the pending bill, U.S. Coordinator for Refugee Affairs Dick Clark stated:

> Until now we have carried out our refugee programs through what is essentially a patchwork of different programs that evolved in response to specific crises. The resulting framework is inadequate to cope with the refugee problems we face today. . . . The combination of conditional entry and parole procedures has become increasingly cumbersome and inadequate over the years. In both the Administration and Congress we have come to see the need for a comprehensive and long term policy.[26]

The bill that subsequently emerged from Congress was signed into law on March 17, 1980, by President Carter. Known as the Refugee Act of 1980, it constituted a major change in the U.S. immigration system.[27]

The act redefined the term *refugee* to include all of the criteria contained in the U.N. convention (1951) and protocol (1967) on refugees. Specifically, it defined a refugee as "any person who is outside any country of such person's nationality . . . and who is unable or unwilling to avail himself or herself to the protection of that country because of persecution or a well-founded fear of persecution on account of race, religion, nationality, membership in a particular group or political opinion." In addition, the act enlarged the definition to include persons who are within their country of nationality and who are also subject to persecution. The latter grouping—those who were "within their country of nationality"—was restricted, however, to persons who were specifically designated as refugees by the president of the United States and not self-proclaimed by the individuals themselves. Otherwise, it was felt, endless numbers of persons from groups in many nations could lay claim to refugee status. Persons who had contributed to the persecution of others were deemed ineligible to be refugees themselves.

Having broadened the definition of the term *refugee,* the critical question for immigration policymakers was how many persons to admit each year under these new terms. After extensive debate on various proposals, Congress repealed the "conditional entry" provisions of the Immigration Act of 1965 (which meant that there would no longer be a seventh preference category). As a result, the ceiling on immigrants was reduced from 290,000 to 270,000 persons. The entry of refugees since 1980 has been governed by an admissions system that is entirely separate from the preference categories of the nation's immigration statute. From 1980 to 1982 up to 50,000 refugees could be admitted each year by the president. This ceiling was considered to be "the normal flow." The number was arbitrarily selected on the basis that between 1956 and 1979 the average annual number of refugees admitted to the United States under the parole provision was 44,670. With the exception of the Indochinese refugees, the ceiling of 50,000 refugees a year would have accommodated all of the yearly refugee admissions between 1956 and 1979. The aggregate effect of the elimination of the seventh preference category and the simultaneous reduction of the worldwide immigrant ceiling to 270,000 was that with the addition of up to 50,000 refugees a year a new total—320,000 immigrants and refugees—would be admitted each year under quotas. This new total was approximately the same as the previous aggregate total of immigrants (i.e., 290,000 quota immigrants a year, 17,400 of whom were refugees) plus the average annual number of refugees admitted as parolees between 1956 and 1979. Hence, supporters of the seemingly high refugee figure in the Refugee Act of 1980 argued that in fact "there would be no actual increase in the immigration flow as a result of the Refugee Act."[28]

President Carter had asked that the law allow the president to admit refugees in excess of the 50,000 ceiling if world events seemed to dictate such a course. To do so, however, the president would have had to specify the additional number of refugees to be admitted in advance of the beginning of the next fiscal year and after consultation with Congress. Fearing that the proposal was too open-ended as to what the ultimate number of refugees would be, Congress included in the act a "sunset" provision that abolished the 50,000 normal flow at the end of fiscal year 1982. The legislation also stipulated that as of October 1, 1982, the president would be required to state in advance the total number of refugees he wished to admit and that he must consult with Congress through "personal contact" with specifically designated representatives as to the appropriateness of the requested number. Congress, in turn, was required to hold hearings on the number. In addition, the bill required that the president assign geographic allocations to refugees from different parts of the world in order that no one group could use all the available visa slots. It is important to note that these assigned figures are ceilings. They are not goals. Consequently, there is no obligation to reach the totals. In fact, the refugee program is administered in such a way as to be deemed satisfactory if the ceilings are not achieved, for "the underlying principle is that refugee admissions is an exceptional *ex gratia* act provided by the United States in furthering foreign and humanitarian policies."[29] Accompanying the numerical recommendations there is a requirement that the president simultaneously submit an analysis of the anticipated economic and social impact of the number of refugees he wishes to admit as well as detailed plans for their resettlement and the cost of such plans.

In compliance with these provisions, President Carter notified Congress in September 1980 that he intended to admit 217,000 refugees during fiscal year 1981. Of this total, 50,000 refugees were to be admitted under the "normal flow" provisions of the act while an additional 167,000 refugees were to be admitted as an emergency humanitarian gesture. President Carter also proposed continuing the practice of admitting 14,000 Indochinese immigrants a month. This meant that of the 217,000 refugees admitted, 168,000 would be Indochinese.

For fiscal year 1982 the Reagan administration asked for permission to admit a total of 140,000 refugees. The geographic allocation of the proposed admissions is shown in Table 26. Table 26 also shows that the actual number of refugees admitted during fiscal year 1982 totaled 99,200, or 40,800 below the authorized ceiling for that year. One explanation for the lower number of admissions was that the level of admissions from East Asia was significantly below what had been anticipated. In part this was due to the fact that a new coalition of leaders was formed in 1982 by exiled Cambodian forces that included Norodom Sihanouk. Sihanouk pledged to lead his people back home to the territory occupied by Vietnamese troops.[30] The decline in the number of Indochinese refugee admissions also reflected the fact that in 1982 the Reagan administration tightened some of the admissions regulations in such a way as to block the entry of persons from this region who did not have family or other ties to the United States. Faced with the dreary conditions that existed in the refugee camps in Thailand and having only a bleak chance of being accepted elsewhere, many persons without such ties apparently began to drift back into Kampuchea.[31] Aside from the reduction in the number of East Asian refugees, new controls

TABLE 26. PROPOSED CEILINGS AND ACTUAL REFUGEE ADMISSIONS
TO THE UNITED STATES DURING FISCAL YEAR 1982 AND
FISCAL YEAR 1983 BY AREA OF ORIGIN

Area of Origin	Fiscal Year 1982		Fiscal Year 1983	
	Proposed Ceiling[a]	Refugee Admissions	Proposed Ceiling	Refugee Admissions
Africa	3,500	3,500	3,000	2,643
East Asia	96,000	75,000	68,000	51,476
Eastern Europe and the Soviet Union	31,000	14,000	17,000	13,382
Latin America and the Caribbean	3,000	700	2,000	715
Near East and South Asia	6,500	6,000	8,000	5,435
Total	140,000	99,200	98,000	73,651

Source: The data for 1982 are from U.S. Department of State, Office of the U.S. Coordinator for Refugee Affairs, "Proposed Refugee Admissions and Allocations for Fiscal Year 1983" (Washington, D.C., 1983, mimeographed), p. 11. The data for 1983 were supplied by telephone by the U.S. Immigration and Naturalization Service, Office of Public Relations, March 20, 1984.

[a]These figures were slightly revised during the course of the fiscal year from the original ceilings. The total was not affected by these changes, however, for increases in some figures were offset by decreases in others.

imposed by the Soviet Union on emigration during 1982 resulted in fewer Soviet Jews' and Armenians' being permitted to leave the U.S.S.R., and thus the refugee ceiling for that nation was not achieved either. Finally, the number of refugees admitted from Latin America also was significantly below the authorized ceiling for that region.

Similarly, the Reagan administration recommended a ceiling of 98,000 refugees for fiscal year 1983. As shown in Table 26, the strongest geographic category continued to be East Asia. The number of refugees actually admitted was 73,651. The explanations for the shortfall in 1983 are the same as those for 1982.

Likewise, prior to the beginning of fiscal year 1984, the Reagan administration proposed a ceiling of 72,000 refugees. The geographic distribution of these proposed admissions is shown in Table 27.

The Refugee Act of 1980 specified that all refugees who were admitted to the United States would be allowed to adjust their status to that of permanent-resident aliens after one year. This change cut in half the two-year waiting period that had been imposed for the various ad hoc refugee admission programs enacted since the 1950s.

Having enacted what it believed was a more flexible admissions procedure for accommodating massive numbers of refugees, Congress sought assurances that the parole authority of the attorney general would be used only as it had originally been intended—for individual emergency cases. Thus an amendment was

TABLE 27. PROPOSED CEILINGS FOR REFUGEE ADMISSIONS FOR FISCAL YEAR
1984 BY AREA OF ORIGIN

Area of Origin	Proposed Ceiling
Africa	3,000
East Asia	50,000
East Europe and the Soviet Union	12,000
Latin America and the Caribbean	1,000
Near East and South Asia	6,000
Total	72,000

Source: "U.S. Sets New Limits on Refugees," *New York Times,* September 27, 1983, p. A-3.

added to the statute. After May 15, 1980, the attorney general would be forbidden to use the parole authority to admit refugees unless a "compelling reason" that was in "the public interest" with respect to a particular individual dictated that this person be admitted as a parolee rather than as a refugee.

A SPECIAL CASE: ASYLUM

Prior to passage of the Refugee Act of 1980 the immigration statutes of the United States contained no specific provision for granting asylum to individuals who were already in the United States and who feared they would be persecuted if they returned to their homeland. U.S. aid to refugees was restricted to persons who were temporarily residing in some other nation of "first instance" after fleeing their homeland. Thus, refugees could be screened with respect to their eligibility for admission before being physically admitted to the United States. The only existing authority that came close to being an asylum policy was a section in the Immigration and Nationality Act of 1952 that allowed the U.S. attorney general to block the deportation of an alien who was already in the United States if he believed that the alien would be subject to persecution on the basis of race, religion, or political opinion if he or she were be forced to return home.

The Refugee Act of 1980 instituted a new procedure for handling asylum requests. It authorized the attorney general to grant asylum to an alien who was already in the United States if the individual applied for asylum and if the attorney general determined that the individual could be classified as a refugee. The asylee status could be revoked at a later time if it was determined that the conditions in the alien's homeland had changed such that the status was no longer warranted. Of the 50,000 persons who were to be admitted annually under the original terms of the act, up to 5,000 could be asylees.

As events within a month after passage of the act would vividly demonstrate, however, the asylum section was the weakest aspect of the legislation. Clearly the implications of these provisions had not been thought through. In 1980, 5,800 applications for asylum were filed, but by early 1984 the number of asylee applications pending had skyrocketed to 170,000.

The Cuban Crisis of 1980

The president's signature on the Refugee Act of 1980 had hardly dried when events in the Caribbean essentially abrogated its provisions. As usual, the legislation had been formulated on the basis of past circumstances and experiences. The possibility that the United States itself might become a country of "first instance" for massive numbers of persons—all arriving within a very short period of time and all claiming asylum—had never been contemplated. This, however, was precisely what happened between late April and the middle of June 1980.

During the late 1970s the two major agricultural crops of Cuba—sugar cane and tobacco—sustained serious production shortfalls. There were also signs that the Cuban government was having difficulty providing sufficient economic and educational opportunities for the nation's young people. The result was "a rising tide of restlessness and dissatisfaction, particularly among those Cubans with relatives in the United States."[32] Beginning in 1979 the Peruvian and Venezuelan embassies in Havana were confronted by numerous Cubans seeking asylum. In the early months of 1980 several violent incidents occurred. Some involved the asylum-seekers' use of trucks and buses to crash through the gates of these embassies despite the presence of armed Cuban guards there. In early April a Cuban guard was shot and killed in one of these attempts. Protesting the Peruvian officials' willingness to grant asylum to persons who made it onto the grounds of their embassy, Premier Castro on April 4, 1980, ordered that the Cuban guards be removed from the embassy gates. He also announced that anyone in Cuba who wished to seek a Peruvian visa could do so and leave Cuba. Within the next few days 10,000 persons crowded onto the grounds of the embassy. Health and feeding conditions deteriorated rapidly. It was unlikely that Peru would be able to resettle all the persons who were seeking asylum and it was unclear exactly how many more might ultimately request such a move. The government of Costa Rica indicated that it was willing to serve as a temporary way station for some of these persons until an international relocation effort could be organized. President Carter indicated that under the terms of the Refugee Act of 1980 the United States would accept 3,500 of the refugees from the Peruvian Embassy as its part of an envisioned international cooperative movement. Eight other nations agreed to accept the remaining 6,750 refugees. Beginning on April 14, 1980, flights from Cuba to Costa Rica transported an average of 1,000 persons a day for five days. When the planes landed in Costa Rica, they became the center of worldwide publicity, which created a disparaging image of contemporary life in Cuba. On April 18, 1980, the Cuban government suddenly suspended refugee flights.

On April 20, 1980, Premier Castro announced on radio that all Cubans who wished to emigrate to the United States were free to board boats at the port city of Mariel, about 20 miles from Havana, and go.

Within hours of the broadcast, which was received in southern Florida, a flotilla of boats of all descriptions began to stream toward Mariel from Florida, and on April 21 the first boat returned to Key West. Many of the persons who left Cuba were relatives of persons already in the United States, but it was also the case that "a deliberate policy of forcing acceptance of several non-relatives for every relative on board" was also in effect.[33] Some of these nonrelatives were persons who had fled to the Peruvian Embassy, but others—including convicted criminals—came from a variety of state-run institutions. The number of Cuban refugees soon soared, from several hundred a day in late April to over a thousand a day by early May.

On May 5, 1980, in a speech before the League of Women Voters, President Carter stated: "Ours is a nation of refugees. We will continue to provide an open heart and open arms to refugees seeking freedom from Communist domination brought by Cuba."[34] The next day, however, responding to a request by the governor of Florida, the president declared that "a state of emergency" existed in southern Florida. Accordingly, the area received federal assistance to defray some of the costs of accommodating the influx of refugees. By May 9, 1980, 30,127 persons had arrived in southern Florida and the massive scale of the movement was finally recognized. Moreover, the dangers of overcrowding, as well as the lack of sufficient safeguards on what were essentially pleasure boats designed for families, became apparent. Thus, on May 14, 1980, President Carter moved to halt the sealift. Ostensibly, his reason for this seeming reversal in attitude was that he wanted to find a better and safer way of conducting the transfer. No doubt the request was also an effort to reduce the size of the flow and to allow the government time to develop an appropriate policy of accommodation and seek international assistance in distributing the people to other nations as well. On May 8 and 9, an international conference had convened hastily in San José, Costa Rica. At that meeting eighteen nations had agreed to accept some of the Cubans, but none had agreed to take more than a few hundred persons.[35] Thus, the burden of trying to stop the flow of refugees as well as to accommodate the Cubans who were already ashore fell largely upon the United States.

Technically speaking, the Cubans who were boatlifted to southern Florida were illegal immigrants and the citizens who conveyed them were "smugglers." The Carter administration did not treat the Cubans as illegal aliens, however, and initially no action was taken against those who transported them. Indeed, the INS immediately accepted these Cubans' applications for a status classification, granted them visas, and authorized them to work. Deciding what status to assign to the Cubans, however, proved to be very difficult. The administration declined to classify all of them as refugees. They were already in the United States, and the administration wanted to avoid setting a precedent that might lead persons from other countries in the world to think that they could simply enter the United States without documents and claim to be refugees.[36] Thus the initial 3,500 persons who had been at the Peruvian Embassy and entered the United States by way of Costa Rica, where they were screened for eligibility, were classified *as a group* as refugees. But those who had come directly to Florida from Cuba by boat were classified as "applicants for asylum" rather than as refugees. The same policy was applied to the Haitians, who also were streaming in on boats during this period. The Refugee Act of 1980 had provided for the assignment of asylee status to persons already in the United States, but the use of that classification had been intended for individuals, not for massive groups of persons. Declaring the flotilla Cubans and Haitians to be "applicants for asylum" meant that each would have to be interviewed individually to determine his or her eligibility for asylee status. The situation in May 1980 was deemed by the administration to be "a very special emergency situation."[37]

Meanwhile the Carter administration continued to be unsuccessful in its efforts to arrange for U.S. officials to interview persons in Cuba to determine their eligibility for refugee status (as had been permitted during the "freedom flight" era, 1965–1973) or to arrange for an orderly process that might regularize the flow. Thus, the "freedom flotilla" continued despite efforts that began in mid-May to crack down on those who were providing the transportation. The U.S. government's efforts included impounding the private boats that were being used as well as levying a $1,000-per-person fine against the captains of the boats. By mid-June the deterrents imposed by the U.S. government as well as a change in the attitude of the Cuban government toward the exodus resulted in a sharp reduction in the number of Cubans who reached the United States. The total number of arrivals as of that date was close to 123,000. Almost 3,000 persons a month continued to escape until September 1980, when the flow ceased. Thus, more than 130,000 Cubans were involved in the flotilla movement. This number constituted about 1.5 percent of the entire population of Cuba at that time.

On June 20, 1980, the U.S. attorney general established a new temporary status, "Cuban-Haitian Entrant (Status Pending)," for the boatlift refugees who had arrived by that date and issued them a temporary six-month parole into the United States. Eligibility for this status was later extended to all persons who had arrived as of October 10, 1980. During this interval the administration sought to have Congress give statutory basis to this emergency classification, but Congress declined to do so. On January 15, 1981, before leaving office, Attorney General Civiletti extended the parole status of these refugees for an additional six months, to July 15, 1981. The Reagan administration subsequently proposed that all such persons who were found to be eligible for admission be given a "renewable term entrant" status. This status could be renewed after three years, and after five years such persons could apply to become permanent-resident aliens.[38] No congressional action was taken on this proposal, however. What to do with those who were found to be ineligible for admission—about 3,000 persons as of mid-1982—remained an open question because Cuba refused to allow any of its citizens who had left the country to return. As of May 1983, 1,024 of these Cubans were still being held in detention centers or prisons, 100 were in mental institutions, and 1,520 had been released from detention but had been judged unfit to become permanent residents of the United States. Accordingly, the Reagan administration directed that Cuba accept 789 of these people immediately (and others later), but to date there has been no sign that Cuba would agree to this.[39] Lawyers for these Cubans, however, had indicated that they plan to appeal any such deportation order on the grounds that the deportees would be subject to persecution if they returned to Cuba.[40] Thus, even if Cuba should relent, the question of what to do with the Cubans who have been found to be ineligible for immigration or refugee status in the United States will remain.

The Simpson-Mazzoli bill would permit all Cubans and Haitians who entered the United States in 1980 and 1981 and who are still residing in this country to adjust their status to that of permanent-resident aliens. Thus, passage of this legislation would end the uncertainty that has plagued this particular issue since it arose, even though it would hardly serve as a permanent solution to the policy problem that the broader issue of refugee admissions has raised. Yet in early 1984 the fate of the Simpson-Mazzoli bill remained uncertain, and the status of these refugees became the subject of a series of controversial political ploys. In early February 1984 the Reagan administration announced that it planned to offer to the Cubans whose status was still pending the opportunity to become permanent-resident aliens but that it would not do this for the similarly situated Haitians.[41] It was later revealed that INS officials and Department of Justice lawyers had concluded that the Cuban Adjustment Act of 1966 was applicable only to the Cubans who entered during the Mariel boatlift era, and that none of the act's provisions could be extended to the Haitians. A number of Cubans had already filed lawsuits to adjust their status, but the INS had not acted on them because the provisions of the pending Simpson-Mazzoli bill would make such action unnecessary. Whether the Reagan administration actually has the power to extend resident-alien status to the Cubans while denying it to the Haitians is open to question, for it was generally assumed that the Refugee Act of 1980 superseded the refugee adjustment processes of earlier legislation.

The Reagan administration's announcement was immediately labeled a political gambit designed to gain favor with Cuban voters (though not with the Cubans whose status would be changed, since resident aliens cannot vote). Congressman Peter W. Rodino, chairman of the Judiciary Committee of the House of Representatives, charged that any attempt to treat the Cubans and the Haitians differently would "violate fundamental fairness."[42] Accordingly, Rodino introduced a bill that would provide the identical opportunities to the Haitians who have been included in the special "Cuban-Haitian entrant (status pending)" category. Rodino claimed that such a measure was necessary to avoid divisiveness between Cubans and Haitians in the Miami area, where both groups have clustered.[43]

Under the Simpson-Mazzoli bill that passed the Senate in 1983, the Cuban Adjustment Act of 1966 would be repealed and all Cubans and Haitians who had entered in 1980 and 1981 would be treated the same as persons who were eligible for the amnesty provisions of the bill. Under the June 1984 House version of the bill, however, the Cuban Adjustment Act would be unequivocally restored for all past and future refugees from Cuba. Adjustment would also be permitted to all Haitians who had entered in 1980 and 1981. This would mean that all persons covered by these provisions would be immediately eligible for all the federal assistance programs that are available to refugees and that therefore they would be exempted from the general ban against benefit eligibility that applies to all other persons who are granted amnesty under the bill.

It should be noted that these adjustment programs, if carried through, would not affect the status of the Cubans who are still being held in a federal prison in Atlanta and those who have been released but who belong to classes of persons who are ineligible for U.S. citizenship. Since Cuba still refused to allow them to return home, their fate would remain in limbo.

Distinguishing between Political and Economic Motivations

One of the most perplexing dimensions of refugee and asylee policy has been the determination of U.S. policymakers to distinguish between the political and economic motivations of the persons involved. Both the United States and the United Nations define refugees and asylees as persons fleeing from political persecution. Neither includes economic motivations within this definition. The issue, in fact, did not arise prior to the late 1970s. The Hungarians, Chinese, Cubans, as well as most refugees from Indochina, were perceived to be political refugees. But then circumstances began to change.

THE INDOCHINESE: POLICY EQUIVOCATION

Prior to passage of the Refugee Act of 1980, there was no need to determine the motivation of refugees from Indochina—fleeing from Communist countries was considered grounds for automatic admission to the United States. But after passage of this legislation, the admission of such refugees was no longer automatic. An effort was initiated to apply the new definition of *refugee*. By mid-1981, through its screening of the persons who remained in the refugee camps of Southeast Asia, the INS had determined that about 16 percent (or about 30,000 persons) had fled Vietnam, Laos, or Kampuchea for economic reasons rather than for fear of political persecution. These persons had been "deferred" from admission to the United States. As a result, the government of Thailand (the country where most of these refugees had accumulated) threatened to cease receiving any refugees at all if the United States rescinded its implied agreement to admit them. In light of this threat, the U.S. Department of State intervened and claimed that the INS's effort to distinguish between economic and political refugees constituted "a fundamental change in our Indochinese refugee policy."

Secretary of State Alexander Haig stated that this change in policy had "political and foreign policy implications" and that

> at its heart, the issue revolves around the nature of the Indochinese regimes. These regimes are, by policy and practice, totalitarian and revolutionary. They seek totally to reorganize society, disenfrancising whole classes of citizenry. Their definition of loyalty is unquestioning adherence to the policies, edicts, and procedures laid down by the state. It is to such totalitarian states and the kind of punishment that they mete out that we doom people to return, if we accept and carry to its logical consequences the INS action. In my view, this Administration does not wish to be seen as contributing to the creation of that kind of tragedy.[44]

Attorney General William French Smith agreed with Haig's views and ordered the INS to reverse its efforts to determine the motivations of Indochinese refugees. He noted: "We now concur, that persons coming out of Vietnam, Laos, and Cambodia and processed by the Department of State . . . are presumed to be refugees by INS and therefore admissible to the United States."[45] The only exceptions would be individual Indochinese who were found to belong to an excludable class of persons under the nation's basic immigration statutes. This policy led to charges of favoritism. As a result, the Reagan administration announced a year later that as of April 30, 1982, Indochinese refugees would be subject to the identical procedures applied to all other refugees. By then, of course, the number of refugees fleeing to Thailand had declined substantially from previous levels.

THE CUBANS: DENIAL OF A DISTINCTION

As noted earlier, the Mariel boatlift brought more than 130,000 Cubans to the United States in the six months following enactment of the Refugee Act of 1980. In the process of reviewing the individual situations of the Cubans who were seeking classification as asylees, the issue of motivation naturally arose. Over the years the position of the Justice Department has consistently been that Cuban refugees are motivated by fear of political persecution and the desire for family reunification. This position was typified by the following exchange between the attorney general and a member of the Senate Judiciary Committee in September 1980:

> *Senator Thurmond:* "I believe there are 125,000 Cubans that have come here."
> *Mr. Civiletti:* "That is about right."
> *Senator Thurmond:* "Don't you think that most of those people really came to improve their economic situation?"
> *Mr. Civiletti:* "I do not know but I do not think so. I think they had other motives."[46]

The fact is that no serious effort has ever been made to apply the "economic versus political refugee" distinction to Cubans. Since Cuba to date has refused to allow persons who left to return, the issue is not really moot. The only alternative to allowing them to stay, should the United States try to apply this distinction to Cubans, would be to attempt to resettle in other nations any Cubans already in the United States who have been classified as economic refugees.

THE HAITIANS: APPLICATION OF A PRINCIPLE

It is to Haitians that the definition "economic refugees" has been applied in earnest. As mentioned in Chapter 5, Haiti is regarded as a major source of illegal immigrants to the United States. During the Mariel boatlift of 1980 a number of boatloads of Haitians arrived with those from Cuba. Since Cuba and Haiti are neighboring islands and both have long been ruled by dictators—one representing the political left and the other the political right—it was unavoidable that comparisons of the treatment of persons fleeing from each would be made. Successive U.S. administrations have consistently contended that Haitians are illegal immigrants while Cubans are refugees and asylees. This difference in treatment has caused countless legal and political difficulties. It has also evoked charges of racism because the Cubans have tended to be white while the Haitians are black.

To gain perspective on this issue, it is necessary to examine briefly the history of U.S. relations with Haiti. Occupying the western third of Hispaniola, the Republic of Haiti was the second nation in the Western Hemisphere (the United States was first) to gain independence from colonial domination. After securing its independence from France in 1804, Haiti experienced years of government turmoil, however. Efforts were repeatedly made by various internal political factions to take control of the country. Assassinations of political leaders were frequent. In the early twentieth century, U.S. business interests began to invest heavily in the country. It was also the case that Haiti occupied a strategic position relative to one of the key approaches to the newly opened Panama Canal. Hence, for a variety of reasons, the United States sent its marines to occupy the country in 1915 just prior to its entry into World War I. The marines remained until 1934. During this period a treaty was signed that gave the United States complete control over Haiti's financial and political affairs. Also during this interval the minority mulatto elite, which comprises only about 5 percent of the Haitian population, gained political control of the country, a control which it has never relinquished. The U.S. Marines introduced forced physical labor for the construction of public facilities during their stay in Haiti. After the withdrawal of the marines in 1934, the United States maintained direct financial control over Haitian affairs until 1941 and indirect control until 1947. In September 1957, after a number of governments had come and gone, François Duvalier ("Papa Doc") was elected president. The next year, in the aftermath of an unsuccessful coup to oust him, Duvalier organized the Tontons Macoutes, an extralegal terrorist squad, to squelch opposition to his regime. Soon thereafter he had himself elected "president for life." His rule was harsh. Upon his death in 1971 he was succeeded by his nineteen-year-old son, Jean-Claude ("Baby

Doc'') Duvalier, who also was designated president for life. Soon after taking office, the new president announced that there would be some liberalization with respect to the government's human rights practices, but apparently little real change occurred.[47] It is also alleged that the new Haitian administration turned its efforts to securing domination of the political affairs of the rural areas of the country, where about 80 percent of the population lives; historically, political control had been exercised primarily in the nation's urban areas. As a result of the repression that ensued, illegal immigration to the United States began in 1972 and has continued ever since. It is an 800-mile boat trip across open ocean from Haiti to southern Florida.

The moment the first boatload of Haitians arrived on the coast of Florida on December 12, 1972, the issue of whether Haitians were to be treated differently from Cubans was raised. An editorial in the *Miami News* on December 15, 1972, stated prophetically:

> A moment of truth has arrived for our local immigration officials who so casually go about their almost daily task of processing Cuban citizens landing in South Florida after having escaped the Castro regime. Should the procedure be any different for the dark-skinned Haitians? The action taken in this case will be watched by people across the country and even the world. . . . To refuse the pending request of the dark-skinned Haitians would be racism and surely our government is not racist or is it?[48]

The initial response of the INS to the Haitians' arrival was to declare that they were illegal immigrants and that they were not entitled to refugee status. Acknowledging that Haiti was the "poorest country in the Western Hemisphere," the Department of Justice and the Department of State nevertheless held that the Haitians were fleeing from poverty and not from the threat of political persecution. According to their reasoning, being poor (per capita income in Haiti was only $275 in 1980) did not entitle an individual to be admitted to another nation. Economic refugees are not sanctioned under any U.S. immigration statute. Moreover, these agencies argued, the Haitian government—unlike Cuba—was willing to take back any persons the INS decided to deport.

Since 1972 a policy debate has raged over the distinction between political and economic refugees from Haiti. The Haitian government has consistently been judged to be repressive by a wide range of international organizations, including the Inter-American Commission on Human Rights of the Organization of American States, the Lawyers Committee for International Rights, and a number of religious and citizens groups.[49] Yet in 1979 a U.S. Department of State study team concluded that "most Haitian migrants come to the U.S. drawn by the prospect of economic opportunity and are not fleeing political persecution."[50] The following is an excerpt from its report:

> One must also express some admiration for those willing to brave the substantial risks of a long voyage in a small boat in order to improve their lot and that of their families. In today's world, however, immigration doors are not open to all would-be immigrants, and economic motives, however admirable, do not

translate into a right under the Protocol to asylum. Barring a legislative change, individuals in these circumstances are not entitled to remain in the U.S. as refugees.[51]

The study team did acknowledge that "some who leave Haiti might very well establish that their fear of political persecution is well founded," but it noted that a "close examination of the facts in each case" would be required before such a distinction could be made. In 1983 W. Scott Burke, director of the asylum program for the U.S. State Department, reaffirmed this position: "My view is that most who leave Haiti do so for economic reasons and have never been attacked for political reasons. I would want to escape too. I'd probably hop on a boat too. But that doesn't mean I'd have a fear of persecution."[52]

Spokesmen and lawyers for the Haitians contend that it is impossible to distinguish between political and economic motivations for leaving Haiti because there are laws on the books in Haiti that prohibit citizens from complaining about economic problems. They argue that the oppressive political system of the country creates economic refugees. According to their reasoning, human rights abuses are one of the "push" factors that lead to massive out-migration from a country.

In the years following 1972 several hundred Haitians were returned to their homeland through the use of the voluntary departure and formal exclusion proceedings of the INS. The majority of the Haitians who entered the United States, however, have used this nation's legal system to challenge the INS's efforts to treat them as illegal immigrants. By the early 1980s, for instance, 15,000 cases of Haitians claiming to be political refugees were pending in Miami alone and only about 50 Haitians had been granted that status.[53] The Carter administration refused to exercise its parole authority for Haitians as a group. The only alternative, therefore, was for the INS to use the case-by-case approach, which opened the way for the Haitians to seek judicial review and appeal. That option has generally been exercised, and as a result the individuals involved have remained in the United States during the lengthy appeal process.

During the five-month Mariel boatlift, a number of boatloads of Haitians seeking admission to the United States also arrived. The Carter administration decided to treat the Cubans and Haitians who arrived during this period identically.[54] Namely, as stipulated in the asylum provisions of the Refugee Act of 1980 the case of each individual would be reviewed to determine whether the threat of political persecution actually existed. Haitians who entered the country between April 22 and October 10, 1980, were included in the administration's request for a special, one-time "Cuban-Haitian Entrant (Status Pending)" classification, which would have permitted them to enter through channels outside the normal immigration system (though, unlike the Cubans, the Haitians would have had to prove that they would be subject to persecution if they returned to their homeland). The administration's request was denied, however, and the 6,000 Haitians who entered during that period joined the ranks of their countrymen who were awaiting the disposition of their individual cases. In most instances, negative decisions in these cases were appealed.

The Reagan administration, in addition to continuing the effort to secure special legislation to adjust the status of the Cubans and the Haitians (i.e., those who were successful in their claim for asylum), initiated a controversial policy of deterrence to prevent more Haitians from immigrating illegally. In the fall of 1981 the U.S. Coast Guard was ordered to begin interdicting refugee boats on the high seas and to turn them back before the Haitians could actually touch U.S. soil and lay claim to being asylees. The Department of Justice adopted a policy of sending apprehended Haitians to various detention camps around the country instead of keeping them in Florida to await their hearings. These initiatives, together with the widespread publicity given in Haiti to the drowning of thirty-three Haitians whose boat sank off the coast of Florida on October 26, 1981, contributed to a sharp decline in the number of Haitian immigrants by the end of 1981.[55]

Another feature of the Reagan administration's policy of deterrence was its decision in May 1981 to hold all Haitians who subsequently arrived illegally in the United States in detention centers. They would no longer be released to private sponsors—churches, community groups, or individuals—while their cases were pending. Subsequently, a federal court in Florida ruled that each of the individuals for whom hearings were held by the INS had to be represented by a lawyer. As a result of this decision and the tendency of lawyers to appeal all adverse decisions affecting their clients, the length of time that these Haitians spent in detention camps tended to increase. By mid-1982 there were 2,025 Haitians in such centers.[56] This practice aroused bitterness among the Haitians as well as among individuals and groups who sympathized with their cause. It was described as racist and discriminatory against Haitians, and the entire detention policy became the topic of yet another court case.[57]

The Department of Justice repeatedly denied the charges that the detention policy was discriminatory and racist. It argued that Haitians were treated "specially" (but not discriminatorily) because they were economic refugees and therefore were illegal immigrants, not political refugees. Attorney General Smith announced that the Haitians could leave the detention centers "any time they want to—all they have to do is go home."[58]

Anticipating that the policy of holding Haitians in detention centers would not be upheld in the aforementioned court challenge, the Reagan administration on June 14, 1982, reversed itself.[59] On that day Attorney General Smith issued new guidelines to the INS that would allow Haitians to be paroled if they were represented by an individual lawyer, if they had a "responsible sponsor," and if assurances could be made that the individual would appear at exclusionary hearings when they were scheduled. Acceptable assurances included a pledge by relatives or by persons of long-standing residence in the community or the posting of a reasonable bond. The question of "reasonable bond," however, was cause for concern among the lawyers and community supporters of the Haitians.

Moreover, except for the bonding requirement, the "new" policy was essentially a return to the old policy that existed prior to May 1981. Government officials complained that this earlier policy had been "abused" and had led to "more, not less illegal immigration."[60] For this reason they pledged that the "new" policy would be monitored and that if the Haitians did not appear at their exclusionary hearings, the policy would be rescinded.

As it turned out, the court did rule against the Reagan administration's policy of holding Haitians in detention camps, but the decision was very narrowly drawn. The ruling issued by the federal district court on June 18, 1982, was made on purely procedural grounds.[61] To the dismay of supporters of the Haitians' cause, the court ruled that the policy was not discriminatory in its implementation. Moreover, the Haitians who had not yet had a hearing were to be eligible for parole only because under the Federal Administrative Procedure Act of 1946 a federal agency is prohibited from adopting any substantive rule unless it first gives notice and provides the opportunity for interested persons to comment on the proposed rule. Because these procedures had not been strictly adhered to, the court ruled that the Haitians should not have been denied the right of being released to sponsors pending the outcome of their hearings. With regard to the controversial issue of race discrimination, the court found that the contention was without merit. Specifically, it stated:

> The evidence shows that the detention was not directed at the plaintiffs because they were black and/or Haitians but because they were excludable aliens unable to establish a *prima facie* claim for admission and that non-Haitians were detained pursuant to this policy as well. The mere fact that more Haitians were detained and kept in detention for longer periods than aliens of other nationalities does not render the policy discriminatory.[62]

Neither side was satisfied with the court's decision. The Haitians had won a temporary reprieve from detention, but the ruling had been based on only a procedural flaw. The government had lost the case, but it had not been found to be acting in a discriminatory manner.

Because of the importance attributed to this legal encounter, and in conjunction with an affidavit filed by the governor of Florida claiming that between 20,000 and 40,000 Haitians were poised in the Bahamas for possible flight to Florida to claim asylum, the U.S. Department of Justice sought a stay of the order to release the Haitians. On July 13, 1982, a three-judge panel of the U.S. Court of Appeals for the Eleventh Circuit denied the request.[63] Subsequently, the government decided not to carry its appeal of this denial to the Supreme Court.[64] It did, however, decide to appeal the original district court decision. On July 23, 1982, the first two Haitians who had been detained were released. Simultaneously, the Justice Department reaffirmed its intention to detain persons who entered the country illegally in the future and it announced that new rules had been enacted to correct the procedural flaw that had been the basis of the district court's decision. As a spokesman for the department noted, "The day of just coming into this country and getting-in whether you have a right to be here or not is over."[65] With respect to Haitians, he stated:

> There is no civil strife going on in Haiti that I know of. Haiti may be poorer than some of the other Latin American countries but it is not a situation of tremendous political foment.
> They are coming for sympathetic reasons. They are poor. However, I fear that if you open the political asylum process to those with only an economic claim, you are going to swallow up political asylum because two-thirds of the world would have a valid economic claim to come to this country.[66]

The Justice Department also claimed that it had been assured by the Haitian government that returnees would not be harmed.

By late August 1982, however, less than half of the Haitians who had been held in detention centers had been released. Difficulty in finding sponsors was cited as the reason for the delay. Lawyers for the detainees again sought a hearing to consider whether "the spirit" of the initial order was being followed. Several of those who had been released had subsequently been returned to detention for failing to report to sponsors as scheduled or to appear at their formal asylum hearings.[67] The first Haitian among the released group to have an asylum hearing lost his claim and was ordered to leave the country, but he filed an appeal, which under existing U.S. court procedures could take years to complete.[68] Such was the pattern in most subsequent asylum hearings. By the early fall of 1982 all the Haitians who had been held in detention camps had been released. Their petitions for asylum brought the total number of Haitian asylum requests pending in the court system at that time to 5,200. In the spring of 1983 two more boatloads of Haitians landed on the coast of Florida. They were the first such arrivals since October 1981 and may portend a renewal of this pattern.

Despite having been forced to release the Haitians it had held in detention, the INS decided to appeal the court ruling against its detention policy. In the appeal the lawyers for the Haitians did not question the right of the government to detain people who entered the country without proper documents. Rather, they reiterated the claim that the INS policy was being implemented in a discriminatory manner against Haitians because of their race and national origin, which violated their Fifth Amendment rights under the U.S. Constitution. The INS denied this charge and argued that the policy of detention was meant to be applied "across the board." On April 12, 1983, in Atlanta, a three-member panel of the U.S. Court of Appeals for the Eleventh Circuit ruled in favor of the Haitians.[69] In this decision, the court ruled that "there was ample rebutted evidence that the plaintiffs [i.e., the Haitian detainees] were denied equal protection of the laws." In other words, the court ruled that the government had acted in a discriminatory manner in implementing its detention policy. The court also ruled that the detainees had not been fully informed of their rights to petition for political asylum and to have adequate legal counsel. Accordingly, the appeals court ordered that those Haitians who had been released pending hearings on their individual cases should remain free. The court order also meant that about 100 Haitians who had arrived since the others were freed and who had been held in detention were also to be freed. Moreover, the implications of this decision reach beyond the case of the Haitians. As one of the lawyers for the Haitians stated after the decision was announced, "We think this decision is going to be a landmark case in the immigration field." He went on to explain that the decision "establishes the right of the protection of the U.S. Constitution to aliens who have been incarcerated; it has substantial implications for Salvadorans, Nicaraguans—anyone who is going to the States."[70]

In September 1983, however, the federal government requested that the case be heard by the full (twelve-member) Eleventh Circuit Court of Appeals. Because of the significance of the case, the court acceded to the request, and on February 28, 1984, it issued its ruling. It reversed the earlier decision of its three-member panel.[71] The court held that nonresident aliens are not entitled to the rights granted under the U.S. Constitution but are entitled to the privileges conferred on them by Congress. In this case, the Haitians are entitled to a hearing, the advice of counsel, and a review of an exclusion order if necessary. The decision indicated that the president and the attorney general have the primary responsibility for protecting the nation's borders, while the courts are restricted to the narrow role of review. According to the ruling, nonresident aliens need not be notified by INS officials of their right to request asylum but they can challenge their treatment by these officials if they feel it is discriminatory. The appeals court asked the original district court in Miami to determine if the INS had made any of its decisions on the asylum requests of the Haitians on discriminatory grounds. This decision also applied to the Haitians who were still being held in detention centers and of course would apply to all other persons who subsequently enter the United States from any country under similar circumstances.

Responding to the circuit court ruling, the attorneys for the Haitians stated that "the appeals court decision doesn't mean anything" because it is not final.[72] They indicated that they would appeal the decision to the U.S. Supreme Court. They also expressed optimism that the legislation introduced by Congressman Rodino in 1984 to grant all Haitians and Cubans who entered prior to 1982 the status of permanent-resident aliens would be passed. Indeed, if this happens, the concerns of the individuals involved in this case will become moot, but the larger question of determining the status of refugees who entered the United States from any country *after* 1982 will remain.

Resettlement Assistance

Unlike all other legal and illegal immigrants to the United States, refugees and the communities in which they have located have benefited from a series of private and public assistance programs. The initial efforts to assist the refugees who were admitted under the various ad hoc programs of the World War II era were primarily handled by private, nonprofit, voluntary agencies. These agencies assumed responsibility for sponsoring individual refugees and for meeting their initial resettlement needs. Often, during this period, these agencies received no financial assistance from the public sector for the expenses they incurred. When the Hungarian refugee crisis arose in the 1950s, voluntary agencies were again called upon to be the primary assistance vehicles in various local U.S. communities. These private agencies have been given major credit for the rapidity and relative ease with which the Hungarians were integrated into the society and labor markets of the United States.[73] Some federal funds were made available to these agencies to help them cover the health-care and transportation expenses of the refugees. In addition, federal aid was provided to Hungarian refugees abroad. At the time, however, the authorization legislation expressly noted that this federal assistance was not intended to constitute a precedent.[74] In fact, it did.

In the case of the Cuban and Indochinese refugees of the 1960s and 1970s, the federal government expanded its practice of contracting with voluntary agencies to aid in the resettlement process. In some instances these agencies provided the services directly to the refugees; in others, the agencies helped refugees apply for the public programs that are generally available. The scale of public assistance was much more extensive for the Indochinese than for the Hungarians, the Cubans, or refugees from other nations. Assistance for the Cubans was authorized by specific sections of the Migration and Refugee Act of 1962. For the Indochinese, the Indochina Migration and Refugee Assistance Act of 1975 served this purpose.

The types of services provided to the Cubans and the Indochinese were similar. Those in need of aid who were aged, blind, or disabled were granted eligibility for the Supplemental Security Income (SSI) program financed by the federal government on the same basis as citizens. Federal funds were added to compensate any state that made supplemental income payments in excess of the minimum federal SSI level. The same procedures applied to refugees who were eligible to participate in the Aid to Families with Dependent Children (AFDC) program, which is financed jointly with federal and state funds. Full federal funding was provided for medical assistance given to needy refugees under the prevailing Medicaid program in each state. Federal aid was also provided to Indochinese refugees for special English-language programs as well as certain employment services. While unaccompanied refugee children were cared for within state and local government welfare systems, federal funding covered the cost of this care. The Indochinese Refugee Children Assistance Act of 1977 provided direct financial payments to school districts for each Indochinese refugee child enrolled in a school district. It also provided federal funds to support adult education programs for school districts that served needy Indochinese refugees.

In 1980 the specific federal refugee assistance programs for individual refugee groups were consolidated into a general refugee eligibility assistance program as defined in the Refugee Act of that year. This legislation set the length of time that a refugee could be eligible for resettlement assistance at thirty-six months after the refugee's admission to the United States. In 1982, as part of its budget-cutting initiatives, the Reagan administration succeeded in reducing the period of eligibility for federal refugee assistance to eighteen months. When that limitation took effect on April 30, 1982, thousands of refugees lost eligibility for further assistance. In Florida alone it was estimated that 32,000 refugees from Cuba and Haiti were affected. Consequently, on May 4, 1982, officials of Florida's state welfare agency sent a letter to those persons who were being cut off from further assistance. The letter listed ten other states that had more liberal state welfare programs for which these refugees might qualify if they moved to them.[75] A spokesman for the governor of Florida charged that "the federal government [was] being unfair and capricious in its treatment of Florida, the state with the most refugees."[76] The action by Florida infuriated officials in most of the states where it had been suggested the refugees might relocate. In New York, however, a spokesman for the Department of Social Services made a conciliatory response that aptly described the crux of the dilemma. "We are not blaming Florida," he said. "The root of the problem for the states and for the refugees is the Federal policy."[77] It is not expected that many refugees in Florida will take it upon themselves to relocate, and this means local and state officials in Florida are going to have to cope with ensuing refugee problems themselves.[78]

In addition to federal assistance, refugees are eligible for state-administered income transfer programs such as worker compensation, general income assistance, and temporary disability insurance.[79]

As long as refugees and asylees continue to constitute a substantial portion of the total flow of immigrants into the United States, it is only fair that the federal government should assume the full financial responsibility for their accommodation in local communities. Most of the nation is unaffected by refugees and can therefore afford the luxury of passing judgment on refugees on the basis of abstract humanitarian considerations. In those states and localities where refugees cluster, however, the economic, political, and social costs of refugee accommodation are substantial. The same can be said of the need to protect the particular citizen workers in these localities who must compete with large numbers of refugees for jobs. Hence, given the fact that refugees are supposedly admitted in response to national interests, their associated economic costs should be assigned to the nation as a whole as well. To this end, the National Governors' Association adopted a resolution in February 1982 that stated the following corollary: "If the federal government is unwilling to fund the necessary services, then it is incumbent upon the federal government to decrease the flow of refugee admissions."[80]

Perhaps even more troubling for policymakers is the fact that many social services that refugees require exceed benefits that needy citizens are eligible to receive. Hence, refugee accommodation serves to underscore the need for national commitment to full employment policies and to human resource development programs for all workers in the nation. Without such a commitment, the humanitarian idealism that surrounds refugee accommodation will be severely tarnished. In a labor market that is increasingly placing stress on education and skills, this idealism will quickly wane if citizen workers are adversely affected by refugees. The same disillusion will set in among refugees if they are left to fend for themselves in a social and economic environment in which they are ill-prepared to live and work. Unfortunately, the very localities in which refugees have tended to cluster already have a surplus of unemployed and economically disadvantaged citizen workers.

The Effects of Refugees on the U.S. Labor Market

The literature on the precise employment effects of refugees in the United States is very limited. Presumably the studies that have been made on the employment and earnings effects of the foreign-born population include some data on refugees, but in fact this literature to date has been based largely on 1970 census data and other sample data from the early 1970s. In other words, the large influxes of refugees in the late 1970s and early 1980s have yet to be analyzed. It is even likely that the 1980 census missed most of the Mariel and Haitian refugees in Florida, for the census was taken largely in early April 1980 and the major movements of these two groups occurred in May and June 1980. Hence, one is left with a largely disparate literature on specific groups at specific times.

One theme does run through the existing labor market literature on refugees, however, regardless of their ethnic background. As Barry Stein noted in his study of Vietnamese workers: "Generally, the higher one's former occupational status, the worse the adjustment. As occupational status declines, the likelihood increases that one will attain or surpass former levels."[81] A downward occupational bumping—especially among professional, technical, and skilled workers—is a recurring theme in the available literature. The obvious tendency is for the unskilled refugees to have the least difficulty finding similar unskilled work. It is therefore likely that the brunt of the effect of refugees on U.S. labor markets is borne by the substantial number of unskilled citizen workers with whom the refugees compete. This competition is further exacerbated by the fact that refugees have tended to concentrate in essentially the same few states and the same few central city labor markets that have received the most legal and illegal immigrants.

THE HUNGARIANS

The number of Hungarian refugees who fled to the United States in the mid-1950s was relatively small compared to the Cuban, Indochinese, and Haitian inflows that would come later. In the mid-1950s the U.S. unemployment rate (in the 4–5 percent range) was relatively low. Most of the Hungarians "were sufficiently skilled so that jobs could be quickly found for the majority of them."[82] Where difficulties did occur, they usually involved refugees who had to take positions requiring less skill or less responsibility than they had held before coming to the United States. The most difficult barrier to adjustment, however, was language. Knowledge of English separated the refugees who entered and adjusted to the labor force satisfactorily from those who did not.

When the Hungarian refugees entered the United States in the mid-1950s, there was already a sizable population of Hungarians living in the nation (in the 1950 census about 268,000 residents of the United States reported that they had been born in Hungary). About 70 percent of these Hungarians lived in New York, Ohio, Pennsylvania, and New Jersey. It is not surprising, therefore, that 60 percent of the Hungarian refugees of the mid-fifties settled in these same four states.[83] California was the only state to receive an appreciable number of Hungarian refugees that did not already have a sizable Hungarian population.

THE CUBANS

As mentioned earlier, the Cubans who arrived in the United States in the years immediately following the Castro takeover were considered to be "golden exiles." They, like the Hungarians, were relatively highly skilled and trained. Most of them settled in the Miami area. They were the first group to become the object of deliberate federal government efforts to provide refugee resettlement assistance.

The majority of the Cuban refugees who entered the United States between 1957 and 1977 settled in Florida.[84] Substantial numbers also settled in New Jersey and California, which had relatively small Cuban-heritage populations prior to this inflow of refugees. New York also witnessed an increase in its Cuban population during this period, but it already had a large Cuban population, and in relative terms, it did not receive a substantial number of Cuban refugees during this era.

Federal efforts to disperse the Cuban refugees failed. The Mariel boatlift Cubans settled primarily where the "golden exiles" had—in Florida, New York, and New Jersey.[85] As a group, however, the Mariel refugees were far less skilled and trained than the "golden exiles" had been. In addition, two-thirds of them were male. They tended to be craft workers, operatives, and laborers— occupations that "possibly reflect[ed] the reported significant cutbacks in educational enrollments in Cuba"—especially at the university level.[86] Fewer than 5 percent of these persons could speak English. As of March 1981, 72 percent of the Cubans who had arrived from Mariel were living in Florida, 6.5 percent had moved on to New Jersey, and 5.1 percent had settled in New York. Among the Mariel refugees there were some convicted felons and some aged and infirm persons. These groups added to the social costs of the adjustment process, for they were unable to become self-supporting members of their communities.

THE HAITIANS

The Haitians who sought refugee and asylee status in 1980 and 1981 were almost uniformly persons with few skills and little education. Many were from rural backgrounds. They were often illiterate in Creole French (their native tongue) and generally knew very little English. In a study prepared by the U.S. Department of Health and Human Services in 1981, researchers found that of 18,439 Haitians for whom occupational data were available, 27 percent worked primarily in agriculture. The next largest group consisted of government workers (19.9 percent).[87] The rest represented various other largely unskilled occupations. Of those for whom educational data were available (i.e., 6,096 persons), more than half (3,194) had less than an elementary-school education. Of the 45,573 Haitians for whom the INS had names, 70.7 percent reportedly lived in Florida (59.2 percent in three counties of southern Florida). The next highest percentage—0.6—lived in New York. For 28.5 percent of the names, however, the INS had no address. Many of these persons were believed to be residents of Florida.

THE INDOCHINESE

The admission of refugees from Indochina was not a particularly welcome event in the United States. The attitudes of Americans toward the war in Southeast Asia had, by the mid-1970s, turned bitter, and some of this ill will spilled over into a "feeling of ambivalence—even hostility—about these refugees."[88] The Indochinese who arrived prior to 1978 were generally well educated and had formerly held occupations of relatively high status. Most were from urban backgrounds and many had some knowledge of English.[89] Those that came after 1978, however, were decidedly different in each of these regards. They were less well educated, poorly skilled, spoke little English, and often were from rural backgrounds. Consequently, labor force participation rates declined sharply for men and even more severely for women among those who entered after 1978 compared to those who entered between 1975 and 1978.[90] The labor force participation rates for persons from Laos and Kampuchea were far worse than the rates for persons from Vietnam. All three groups, however, fared worse than the comparable age and sex cohorts of U.S. citizen workers. Initially, the U.S. government sought to disperse the Indochinese refugees in order to minimize any adverse economic impacts on local employment and social services. In a conscientious effort to prevent the clustering that had characterized the settlement of Cuban refugees, the government enlisted the aid of nationally established volunteer organizations (e.g., United States Catholic Charities, Church World Service, American Council for Nationalities Service, and the Lutheran Immigration and Refugee Service), but due in part to secondary migration (i.e., regrouping), this attempt failed. Consequently, the refugees from Southeast Asia also have tended to cluster. Of the 394,979 Indochinese refugees who had been admitted to the United States as of August 15, 1980, 126,348 (or 32 percent) had settled in

California and 35,450 (or 9 percent) had settled in Texas.[91] In addition, there has been extensive urban clustering within these states and the others where the Indochinese have located.

The Need for Additional Reforms

Recognition of the fact that refugee flows are an important component of immigration has come late to U.S. policymakers. Legislation has slowly evolved, however, and refugee flows are no longer viewed as irregular and exceptional happenings that require only ad hoc responses. Given the increases that have occurred in refugee populations worldwide, it is certain that refugee accommodation will be a permanent feature of the U.S. immigration system. It is also apparent that refugee policy has become intertwined with the question of illegal immigration.

The Refugee Act of 1980 was passed almost a year prior to the issuance of the final report of the Select Commission on Immigration and Refugee Policy. As a result, most of the commission's key recommendations pertaining to refugee policy had already been incorporated into the act by the time the commission ended its work. Thus, the commission endorsed the act in terms of its definitions, the number of visas it allocated to refugees, and the process it recommended for distributing these visas.[92] As for mass asylum admissions similar to the Cuban and Haitian experiences, the commission had little of substance to add. It called for interagency planning for possible future emergencies and it endorsed the concept of individual case review of asylum requests. It did suggest, however, that the review process could be expedited by developing and using group profiles, a task it recommended that the Department of State undertake. The commission's report included no recommendations of consequence concerning how to overcome the judicial bottleneck caused by the review of individual cases; the subsequent number of appeals of most adverse decisions; and the extended length of the appeal process.

Thus, the reform issues that need to be addressed include the judicial bottleneck, the need to relate the number of refugee and asylee admissions to overall immigration flows, the possibilities of relocation to other nations, and the "push" factors that make people want to leave their homelands.

THE JUDICIAL REVIEW PROBLEM

Since 1980 it has been apparent that the asylum provisions of the Refugee Act are subject to abuse. As Terrance Adamson, a former Justice Department official associated with this area of the law, remarked in 1983, "Sheer numbers [of persons] now get in the way of this country's tradition of offering welcome and shelter."[93] He added that "there have to be limits and that's where Congress should be involved—giving guidance."[94] As for the immediate future, the problem of the huge backlog of asylum requests and appeals pending in the nation's administrative and judicial channels may well be alleviated by the amnesty provisions for Cubans and Haitians who entered in 1980 and 1981, as provided by the pending Simpson-Mazzoli bill. If the applicants are found to be true refugees, they will be admitted; if they are found to be illegal immigrants, most (depending on the effective date of the forgiveness provisions) will be eligible for amnesty. Under this arrangement, many refugees will win either way. Despite this short-term political tonic, however, the basic problem will remain unaddressed. It can be anticipated that even if the sense of urgency surrounding the asylum issue is eliminated, a new backlog of requests for asylum will soon develop.

The difficulty, of course, lies in determining which persons seeking asylee or refugee status have a well-founded fear of persecution in their homelands and which are simply illegal immigrants pretending to be refugees. If U.S. officials forcibly returned persons to their homelands and the lives of these persons were imperiled as a result of that action, the nation would be guilty of the diplomatic sin of *refoulement*. But if these officials honored every claim that a person would be persecuted if he or she were returned home, they would invite massive abuse of the nation's immigration laws. As the *New York Times* succinctly editorialized: "But what if they are not legitimate refugees? Then they are just another form of gate-crasher, ready to confuse refuge and subterfuge. To send them home would only be fair, signaling to other would-be illegal immigrants that Americans are compassionate but not suckers."[95] The only way out of this moral thicket is to create an expeditious review procedure and see to it that it is conducted by an informed and independent body.

To this end, the drafters of the Simpson-Mazzoli bill of 1982 proposed a summary exclusionary proceeding without judicial appeal of substantive decisions for persons who enter the country without documents and request asylum. An initial hearing would be held by specially trained hearing officers in the Department of Justice—but outside the jurisdiction of the Immigration and Naturalization Service—and appeals would be limited to a newly created U.S. Immigration Board (USIB) within the department. The attorney general would be authorized to review any decisions made by this board, but only if he or she changed the board's decision could an appeal be made to the U.S. Circuit Court of Appeals. The practice of denying refugees direct access to the nation's court system was deemed to be "consistent with the practices of most other countries."[96] When the bill was reintroduced in 1983, the administrative hearing officers (now called "immigration judges" in the Senate bill and "administrative law judges" in the House bill) and the creation of the USIB were retained. In the final version of the bill that cleared each house of congress, summary exclusion procedures were established for an alien who arrives in the United States and does not have a visa, a legal basis to enter, and who does not specifically request asylum. Such aliens may be sent back to their native land without any recourse to the U.S. judicial system. For those who arrive and specifically request asylum, an exclusion hearing would be permitted, but it would be restricted to the issues raised in the individual's asylum petition. No class-action cases would be permitted. Appeals of negative decisions could be made to the court system, but they would be restricted to procedural issues or constitutional errors. Appeals of substantive issues, however, would not be allowed. The number of appeal levels for asylees would be reduced from the prevailing seven levels (which is currently more than the number of appeals permitted to convicted murders) to four. It is anticipated that these procedures would reduce the backlog problem in the future.

There is, of course, no way to avoid the human judgment that is required to decide who is a legitimate refugee and who is an illegal immigrant. Some organization of human beings must ultimately be entrusted with that responsibility. There are only two alternatives: an agency within the immigration bureaucracy or the nation's court system. From 1980 to 1983 the courts became increasingly bogged down in the task of assuring due process. As a result, the asylum process degenerated into a chaotic, costly, and time-consuming process that has shown no signs of improvement and, if not rescued by the granting of mass amnesty, will only get worse. It would seem, therefore, that reliance upon the trained bureaucracy, with appeal to the courts being restricted to procedural and constitutional issues, should be tried. Many civil libertarians, however, distrust bureaucratic decision makers, as do various legal groups that have a substantial financial stake in procedures that place greater reliance upon the courts to make such decisions. But as the commissioner of the INS, Alan C. Nelson, has argued,

> Because the judicial process is inherently protracted, invoking it to adjudicate asylum cases is likely to result in precisely what the legislation seeks to cure: paralysis of the system, so that arriving in the U.S. and filing an asylum claim creates *de facto* refugee status and admission to the country.
>
> Such an outcome is unfair to *bona fide* claimants who deserve speedy resolution of their claims; to the spirit and purpose of immigration reform; and to the integrity of our system of laws.[97]

The civil liberties issues associated with due process are obviously complex, but as matters now stand the intent of the nation's refugee policy is being subverted by the application and possible abuse of judicial procedures. Adherence to a strict standard of protecting all the rights of all applicants for political asylum and all illegal aliens threatens the efficacy of the nation's entire immigration system. Speaking of this quandary, Michael Teitelbaum has written:

> Surely illegal immigrants are entitled to all basic human rights, e.g., the right to humane treatment while in custody, the right of *habeas corpus,* and so on. Yet, realistically, if every technical aspect of due process, including the right of appeal right up to the Supreme Court is to be guaranteed persons walking across an open border or landing in a small boat on an unpatrolled beach, enforceable immigration laws cannot exist in a practical sense.[98]

Teitelbaum also reverses the equity issue by pointing out that it is law-abiding persons who are actually hurt by the prevailing practices. He argues that ''support for such an absolutist position implies an elemental unfairness—the full panoply of legal rights are to be granted to persons who violate the law, but similar rights of appeal are not given to others who respect the law and apply for legal entry but have not yet entered the country.''[99]

THE INCLUSION OF REFUGEES IN THE NATION'S AGGREGATE IMMIGRATION CEILING

At the present time, refugee admissions to the United States are not numerically regulated as are all other categories of legal immigrants. Consequently, the president's position is extremely awkward. Given the immense size of the world's refugee populations, he is often under severe political pressure to admit large numbers of refugees to the United States each year. This pressure is exerted by the governments of the countries where the refugees are located. It is also brought to bear by citizens groups that are ethnically similar to the refugee groups and that seek to have these people admitted through channels outside the legal immigration system. Such pressures can contribute to decisions that are politically expedient but that often defy the logic of a regulated immigration system. Accepting the desirability of seeking to accommodate refugees cannot mean that whatever happens is acceptable. If U.S. immigration policy is to have any meaning at all, increases in the number of refugees and asylees admitted will require concurrent modifications in the nation's legal immigration ceilings. In short, the decision to increase the number of refugees admitted in a given year will require that the number of legal immigrants admitted be reduced by the same magnitude. Otherwise, as experience has shown, the notion that the nation is in control of the situation will quickly become a delusion.

RELOCATION TO OTHER COUNTRIES

The quest to find alternative solutions to the refugee/asylee problem has led to a suggestion that actually harks back to the Migration and Refugee Assistance Act of 1962. As stated in that legislation, the only policy alternative to simply accepting all persons who have arrived in the United States is to attempt to relocate to other nations the surplus of persons above the number the nation agrees to receive.[100] The inducement for other nations to accept these refugees as immigrants would be twofold: they would truly need more settlers, and the United States would underwrite the refugees' resettlement expenses. Application of this policy was actually proposed in 1982 with regard to the Haitian situation. Specifically, Belize (formerly British Honduras, which gained its independence in 1981) expressed such an interest to the United States. Belize is relatively underpopulated and needs farmers to cultivate its extensive fertile farmland.[101] Belize officials stated a specific interest in ''people of African descent'' to help it maintain its prevailing racial balance between blacks, mestizos, and native Indians. Because most of the Haitians entering the United States have been from farming backgrounds and all are black, the Belize government expressed a willingness to explore the topic. It was understood that as part of the agreement, the United States would bear a substantial portion of the financial costs of resettlement and that it would provide assistance in developing a cattle industry and the industrial capacity to process food. A major unknown in the proposal, however, is the fact that one of Belize's neighbors—Guatemala—has not recognized the right of Belize to exist as an independent nation. Guatemala believes that Britain artificially carved its former colony out of land that rightfully belonged to Guatemala.[102] No doubt one of the unwritten reasons why Belize is interested in Haitians as settlers is its fear that it may in the near future need more people to secure its very existence.

ADDRESSING THE "PUSH" FACTORS DIRECTLY

The interplay of the political and economic motivations of refugees and asylees seems to dictate that a long-term strategy to reduce the inflow of these immigrants must address the "push" factors that are operative in their homelands. With respect to the economic issues involved, the Reagan administration succeeded in passing legislation in 1982 and 1983 to assist economic development in the Caribbean Basin and to enhance trade in that region.[103] These steps may reduce some of the pressures that cause illegal immigrants and refugees to flee from this region to the United States. If it is the case that political forces are the dominant causes for persons to flee their homelands, however, reliance on economic measures alone to reduce these flows may prove to be futile. It seems obvious that the United States must continue to insist that the nations of the Caribbean region adhere to basic human rights tenets and rely upon democratic practices. In addition, it is hoped that the United States would continue to insist that the governments of the region—regardless of their political ideologies—practice policies that reflect a respect for human life. Saying this, of course, is easier than specifying how to accomplish these goals. Still, recognizing the necessity of including these considerations within the nation's panoply of efforts to create a meaningful immigration policy is certainly the first step. Through its foreign policy the United States must constantly exert pressure on these nations to pursue these goals. If it neglects these efforts, the result will surely be an increase in the number of persons who are forced to seek freedom by fleeing from their homelands to the United States.

Delay in the Search for a Permanent
Refugee-Asylee Policy

At the time of its passage the Refugee Act of 1980 was authorized to last until September 30, 1983. It was understood that it represented a temporary solution to the problem of refugee admissions. Having congressional committees consult with the administration prior to each fiscal year on the number of refugees to be admitted can hardly be considered a satisfactory permanent way of addressing the issue. In 1982, when the Simpson-Mazzoli bill was introduced, the advocates of immigration reform anticipated that it would be enacted in that year. Following its passage, they intended to address a new immigration reform issue—the crisis in refugee-asylee policy as outlined in this chapter.[104] The Simpson-Mazzoli bill did not pass in 1982, however, nor was Congress able to vote on the bill when it was reintroduced in 1983. Hence, shortly before the Refugee Act of 1980 was due to expire, it was extended by Congress for one more year—to September 30, 1984. Because the House of Representatives did not pass its version of the Simpson-Mazzoli bill until June 1984 and because the effort to reconcile the differences between the Senate and the House bills will take additional time, it is likely that the Refugee Act of 1980 will have to be extended again. Consequently, the urgent need to establish a permanent refugee-asylee policy will be postponed until 1985—or later if the Simpson-Mazzoli bill does not pass in 1984.

CHAPTER 7

Immigration-Related Policies and U.S.-Mexican Border Labor Markets

$\mathbf{H}$aving considered the major immigration policies of the United States in the preceding chapters, let us turn now to several immigration-related policies. Discussion of these policies is often omitted from immigration studies, but they have specific impacts on the labor markets of the border regions of the nation and thus deserve prominence equal to that given to policies pertaining to legal immigrants, illegal immigrants, nonimmigrants, and refugees. Within their own realms of influence, these microcosmic immigration policies often exert even stronger effects on the prevailing employment and wage conditions of workers than the previously discussed macrocosmic policies.

The land border the United States shares with Canada is much larger than that which it shares with Mexico, but the nation's immigration-related policies have a greater impact along its southwestern border than along its northern boundary.[1] The primary reasons for this are two: the population of Canada is far smaller than that of Mexico; and the differences in standard of living between Canada and the United States are slight compared to those that separate Mexico and the United States. Hence, the pressures that lead persons to enter the United States (legally or illegally) are far less pronounced along the nation's northern border than along its southern border. Consequently, the border policies that are in effect along the U.S.-Mexican border will be closely examined here.

The U.S.-Mexican Borderland

To anyone who visits the borderland that separates Mexico and the United States, the stark differences in living conditions and in economic opportunity are immediately apparent. The U.S. side of the border generally seems quite affluent compared to the Mexican side. This impression is deceiving, however, for the communities on both sides of the border are anomalies. Despite how bad conditions appear to be on the Mexican side, the border states and border cities of Mexico have the highest income levels of any area in Mexico outside the Federal District (i.e., Mexico City).[2] In contrast, despite the fact that life in U.S. border communities appears to be prosperous, many of these communities typically rank among the poorest metropolitan areas in the entire United States. Thus, the border separates Mexican cities that in economic terms are comparatively well-off relative to the rest of Mexico from U.S. communities that are very poor relative to the remainder of the United States. An understanding of this paradox is crucial to any discussion of the effects of U.S. immigration policies on the labor markets of these forgotten regions. The Mexican government tends to ignore its borderland communities because there are far greater human and economic claims elsewhere for it to address. Likewise, the U.S. government is often oblivious to the disproportionate poverty and unemployment that characterize its border communities. The U.S. Southwest is generally a quite prosperous region, and the unique problems of these border communities are hardly noticed in the four states that comprise the nation's southwestern border. Indeed, Ellwyn Stoddard has observed that poverty along the southwestern border "is one of the best kept secrets in America."[3]

Twenty-five counties in four states comprise the southwestern U.S. border region. As can be seen in Table 28, the rate of population growth in the border states has in almost every instance substantially exceeded the population growth of the United States as a whole in the decades 1960–1970 and 1970–1980. Even more important is the fact that the growth in the population of the twenty-five

TABLE 28. POPULATION GROWTH IN SOUTHWESTERN BORDER STATES AND IN LARGEST BORDER COUNTIES IN EACH STATE, 1960, 1970, AND 1980

Border State	Largest Border Counties	Population			Percentage Change	
		1960	1970	1980[a]	1960–1970	1970–1980
Arizona		1,302,161	1,770,900	2,714,013	36.0	53.3
	Pina	265,660	351,667	531,896	32.0	51.2
California		15,717,204	19,953,134	23,668,562	18.6	27.0
	San Diego	1,033,011	1,357,854	1,858,217	31.4	36.8
	Imperial	72,105	74,492	91,708	3.3	23.1
New Mexico		951,023	1,016,000	1,290,551	27.0	6.8
	Dona Ana	59,948	69,773	95,861	16.4	37.4
Texas		9,579,677	11,196,730	14,152,339	16.9	26.4
	El Paso	314,070	359,291	478,834	14.4	33.3
	Webb	64,791	72,859	99,027	12.5	35.9
	Hidalgo	180,984	181,535	277,278	0.3	52.7
	Cameron	151,098	140,368	208,125	−7.1	48.3
	All 25 border counties	2,363,804	2,862,370	3,995,055	21.1	39.6
United States		179,323,175	203,302,031	226,504,825	11.4	13.3

Source: Reprinted from Kathleen Brook and James T. Peach, "Income, Employment, and Population Growth in the U.S.–Mexico Border Counties," *Texas Business Review,* May–June 1981, p. 137, by permission of the Bureau of Business Research, University of Texas at Austin. Copyright © 1981, Bureau of Business Research, University of Texas at Austin.

[a]Figures for 1980 are preliminary census data.

border counties has with few exceptions significantly exceeded the rapid population growth of the border states of which they are a part. Because the climate of the entire borderland region is extremely arid, the population of the region is for the most part clustered into scattered oasis communities. Thus the labor markets of the border region should be viewed as an archipelago of geographically dispersed groupings rather than as an integrated and interrelated continuum. The eight largest border counties, for instance, account for 91 percent of the southwestern border population of the United States. Even within these counties the population is highly concentrated into urban enclaves.

The growth of the labor force in these twenty-five border counties reflects the region's population trends. Between 1970 and 1978, the number of employed persons increased by 39.9 percent compared to a 22.7 percent increase for the nation as a whole.[4] Unemployment in the region is consistently higher than the national rate. Of particular interest is the fact that the unemployment rate differential between the border labor markets and the national labor market is greatest when the national unemployment rate is low. When the national rate increases, so does the border rate, but less rapidly, so that the differential narrows considerably.[5] In other words, the persistently high unemployment rate along the border reflects a long-term structural imbalance—an imbalance to which U.S. immigration policy, in all its forms, undoubtedly contributes.

With regard to personal income, the border counties are consistently below the levels of the rest of the United States. In 1978 the average personal income in these counties was $6,797, while for the nation as a whole it was $7,840.[6] San Diego County, the largest of the border counties, actually exceeded the national average, but it was the only one of the twenty-five border counties to do so. Moreover, in 1978 the three poorest U.S. counties that were classified as metropolitan areas were located in the border region, as was the nation's poorest rural county.

Mexico's border region is comprised of six massive states that, like their U.S. counterparts, extend far into the interior of the country. Along the border proper there are thirty-five municipalities. Each of these municipalities is linked to a corresponding border city on the U.S. side. Over 75 percent of the population of the Mexican border region lives in seven of these municipalities, and three of them—Juarez, Mexicali, and Tijuana—account for about half of the total border population. The arid climate of the region undoubtedly explains this clustering, but the political border itself is responsible for the actual location of the municipalities. Without the border there would be no reason for any of the municipalities to be located where they are.

The population of the Mexican border municipalities has consistently increased more rapidly than the population of Mexico as a whole.[7] The birth rate in the border municipalities is higher than the national birth rate, and the mortality rate is lower.[8] Another key factor in the rapid growth of the borderland population has been internal migration to these northern cities and towns. As of 1970, almost one-third of the population of these border municipalities had come from

TABLE 29.   POPULATION TRENDS IN SELECTED MAJOR MEXICAN MUNICIPALITIES
ALONG THE U.S.-MEXICAN BORDER, 1950–1980

Mexican Municipality (and U.S. City and State Opposite)	Population				Percentage Change		
	1950	1960	1970	1980	1950–1960	1960–1970	1970–1980
Juárez (El Paso, Tex.)	131,308	276,995	424,350	671,500	111	53	58
Matamoros (Brownsville, Tex.)	128,347	143,043	186,146	247,200	11	30	33
Mexicali (Calexico– El Centro, Calif.)	124,362	281,333	396,324	573,000	126	40	45
Nuevo Laredo (Laredo, Tex.)	59,496	96,043	143,784	248,300	61	50	73
Tijuana (San Ysidro– San Diego, Calif.)	65,364	165,690	340,583	734,300	153	105	116

Sources: Mercametrica de 75 Ciudades Mexicanos, 4th ed., vol. 1 (Mexico City: Mercametrica Ediciones, 1980); and Richard W. Wilkie, "The Populations of Mexico and Argentina in 1980: Preliminary Data and Some Comparisons," in *Statistical Abstract of Latin America,* vol. 21, ed. James Wilkie and Stephen Haber (Los Angeles: UCLA Latin American Center Publications, University of California, 1981), table 3900, p. 640.

other communities in Mexico, and almost half of these migrants had come in the preceding eleven years.[9] It is highly likely that the number of migrants has increased since that time. Table 29 shows the population growth trends for the five largest Mexican border municipalities from 1950 to 1980. These trends have exerted immense labor market pressures throughout the Mexican border region, and with regard to such concerns as unemployment, irregular employment opportunities, underemployment, and poverty, "the greatest problems found in the border region are naturally localized in these urban areas."[10] It is in this context that the discussion of U.S. immigration and border labor market policies will proceed.

Border Commuters

In the border regions of Mexico and Canada, workers have long chosen to live there but to seek work in one of the border labor markets of the United States. Actually, relatively few Canadians are involved in this process, for their standard of living is similar to that of Americans. In the Mexican border region, however, the phenomenon of border commuters is common.

Border commuters are a subgroup of the larger immigration classification known as permanent-resident aliens and which has been discussed in earlier chapters. Resident aliens are foreign-born nationals who apply for permission to live and work in the United States on a permanent basis. They retain their original, foreign citizenship. After a waiting period of five years, they may apply for U.S. citizenship, or they may remain resident aliens indefinitely. A substantial number of resident aliens never elect to become naturalized citizens. In fact, resident aliens from Mexico have the lowest naturalization rate (less than 5 percent) of any immigrant group in the United States.[11]

All resident aliens are issued a card from the INS that is officially known as the I-151 card. Issuance of these cards was officially sanctioned by Congress in the Alien Registration Act of 1940.[12] By 1981, 5.3 million resident aliens were registered with the INS. Nearly 75 percent of them resided in six states (California, New York, and Texas account for over half of the total) and Mexicans constituted the largest ethnic cohort (20 percent of the total). Over 75 percent of all resident aliens from Mexico resided in California and Texas, and many lived along the U.S.-Mexican border.[13]

There are, in fact, two types of resident aliens. The larger group is composed of persons who live and work on a permanent basis in the United States. Members of the other group work regularly in the United States but reside permanently either in Mexico or in Canada. The latter are called "commuters" or, more commonly, "greencarders" (so named because each time they cross the border they must show their I-151 card, which originally was green but now is blue). The important distinction is this: all commuters are "greencarders," but most "greencarders" are not commuters.

At the risk of confusing the issue, it is important to note that there are also two types of commuting "greencarders." One is the commuter who crosses the border on a daily basis. The other is the person who works in the United States on a seasonal basis. Generally speaking, the daily commuter is the one whose presence impacts on the economy of the U.S. border regions—especially the southwestern border region. The seasonal commuter generally travels much farther inland and returns to his or her home in Mexico only during the off-season of the industry in which he or she is employed. The impact of seasonal commuters—who tend to work in construction, farming, and the tourist industry—is diluted by the fact that their jobs are scattered throughout the Southwest and in other parts of the nation as well. Daily commuters, however, do not travel very far inland, and thus their impact on border labor markets is significant. David North has aptly observed that the daily commuter "is this generation's bracero."[14]

Due to the extreme difference between the standard of living of Mexico and that of the United States, commuters from Mexico are often willing to work for wages and under conditions that a person who must confront the daily cost of living in the United States on a permanent basis would find impossible to accept. Commuters have a real income advantage and for this reason have less incentive to seek higher wages or better working conditions.[15] In addition, commuters often act as strikebreakers in labor disputes along the border and accordingly are one reason for the scarcity of unions in the region. As a 1981 study of the labor market in Brownsville, Texas—where 20 percent of the labor force was composed of daily commuters from Mexico—noted: "Mexican commuters constitute an important labor source in the event of a strike. Indeed, they have often served as a strike-breaking force. The knowledge among local workers that they can and will be replaced if they walk out obviously subverts labor militancy."[16] A study in 1970 placed the number of daily commuters from Mexico at 70,000.[17] This meant that roughly one out of every eleven people employed in the southwestern border region in 1970 was a commuter. The number of commuters has undoubtedly increased since that time. Obviously, a work force of such magnitude exerts a tremendous impact on the labor markets of these communities. In a 1967 study of border commuters, the U.S. Department of Labor concluded that "the factors which produce low wages are commonly present in the border towns and quite often are interrelated with the alien commuter problem."[18]

To date, only one detailed field study has focused specifically on the occupational patterns of "greencarders." It was conducted by David North in 1970.[19] Table 30 shows the occupational distribution that was reported in that study. North based his analysis on personal interviews with 400 persons who were randomly selected from a list of 40,176 commuting "greencarders." The interviewees were selected from names on this list in November and December 1967 using a procedure whereby a grommet (a small metal ring) was stamped through their greencard as they passed over the border from Mexico to work in the United States. The grommet was used to separate commuting "greencarders" from other "greencarders" who crossed the border during this interval (i.e., people who lived permanently on the U.S. side of the border). North found that com-

TABLE 30.   OCCUPATIONS OF MEXICAN BORDER COMMUTERS, 1969

Occupation	Percentage of Commuters in Occupation
Professional	1.0
Clerical, managerial, and sales	7.8
Skilled	
Nonagricultural	11.8
Agricultural	1.5
Semiskilled	
Operators (garment industry)	5.0
Other	2.8
Unskilled	
Nonagricultural	8.0
Agricultural	39.2
Service	
Domestic	6.5
Other	16.4
Total	100.0

Source: David S. North, *The Border Crossers: People Who Live in Mexico and Work in the United States* (Washington, D.C.: TransCentury Corp., 1970), p. 111. Data were derived from interviews with 400 green-card commuter-workers conducted across the border in 1969.

muting "greencarders" were employed in every occupational category but were concentrated in unskilled jobs. The largest percentage were unskilled agricultural workers. He concluded that commuting "greencarders" adversely affected citizen workers in four major ways: by lessening employment opportunities, lowering wages, reducing the incidence of unionism, and contributing to the seasonal migration of citizen workers who had to find jobs elsewhere.[20]

Because of the unfair real income advantage that commuting workers have over resident workers (i.e., citizens and permanent-resident aliens who live and work on the U.S. side of the border) in the competition for jobs, the legitimacy of the commuting workers' status has long been disputed. To understand the nature of this controversy, it is first necessary to understand why and how the commuter phenomenon evolved. As discussed in Chapter 2, prior to 1917 there were no restrictions on the number of immigrants that could be admitted to the United States except in the case of Asians. In 1917 and 1921, however, temporary restrictions were imposed on admissions from the Eastern Hemisphere, and shortly thereafter, with passage of the Immigration Act of 1924, the nation's first permanent numerical ceilings were established. Persons from the Western Hemisphere were not included in the quotas established by the 1924 act, but the new law stipulated that all persons entering the United States be classified as "immigrants" or "nonimmigrants." "Immigrants" were defined as all entrants except "nonimmigrants," who were visiting the nation temporarily "for business or pleasure." For a short interval, workers who lived in Mexico but commuted to jobs in the United States were classified as "nonimmigrant visitors," who were free to cross the border "for business." In 1927, however, an arbitrary administrative decision of the INS resulted in the reclassification of these persons as "immigrants." The U.S. Supreme Court upheld this decision in 1929 with the famous ruling that "employment equals residence" (thereby neatly avoiding the permanent-residency requirement of the nation's immigration statutes).[21] As indicated earlier, the use of resident-alien cards began with passage of the Alien Registration Act of 1940.

In addition to the fact that they do not live in the United States, there are several other ways in which commuting "greencarders" differ from all other permanent-resident aliens: (1) if commuting "greencarders" remain unemployed for more than six months, they lose their classification as "immigrants"; (2) they may not serve as strikebreakers; and (3) they may not count the time they live outside the United States as part of the five-year waiting period for eligibility to apply for U.S. citizenship. In reality, these differences are of absolutely no consequence. The unemployment restriction is not enforced; the anti-strikebreaker rule is so easily circumvented that it is essentially meaningless; and, as has already been noted, most Mexican "greencarders" have absolutely no interest in becoming American citizens.

Establishing residency requirements for "greencarders" has long been the subject of extensive controversy. It has been charged that the Immigration Act of

1965 actually forbids the practice of commuting since it limits the right of reentry to persons who are "returning to an unrelinquished lawful permanent address."[22] Before 1965 the INS reasoned that any commuter who had been accorded the "privilege of residing permanently" was entitled to leave and reenter the country at will. The Immigration Act of 1965, however, altered the language of the previous statutes. The amended language restricted informal entry to "an immigrant lawfully admitted for permanent residence who is returning from a temporary visit abroad." Accordingly, Sheldon Greene concluded: "No distortion of the English language could result in a finding that the commuter was entering the United States after a temporary visit abroad to return to his principal, actual dwelling place. Rather, the commuter was simply leaving his foreign home and entering the United States to work."[23] He argued that in 1965 the practice of border commuting was "actually prohibited."

In November 1974, however, the U.S. Supreme Court rejected the aforementioned logic by upholding the INS's position that daily and seasonal commuters are lawful permanent residents returning from temporary absences abroad.[24] Essentially the Court said that it was not going to overthrow fifty years of administrative practices with a judicial decree. If Congress wanted to outlaw border commuting, it would have to act in a specific legislative manner.

The U.S. Department of State has consistently contended that any interruption in the commuter program would seriously harm relations between Mexico and the United States. Testifying before Congress in 1963, former Secretary of State Dean Rusk contended that the adjacent border towns and cities of the two nations "have grown into single economic communities" and that "a disruption in the life of these communities would do real harm to good neighbor relations in the area."[25] It is also true, however, that the sanctioning of border commuters means that the citizen workers of the region must compete directly with them. As Fred Schmidt has noted, "The United States worker who competes with the traffic of workers from Mexico is caught in a situation where he pays a substantial part of what the Secretary of State regards as a form of foreign aid to a neighboring nation."[26]

Resident aliens who commute could, of course, simply move across the border and establish a residence in the United States. They enjoy real income benefits from living in Mexico and working in the United States, however, and this gives them an advantage over the U.S. citizens with whom they compete for jobs. Most Mexican commuters have no intention of becoming U.S. citizens. They simply continue to avail themselves of a loophole in U.S. immigration policy that has for years adversely affected citizen workers in the nation's southwestern border region.

In passing it is important to note that the U.S. Supreme Court ruled in 1973 that the bans against discrimination in the Civil Rights Act of 1964 do not apply to alienage.[27] Hence, it is legally permissible for employers in the private and public sectors to discriminate against permanent-resident aliens in the hiring, firing, and promotion of workers so long as discrimination is not alleged on other grounds. In its ruling, the Court drew a distinction between national origin, which is specifically protected under the provisions of the Civil Rights Act, and noncitizenship, which it chose to exclude from this protection. In 1976 President Gerald Ford issued Executive Order 11935, which banned the employment of permanent-resident aliens in the federal civil service. Congress, however, has since exempted certain governmental units from this ban. The exemptions pertain primarily to positions in scientific research, the foreign service, and technical research, but they apply to most postal employees as well. In addition, a number of states have passed laws that forbid resident aliens to hold certain jobs. In New York, for instance, they may not be employed as teachers or as state troopers. A California law that forbade aliens to hold any type of "peace officer" position (a broad category that includes welfare investigators, park rangers, and the state's Board of Dental Examiners) was upheld by the U.S. Supreme Court by a 5-to-4 vote in 1982.[28]

It should also be mentioned that the alienage issue became part of the 1983 congressional debates on the Simpson-Mazzoli bill. In the version of the bill that passed the House of Representatives a floor amendment by Congressman Barney Frank (D., Mass.) was approved that would reverse the current exclusion of alienage from coverage by the Civil Rights Act of 1964. Patterned on the provisions of the National Labor Relations Act, the amendment would create a new legal concept called "unfair immigration related employment practices." The new concept would make employers of four or more workers liable for discrimination on the basis of "national origin or alienage." There is no such provision in the Senate version of the bill. If accepted in the final bill (and if that bill is ultimately passed), this provision would reverse the 1973 Supreme Court decision that excluded alienage from coverage by the Civil Rights Act of 1964. It would also negate the previously mentioned executive order issued by President Ford and it could nullify any state laws that prohibit the hiring of aliens for certain public jobs. (The latter point would probably have to be settled by the courts.) The amendment also calls for the creation of a new position—that of an enforcement officer called a "special counsel"—to investigate charges of discrimination on the basis of alienage and any charges of employment discrimination that might arise following the enactment of the employer sanctions provision of the Simpson-Mazzoli bill (e.g., the charge that an employer refused to hire a Hispanic citizen for fear that he or she might be an illegal immigrant). The "special counsel" would bring such charges before the new administrative appeals body that the Simpson-Mazzoli bill seeks to create to handle requests for asylum. It should be realized, however, that duties pertaining to employment practices and discrimination issues require a degree of expertise that immigration officials do not have. The attempt to assign these duties to INS officials only emphasizes the need to transfer immigration matters from the Department of Justice to the Department of Labor (as will be advocated in the next chapter).

"Visitor-Workers"

The status of another, more pernicious, category of commuting Mexican workers is not debatable, it is simply illegal. Nonetheless, these persons pass through legal checkpoints by the thousands each day to work in U.S. border towns. They are not citizens of the United States nor do they have any claim to citizenship. For lack of a better name, let us call them "visitor-workers." Technically, "visitor-workers" are part of the "nonimmigrant" classification that was created under the Immigration Act of 1924. Technically, their presence in the United States constitutes a foreign-worker program, but it is seldom discussed as such.

The "visitor-worker" phenomenon exists because citizens of Mexico who live permanently in Mexican border towns are accorded special privileges to enter the United States at will. These Mexican citizens request an I-186 card from the INS. The cards are white, and as one would expect, the bearers of the card are known as "whitecarders." The I-186 card is issued to "legal visitors," or "border crossers." Technically, the bearer of the I-186 card is permitted to stay in the United States for up to 72 hours on any visit, may travel no farther than 25 miles from the border, and is specifically forbidden to seek employment or to be employed anywhere in the United States.

In fact, however, there is little to stop "whitecarders" from working, and many do. Prior to January 1, 1969, a white card was valid for only four years. Since that time the cards have not been dated, and thus they bear no expiration date. The INS claims that the renewal procedures are too time-consuming and costly. As can be imagined, the result is that many Mexican workers under the guise of "visitors" regularly cross the border to work.[29] Given the immense number of persons who cross at border checkpoints each day as well as the pressure to expedite that flow, little can be done by INS officials to police the prohibition against working that is supposedly a condition for issuance of the I-186 card.

Despite the fact that the "visitor-worker" phenomenon is well known to all who are familiar with conditions in the U.S.-Mexican border region, it is the least-studied aspect of the nation's immigration policy. Typically, "visitor-workers" are day workers or live-in workers. It is not uncommon in many border cities for even lower middle class families to have full-time maids.[30] As North has so poignantly put it, "There is no 'servant problem' on the border."[31] Because "visitor-workers" are illegal aliens, they seldom complain about their wages and working conditions. It is widely believed that Mexican "visitor-workers" are disproportionately women and that they crowd into occupations for which there is already a surplus of available labor. Their numbers are small compared to the total number of Mexicans who daily cross the border into the United States, but it is likely that they constitute a significant percentage of the persons who are employed in the occupations in which they work.

Exactly how many "whitecarders" there are remains a mystery. The INS reports that over 2.2 million cards were issued in the southwestern border region between 1960 and 1969.[32] There is no way to estimate how many have been issued since that time. A congressional committee has reported that a total of 1,323,380 persons used these cards to enter the United States in 1977.[33] How many of these persons were legitimate visitors and how many used their cards to gain access to jobs is unknown. The fact that statistics on "greencarders" and "whitecarders" are either vague or completely nonexistent was labeled "astonishing" by the 1970 UCLA Mexican-American Study Project.[34]

In passing it should be noted that the "white card" is also used by other types of illegal immigrants to cross the border. Having entered the United States, such persons often simply mail the cards back to Mexico and then move farther north (beyond the 25-mile "whitecarder" zone).[35] That way the cards cannot be confiscated (in the event the bearers are apprehended). If caught, these persons simply indicate that they are illegal immigrants and ask for voluntary departure processing. Back in Mexico the original white cards are waiting for them to use again.

The "Twin Plants" Program

Following the termination of the bracero program on December 31, 1964, the United States and Mexico began to seek other methods to assist Mexico in adjusting to the new labor market conditions in its border communities. The population of the Mexican border cities had grown immensely during the life of the bracero program, and the newly displaced braceros exacerbated the already severe problems of unemployment, underemployment, and poverty in the Mexican border communities.

In May 1965 Mexico passed the Border Industries Program (Ia Programa de Industrialización Fronterizo). The Mexican government had noted that the tariff codes of the United States allowed foreign-based subsidiaries of 100 percent U.S.-owned firms to assemble products whose parts were originally manufactured within the United States. It opted to participate in such a plan. Under special value-added tariff schedules, the products assembled in Mexico would then be shipped back to the parent firm in the United States for "finishing" and sale. Similar programs were already in effect in Taiwan, Hong Kong, South Korea, Haiti, and Puerto Rico.

Because of the tandem relationship of the firms involved, the endeavor has been referred to in the United States as the "twin plants," or "in-bond," program. In Mexico it is popularly called the "*maquila* program" and the plants are called *maquiladoras*. *Maquila* is the term used in Mexico to describe the payment of grain that a farmer gives to a miller for the milling services he provides the farmer. In this instance it is the price Mexico feels it must pay to attract the American firms that can provide its citizens with much-needed job opportunities.

The Mexican government felt that this type of program would be especially advantageous for Mexico because of this nation's proximity to the United States. It anticipated that lower transportation costs to and from the United States would make a Mexican-based program more attractive to U.S. firms than similar programs in other nations. It also believed that the long-term prospects for such an arrangement would be good in Mexico because Mexican-U.S. trade relationships have consistently been increasing both in scope and in the dollar value of goods. As Donald Barrensen has written:

> Many U.S. manufacturers who want to operate in foreign countries with low labor costs are apprehensive about the likely increase of restrictions on manufactured imports to protect and stimulate U.S. domestic employment. It is believed that such restrictions would not be applied to imports from Mexico because of [the] special conditions [that exist] between the two countries.[36]

In order to implement the twin plants program, a number of modifications had to be made in Mexico's laws, which included stringent regulations concerning the operation and taxation of foreign firms within its territory.[37] Hence, it was not until June 1966 that the program became operative. A free-trade zone, 12.5 miles wide, was established along the Mexican side of the entire 1,945-mile-long U.S.-Mexican border. In March 1971 a coastal strip along the Gulf of Mexico was added to this zone, and in November 1972 the Mexican government abolished the geographical limitations of the program and enlarged its scope to include the entire nation. These efforts to encourage dispersal were not successful, however. Most of the twin plants have remained in the border region because such locations keep transportation costs at a minimum and because plant supervisors and technicians—who usually are U.S. citizens—prefer to live on the U.S. side of the border and to be able to commute to their jobs.

The continuation of the program, of course, depends entirely upon the permissiveness of the laws of the United States. The relevant provisions of the U.S. tariff code are sections 806.30 and 807.00. The former, enacted in 1953, applies to the assembly of products made of metal components originally manufactured in the United States. The latter provision was adopted in 1963 and simply gave legal sanction to the already existing practice whereby a variety of products produced by U.S. firms could be exported for assembly in other countries and then returned for sale in the United States if the condition of the parts had not changed. Under both of these tariff provisions, a duty is assessed only on any value that is added to such products, and under the twin plants program, that is basically nothing more than the wages paid to the workers who do the assembly work. As can be seen in Table 31, the wages for unskilled work in Mexico are quite low relative to prevailing U.S. wages. Hence, there is a strong financial incentive for Mexican workers to participate in the twin plants program. Moreover, although Mexican wages in the relevant industries are about one-third the

TABLE 31.   MINIMUM DAILY WAGE FOR UNSKILLED LABOR IN
MEXICAN BORDER STATES AND CITIES, 1981

State	Cities	Minimum Daily Wage for Unskilled Labor (in U.S. Dollars)
Baja California	Tijuana, Ensenada, Tecate, Rosario, and Mexicali	9.04
Sonora	San Luis Rio Colorado	9.04
	Nogales and Agua Prieta	8.61
Chihuahua	Ciudad Juárez	9.04
	Chihuahua	7.32
Coahuila	Ciudad Acuña and Piedras Negras	7.32
Tamaulipas	Matamoros, Nuevo Laredo, and Reynosa	8.61

Source: Reprinted from Donald W. Barrensen, "Mexico's Assembly Program: Implications for the United States," *Texas Business Review,* November–December 1981, p. 256, by permission of the Bureau of Business Research, University of Texas at Austin. Copyright © 1981, Bureau of Business Research, University of Texas at Austin.

comparable wages in the United States,[38] the participating U.S. firms are supposed to pay 50 percent more than the prevailing legal minimum wage in each Mexican city. Whether Mexican workers are in fact paid at these levels is a matter of speculation, for enforcement is scant and corruption in enforcement is notorious. The fact remains that the wage differences for unskilled U.S. and Mexican workers are immense, and the drastic devaluations of the peso that occurred in 1982 have significantly widened the differential.

A significant boost to the growth of the twin plants program occurred in 1970 when the U.S. Tariff Commission released a special report on the employment impact of sections 806.30 and 807.00 of the nation's tariff code.[39] The report was made following President Richard Nixon's request in August 1969 that the commission conduct a detailed inquiry. In its report the commission noted that the aggregate benefits exceeded the aggregate costs to the *nation* and recommended that the tariff provisions remain as they were. It did not, however, attempt to assess the benefits and costs to the border communities of the United States and their workers.

In the wake of the Tariff Commission's report, the number of U.S. firms participating in the twin plants program increased sharply. By 1972, 345 twin plants were operating with a total labor force of more than 46,000 workers.[40] Many of the participating businesses are among the nation's largest corporations (e.g., Bendix, Honeywell, Lockheed, RCA, Samsonite, and Zenith). It is estimated that in 1972 they collectively produced $400 million worth of goods. By

1980 the number of assembly plants had grown to 556, the number of employees was 112,277, and total production was estimated at \$2.3 billion worth of goods.[41]

Ironically, the twin plants program is a contradiction of Mexico's long-range border economic development strategy. In 1960 Mexico enacted its National Frontier Program (Ia Programa Nacional Fronterizo, or PRONAF), which sought to diversify the economy of its northern states as part of an effort to reduce its dependence on the U.S. economy. The twin plants program, however, has sharply increased that dependence.[42] The size of the twin plants program has varied with the cycles of the U.S. economy. In fact, noted Mexican economists have warned (to no apparent avail) that "the Mexican government is running a great risk in depending on this type of manufacturing for the industrial development of the border region and gearing its employment policy toward it."[43] The restrictive assembly jobs do not stimulate additional economic activity since, by definition, no locally related industries are involved. Moreover, prior to Mexico's imposition of stringent exchange controls and import restrictions in the summer of 1982, much of the income received by Mexican twin plants workers was spent on consumer nondurables on the American side of the border. A 1981 study of the spending patterns of Mexican twin plants workers in Ciudad Juárez estimated that they spent 70 percent of their wages across the border in El Paso, Texas.[44] These expenditures probably created some employment in the low-wage retailing and service sectors of the U.S. border communities that might otherwise not have existed, but to the degree that this happened, even fewer benefits from the twin plants program accrued to Mexico.

With the far-reaching controls that were imposed during the summer of 1982 and the sharp devaluations of the peso that occurred that year, spending by all Mexicans in border communities was sharply curtailed. These spending reductions led to extensive layoffs of workers and the closing of some companies in the U.S. border cities.[45] This means that the few employment benefits that accrued to U.S. workers from the expenditures of twin plants workers in these cities have largely evaporated—at lease for the time being.

It is easy to understand why Mexico continues to participate in the twin plants program. Despite the fact that the program conflicts with the Mexican government's long-range economic development objectives, there are jobs and foreign exchange to be gained from it in the short run. It is not clear, however, why the United States should encourage such an undertaking through its own tariff policies without offering the slightest compensation to its own border citizens, whose opportunities for employment probably are retarded, and certainly are not helped, by the existence of the program. Relative to the rest of the country, the supply of labor and the working conditions that prevail in all the major U.S. border communities should long ago have turned the region into an industrial magnet. The fact that the region is instead one of the most economically depressed areas in the nation is proof that something is awry.[46] The U.S. tariff policies that give special preference to products assembled in Mexico are part of the explanation for the perpetuation of this regional poverty. For an American enterprise, any possible economic advantage of locating in one of the border communities on the U.S. side is always nullified by the even greater economic advantage of locating on the Mexican side.

The twin plants program was allegedly conceived to meet the needs of unemployed males (i.e., the former braceros), but the nature of the assembly work is such that 80–90 percent of the employees have consistently been young women.[47] In many instances, therefore, the program has absorbed some of the surplus of female laborers who would otherwise remain unemployed or might not even attempt to enter the labor force. There is also some evidence that the program has contributed to internal migration to Mexico's border region, but it is difficult to attribute the decision to migrate to just one cause.[48] Nevertheless, for young Mexican women, who are expected to live at home, the intended location of the family is likely to be the dominant consideration.

Technically, of course, U.S. tariff codes are not part of the nation's immigration system. Discussion of the twin plants program has been included here because Mexico's participation was originally prompted by the termination of the bracero program and because the effects of the twin plants program impinge upon the economy of the border region of both Mexico and the United States. The search for an understanding of the factors that give rise to immigration— both legal and illegal—as well as the impacts of such movements, requires that we review all governmentally determined immigration-related policies as well.

CHAPTER 8

U.S. Immigration Policy
in the 1980s

Having discussed the evolution of each of the major components of the nation's immigration policy, it is appropriate to conclude by relating this policy to contemporary labor market trends. As noted earlier, immigration in all its forms has since the 1960s gradually reemerged as a major cause of the growth of the U.S. population and labor force. A new era of mass immigration is now in progress, and all indications are that this trend will continue and perhaps even intensify. Concurrently, the expanding labor force of the United States is undergoing a radical transformation in both the character of the demand for labor and the composition of the available supply of labor. In this concluding chapter, therefore, we will address the reality that the public policymakers of the nation have as yet refused to face—the fact that mass immigration has economic as well as political implications. It is essential that U.S. immigration policy be reconciled with contemporary labor market requirements. To maintain the status quo is to invite an inevitable negative reaction to all forms of immigration. The nation's policymakers cannot continue to treat immigration as a political abstraction that functions in a vacuum devoid of economic implications. On the contrary, immigration is a change-creating process. It is affected by prevailing labor force trends, but it is also capable of influencing the future course of those trends.

Immigrants are not ornaments in our society. They are human beings who, regardless of what motivated them to leave their homelands, need to find a means of support in this country. If the current influx of immigrants were of minor proportions, as was the case in the 1930s and 1940s; if the rate of growth of the U.S. labor force were slow; if occupational employment patterns were stable; and if the composition of the available labor supply were inconsequential to contemporary economic and social expectations, reconciliation of the nation's immigration policies with its broader economic policies would not be necessary. As will be shown, however, such a reconciliation is long overdue. Labor force parameters have changed significantly in the past twenty years, and it is time to place immigrants within the broader matrix of factors that influence the economic welfare of the nation. Immigration policy is too important to be scrutinized only in terms of its political acceptability. It needs to be held accountable for its economic impacts as well.

A Brief Review of the State of U.S. Immigration Policy

In mid-1984, the U.S. immigration system continues to function with assiduous disregard for the derivative labor market implications of its individual policies. The policies pertain to legal immigrants, nonimmigrant workers, refugees, illegal immigrants, and border commuters, but none addresses the impact of immigrants on the American labor force and on U.S. labor markets.

With regard to legal immigrants, the number admitted each year is fixed by an overall ceiling. Each year, however, the ceiling is exceeded because the immediate relatives of immigrants also are admitted, and as of 1984 they were not counted. Eighty percent of the legal immigrant admissions are based on the politically popular concept of family reunification. Only 20 percent of the admissions are based on an actual need for the occupational skills of the immigrants in U.S. labor markets. No geographic restrictions are placed upon legal immigrants whereby their admission would be conditional upon their willingness to settle in local labor markets where there are shortages of workers with similar occupational backgrounds or away from areas where there are surpluses. Consequently, immigrants tend to cluster in relatively few cities in relatively few states. Their contribution to these labor markets is therefore purely accidental and may even be detrimental. It can in no way be argued that U.S. immigration policy is designed to meet the skill and educational requirements of the local labor markets where legal immigrants tend to reside and seek employment. In sharp contrast to the policies of the few other industrialized nations that admit sizable numbers of immigrants, the U.S. immigration system functions largely without regard for these considerations. During earlier eras, when most of the jobs that needed to be filled were unskilled in nature, there was no need to be particularly concerned about the labor market adjustment of immigrants. As will be shown, however, such a random process is not justified in an era when the number of unskilled jobs is declining (and unskilled workers are in surplus) and the number of skilled jobs is increasing (and skilled workers are in short supply).

In contrast to the policies of other immigrant-receiving nations, U.S. immigration policy makes no allowance for cyclical swings in the nation's employment levels. The number of legal immigrants admitted to the United States is fixed; no consideration is given to whether U.S. unemployment levels are high or low, declining or rising. Instead of providing for an administrative agency that would adjust the annual ceiling to meet short-term employment fluctuations, Congress mandated a figure that is reviewed only every couple of decades. Obviously this process makes no allowance for the need to increase the supply of labor during periods of labor shortage and to decrease the supply during periods of labor surplus. With immigration in all its forms accounting in recent years for an influx of over one million persons a year, it can hardly be said that these annual infusions into the U.S. labor force and population are insignificant. Moreover, because these immigrants are concentrated in selected states and urban labor markets, they undoubtedly give rise to employment and wage conditions that would not prevail in their absence.

With regard to nonimmigrant workers, who are ostensibly admitted to work temporarily in low-wage industries, U.S. policy reflects a political genuflection to special interest groups rather than a logical response to demonstrated economic needs. The number of nonimmigrant workers involved is small, but the impact of temporary-worker programs on employment opportunities and wages in selected labor markets is often substantial. The longer these programs are allowed to persist, the more addicted the employers in these industries will become to their cost benefits and the less likely it will be that competitive forces will ever succeed in making jobs in these industries attractive to citizen workers. In fact, employers in these industries bring to pass the self-fulfilling prophecy that citizen workers are unavailable for these types of jobs. Certainly there is no demonstrated need for a new large-scale foreign-worker program for the agricultural industry as provided in the version of the Simpson-Mazzoli bill that passed the House of Representatives in June 1984.

At the present time there is no limit on the number of refugees admitted or the number of asylees permitted to remain in the United States. The flow of refugees and asylees has increased dramatically in recent years, and, as experience has shown, their numbers can escalate at any given moment. Because there are no fixed refugee ceilings, there is currently no way to force a discussion of priorities. Given the size of world's refugee populations and the paralysis imposed by the U.S. judicial system with respect to asylum procedures, it can be anticipated that refugees and asylees will continue to comprise a substantial portion of the nation's annual immigration flow. If their numbers continue to grow and if their patterns of settlement do not change, they, too, will increasingly affect employment and wage patterns in selected labor markets of the nation.

In the southwestern border region of the United States, commuting workers from Mexico as well as Mexican "visitors" (who work with impunity despite bans against their seeking employment) comprise a significant portion of the labor force and have had a negative economic impact on the region's citizen workers. Despite the fact that this region is among the most poverty-stricken in the entire United States, no effort has been made to restrict the job-seeking activity of these persons.

In truth, the prevailing immigration policies of the nation are honored more in the breach than by adherence to their terms. Illegal immigration probably adds more workers to the labor force each year than do all the other categories of immigrants combined. It would appear that it is the sizable low-wage labor markets of the nation that must seek to accommodate this infusion of additional job-seekers. Sadly, millions of citizen workers have been forced to compete with illegal immigrants in these same labor markets. Because the nation's low-income citizen workers have been the nominal target of many public policy measures designed to overcome the causes of their plight, it is blatantly counterproductive to tolerate the uncontrolled entry of illegal immigrants into direct competition with them. Moreover, the creation of a sizable subpopulation of illegal immigrants, who because of their status live in fear and are denied the political rights of citizens, can hardly be in the nation's long-term interests.

Individually and collectively, the aforementioned policies of action and inaction affect not only the immigrants themselves but also the employment opportunities of citizen workers, the quality of life of many U.S. communities, and, ultimately, the welfare of the nation as a whole.

The fact that the United States continues to accept a substantial number of legal immigrants and permanent refugee settlers is a feature that sharply distinguishes it from other industrialized nations. This characteristic has been, and should continue to be, a positive feature of U.S. immigration policy. As the Select Commission on Immigration and Refugee Policy concluded, however, the nation can no longer afford to receive *unlimited* numbers of immigrants.[1] Immigration policy, like all other U.S. economic policy measures, must be held accountable for its labor market ramifications.

Labor Force Trends during the Fourth Wave of Mass Immigration

The resurgence of immigration that has occurred since 1965 has exactly paralleled unprecedented changes in both the size and composition of the labor force and population of the United States. An awareness of these changes is essential to an understanding of the context in which the renewed mass immigration has occurred.

THE GROWTH OF THE LABOR FORCE

Beginning in the mid-1950s, accelerating in the mid-1960s, and continuing through the 1970s and early 1980s, the size of the civilian labor force of the United States has expanded at a rate that has exceeded even the most optimistic projections of labor market forecasters. The magnitude of the increase has itself become a problem for policymakers in their efforts to design a full-employment strategy for the nation. Between 1955 and 1980 the civilian labor force grew from 65 million to 104.7 million workers. In terms of annual growth, it gained an average of 1.6 million workers a year over that time span. This long-term annual increase, however, masks the fact that there was also a significant stepwise climb in the annual averages during this period. Interim estimates indicated that between 1955 and 1964 the civilian labor force increased by an average of 888,000 workers annually; from 1964 to 1973 it increased by an average of 1.8 million workers a year; and from 1973 to 1980 it averaged 2.2 million new workers a year. Then, in 1980, U.S. census data revealed that the labor force growth for the 1971–1980 period had been significantly underestimated. The actual growth of the labor force over the decade was 2.3 million workers higher than the interim estimates.[2] Illegal immigration may partially explain the unprecedented magnitude of this error in the most sophisticated labor force data collection system available to the nation.

In 1980 the Bureau of Labor Statistics (BLS) of the U.S. Department of Labor issued its long-term labor force projections for 1979–1985 and 1979–1995. The forecasts included a low, an intermediate, and a high growth projection. In the BLS's intermediate scenario, the labor force was projected to reach 115 million by 1985 and 128 million by 1995 (or an annual growth of about 2 million to 1985 and 1.25 million from 1985 to 1995).[3] In the past, however, all BLS projections of future labor force growth have erred on the low side. Moreover, the BLS candidly admits that "there is no way of ascertaining what portion of undocumented workers, if any, are currently [i.e., in 1980] accounted for in existing labor force data."[4] Consequently, in making its projections of the growth of the labor force from 1980 to 1995, the BLS did not allow for the future influx of illegal immigrants.[5] This conscious omission guarantees that once again its long-range projections of labor force growth will prove to be considerably understated. Furthermore, in making its forecasts the BLS used as its estimate of net legal immigration the figure of 400,000 immigrants and refugees a year and a labor force participation rate of 63.7 percent of those persons aged sixteen years and older. Data for the 1970s and early 1980s indicate that both of these estimate assumptions are grossly understated. Indeed, in 1984 the BLS issued "a second look" at its earlier projections and reported a significant upward revision.[6] Its 1984 intermediate projection of labor force growth is 124.9 million by 1990 and 131.4 million by 1995—or 3.8 million more than it estimated in 1980. The revised estimates project an annual increase of 1.8 million workers through 1990 and 1.3 million from 1990 to 1995. The upward revisions were based on corrections reported in the 1980 census that were not available when the earlier estimates were made. The 1984 estimates do not contain any adjustments for the effects of immigration other than those that were made in the 1980 forecast and, as noted, those unrealistic assumptions virtually guarantee that even the revised estimates will prove to be too conservative.

The quantum increases in immigration that have occurred since 1965 have paralleled unprecedented annual increases in the size of the nation's citizen labor force. The factors that have contributed to the latter include the attainment (beginning in 1964 and lasting through 1979) of labor force entry age by the post–World War II "baby boom" generation; a long-term increase in the labor force participation rate of youths; and the change in societal values with respect to the acceptance of women in the work place and the increase in the number of women (especially married women) who choose to participate in the labor force.

THE COMPOSITION OF THE LABOR FORCE

The age cohort of the U.S. population that grew most rapidly from the mid-1960s until 1980 was the youth population (ages sixteen to twenty-four years). Between 1965 and 1979 this cohort increased in size at an annual rate of 3.9 percent, the prime labor force age group (ages twenty-five to fifty-four) increased at an annual rate of 2.2 percent, and the older cohort (over fifty-five) increased annually by 0.4 percent. By 1980, however, the size of the youth cohort had began to decline and its significance will continue to diminish between 1980 and 1995. Over this interval, in fact, the youth cohort will actually decrease in numbers at an average rate of 0.9 percent a year.[7] Unfortunately, however, the anticipated aggregate decline in the size of the youth cohort between 1980 and 1995 masks a serious compositional shift that is taking place within this cohort. Namely, the aggregate decline in the youth cohort reflects a sharp decline in the expected number of white youths. Because the birth rates of blacks and Hispanics did not begin to decline until much later than the rate for whites, and the rate of this decline during the 1960s and 1970s was much slower than that of whites, the number of black and Hispanic youths will continue to increase throughout the 1980s and into the early 1990s. Thus, youth unemployment—which has been a serious national problem since the mid-1960s—will continue to be a serious issue throughout the 1980s for minority youths even though the size of the youth cohort itself will decline sharply.[8] Moreover, given the fact that minorities and immigrants tend to concentrate in the same geographic—mostly urban—areas, it is likely that many minority youths will have to compete with illegal immigrants and some portion of the growing population of refugees and asylees for entry-level jobs.

At the national level, the advancement of the large youth cohort of the 1965–1979 era from their teenage years into their prime working age years during the 1980–1995 era has already been heralded as "demography's glad tidings" for the economy.[9] This shift portends a significant "productivity bonus" for the nation. It is projected that by 1995 more than 70 percent of the U.S. labor force will be in the prime working age bracket.[10] This means that the nation will be confronted with the need to provide permanent jobs (as opposed to the temporary, or transitional, jobs usually held by the youth cohort) on a scale that has never been required before. Thus there will be a "pig in the python," so to speak, over the next fifteen years, for the largest labor force cohort will consist of workers who have the highest labor force participation rates and the strongest commitment to their jobs. Realization of the anticipated "productivity bonus" associated with this demographic shift will of course depend on whether the workers in this cohort can find jobs. The pursuit of full employment which has proved to be an elusive goal during the 1970s and early 1980s, can only be made more difficult in the remainder of the 1980s by the need to provide jobs for so many prime age workers. Given the limited number of quality jobs that exist at any given time, it is already likely that many job-seekers will not be able to secure the types of jobs they want, and for those who do, it is unlikely that they will advance as rapidly as they hope to or as others have done in the past. Some work-seekers will be bumped downward into jobs for which they are overqualified. Others may be pushed out of the ranks of the employed and into active competition with the poorly qualified and with the least experienced job-seekers for any type of job that might become available. Accordingly, it is unlikely that there will be any shortage of workers for unskilled and semiskilled jobs in the foreseeable future.

The societal tension associated with the competition for access to jobs and for advancement in jobs during the 1980–1995 interval will be exacerbated by the need to enlarge the share of jobs, and improve the types of jobs, held by racial and ethnic minorities and by women. Because the civil rights movement and the feminist movement have increasingly turned their attention to economic goals, the labor market has naturally emerged as the primary arena in which to accomplish their objectives. As matters now stand, the BLS projects that the black labor force will grow at twice the annual rate of the white labor force from 1980 to 1995 (2.5 percent versus 1.2 percent per year respectively).[11] The BLS has not issued a long-term projection for Hispanics as a separate group (traditionally they are included in data on whites). But given the fact that fertility rates for Hispanics are much higher than those for blacks, and that a disproportionate number of Hispanics are immigrating to the United States relative to blacks, it is certain that the growth rates for the Hispanic labor force in the next fifteen years will exceed those for blacks.[12] As for women, they are expected to account for over two-thirds of the growth in the labor force during the same period.[13] In 1975, women constituted 40 percent of the labor force, but it is estimated that by 1985 this figure will rise to 45 percent and by 1995, to 47 percent.

Thus it is clear that in the last two decades of the twentieth century the labor force of the United States will be confronted with immense internal pressures to change its racial and gender patterns of employment. The effort to bring about these changes will be hampered if the nation's immigration policy continues to ignore the labor market consequences of its implementation.

The Supply of Unskilled Workers

Because the size of the nation's youth cohort is expected to decline during the 1980s and because the aspirations of many female and minority workers are rising to ever-higher levels, some analysts have forecast that the nation will soon face a shortage of unskilled and low-wage workers. In many ways it would be a blessing if such a shortage did occur, for it is hard to imagine an easier economic problem to solve. Given the rapidly declining quality of public education in the United States, however, it is more likely to be the case that many of the nation's youths (especially those in central cities and in rural areas) will be poorly prepared for the jobs that will become available in our increasingly technologically oriented society in the 1980s and 1990s. In 1983 the National Commission on Excellence in Education warned that the decline in the quality of education and training has been so rapid and so pervasive that the long-term welfare of the nation is "in peril."[14] Consequently, when one views the data in that report which show the magnitude of the dropout and pushout problem, as well as the low achievement scores of the graduates of many of the nation's schools, it is hard to imagine that there will ever be a shortage of new job-seekers at the lower end of the skill ladder. The reforms needed to reverse this decline in the quality of public education will require a substantial infusion of tax dollars as well as major changes in the educational process. At the present time the nation does not appear to be prepared to respond to these needs, but even if it should, it is probably already too late for most of the youth who will enter the labor force in the remainder of the 1980s.

If by chance the miracle of economic miracles does occur and the United States achieves full employment, and if under these special circumstances labor shortages in certain unskilled occupations do occur, there is a preferable alternative to illegal immigration as a means of filling these needs. That is, of course, to use the front door to the nation's labor force and simply increase legal immigration under the occupational admission categories of the existing immigration statutes. At present, only highly skilled and educated immigrants are admitted under these provisions in response to perceived labor market shortages, but there is no reason why the legal immigration system and the refugee admissions program could not be adapted to meet real shortages of unskilled workers as well.

The use of illegal immigration as a means to supply unskilled workers to the U.S. labor force is totally unjustifiable. When there are no real labor shortages, the illegal immigrants harm the employment and income opportunities of citizen workers; if real shortages exist, the correct course would be to enlarge the flow of legal immigrants and refugees who are unskilled and poorly educated. The labor force of the world is crammed with unskilled workers and refugees who, experience shows, would be more than willing to emigrate to the United States if given the opportunity to fill such a vacuum.

Employment Trends during the Fourth Wave of Mass Immigration

In addition to the dramatic changes that have taken place in the demographics of the labor supply of the United States since the 1960s, even more consequential long-term changes have been occurring in the demand for labor. The American economy is in the midst of a radical transformation in the types and locations of jobs that are available, and as a result the nation's employment patterns are rapidly changing. Because employment is one of the principal reasons immigrants come to the United States, it is important that the supply of labor provided by immigration be responsive to these emerging trends. If it is not responsive, immigration could retard the formidable adjustment process that confronts the citizen labor force, a process that already involves secular shifts in job opportunities and persistently high unemployment rates.[15]

The first of these structural changes pertains to the rapidly declining significance of the goods-producing sector of the economy. Agriculture, the dominant employment sector of the U.S. economy in the nineteenth century, has been a consistently negative source of employment since the end of World War II. Between 1960 and 1980—the period of renewed ("fourth wave") mass immigration to the United States—the number of agricultural workers employed in the economy declined steadily from 5.4 million to 3.3 million. More importantly, as shown in Table 32, the nonagricultural industries that comprise the remainder of the goods-producing sector of the economy have barely been able to show any absolute gain in employment during this long period. In relative terms, all the goods-producing industries have declined significantly in terms of the percentage of the nation's jobs they provide to the economy. Conversely, as also is shown in Table 32, the five industries that comprise the service sector of the economy have experienced significant increases in the absolute number of persons they employ, and four of the five have also dramatically increased their relative share of the nation's total employment.

Although the goods-producing sector and the transportation industry in the service sector provided most of the nation's employment opportunities during the "third wave" of mass immigration (1890–1914), they are now unable to provide as many jobs and their occupational structure is shifting away from blue-collar employment and toward white-collar employment. Moreover, the effects of automation and computerization, as well as the prospects for the rapid introduction of robots (at least in manufacturing), imply that future increases in output in the goods-producing sector will likely be accomplished with far fewer labor inputs.[16] Consequently, the growing U.S. labor force has increasingly had to turn to the service industries to find employment. As of 1980, over two-thirds of the nation's nonagricultural labor force was employed in the service sector. Generally speaking, in the past the goods-producing industries provided a disproportionate demand for the nation's unskilled and semiskilled workers while the service sector tended to provide a relatively greater demand for the more skilled and educated workers.

The second major structural shift in employment patterns pertains to the occupational composition of the economy. Table 33 shows that the ratio of nonproduction to production workers has increased in every sector of the private economy since 1960. This shift also represents a relative increase in the job opportunitites available for the more skilled and educated workers in the labor force. Since 1976, employment in white-collar occupations has exceeded 50 percent of all occupations in the U.S. economy. A study of the occupational growth patterns of the economy from 1972 to 1980 revealed that of the approximately 176 different occupations that increased in size during this period, 20 occupations accounted for half of the total growth.[17] White-collar employment—spurred by rapid growth in the professional, technical, managerial, and administrative occupations—achieved the largest gain, 30 percent; blue-collar employment edged ahead by only 7.8 percent; service employment increased by 18.2 percent; while the number of farmworkers declined by 11.9 percent over this time span.

The ten occupations that experienced the greatest absolute increases in employment were (in order of magnitude) secretaries, cashiers, registered nurses, cooks, truck drivers, accountants, engineers, computer operators, bookkeepers,

TABLE 32. EMPLOYEES IN NONAGRICULTURAL ESTABLISHMENTS BY INDUSTRY, 1960, 1970, AND 1980 (in thousands)

| | Total Nonagricultural Employment | | Goods-Producing Industries | | | | | | Service Industries | | | | | | | | | |
| | | | Mining | | Construction | | Manufacturing | | Transportation, Communications, Utilities | | Trade | | Finance, Insurance, Real Estate | | Personal Services | | Government (Civilian Employees) | |
Year	No.	%	No.	%	No.	%	No.	%	No.	%	No.	%	No.	%	No.	%	No.	%
1960	54,189	100	712	1.3	2,926	5.4	16,796	31.0	4,004	7.4	11,391	21.0	2,629	4.9	7,378	13.6	8,353	15.4
1970	70,880	100	623	0.9	3,588	5.1	19,367	27.3	4,515	6.4	15,040	21.2	3,645	5.1	11,548	16.3	12,554	17.7
1980	90,658	100	1,025	1.1	4,469	4.9	20,363	22.5	5,155	5.7	20,573	22.7	5,162	5.7	17,740	19.6	16,171	17.8

Source: U.S. Department of Labor, *Employment and Training Report of the President, 1981* (Washington, D.C.: GPO, 1981), table C-1, p. 211.

TABLE 33. NONPRODUCTION WORKERS ON PRIVATE PAYROLLS AS A PERCENTAGE OF TOTAL EMPLOYMENT IN EACH INDUSTRIAL DIVISION, 1960, 1970, AND 1980

Year	Total Percentage of Nonagricultural Private Sector Employment	Industry						
		Mining	Construction	Manufacturing	Transport, Communication, Utilities	Trade	Finance	Service
1960	16.0	19.9	14.7	25.1	N.A.[a]	9.4	18.4	N.A.
1970	17.4	24.1	16.7	27.5	13.3	11.1	21.0	9.2
1980	18.7	25.6	21.3	29.9	16.5	12.3	24.4	11.0

Source: Employment and Training Report of the President, 1981 (Washington, D.C.: GPO, 1981), table C-3, p. 213.
[a]N.A. = not available.

and computer specialists. The six occupations that experienced the highest percentage increased between 1972 and 1980 were computer systems analysts, computer operators, welfare service aids, authors, psychologists, and research workers. The ten occupations that sustained the largest absolute decreases (in order of magnitude) were delivery workers, cleaners and servants, farm owners, unpaid family farmworkers, garage and gas station attendants, sewers and stitchers, child-care workers, textile operatives, telephone operators, and stenographers. The six occupations that sustained the greatest absolute losses (at least 60,000 fewer jobs over the interval) were delivery workers, cleaners and servants, farm owners, farm laborers and unpaid family farmworkers, garage workers, and sewers and stitchers.

Given the chronic deficiencies of the nation's immigration data, it is very difficult to pinpoint exactly where immigrants fit into this emerging occupational structure. As discussed in Chapter 3, the meager amount of research that has been done on the contemporary employment and earnings experiences of legal immigrants is based on data for 1970 or earlier years. Many heroic assumptions had to be made by the few scholars who were willing to base their conclusions on these data. Both the size and the composition of the flow of legal immigrants have changed significantly since 1970. Moreover, the full effect of the Immigration Act of 1965 was not felt until after 1970. In the 1970s and early 1980s the Western Hemisphere has emerged as the major source of legal immigrants. The educational and skill levels of Western Hemisphere immigrants have been found to be substantially lower than those of the Eastern Hemisphere immigrants who dominated the pre-1970 immigrant flows. Likewise, as was also pointed out in Chapter 3, the ethnic composition of immigrants from the Eastern Hemisphere has changed substantially since 1970. The proportion of Eastern Hemisphere immigrants from Europe (who have had relatively high human capital endowments) has declined sharply while the proportion from Asia (who have had relatively lower human capital endowments) has risen sharply.

The immigration studies that were based on pre-1970 imply that the occupational profile of immigrants corresponds roughly to the occupations of the American labor force that are expanding. This conclusion is dubious, however. Although the legal immigration system does provide workers to meet labor market needs, the family reunification principle controls 80 percent of the available visas, and thus the above result is largely coincidental. Moreover, the overt nepotism of the prevailing legal immigration system, as well as the tendency of the system to favor those who have the time and money to master its complexities, raises questions about the system's fundamental fairness, questions that transcend purely labor market considerations.

The impact of refugees on U.S. labor markets is even less clear than the effect of immigrants who are admitted under the preference system. As discussed in Chapter 6, prior to 1973 refugees from Europe, the Soviet Union, and Cuba came from occupational and educational backgrounds that qualified them for employment in the occupations that were expanding in that era. The refugees who came from Cuba in the late 1970s and early 1980s do not appear to have these qualifications, however, nor do most of the refugees who entered from Southeast Asia in the late 1970s and who continue to be admitted in substantial numbers in the early 1980s.

As for the illegal immigrants who are entering from Mexico and the Caribbean Basin, it appears that they are crowding into the occupations that have shown the greatest decline in employment in recent years. To the extent that this is true, they are in direct competition with poorly skilled citizen workers who are struggling to find work in these same occupations. There is little or no evidence to suggest that illegal immigrants are seeking employment in the expanding occupations of the economy.

The third significant structural change in U.S. employment patterns that has paralleled the renewal of mass immigration pertains to the geographic shift that has occurred in job opportunities. This structural shift has resulted primarily from major changes in the location of the defense operations of the federal government; the declining competitiveness of certain basic industries due to enhanced international competition; and the general decentralization of employment that has characterized the growth of service industries since the late 1950s. In 1980 a study of the changes that had occurred in the geographic distribution of employment between 1968 and 1978 revealed that while overall employment increased by 24.3 percent during these years, the geographic distribution of this growth was extremely unequal across the country.[18] Employment in the northeastern states grew by only 10.7 percent and in the north-central states by 18.8 percent, while in the southern and western states it grew by 32.6 percent and 39.7 percent, respectively. The response of workers to these regional growth patterns triggered a substantial internal migration. In terms of net migration (the difference between the number of persons moving into and out of a particular region), the northeastern states sustained a loss of 2,384,000 persons and the north-central region lost 2,034,000 persons, while the southern states gained 2,655,000 persons and the western states gained 1,763,000 persons. Unfortunately, but typically, this study did not include any data on immigration. It simply stated that immigration "has been particularly important in the South and West."[19]

As noted in the earlier chapters of this volume, the available research on the settlement patterns of immigrants indicates a strong tendency toward clustering. Legal immigrants and refugees have tended to settle in the central city labor markets of half a dozen states, and illegal immigrants have shown a pronounced tendency to reside and seek work in these same localities. From the standpoint of the immigrants, this clustering has facilitated their assimilation to the American way of life and the nation's economy.[20] The particular communities that receive immigrants, however, are called upon to provide jobs, housing, and related community services. As indicated earlier, the urban labor markets of California, Texas, and Florida have since the 1960s been the primary destinations not only of immigrants but also of record numbers of citizen migrants. At the other extreme, some of the urban labor markets of New York, Illinois, and New Jersey have been the destinations of many immigrants during periods when the employment opportunities and population of these metropolitan areas have been in a state of secular decline. In both instances immigration has complicated rather than eased the labor market adjustment process. With little or no federal assistance, these few states and localities bear the burdens imposed by the mindlessness of federal immigration policy.

The Internationalization of the Domestic Economy

One of the most pronounced changes in the U.S. economy began in the 1970s and is likely to continue into the foreseeable future. That change is the internationalization of the domestic economy. Enhanced foreign competition has become a fact of contemporary life. While international trade accounted for 9 percent of the U.S. gross national product in 1950, by 1980 its share had increased to 25 percent. In 1982, over half of all profits for American corporations came from foreign sales and investments; international trade involved a third of the production of all U.S. cropland and a fourth of the nation's farm income; and one-sixth of all jobs and about 70 percent of all manufactured goods in the United States were in direct competition with imports.[21] Similarly, it is conservatively estimated that legal and illegal immigrants and refugees accounted for 25–50 percent of the growth in the U.S. population that occurred during the 1970s.

The forces that led to the internationalization of the U.S. economy have been at work since the end of World War II. One of the most important of these was the relative position of the United States in the world economy and the nation's advocacy of a relatively free international trading system. The United States joined with other countries to form institutions to facilitate international trade and finance—the General Agreement on Trade and Tariffs (GATT), the International Monetary Fund, and the International Bank for Reconstruction and Development (i.e., the World Bank). It also established special unilateral aid programs for the reconstruction of Western Europe and Japan following World War II.

The dominant role of the United States in the world economy made it possible for American interests to impact strongly on international economic institutions and policies. By 1950 the U.S. gross national product accounted for over half of the world's gross production of goods and services. The American economy had been greatly strengthened during World War II while the economies of all the other major industrial nations had been devastated. The United States emerged from World War II with a backlog of technology that provided the basis for an unprecedented rate of growth in productivity and total output that remained unchallenged until the 1970s. The dollar became the currency of international commerce and English became the dominant language of international transactions. The international trading system was also strengthened during this era by information, communications, and transportation advances that integrated world product, commodity, and capital markets.

The nature of economic interdependence is such that actions taken in one nation are transferred to other nations. For example, in the years following World War II a number of countries adopted export-driven industrial policies that were designed to develop key industries, and by the 1970s many of these key industries had come into direct competition with American firms. The industrial policies that caused these foreign firms to become competitive in international markets included protecting domestic firms from outside competition until they had built a greater capacity than could be sold in domestic markets; various subsidy arrangements, especially the subsidization of capital costs; and the prohibition of foreign investments in domestic markets unless the foreign firms making those investments agreed to share desirable technologies.

These policies have not been limited to industrialized countries such as Japan and the nations of Western Europe. Less economically developed countries— Mexico, Korea, Brazil, and Taiwan for instance—also have adopted export-driven industrial policies to help them either penetrate American markets or compete with American products in other foreign markets. These countries have sought to develop capital- and energy-intensive export industries, but such industries create very few jobs in the domestic economy and even serve to displace labor, especially from agriculture. At the same time, export-driven industrial policies have improved these nations' communications systems, exposed their people to higher living standards, and raised expectations which because of rapid population growth cannot be realized. The logical consequence of these developments has been an increased desire on the part of many persons in these countries to emigrate to other countries. People tend to seek more attractive job opportunities if they are accessible. Because the United States is the most open of the industrialized countries and because its immigration policies have been so lax, it has received in recent years more immigrants and refugees than the rest of the industrialized nations combined. The number of immigrants from Mexico has been particularly high, but as has been shown, emigration pressures have intensified in many other countries as well. Thus, the need to coordinate U.S. immigration policy with the nation's other economic policies has become even more acute in the wake of these international developments.

The Need to Synchronize Immigration Policy with Other Economic Policies

The current immigration policy of the United States was largely conceived in the early 1950s and the mid-1960s, periods when immigrants did not have a particularly significant impact on the economy of the nation. In those years the major concerns of policymakers were the political views of would-be immigrants (in the 1950s) and repeal of the national-origins system (in the 1960s). The percentage of the nation's population that was foreign-born had declined in every census from 1920 to 1970. In the 1950s and early 1960s the U.S. labor market was beginning to show the early signs of the major structural shifts in its industrial, occupational, and geographic employment patterns that were to become pronounced in subsequent years. In the 1970s the full effects of enhanced foreign competition on domestic employment began to be felt.

Clearly the immigration laws that were enacted in the early 1950s and mid-1960s manifested a complete disinterest on the part of policymakers in the labor force implications of the legislation. In fact, this lack of concern about the impact of immigration on the broader economic dimensions of American life was apparent in 1940, when the president shifted responsibility for immigration matters from the U.S. Department of Labor to the U.S. Department of Justice. The former agency gives priority to the employment and income implications of the statutes it administers and it has traditionally relied on a trained bureaucracy to resolve difficult and contested issues. The latter agency has neither the expertise nor the desire to give priority to labor market considerations in the design and implementation of the nation's immigration statutes and it tends to defer to the judicial system for solutions to problems.

By the 1970s and early 1980s, however, all forms of immigration had increased dramatically, and the 1980 census reported a notable increase in the foreign-born population of the nation. Moreover, the census showed that the composition of the total immigrant population had changed substantially since 1970 in terms of the skills, education, and experiential backgrounds that immigrants were bringing to U.S. labor markets. The magnitude and character of the immigration that has occurred since the 1960s has introduced so many new challenges that it has essentially overwhelmed the nation's extant immigration laws and related administrative procedures. In the absence of any serious effort to forge an immigration policy based on labor market considerations, immigration policy continues to function as a "wild card" among the nation's key labor market policies. Unlike all other categories of economic policy (e.g., fiscal policies, monetary policies, employment and training policies, education policies, and antidiscrimination policies), where attempts are made by policymakers to orchestrate the diverse policy elements into a harmony of action to accomplish particular objectives, immigration policy has been allowed to meander aimlessly.

The United States could probably continue to exempt immigration policy from accountability for its direct effects on the nation's economic welfare if it were not for the major structural changes and external competitive forces that have caused such upheaval in the traditional employment patterns of the nation in recent years. These changes, however, clearly indicate that the nation can no longer afford a policy of inaction.

The reforms that are needed to make U.S. immigration policy serve the economic welfare of the nation were discussed in detail in the preceding chapters of this book. What follows is a brief summary of the major issues. With respect to the annual levels of immigration, there do need to be ceilings, but these ceilings should be flexible and responsive to the trends in unemployment in the nation. As is the case in Canada and Australia, the annual immigration ceiling should fluctuate inversely with the number of unemployed. An absolute ceiling should be legislated, but the precise number of immigrations admitted in any given year should be determined administratively. Implicit in this recommendation is the transfer of the administrative responsibilities for immigration policy back to the U.S. Department of Labor (or some new agency that might be created to administer and coordinate all of the nation's human resource development policies). The immigration responsibilities of the Department of Justice should be limited to border management and naturalization procedures.

The thrust of policies to affect the composition of the legal immigrant flow should revert to the emphasis on occupational preferences that characterized the immigration system from 1952 to 1965. Family reunification should remain an admissions criterion, but it should not be the primary factor as has been the case since 1965. No other nation in the world allows a nepotistic doctrine to dominate its admissions system. In particular, the fifth preference category, which reserves up to 24 percent of all available visas for adult brothers and sisters of U.S. citizens, should be abolished. Not only has this category become one of the largest contributors to the backlog of visa applicants but it has also been widely abused through the use of fictitious family arrangements and forged documents. In the original Simpson-Mazzoli bill (1982), deletion of the fifth preference category was recommended, but as a result of subsequent political compromises this effort was abandoned. Adult brothers and sisters of immigrants should still be eligible for admission but they should have to compete for available visas on equal grounds with other adult applicants. Abolishing the fifth preference category would allow the number of occupational preference visas to be increased and would probably enhance the opportunities for more "new seed" immigrants to enter the nation. It should be noted, however, that these changes in the family reunification category would not alter the entry privileges of immediate family members. It is also recommended that admissions under the occupational preference category be increased to at least the pre-1965 level—50 percent of the available legal immigrant visas. In addition, the occupational preference category should be expanded to include the entire range of skill levels, and full discretion should be given to the administering agency to decide which skill, education level, or occupation is in greatest demand at any particular time. This discretionary power should also include the right to give preference to immigrants who are willing to settle in regions where labor is scarce.

The refugee and asylee policies of the nation are the most difficult to integrate into a policy design that focuses on economic priorities. Obviously the United States should continue to participate in worldwide efforts to absorb and assist in the resettlement of refugees. Experience clearly indicates, however, that some limitations must be placed on the number of refugees admitted and on where they are to be located.

The practice of legislatively ratifying what has already happened can hardly be called a policy, yet too often since 1965 this is what has occurred. The number of refugees and asylees admitted should be included in the total number of immigrants admitted to the United States each year or separate legislation should establish a fixed ceiling for these admissions. In either event, it should be clearly understood that when special circumstances arise, more refugees will be admitted and more asylees will be permitted to stay, but that offsetting reductions will be required in the number of legal immigrant admissions so that the established administrative ceiling for any given year will be maintained. There is no sense establishing the concept that total immigrant flows should fluctuate with domestic labor market conditions if the entire process can be easily undermined by flows from an unregulated source. If a truly extraordinary situation should develop, Congress could legislate a temporary increase in the numerical boundaries to accommodate such a circumstance. This power, however, should not be within the province of any administrative agency of government or at the discretion of the president. It is also vital that the full cost of financing the adjustment of refugees to American economic life be borne by the federal government. Policies that are implemented in the name of the national interest should not impose economic hardship on any specific community or region of the nation or on any particular segment of the labor force.

The preceding suggestions are predicated on the assumption that a full-scale effort will be mounted to end the flow of illegal immigrants into the United States. If the nation's immigration policies are not reshaped to work in tandem with general economic policies, the entire reform process will be easily circumvented. The various reforms should address both the "push" and the "pull" factors that contribute to illegal immigration. They should include deterrent as well as prevention measures. Enforcement of whatever measures are ultimately adopted should be given high priority in terms of providing the funds and manpower required to fulfill these duties. Concomitantly, because of the need to legalize the status of the large number of illegal immigrants who entered the country when its policies were ambivalent, a one-time-only amnesty should be offered to these persons.

In sum, U.S. immigration policy needs to be synchronized with all other policies that are designed to accomplish full employment, strengthen the domestic economy, and enhance the development of the nation's human resources. A liberal and nondiscriminatory immigration policy should continue to be a hallmark of American society, but that policy must truly contribute to—not contravene—the nation's domestic economic interests.

Grounds for Denial of Immigrant Status, the United States, 1984

1. Mentally retarded
2. Insane
3. One or more attacks of insanity
4. Afflicted with psychopathic personality, or sexual deviation, or a mental defect
5. Narcotic drug addicts or chronic alcoholics
6. Afflicted with any dangerous contagious disease
7. Physical defect, disease, or disability affecting ability to earn a living
8. Paupers, professional beggars, or vagrants
9. Crimes of moral turpitude
10. Convicted of two or more non-political offenses with imposed aggregate sentences of five or more years
11. Practice or advocate the practice of polygamy
12. Prostitutes or procurers
13. Seeking admission to engage in an immoral sexual act
14. Uncertified skilled or unskilled labor
15. Likely to become a public charge
16. Excluded and deported within one year
17. Previously arrested and deported
18. Stowaways
19. Obtained visa or seeks to enter U.S. by fraud or willful misrepresentation
20. Immigrant without valid visa
21. Issued visa outside of preference system
22. Ineligible for citizenship or evaded military service in time of war or national emergency
23. Past conviction for drug possession or trafficking
24. Arrival by vessel or aircraft of non-signatory line
25. Illiteracy
26. Nonimmigrants not in possession of valid passports or other suitable travel documents
27. Intent to engage in activities prejudicial to the public interest
28. Anarchists, communists, or other political subversives
29. Entering to engage in espionage, sabotage or other subversive activity
30. Alien accompanying another alien ordered to be excluded and deported whose protection or guardianship is required by the alien ordered excluded and deported
31. Aliens who have encouraged, induced, assisted, abetted or aided other aliens to enter U.S. in violation of the law
32. Foreign medical school graduates
33. Nazi war criminals

Source: Section 212(a) of the Immigration and Nationality Act of 1952, as amended in subsequent years.

Estimates of the Size of the Illegal Immigrant Population of the United States, 1974–1981

Estimate (in millions)	Year of Estimate	Source and Date of Publication	Methodology
1.6	1970	Goldberg (1974)[a]	Compared the 1970 Mexican census count with the number expected to result from counting births, deaths, and legal immigrants since 1960 census.
3.9 (from a range of 2.9–5.7 million persons 18–44 years old)	1973	Lancaster and Scheuren (1978)[b]	Households categorized in a 1973 Current Population Survey sample by whether they were on file as contributors to or recipients of any of three social security and internal revenue categories.
0.6–4.7 (white males 20–44 years old)	1975	Robinson (1980)[c]	Analyzed trends in selected state death rates from 1950 to 1975 and compared results with actual number of deaths in selected states.
0.4–1.2	1975	Heer (1979)[d]	Analyzed change between 1970 and 1975 in Mexican-origin population as estimated in Current Population Survey and adjusted figures for both natural increases and legal immigration.

Study	Year(s)	Estimate	Method
Vining (1979)[e]	1974–1977	0.18–0.38 (number of overstays by air)	Analyzed data on air passenger arrivals and departures.
Morris and Mayio (1980)[f]	1977	4.3–6.2	Analyzed Mexican adjustments of INS apprehension data in order to secure an estimate of those who had entered without inspection.
Warren (1981)[g]	1979	1.025–1.475 (illegal aliens included in Current Population Survey)	Compared estimates of foreign-born respondents to November 1979 Current Population Survey who reported they had immigrated since 1970 with two INS population counts: (1) the number of legal immigrants and refugees admitted since 1970; and (2) the number of aliens reporting addresses in 1980.

Sources: A selection of the major studies cited in U.S. General Accounting Office, *Problems and Options in Estimating the Size of the Illegal Alien Population* (Washington, D.C.: U.S. General Accounting Office, 1982), app. II, pp. 26–27:

[a]H. Goldberg, "Estimates of Emigration for Mexico and Illegal Entry into the United States, 1960–1970, by the Residual Method" (Georgetown University, Center for Population Research, Washington, D.C., 1974).

[b]C. Lancaster and F. J. Scheuren, "Counting the Uncountable Illegals: Some Initial Statistical Speculation Employing Capture–Recapture Techniques," in *Proceedings of the Social Statistics Section, American Statistical Association, 1977* (Washington, D.C.: ASA, 1978), pp. 530–35.

[c]J. G. Robinson, "Estimating the Approximate Size of the Illegal Alien Population in the United States by the Comparative Trend Analyses of Age Specific Death Rates," *Demography* 17 (May 1980): 159–76.

[d]D. M. Heer, "What is the Annual Net Flow of Undocumented Mexican Immigrants to the United States?" *Demography* 16 (August 1979): 417–23.

[e]D. R. Vining, *Net Migration by Air: A Lower-Bound of Total Migration to the United States,* Working Papers in Regional Science and Transportation no. 15 (Philadelphia: University of Pennsylvania, 1979).

[f]M. D. Morris and A. Mayio, *Illegal Immigration and United States Foreign Policy* (Washington, D.C.: Brookings Institution, 1980).

[g]R. Warren, "Estimation of the Size of the Illegal Alien Population in the United States" (paper presented at the Census Advisory Committee Meeting of the American Statistical Association, Washington, D.C., November 1981).

Estimates by Mexican Scholars
of the Extent of Illegal Immigration
to the United States, 1979

Responding to claims made in the United States in the 1970s that significant increases were occurring in the number of illegal immigrants from Mexico, the Mexican government supported two research studies to determine the size of the flow. These studies were conducted by scholars associated with the Centro Nacional de Información y Estadísticas del Trabajo (CENIET), an organization that is roughly equivalent to the National Assembly of Sciences in the United States.

One study, a survey of emigrants, was conducted from December 1978 through January 1979.[1] Sample households in the northern border states of Mexico were asked whether any members of their families over the age of fifteen were currently in the United States looking for work legally or illegally. The study estimated that about 400,000 Mexicans could be so classified. One of the drawbacks of this technique, of course, is that it assumes that respondents will answer such questions honestly. The technique is also limited by the fact that whole families that have already moved to the United States as well as persons who live outside the survey area are not counted.

The second study consisted of interviews by CENIET scholars of a sample of illegal immigrants whom the INS had apprehended and returned to Mexico.[2] The immigrants were asked how long they had stayed in the United States; how many times they had been apprehended and returned to Mexico; and how many times they had not been apprehended but had returned. The study concluded that between 500,000 and 1.2 million Mexicans were living in the United States illegally in 1977. This methodology also is limited, for it cannot measure those persons who have permanently emigrated and it does not take into account nonapprehended illegal immigrants who voluntarily return to Mexico on either a temporary or permanent basis. Finally, it too is dependent upon the willingness of the participants to answer the survey questions truthfully.

Notes

CHAPTER 1. THE STUDY OF U.S. IMMIGRATION POLICY

1. John Herbers, "Census Data Show Gains in Housing and in Education; Summary Also Indicates Rise in Foreign-Born Population," *New York Times,* April 20, 1982, p. A-1.

2. Leon F. Bouvier, *The Impact of Immigration on the Size of the U.S. Population* (Washington, D.C.: Population Reference Bureau, 1981), p. 1.

3. Leon F. Bouvier, *Immigration and Its Impact on U.S. Society* (Washington, D.C.: Population Reference Bureau, 1981), p. 23.

4. Select Commission on Immigration and Refugee Policy, *U.S. Immigration Policy and the National Interest* (final report) (Washington, D.C.: GPO, 1981), p. 2.

5. Ibid.

6. Ibid., pp. 5, 10.

7. United Nations, "Universal Declaration of Human Rights," adopted by the General Assembly on December 10, 1948.

8. Philip L. Martin and Alan Richards, "International Migration of Labor: Boon or Bane?" *Monthly Labor Review,* October 1980, p. 4.

9. David S. North and Allen LeBel, *Manpower and Immigration Policies in the United States* (Washington, D.C.: National Commission for Manpower Policy, 1978), p. 40.

10. Ibid.

11. Select Commission on Immigration and Refugee Policy, *U.S. Immigration Policy* (final report), p. 5.

12. Robert Pear, "Final Action on Immigration Bill Seen as Unlikely before Late July," *New York Times,* June 22, 1984, p. A-11.

13. Vernon M. Briggs, Jr., "Special Labor Market Segments," in *Manpower Research and Labor Economics,* ed. Gordon L. Swanson and Jon Michaelson (Beverly Hills, Calif.: Sage Publications, 1979), pp. 243–76.

14. National Commission on Employment and Unemployment Statistics, *Counting the Labor Force* (Washington, D.C.: GPO, 1979), p. 101. The commission expressed particular concern about the lack of data on illegal immigrants. This concern is very important, but the lack of good data on legal immigrants, nonimmigrants, and refugees in the labor market also hampers effective evaluation of their respective influences on selected labor markets. It also limits the ability of policymakers and scholars to judge conclusively the adjustment experiences of the immigrants themselves.

15. U.S. Congress, House Select Committee on Population, *Legal and Illegal Immigration to the United States* (Washington, D.C.: GPO, 1978), p. 47.

16. Ibid., p. 48.

17. Silvano Tomasi and Charles B. Keely, *Whom Have We Welcomed? The Adequacy and Quality of United States Immigration Data for Policy Analysis and Evaluation* (Staten Island, N.Y.: Center for Migration Studies, 1975).

18. House Select Committee on Population, *Legal and Illegal Immigration to the United States,* pp. 48–49.

19. Ibid., p. 50.

20. Ibid.

21. Select Commission on Immigration and Refugee Policy, *U.S. Immigration Policy and the National Interest: Staff Report* (supplement to the final report) (Washington, D.C.: GPO, 1981), pp. 25–26.

22. Wayne A. Cornelius, "Undocumented Immigration: A Critique of the Carter Administration's Policy Proposals," *Migration Today,* October 1977, p. 6.

23. House Select Committee on Population, *Legal and Illegal Immigration to the United States,* p. 13.

24. John Dunlop, "Policy Decisions and Research in Economics and Industrial Relations," *Industrial and Labor Relations Review,* April 1979, pp. 275–82.

25. Melvin W. Reder, "Chicago Economics: Permanence and Change," *Journal of Economic Literature,* March 1982, p. 30.

26. Henry C. Simons, *Economic Policy for a Free Society* (Chicago: University of Chicago Press, 1948, p. 251.

27. Reder, "Chicago Economics," p. 31.

28. Ibid.

29. John Kenneth Galbraith, *The Nature of Mass Poverty* (Cambridge: Harvard University Press, 1979), p. 136.

30. Dunlop, "Policy Decisions," p. 275.

31. For example, see Barry Bluestone and Bennett Harrison, *The De-industrialization of America* (New York: Basic Books, 1982); Mancur Olsen, *The Rise and Decline of Nations: Economic Growth, Stagflation, and Social Rigidities* (New Haven, Conn.: Yale University Press, 1982); Robert B. Reich, *The Next American Frontier* (New York: Times Books, 1983); and Michael Wachter and Susan Wachter, eds., *Toward a New U.S. Industrial Policy* (Philadelphia: University of Pennsylvania Press, 1981).

CHAPTER 2. THE QUEST FOR A POLICY ON IMMIGRATION, 1787–1965

1. *Elkie v. United States,* 142 U.S. 651 (1892).

2. *De Canas v. Bica,* 424 U.S. 351 (1976).

3. U.S. *Constitution,* Art. 1, sec. 9.

4. 2 Stat. 426.

5. Stanley M. Elkins, *Slavery* (New York: Grosset and Dunlap, 1959), p. 49.

6. U.S. Department of Labor, *Employment and Training Report of the President, 1976* (Washington, D.C.: GPO, 1976), table AA-1, p. 375; and U.S. Department of Commerce, Bureau of the Census, *1980 Census of Population and Housing: Provisional Estimates of Social, Economic, and Housing* Characteristics (Washington, D.C.: GPO, 1982), table P-2, 14–19.

7. W. E. B. DuBois, *The Suppression of the African Slave Trade to the United States of America, 1638–1870* (New York: Schocken Books, 1969), pp. 152–53.

8. Ibid., pp. 108–18.

9. Select Commission on Immigration and Refugee Policy, *U.S. Immigration Policy . . . Staff Report* (supplement to the final report), p. 169.

10. Barbara M. Tucker, "The Force of Tradition in the Southern New England Textile Industry, 1790–1860" (unpublished manuscript, 1982, mimeographed), p. 197. (Note: This manuscript will be published by Cornell University Press under the title *Samuel Slater and the Origins of the American Textile Industry* in late 1984 or early 1985).

11. Ibid., p. 198.

12. Ibid., p. 187.

13. Mary R. Coolidge, *Chinese Immigration* (New York: Holt and Co., 1909); and Rodman W. Paul, "The Origins of the Chinese Issue in California," *Mississippi Valley Historical Review*, 1938, pp. 181–96.

14. Philip Taft, *Organized Labor in American History* (New York: Harper and Row, 1964), p. 301.

15. DuBois, *Suppression of the African Slave Trade*, pp. 162–67; see also p. xx.

16. Department of Labor, *Employment and Training Report of the President, 1976*, table AA-6, p. 379.

17. Stanley Lebergott, *Manpower in Economic Growth* (New York: McGraw-Hill, 1964), p. 27.

18. Ibid., pp. 154–55.

19. Ibid.

20. Joseph G. Rayback, *A History of American Labor* (New York: Free Press, 1966), pp. 119–20.

21. Taft, *Organized Labor*, p. 304.

22. Ibid., p. 303.

23. 22 Stat. 58.

24. See Appendix A for a list of the exclusions that continue to be effect as of 1984.

25. 23 Stat. 332.

26. Taft, *Organized Labor*, p. 305.

27. Ibid.

28. Samuel P. Orth, "The Alien Contract Law and Labor Law," *Political Science Quarterly*, March 1907, p. 60.

29. Ruth Allen, "The Capitol Boycott: A Study in Peaceful Labor Tactics," *Chapters in the History of Organized Labor in Texas* (Austin: University of Texas, 1912), p. 46.

30. Ibid., p. 55.

31. *Henderson v. Mayor of the City of New York*, 92 U.S. 259 (1876).

32. 22 Stat. 214.

33. 26 Stat. 1084.

34. Paul H. Clyde, *The Far East: A History of the Impact of the West on Eastern Asia* (Englewood Cliffs, N.J.: Prentice-Hall, 1958), p. 492.

35. Ibid.

36. Arthur S. Link, *American Epoch* (New York: Alfred A. Knopf, 1956), p. 152.

37. Thomas A. Bailey, *Theodore Roosevelt and the Japanese-American Crisis* (Palo Alto, Calif.: Stanford University Press, 1934). See also Charles E. Neu, *An Uncertain Friendship: Theodore Roosevelt and Japan* (Cambridge: Harvard University Press, 1967).

38. Taft, *Organized Labor*, p. 306.

39. Ibid., p. 308. See also Robert Asher, "Union Nativism and the Immigrant Response," *Labor History*, Summer 1982, pp. 325–48.

40. Oscar Handlin, *Race and Nationality in American Life* (Garden City, N.Y.: Doubleday and Co., 1957), p. 77.

41. Ibid., p. 78.

42. North and LeBel, *Manpower and Immigration Policies*, p. 26.

43. Handlin, *Race and Nationality*, p. 80.

44. U.S. Immigration Commission, *Abstracts of Reports of the Immigration Commission*, vol. 1 (Washington, D.C.: GPO, 1911), pp. 13–14.

45. Handlin, *Race and Nationality*, p. 104.

46. 39 Stat. 874.

47. U.S. Congress, Senate Committee on the Judiciary, *History of the Immigration and Naturalization Service* (Washington, D.C.: GPO, 1980), p. 13.

48. 34 Stat. 596.

49. Senate Committee on the Judiciary, *History of the Immigration and Naturalization Service*, p. 20.

50. Ibid., p. 13.

51. Department of Labor, *Employment and Training Report of the President, 1976*, tables AA-6 and AA-7, p. 379.

52. Lebergott, *Manpower in Economic Growth*, p. 162.

53. U.S. Department of Labor, *Employment and Training Report of the President, 1977* (Washington, D.C.: GPO, 1977), p. 104.

54. Edward P. Hutchinson, *Immigrants and Their Children, 1850–1950* (New York: John Wiley, 1956).

55. Immigration Commission, *Abstracts of Reports*, 1:297–313.

56. Ibid., p. 151.

57. Taft, *Organized Labor*, p. 307.

58. For example, see Madison Grant, *The Passing of the Great Race* (New York: Charles Scribner's Sons, 1916).

59. David Brody, *Labor in Crisis: The Steel Strike of 1919* (Philadelphia: J. B. Lippincott, 1965), pp. 132–33, 135–36.

60. 42 Stat. 5.

61. 43 Stat. 153.

62. Select Commission on Immigration and Refugee Policy, *U.S. Immigration Policy . . . Staff Report* (supplement to the final report), p. 196.

63. W. S. Bernard, "America's Immigration Policy: Its Evolution and Sociology," *International Migration* 2, no. 4 (1965): 235.

64. *Ozawa v. United States*, 260 U.S. 178 (1922). The Supreme Court ruled that previous congressional enactments had restricted eligibility for naturalization to free white persons (1 Stat. 103) and later to persons of African descent (REV. STAT., sec. 2169). This decision held that the ban on the naturalization of other races was still in effect after the enactment of the Naturalization Act of 1906 (34 Stat. 596).

65. Clyde, *The Far East*, p. 500.

66. Senate Committee on the Judiciary, *History of the Immigration and Naturalization Service*, pp. 37–38.

67. Leo Grebler, Joan Moore, and Ralph Guzman, *The Mexican-American People* (New York: Free Press, 1970), p. 519.

68. Ibid.

69. 43 Stat. 240.

70. Senate Committee on the Judiciary, *History of the Immigration and Naturalization Service*, p. 36.

71. Act of March 2, 1929 (P.L. 962).

72. Act of March 4, 1929 (P.L. 1018), as amended in June 1929.

73. Link, *American Epoch*, p. 297.

74. Ibid.

75. Robert D. Patton, *The American Economy* (Chicago: Scott, Foresman and Co., 1953), pp. 292–94.

76. Lebergott, *Manpower in Economic Growth*, p. 163.

77. Link, *American Epoch*, p. 302.

78. Lebergott, *Manpower in Economic Growth*, pp. 163–64.

79. Walter Buckingham, *Automation: Its Impact on Business and People* (New York: Mentor Books, 1961), pp. 17–18.

80. Ibid., p. 18.

81. Dudley Dillard, *Economic Development of the North American Community* (Englewood Cliffs, N.J.: Prentice-Hall, 1967), p. 565.

82. Michael J. Piore, *Birds of Passage: Migrant Labor and Industrial Societies* (Cambridge: Cambridge Univeristy Press, 1979), pp. 157.

83. For example, see Gunnar Myrdal, *An American Dilemma* (New York: Harper and Row, 1962), pp. 185–91.

84. Carey McWilliams, *North from Mexico* (New York: Greenwood Press, 1968), p. 163.

85. Harry E. Cross and James A. Sandos, *Across the Border: Rural Development in Mexico and Recent Migration to the United States* (Berkeley, Calif.: Institute of Governmental Studies, 1981), pp. 6–7.

86. Ibid., p. 10.

87. McWilliams, *North from Mexico,* p. 175.

88. Arthur F. Corwin and Lawrence A. Cardoso, "Vamos al Norte: Causes of Mass Mexican Migration to the United States," in *Immigrants—and Immigrants: Perspectives on Mexican Labor Migration to the United States,* ed. Arthur F. Corwin (Westport, Conn.: Greenwood Press, 1978), p. 46.

89. Cross and Sandos, *Across the Border,* p. 10.

90. George C. Kiser and Martha W. Kiser, *Mexican Workers in the United States: Historical and Political Perspectives* (Albuquerque: University of New Mexico Press, 1979), p. 33.

91. Abraham Hoffman, "Mexican Repatriation during the Great Depression: A Reappraisal," in *Immigrants—and Immigrants,* ed. Corwin, p. 226.

92. Ibid., p. 228.

93. Rodolfo Acuña, *Occupied America* (San Francisco, Calif.: Canfield Press, 1972), pp. 190–93. See also Vilma Martinez, "Illegal Immigration and the Labor Force," *American Behavioral Scientist,* January 1976, pp. 340–43.

94. Hoffman, "Mexican Repatriation during the Great Depression," pp. 232–33.

95. Senate Committee on the Judiciary, *History of the Immigration and Naturalization Service,* p. 43.

96. Ibid., p. 54.

97. Select Commission on Immigration and Refugee Policy, *U.S. Immigration Policy . . . Staff Report* (supplement to the final report), p. 310.

98. U.S. Congress, Senate Commitee on the Judiciary, *The Immigration and Naturalization Systems of the United States* (Washington, D.C.: GPO, 1950).

99. P.L. 82-414; 66 Stat. 163.

100. North and LeBel, *Manpower and Immigration Policies,* pp. 32–33.

101. Ibid., p. 34.

102. U.S. Congress, Senate Committee on the Judiciary, *U.S. Immigration Law and Policy, 1952–1979* (Washington, D.C.: GPO, 1979), pp. 5–6.

103. Ibid., pp. 5–6.

104. President's Commission on Immigration and Naturalization, *Whom We Shall Welcome* (Washington, D.C.: GPO, 1953), p. 263.

CHAPTER 3. THE LEGAL IMMIGRATION SYSTEM, 1965–1984

1. 79 Stat. 911.

2. Elizabeth J. Harper, *Immigration Laws of the United States* (Indianapolis: Bobbs-Merrill, 1975), p. 38.

3. Select Commission on Immigration and Refugee Policy, U.S. Immigration Policy . . . Staff Report (supplement to the final report), p. 321.

4. Senate Committee on the Judiciary, *U.S. Immigration Law and Policy, 1952–1979,* p. 52.

5. Bernard, "America's Immigration Policy," pp. 234–42.

6. Senate Committee on the Judiciary, *U.S. Immigration Law and Policy, 1952–1979,* p. 54.

7. House Select Committee on Population, *Legal and Illegal Immigration to the United States,* p. 10.

8. 90 Stat. 2703.

9. 92 Stat. 907.

10. See Japanese-American Citizens League to Senator Thomas H. Kuchel, September 17, 1965, as printed in U.S. Congress, Senate, *Congressional Record,* 89th Cong., 1st sess., 1965, 3, pt. 18, p. 24503.

11. Walter Fogel, *Mexican Illegal Alien Workers in the United States* (Los Angeles: Institute of Industrial Relations, University of California at Los Angeles, 1978), pp. 38–39.

12. House Select Committee on Population, *Legal and Illegal Immigration to the United States,* p. 40.

13. Ibid.

14. Ibid.

15. David S. North, *Alien Workers: A Study of the Labor Certification Program* (Washington, D.C.: Trans Century Corp., 1971), pp. 95–96.

16. North and LeBel, *Manpower and Immigration Policies,* p. 226.

17. Ibid.

18. 94 Stat. 102.

19. Bureau of the Census, *1980 Census of Population and Housing,* table P-2, p. 14.

20. Bouvier, *Immigration and Its Impact,* p. i (inside front cover).

21. See David S. North and William G. Weissert, *Immigrants and the American Labor Market,* prepared for the U.S. Department of Labor (Washington, D.C.: GPO, 1974), table 9, p. 67; and U.S. Department of Justice, Immigration and Naturalization Service, *1979 Statistical Yearbook of the Immigration and Naturalization Service* (Washington, D.C.: GPO, 1982), table 12A, p. 31.

22. Gregory DeFreitas and Adriana Marshall, "Immigration and Wage Growth in U.S. Manufacturing in the 1970s" (paper presented at the Thirty-sixth Annual Meeting of the Industrial Relations Research Association, San Francisco, Calif. (December 29, 1983). The *Proceedings* of that meeting will be published in mid-1984.

23. Immigration and Naturalization Service, *1979 Statistical Yearbook,* table 6-C, p. 12.

24. Steve Lohr, "Taiwan Tries to Reverse Brain Drain to U.S.," *New York Times,* August 30, 1982, p. A-9.

25. North and Weissert, *Immigrants and the American Labor Market,* p. 19.

26. Ibid.

27. Ibid., p. 20.

28. Ibid.

29. Ibid., p. 25.

30. David S. North, *Seven Years Later: The Experiences of the 1970 Cohort of Immigrants in the United States,* prepared for the U.S. Department of Labor (Washington, D.C.: GPO, 1979).

31. Ibid., p. 12.

32. Ibid., chap. 3.

33. See Barry R. Chiswick, *An Analysis of the Economic Progress and Impact of Immigrants,* prepared for the U.S. Department of Labor (Washington, D.C.: GPO, June 1980). See also idem, "The Effect of Americanization on the Earnings of Foreign Born Men," *Journal of Political Economy,* October 1978, pp. 897–921; and idem, "Sons of Immigrants: Are They at an Earnings Disadvantage?" *American Economic Review,* February 1977, pp. 376–80, as corrected in an erratum, ibid., September 1977, p. 775.

34. Barry R. Chiswick, *The Employment of Immigrants in the United States* (Washington, D.C.: American Enterprise Institute, 1982), p. 2.

35. North, *Seven Years Later,* p. 10.

36. Ibid.

37. North, *Seven Years Later,* p. 87; and North and Weissert, *Immigrants and the American Labor Market,* p. 70.

38. DeFreitas and Marshall, "Immigration and Wage Growth in U.S. Manufacturing in the 1970s."

39. U.S. Department of State, "Active Immigrant Visa Applicants Registered at Consular Offices as of January 1, 1982," Report ICRR49 (Washington, D.C., April 19, 1982, mimeographed). Figures in the subsequent two paragraphs of the text are from this source.

40. U.S. Congress, House Committee on the Judiciary, Subcommittee on Immigration, Refugees, and International Law, *U.S. Consular Operations in Mexico City and Mexican Government Attitudes on Immigration Reform: A Study Trip* (Washington, D.C.: GPO, 1981), p. 9.

41. Office of the White House Press Secretary, "Message of the President to Congress on Illegal Immigration" (Washington, D.C., August 4, 1977, mimeographed).

42. P. L. 95-412.

43. Robert Pear, "What the House Said in Not Voting an Immigration Bill," *New York Times,* December 27, 1982, p. B-12.

44. See Martin Tolchin, "Democrats Bar Action in House on Immigration," *New York Times,* October 2, 1983, p. A-1; and Robert Pear, "O'Neill Says Bill on Illegal Aliens Is Dead for 1983," ibid., October, 5, 1983, p. A-1.

45. Tolchin, "Democrats Bar Action in House on Immigration," p. A-31; see also Martin Tolchin, "Republicans Push Immigration Bill," *New York Times,* October 19, 1983, p. A-25.

46. "President's News Conference on Foreign and Domestic Issues," transcript published in *New York Times,* October 20, 1983, p. A-14.

47. Martin Tolchin, "O'Neill, in a Reversal, Supports Immigration Bill," *New York Times,* December 1, 1983, p. A-19.

48. Robert Pear, "Stockman Warns Immigration Bill May Be Too Costly," *New York Times,* January 19, 1984, p. A-1.

49. Robert Pear, "O'Neill to Delay Debate on Aliens," *New York Times,* May 3, 1984, p. A-9.

50. Robert Pear, "House Girds to Take Up Touchy Immigration Bill," *New York Times,* June 8, 1984, p. A-14.

51. Robert Pear, "House to Debate Immigration Bill Despite Pleas of Hispanic Groups," *New York Times,* June 12, 1984, p. A-1.

52. Mark J. Miller and Philip L. Martin, *Administering Foreign-Worker Programs: Lessons from Europe* (Lexington, Mass.: D. C. Heath and Co., 1982).

53. Charles B. Keely, *Global Refugee Policy: The Case for a Development-Oriented Strategy* (New York: Population Council, 1981), chap. 2.

54. For a more detailed discussion of the Australian and Canadian immigration systems, see The White House, *Preliminary Report of the Domestic Council Committee on Illegal Aliens* (Washington, D.C.: GPO, 1976), pp. 26–31. (Note: This preliminary report was prepared for President Gerald Ford and was subsequently made the final report of the committee after Ford's defeat for reelection in 1976.) See also North and LeBel, *Manpower and Immigration Policies,* pp. 196–201.

55. Canada, Employment and Immigration Commission, *Background Papers on Future Immigration Levels* (a companion report to the annual report to Parliament on future immigration levels) (Ottawa: Ministry of Supply and Services, 1983), p. 43.

56. Ibid.

57. North and LeBel, *Manpower and Immigration Policies,* p. 39.

58. See, e.g., Thomas Bailey and Marcia Freedman, "Immigrant Economic Mobility in an Era of Weakening Employment Relationships: The Role of Social Networks" (paper presented at the Thirty-seventh Annual Meetings of the Industrial Relations Research Association, San Francisco, Calif., December 29, 1983, and to be published in 1984 in the *Proceedings* of those meetings).

CHAPTER 4. NONIMMIGRANT LABOR POLICY

1. Kiser and Kiser, *Mexican Workers in the United States,* chap. 1.

2. Ibid., p. 10.

3. Ibid.

4. George C. Kiser, "Mexican American Labor before World War II," *Journal of Mexican American History* 2 (1972): 130.

5. Ernesto Galarza, *Merchants of Labor: The Mexican Bracero Story* (Charlotte, N.C.: McNally and Loftin, 1964); Richard Craig, *The Bracero Program: Interest Groups and Foreign Policy* (Austin: University of Texas Press, 1971); and McWilliams, *North from Mexico,* pp. 265–67.

6. Mexico, *Constitution of 1917,* Art. 123, par. xxvi.

7. Galarza, *Merchants of Labor,* chaps. 8–16.

8. U.S. Congress, Senate Committee on the Judiciary, *A Report on Temporary Worker Programs: Background and Issues* (Washington, D.C.: GPO, 1980), pp. 47–51.

9. President's Commission on Migratory Labor, *Migratory Labor in American Agriculture: Report* (Washington, D.C.: GPO, 1951), p. 59.

10. Galarza, *Merchants of Labor,* chaps. 12, 13, 15, 16, and 17.

11. Vernon M. Briggs, Jr., *Chicanos and Rural Poverty* (Baltimore: Johns Hopkins University Press, 1973), p. 29.

12. Senate Committee on the Judiciary, *Temporary Worker Programs,* pp. 52–53.

13. Ibid., p. 55.

14. Ibid.

15. Craig, *The Bracero Program,* pp. 195–96.

16. U.S. Congress, Senate Committee on the Judiciary, Subcommittee on Immigration, *The West Indies (BWI) Temporary Alien Labor Program, 1943–1977* (Washington, D.C.: GPO, 1978), p. 8.

17. Ibid.

18. President's Commission on Migratory Labor, *Migratory Labor in American Agriculture,* p. 58.

19. David S. North, *Nonimmigrant Workers in the U.S.: Current Trends and Future Implications* (Washington, D.C.: New TransCentury Foundation, 1980), chap. 1.

20. Edwin P. Reubens, *Temporary Admission of Foreign Workers: Dimensions and Policies* (Washington, D.C.: National Commission for Manpower Policy, 1979), p. 15.

21. Ibid.

22. 8 U.S.C. sec. 1101 (a) (15) (H) (ii).

23. Philip L. Martin and David S. North, "Nonimmigrant Aliens in American Agriculture" (paper presented at the Conference on Seasonal Agricultural Labor Markets in the United States, Washington, D.C., January 10, 1980, photocopy), pp. 12–13.

24. North, *Nonimmigrant Workers,* p. 27.

25. Ibid., pp. 29–30.

26. U.S. Congress, House Committee on Education and Labor, Subcommittee on Labor Standards, *Job Rights of Domestic Workers: The Florida Sugar Cane Industry* (Washington, D.C.: GPO, 1983), p. 17.

27. Martin and North, "Nonimmigrant Aliens in American Agriculture," p. 20.

28. Senate Committee on the Judiciary, *The West Indies . . . Alien Labor Program,* p. 25.

29. Ibid., p. 26.

30. *Frederick County Fruit Growers Assoc., Inc., v. Marshall,* Civil No. 77-0104 (H) (W.D. Va., filed Aug. 30, 1977).

31. Senate Committee on the Judiciary, *The West Indies . . . Alien Labor Program,* p. 36.

32. Ibid., pp. 37–40.

33. Perry R. Ellsworth, "Need for Seasonal Foreign Workers in Terms of Present and Projected Labor Markets" (statement on behalf of the National Council of Agricultural Workers), in Select Commission on Immigration and Refugee Policy, *U.S. Immigration Policy . . . Staff Report* (supplement to the final report), app. F, p. 87.

34. Jo Thomas, "Florida's Refugees Challenging Plan to Use West Indies in Cane Harvesting," *New York Times,* October 11, 1981, p. 22.

35. Ibid.

36. U.S. Congress, House Committee on the Judiciary, Subcommittee on Immigration, Citizenship, and International Law, *Nonimmigrant Alien Labor Program on the Virgin Islands of the United States* (Washington, D.C.: GPO, 1975), pp. 5–6.

37. Ibid., p. 15.

38. Ibid.

39. Ibid., p. 17.

40. Ibid., pp. 33–34. The case was *Hosier v. Evans*, 314 F. Supp. 316 (Virgin Islands, 1970).

41. House Committee on the Judiciary, *Nonimmigrant Alien Labor Program on the Virgin Islands,* p. 36.

42. Mark J. Miller and William W. Boyer, "Foreign Workers in the U.S. Virgin Islands: Lessons for the United States" (paper delivered at the 1980 meeting of the American Political Science Association, Washington, D.C., mimeographed), p. 18.

43. P.L. 97-271.

44. David S. North, *The Virgin Islands Alien Legalization Program: Lessons for the Mainland* (Washington, D.C.: New TransCentury Foundation, 1983), p. 14.

45. Ibid., p. 43.

46. U.S. Congress, House Committee on the Judiciary, Subcommittee on Immigration, Citizenship, and International Law, *The Use of Temporary Alien Labor on Guam* (Washington, D.C.: GPO, 1979), p. 13.

47. Immigration and Nationality Act, sec. 212 (d) (5) (1952).

48. House Committee on the Judiciary, *Temporary Alien Labor on Guam,* p. 25.

49. Ibid., p. 49.

50. Walter J. Haltigan, Regional Administrator, to Floyd E. Edwards, Administrator of the U.S. Department of Labor, cover letter accompanying report entitled "Guam Alien Labor Situation" (San Francisco, Calif., May 16, 1977, photocopy), p. 1.

51. "Guam Alien Labor Situation," p. 18.

52. Ibid., p. 40.

53. W. R. Böhning, *Regularizing Undocumentados* (Geneva: International Labour Organisation, 1979).

54. Ibid., p. 7.

55. Ibid., p. 11.

56. Charles B. Keely, *U.S. Immigration: A Policy Analysis* (New York: Population Council, 1979), pp. 60–62.

57. Ibid., p. 60.

58. Ibid., p. 61.

59. Reubens, *Temporary Admission of Foreign Workers,* pp. 61–68.

60. Ibid., p. 59.

61. Ibid.

62. Ibid.

63. Ibid.

64. Ibid., p. 60.

65. Office of the White House Press Secretary, "Message of the President to Congress on Illegal Immigration" (Washington, D.C., August 4, 1977, mimeographed), p. 6.

66. Eli Ginzberg, Chairman of the National Commission for Manpower Policy, to Secretary of Labor Ray Marshall, May 1, 1979, printed in Reubens, *Temporary Admission of Foreign Workers,* p. 100.

67. Select Commission on Immigration and Refugee Policy, *U.S. Immigration Policy* (final report), p. 227.

68. Ibid., p. 228.

69. Ibid., p. 45.

70. U.S. Department of Justice, "U.S. Immigration and Refugee Policy" (Washington, D.C., July 30, 1981, photocopy).

71. Ibid., p. 5.

72. Joseph Nalven and Craig Frederickson, *The Employer's View: Is There a Need for a Guest-Workers Program?* (San Diego, Calif.: Community Research Associates, 1982), p. 1.

73. "Simpson-Mazzoli Immigration Bill: Back to the Bracero Fiasco," *New York Times,* October 2, 1982, p. A-26 (a letter to the editor from Joaquin G. Avila, president and general counsel of the Mexican American Legal Defenses and Education Fund).

74. League of United Latin American Citizens, "Analysis of Simpson-Mazzoli Legislation H.R. 1510" (an open letter released by the League's Washington, D.C., Office on July 21, 1983), p. 5 (mimeographed).

75. Robert Pear, "House Votes Plan to Admit Aliens to Harvest Crops," *New York Times,* June 15, 1984, p. B-5.

76. "Bill to Curb Illegal Immigration: House Debates Reflect Diversity of Nation," *New York Times,* June 17, 1984, p. A-20.

77. Robert Pear, "House, by 216–211, Approves Aliens Bill After Retaining Amnesty Plan in Final Test," *New York Times,* June 21, 1984, pp. A-1 and D-21.

78. Robert Pear, "Final Action on Immigration Bill Seen as Unlikely before Late July," *New York Times,* June 22, 1984, p. A-11.

79. See Böhning, *Regularizing Undocumentados;* Wayne A. Cornelius, *Mexican Migration to the United States: Causes, Consequences, and U.S. Responses* (Cambridge: Center for International Studies, Massachusetts Institute of Technology, 1978); and Piore, *Birds of Passage,* chap. 2.

80. Nalven and Frederickson, *The Employer's View,* p. 7.

81. Ibid., p. 79.

82. Ibid.

83. Labor Council for Latin American Advancement, "Declaration of Albuquerque and Employment Action Program," *Conference Report of the National Conference on Jobs for Hispanics* (Washington, D.C., August 1979), p. 10 (italics in the original).

84. See "Statement by the National Hispanic Task Force," in Select Commission on Immigration and Refugee Policy, *U.S. Immigration Policy . . . Staff Report* (supplement to the final report), app. H, p. 418; and the statements prepared jointly by the Migrant Legal Action Program and the National Center for Immigrant Rights, ibid., app. F, pp. 19–84.

85. " 'Guest Workers' Plan Assailed as Retreat on Gains," *AFL-CIO News,* December 5, 1981, p. 7.

86. "Mexican Labor Denounces Reagan 'Guest Worker' Plans," *AFL-CIO News,* August 22, 1981, p. 1.

87. United Nations, Economic and Social Council, *The Welfare of Migrant Workers and Their Families* (New York, 1974), pp. 1–8.

88. Philip L. Martin, *Guest-Worker Programs: Lessons from Europe,* prepared for the Bureau of International Labor Affairs, U.S. Department of Labor (Washington, D.C.: GPO, 1980), p. 25.

89. Ibid., p. 9.

90. Gary Freeman, "Immigrant Labor and Working-Class Politics: The French and British Experience," *Comparative Politics,* October 1978, p. 29.

91. Ibid., p. 37.

92. Ibid.

93. "Disputed Citizenship Law in Effect in Britain," *New York Times,* January 2, 1983, p. 4.

94. Ibid.

95. Demetrios G. Papademetriou, "European Labor Migration," *International Studies Quarterly,* September 1978, p. 378.

96. Miller and Martin, *Administering Foreign-Worker Programs,* p. 59.

97. Ibid., p. xviii.

98. Martin, *Guest-Worker Programs,* pp. 8–9.

99. W. R. Böhning, *Basic Aspects of Migration from Poor to Rich Countries: Facts, Problems, Policies* (Geneva: International Labour Organisation, 1976), p. 8.

100. Ibid., p. 9.

101. Ibid.

102. Ray Rist, "The European Economic Community (EEC) and Manpower Migrations: Policies and Prospects," *Journal of International Affairs,* Fall–Winter 1979, p. 202.

103. S. Sassen-Koob, "The International Circulation of Resources and Development: The Case of Migrant Labor," *Development and Change,* October 1978, p. 539.

104. Ibid.

105. Papademetriou, "European Labor Migration," p. 385.

106. Quoted in Miller and Martin, *Administering Foreign-Worker Programs,* p. 71, where the original source is cited as Klaus Lefringhausen, "Wirtschafteselhische Aspekte fuer lokale Aktionen," in *Gastarbeiter-Mitbuerger,* ed. Rene Leudesdorff and Horst Zillessen (Gelnhausen: Burckhardthaus, 1971), p. 192.

CHAPTER 5. ILLEGAL IMMIGRATION

1. For example, see John Davidson, *The Long Road North* (Garden City, N.Y.: Doubleday and Co., 1979); and Julian Samora, *Los Mojados: The Wetback Story* (Notre Dame, Ind.: University of Notre Dame Press, 1971).

2. U.S. Congress, House Committee on International Relations, Subcommittee on Inter-American Affairs, *Hearings, Undocumented Workers: Implications for U.S. Policy in the Western Hemisphere* (Washington, D.C.: GPO, 1978), p. 151.

3. Samora, *Los Mojados,* pp. 46–47.

4. Elliott Abrams and Franklin S. Abrams, "Immigration Policy—Who Gets in and Why?" *Public Interest,* Winter 1975, p. 22.

5. House Committee on International Relations, *Undocumented Workers,* p. 116.

6. Office of the White House Press Secretary, "Undocumented Aliens" (Washington, D.C., August 4, 1977, mimeographed), p. 7. This information was compiled by the U.S. Department of Justice.

7. Maurice D. Van Arsdol, Jr., Joan Moore, David Heer, and Susan P. Haynie, *Non-Apprehended and Apprehended Undocumented Residents in the Los Angeles Labor Market,* prepared for the U.S. Department of Labor (Washington, D.C.: GPO, May 1979), p. 27.

8. U.S. General Accounting Office, *Problems and Options in Estimating the Size of the Illegal Alien Population,* GAO/IPE 82-9 (Washington, D.C.: GPO, 1982), p. 17.

9. L. Meyer, "Aliens Hard to Count," *Washington Post,* February 2, 1975, p. A-12.

10. Quoted in Abrams and Abrams, "Immigration Policy," p. 21.

11. U.S. Department of Justice, Immigration and Naturalization Service, *1974 Annual Report of the Immigration and Naturalization Service* (Washington, D.C.: GPO, 1975), p. iii.

12. Lesko Associates, "Final Report: Basic Data and Guidance Required to Implement a Major Illegal Alien Study," prepared for the U.S. Immigration and Naturalization Service (Washington, D.C., October 15, 1975, mimeographed), p. 15.

13. For example, Kenneth Roberts, Michael E. Conroy, Allan G. King, and George Rizo-Patron, *The Mexican Number Game: An Analysis of the Lesko Estimate of the Undocumented Migration from Mexico to the United States* (Austin: Bureau of Business Research, University of Texas, 1978).

14. National Commission on Employment and Unemployment Statistics, *Counting the Labor Force,* p. 101.

15. U.S. Congress, House Committee on Ways and Means, Subcommittee on Oversight, *Hearings, The Underground Economy* (Washington, D.C.: GPO, 1979), ser. 96-70, p. 243.

16. Jacob S. Siegal, Jeffrey S. Passel, and J. Gregory Robinson, "Preliminary Review of Existing Studies of the Number of Illegal Residents in the United States," prepared for the U.S. Bureau of the Census (Washington, D.C., January 1980, mimeographed), p. 19.

17. Ibid., p. 20.

18. Otis A. Singletary, *The Mexican War* (Chicago: University of Chicago Press, 1960), p. 1.

19. Alan Riding, "Facing the Reality of Mexico," *New York Times Magazine,* September 16, 1979, p. 141.

20. McWilliams, *North from Mexico,* p. 59; and Acuña, *Occupied America,* pp. 80–81.

21. McWilliams, *North from Mexico,* p. 59.

22. Ignacio Bernal, "The Cultural Roots of the Border: An Archaeologist's View," in *Views Across the Border,* ed. Stanley R. Ross (Albuquerque: University of New Mexico Press, 1978), pp. 29–30.

23. Grebler, Moore, and Guzman, *The Mexican-American People,* p. 41.

24. For more details, see Henry B. Parkes, *A History of Mexico* (Boston: Houghton Mifflin, 1969), pp. 285–310.

25. Robert E. Quirk, *Mexico* (Englewood Cliffs, N.J.: Prentice-Hall, 1971), p. 85.

26. Ibid., pp. 86–87.

27. Link, *American Epoch,* p. 171.

28. Quirk, *Mexico,* p. 104.

29. "Mexican Senate Resolution," *Immigration Report,* December 1982–January 1983, p. 2.

30. Steven Ratner, "Mexico's Cambridge Connection," *New York Times,* October 24, 1982, pp. F-1, F-10.

31. Calvin P. Blair, "Mexico: Some Recent Developments," *Texas Business Review,* May 1977, p. 98.

32. Joel Bergsman, "Income Distribution and Poverty in Mexico (Washington, D.C.: World Bank, 1980), p. 41.

33. Ibid., p. 43.

34. Ibid., pp. 17, 20.

35. Alan Riding, "Corruption Again Election Issue in Mexico," *New York Times,* June 29, 1976, p. A-2. See also idem, "López Portillo Proposes and Follows a Code to Ban 'Cancer' of Corruption," ibid., September 6, 1981, p. A-3; and Marlise Simons, "Mexico Probes Land Deal, State Governor Vanishes," *Washington Post,* February 7, 1975, p. A-14.

36. Riding, "Corruption Again Election Issue," p. A-2.

37. Richard Severo, "The Flight of the Wetbacks," *New York Times Magazine,* March 10, 1974, p. 81.

38. See discussion by Carl Rowan, "Mexico's Grimly Determined New Leader," *Washington Post,* December 7, 1982, p. A-23. Richard J. Meislin, "Mexico Carries War on Corruption to Unions," *New York Times,* February 6, 1984, p. A-7.

39. Stephen Engelberg, "U.S. General Asserts Mexico Is the Most Corrupt in Region," *New York Times,* February 27, 1984, p. A-4. The testimony was before the Senate Armed Services Committee.

40. Octavio Paz, *The Labyrinth of Solitude: Life and Thought in Mexico* (New York: Grove Press, 1961), chap. 2.

41. Riding, "Facing the Reality of Mexico," p. 129.

42. Ibid., p. 128.

43. Gene Lyons, "Inside the Volcano," *Harper's,* June 1977, p. 54.

44. Paz, *The Labyrinth of Solitude,* p. 122.

45. Lynda Schuster, "Mexican Peso Falls by 53 Percent against Dollar as Float, New Currency Rules Take Effect," *Wall Street Journal,* December 12, 1982, p. 31.

46. See "Arrests of Illegal Aliens Increase as Mexican Economy Falters," *New York Times,* August 27, 1982, p. A-8; and Judith Cummings, "Patrol Searches Harder as Mexicans Seek Easier Life in U.S.," ibid., August 30, 1982, p. A-10.

47. Lyons, "Inside the Volcano," p. 41.

48. Paul Horgan, *Great River: The Rio Grande in North American History,* vol. 1, *Indians and Spain* (New York: Minerva Press, 1968).

49. Samora, *Los Majados,* p. 10.

50. House Committee on International Relations, *Undocumented Workers,* "Statement on Caribbean Labor Migration," by Virginia R. Dominguez, p. 215.

51. David Lowenthal, *West Indian Societies* (New York: Oxford University Press, 1972).

52. Ibid.; see also Gary Freeman, "Immigrant Labor and Working-Class Politics: The French and British Experience," *Comparative Politics,* October, 1978, pp. 24–41.

53. House Committee on International Relations, *Undocumented Workers,* "Statement on 'Illegal' Caribbean Immigrants: Some Foreign Policy Implications for the United States," by Roy S. Bryce-Laporte, pp. 70–84.

54. House Committee on International Relations, *Undocumented Workers,* statements by Bryce-Laporte and Dominguez.

55. Ibid., statement by Dominguez, p. 216.

56. Ibid., p. 218.

57. Ibid., p. 220.

58. Jorge Bustamante, "Commodity Migrants: Structural Analysis of Mexican Immigration to the United States," in *Views Across the Border,* ed. pp. 183–203.

59. Robert Pear, "Mexicans Oppose U.S. Entry Curbs," *New York Times,* November 21, 1982, p. 13.

60. U.S. Congress, House Committee on the Judiciary, Subcommittee No. 1, *Hearings on Illegal Aliens,* pt. 5, (Washington, D.C.: GPO, 1972), p. 1315.

61. *Diaz v. Kay-Dix Ranch* (1970), as reprinted in House Committee on the Judiciary, *Hearings on Illegal Aliens,* pt. 1 (Washington, D.C.: GPO, 1971), p. 179.

62. U.S. Congress, House Committee on the Judiciary, *Report on the Immigration Reform and Control Act of 1982* (Washington, D.C.: GPO, 1982), p. 205.

63. Ibid.

64. David S. North and Marion F. Houstoun, *The Characteristics and Role of Illegal Aliens in the U.S. Labor Market: An Exploratory Study* (Washington, D.C.: Linton and Co., 1976).

65. Van Arsdol, Jr., et al., *Undocumented Residents in the Los Angeles Labor Market.*

66. Robert A. Peterson and George Kozmetsky, "Public Opinion Regarding Illegal Aliens in Texas," *Texas Business Review,* May–June 1982, pp. 118–20.

67. For example, see Jacquelyne Jackson, "Illegal Aliens: Big Threat to Black Workers," *Ebony,* April 1979, pp. 33–40.

68. North and Houstoun, *Illegal Aliens in the U.S. Labor Market,* p. 128.

69. Van Arsdol, Jr., et al., *Undocumented Residents in the Los Angeles Labor Market,* p. 183. See also "Immigration Policies and Black America: Causes and Consequences" (seminar cosponsored by the Department of Human Development, School of Human Ecology, Howard University, and the Federation for American Immigration Reform, Washington, D.C.: November 3, 1983, mimeographed).

70. Peter B. Doeringer and Michael J. Piore, *Internal Labor Markets and Manpower Analysis* (Lexington, Mass.: D. C. Heath and Co., 1971).

71. Piore, *Birds of Passage.*

72. Cornelius, *Mexican Migration to the United States.*

73. U.S. Congress, Senate Committee on the Judiciary, Subcommittee on Immigration, Refugees, and International Law, and House Committee on the Judiciary, Subcommittee on Immigration and Refugee Policy, *Joint Hearings, Immigration Reform and Control Act of 1982* (Washington, D.C.: GPO, 1982), statement by Malcolm Lovell, Undersecretary of Labor (April 20, 1982), p. 367.

74. Ibid.

75. Nalven and Frederickson, *The Employer's View,* p. 79.

76. Robert Taggert, *Hardship: The Welfare Consequences of Labor Market Problems* (Kalamazoo, Mich.: W. E. Upjohn Institute for Employment Research, 1982), p. 1.

77. North and Houstoun, *Illegal Aliens in the U.S. Labor Market,* pp. 17–26.

78. Donald L. Huddle, "Illegals in the Texas Economy" (Department of Economics, Rice University, Houston, 1982, mimeographed), p. 2.

79. Fogel, *Mexican Illegal Alien Workers in the United States,* p. 100.

80. Robert Hershey, "When is Unemployment 'Natural'?" *New York Times,* October 16, 1982, p. A-6. See also "Reagan Says Joblessness Won't Drop Below 6 Percent," ibid., September 30, 1982, p. D-1.

81. For example, see Evan Maxwell, "U.S.-Mexico Smuggling: The Buying and Selling of Humans," *Los Angeles Times,* February 22, 1977, pt. 1, p. 3.

82. For a discussion of the personal dangers involved, see Samora, *Los Mojados,* and Davidson, *The Long Road North.* In both of these studies the "participant observer" technique was used as the basis for the authors' accounts.

83. "Aliens Left in Desert Die," *Washington Star,* July 7, 1980, p. A-1.

84. "Four Dead among Sixteen Aliens Left in Truck on Texas Road," *New York Times,* October 6, 1982, p. A-16.

85. See the discussion in Gregory Jaynes," U.S. Finds a Big Decline in Refugees from Haiti," *New York Times,* December 6, 1981, p. A-81.

86. Patt Morrison, "Illegal Aliens: Good Wages, Bad Jobs, Constant Fear," *Los Angeles Times,* January 22, 1977, pp. 1, 24.

87. Laura Kierman, "Five Deported Aliens Sue for Md. Wages," *Washington Post,* September 23, 1974, p. C-1.

88. "Arizonian Convicted in Beating of Aliens," *New York Times,* February 24, 1981, p. A-12.

89. "The Hanigan Case," *New York Times,* March 7, 1982, p. 41.

90. Leslie Maittand Werner, "Justice Department Considers Possible Appeal of Sentences in Texas Slave Case," *New York Times,* February 11, 1984, p. 13.

91. "Light Slavery Sentences Being Appealed by U.S.," *New York Times,* March 8, 1984, p. A-18.

92. "Fifth State of the Nation Report by President Luis Echeverría," *Mexican Newsletter,* September 1, 1975, p. 14.

93. David S. North, "The Non-sense of Immigration and Welfare Policies," *Public Welfare,* Winter 1982, pp. 28–35.

94. *Phyler v. Doe,* appeal docketed, No. 80-1538, Sup. Ct., June 15, 1982.

95. 7 U.S.C. 2045 (1976).

96. U.S. Congress, Senate Committee on the Judiciary, Subcommittee on Immigration and Refugee Policy, *Hearings, The Knowing Employment of Illegal Immigrants* (Washington, D.C.: GPO, 1981), pp. 84–86.

97. These were H.R. 16188 in 1972 and H.R. 982 in 1973.

98. *De Canas v. Bica,* 425 U.S. 351 (1976).

99. Senate Committee on the Judiciary, *The Knowing Employment of Illegal Immigrants,* testimony of John Huerta, counsel for the Mexican-American Legal Defense and Educational Fund, p. 151.

100. Select Commission on Immigration and Refugee Policy, *U.S. Immigration Policy* (final report), p. 61.

101. U.S. Congress, House, *Congressional Record,* 97th Cong., 2nd sess., 1982, vol. 128, pt. 151, pp. 10318–54.

102. One summary of positions, "Business Views on Immigration Reform and Employer Sanctions," was prepared by the Congressional Task Force of the Federation for American Immigration Reform (Washington, D.C., September 1982, mimeographed), p. 1.

103. U.S. Commission on Civil Rights, *The Tarnished Golden Door: Civil Rights Issues in Immigration* (Washington, D.C.: GPO, 1980), p. 74.

104. Ibid.

105. See "Phoney ID's: They're Flooding the Country," *U.S. News and World Report*, April 6, 1981, pp. 32–33; and John Toohey and Pat McGraw, "Sophisticated, Phoney U.S. Identification Cards Not Hard to Get," *Denver Post-Sun*, August 2, 1981, p. 33.

106. Gerda Bikales, "The Case for a Secure Social Security Card," position paper prepared by the National Parks and Conservation Association (Washington, D.C., September 1978); and Vernon M. Briggs, Jr., "The Impact of the Undocumented Worker on the Labor Market," in *The Problem of the Undocumented Worker*, ed. Robert S. Landmann (Albuquerque: Latin American Institute, University of New Mexico, 1979), pp. 31–38.

107. P.L. 92-603, sec. 137 (1972).

108. North and Houstoun, *Illegal Aliens in the U.S. Labor Market*, p. 179.

109. Davis S. North, *Keeping Undocumented Workers Out of the Workforce: Costs of Alternative Work Permit Systems* (Washington, D.C.: New TransCentury Foundation, 1979).

110. Select Commission on Immigration and Refugee Policy, *U.S. Immigration Policy* (final report), statement of Commissioner Ray Marshall, pp. 364–65.

111. See U.S. Congress, Senate Committee on the Judiciary, Subcommittee on Immigration and Refugee Policy, *Hearings, Systems to Verify Authorization to Work in the United States* (Washington, D.C.: GPO, 1982).

112. Select Commission on Immigration and Refugee Policy, *U.S. Immigration Policy* (final report), p. 68.

113. U.S. Department of Justice, "Testimony of William French Smith, Attorney General, before the Senate Subcommittee on Immigration and Refugee Policy, July 30, 1981" (mimeographed), pp. 6–7.

114. U.S. Commission on Civil Rights, *Civil Rights Issues in Immigration*, p. 74.

115. Theodore Hesburgh, "Nothing Totalitarian about a Worker's ID Card," *New York Times*, September 24, 1982, p. A-26.

116. U.S. Congress, House Select Committee on Population, *Hearings, Immigration to the United States* (Washington, D.C.: GPO, 1978), "Undocumented Workers and U.S. Immigration Policy," statement by Michael J. Piore, p. 491.

117. North and Houstoun, *Illegal Aliens in the U.S. Labor Market*, p. 128.

118. North, "The Non-sense of Immigration and Welfare Policies," p. 35; see also Van Arsdol, Jr., et al., *Undocumented Residents in the Los Angeles Labor Market*, p. 89.

119. "National Association of Counties on Amnesty," *Immigration Report*, June 1982, p. 2.

120. "Counties Voice Fear of Cost of Alien Legalization," *New York Times*, June 8, 1982, p. A-23.

121. John Fogarty, "Alien Policy Could Cost State," *San Francisco Chronicle*, September 8, 1982, p. 6.

122. "Counties Voice Fear of Cost of Alien Legalization," p. A-23.

123. Ibid.

124. Robert Pear, "Stockman Warns Immigration Bill May Be Too Costly," *New York Times*, January 19, 1984, p. A-19.

125. Tugrul Ansay, "Clandestine Immigration," report prepared for the Council of Europe, Special Representatives Advisory Committee (Strasbourg, July 15, 1975, mimeographed), p. 3.

126. Ibid.

127. See Miller and Martin, *Administering Foreign-Worker Programs*, p. 59.

128. U.S. General Accounting Office, *Information on the Enforcement of Laws Regarding Employment of Aliens in Selected Countries* (Washington, D.C.: GPO, 1982), p. 3.

129. Ibid., p. 4.

130. Ibid., p. 2.

131. Ibid.

132. Ibid.

133. David S. North, *The Canadian Experience with Amnesty for Aliens: What the United States*

Can Learn (Geneva: International Labour Organisation, 1979), p. 4. North's study also reviews the experiences of nations other than Canada.

134. Ibid.

135. General Accounting Office, *Enforcement of Laws Regarding Employment of Aliens,* p. 6.

CHAPTER 6. REFUGEE AND ASYLEE POLICY

1. Peter Kihss, "U.S. Using Tougher Policy on Asylum for Afghans," *New York Times,* May 7, 1982, p. B-3.

2. United Nations, *Convention Relating to the Status of Refugees* (Geneva, July 28, 1951), as amended by the *Protocol Relating to the Status of Refugees* (New York, January 31, 1967).

3. Keely, *Global Refugee Policy,* p. 6.

4. Ibid., pp. 27–28.

5. Ibid., p. 36.

6. Select Commission on Immigration and Refugee Policy, *U.S. Immigration Policy . . . Staff Report* (supplement to the final report), p. 199.

7. 62 Stat. 1009.

8. Helen F. Eckerson and Gertrude D. Krichefsky, "A Quarter Century of Quota Restriction," *INS Monthly Review,* January 1950, pp. 85–98.

9. 67 Stat. 229.

10. Immigration and Nationality Act, sec. 212 (d) (5) (1952).

11. 71 Stat. 639.

12. 74 Stat. 504.

13. Senate Committee on the Judiciary, *U.S. Immigration Law and Policy, 1952–1979,* p. 46.

14. Julia V. Taft, David S. North, and David A. Ford, *Refugee Resettlement in the U.S.: Time for a New Focus* (Washington, D.C.: New TransCentury Foundation, 1979), p. 71.

15. 76 Stat. 121.

16. U.S. Congress, Senate Committee on the Judiciary, *Review of U.S. Refugee Resettlement Programs and Policies* (Washington, D.C.: GPO, 1980), p. 12.

17. Ibid., pp. 12–13, which is a verbatim quotation from U.S. Congress, Senate Committee on the Judiciary, *Amending the Immigration and Nationality Act and for Other Purposes* (Washington, D.C.: GPO, 1965), p. 17.

18. Robert L. Bach, "The New Cuban Immigrants: Their Background and Prospects," *Monthly Labor Review,* October 1980, p. 44.

19. *Silva v. Levi,* No. 76, C4268 (N.D. Ill. Apr. 1, 1978).

20. U.S. Department of Commerce, *Bureau of the Census Provisional Estimates of Social, Economic, and Housing Characteristics* (Washington, D.C.: GPO, 1982), pp. 64 and 22 respectively.

21. Taft, North, and Ford, *Refugee Resettlement in the U.S.,* p. 103.

22. Senate Committee on the Judiciary, *U.S. Refugee Resettlement Programs,* p. 14.

23. Ibid.

24. Senate Committee on the Judiciary, *U.S. Immigration Law and Policy, 1952–1979,* p. 79.

25. Ibid., p. 77.

26. Senate Committee on the Judiciary, *U.S. Refugee Resettlement Programs,* p. 35. The quotation is from the testimony of Dick Clark, U.S. Coordinator for Refugee Affairs, before the committee on March 14, 1979.

27. 94 Stat. 102.

28. Senate Committee on the Judiciary, *U.S. Refugee Resettlement Programs,* p. 38.

29. U.S. Department of State, Office of the U.S. Coordinator for Refugee Affairs, "Proposed Refugee Admissions and Allocations for Fiscal Year 1983" (Washington, D.C., 1983, mimeographed), p. 14.

30. Colin Campbell, "Refugees Moving Back to Cambodia," *New York Times,* October 31, 1982, p. A-5.

31. Ibid.

32. U.S. Congress, Senate Committee on the Judiciary, *Hearings, Caribbean Refugee Crisis: Cubans and Haitians* (Washington, D.C.: GPO, 1980), p. 47. The quotation is from the prepared statement submitted to the committee by Ambassador-at-Large Victor H. Palmieri on May 12, 1980.

33. Ibid., p. 30.

34. "Carter and the Cuban Influx," *Newsweek,* May 26, 1980, p. 23.

35. "Eighteen Nations Move to Assist Exodus," *New York Times,* May 10, 1980, p. A-11.

36. Senate Committee on the Judiciary, *Caribbean Refugee Crisis,* p. 42.

37. Ibid.

38. Department of Justice, "Testimony of William French Smith . . . before the Senate Subcommittee on Immigration and Refugee Policy, July 30, 1981," p. 13.

39. Bernard Gwertzman, "U.S. Bids Cuba Take Several Thousand of Its Exiles Back," *New York Times,* May 26, 1983, pp. A-1, A-6.

40. Reginald Stuart, "Cuban's Lawyers Question Deportation Plans," *New York Times,* May 29, 1983, p. A-22.

41. Robert Pear, "Cuban Aliens, but Not Haitians, Will Be Offered Residency Status," *New York Times,* February 13, 1984, p. A-1.

42. Ibid., p. A-40.

43. "Floridians Seek Residency Status for Haitians, Along with Cubans," *New York Times,* February 13, 1984, p. A-15.

44. Bernard Gwertzman, "Policy That Limits Indochina Refugees Is Reversed by U.S.," *New York Times,* May 31, 1981, p. A-13.

45. Ibid.

46. U.S. Congress, Senate Committee on the Judiciary, *Hearings, U.S. Refugee Programs, 1981* (Washington, D.C.: GPO, 1980), p. 29.

47. Senate Committee on the Judiciary, *Caribbean Refugee Crisis,* p. 55; see also Richard J. Meislan, "Trial in Haiti Puts the Focus on Rights," *New York Times,* August 27, 1982, p. A-3.

48. "Asylum for the Haitians," *Miami News,* December 15, 1972, quoted verbatim in "Haitian Refugees Need Asylum" (briefing paper prepared by the Church World Service, New York, N.Y., April 9, 1980), p. 5. The briefing paper is printed in Senate Committee on the Judiciary, *Caribbean Refugee Crisis,* p. 245.

49. Organization of American States, "Report on the Status of Human Rights in Haiti" (April 17, 1980), and Lawyers Committees for International Human Rights, "Violation of Human Rights in Haiti, 1980," both printed in Senate Committee on the Judiciary, *Caribbean Refugee Crisis,* pp. 66–201.

50. U.S. Department of State, "Report of the Department of State Study Team on Haitian Refugees" (June 19, 1979), p. 14, printed in Senate Committee on the Judiciary, *Caribbean Refugee Crisis,* p. 215.

51. Ibid.

52. Leslie M. Werner, "A Torrent of Requests for Asylum," *New York Times,* July 7, 1983, p. B-6.

53. Senate Committee on the Judiciary, *Caribbean Refugee Crisis,* p. 16.

54. Ibid., p. 28.

55. Jaynes, "Big Decline in Refugees from Haiti," p. A-30.

56. "A Look into Haitian Camps," *New York Times,* May 9, 1982, p. E-4.

57. Gregory Jaynes, "Ruling on Detention of Haitians Expected as Miami Suit Concludes," *New York Times,* May 16, 1982, p. A-34.

58. Ibid.

59. Gregory Jaynes, "U.S. Announces New Policy for Parole of Some Haitians," *New York Times,* June 15, 1982, p. A-24.

60. Ibid.

61. *Louis v. Nelson*, 544 F. Supp. 973 (S.D. Fla. 1982); see also Gregory Jaynes, "U.S. Judge Voids Policy on Detention of Haitians," *New York Times*, June 19, 1982, p. A-4.

62. Ibid.

63. "U.S. Plea on Haitian Refugees Is Rebuffed," *Washington Post*, July 15, 1982, p. A-4.

64. "Justice Decides against Appeal of Court Order Freeing Haitians," *Washington Post*, July 15, 1982, p. A-8.

65. Mary Thornton, "Despite Setback, Administrators Vow to Keep Illegal Aliens Out," *Washington Post*, July 24, 1982, p. A-3.

66. Ibid.

67. "Hearing Is Set in Dispute on Resettling of Haitians," *New York Times*, August 25, 1982, p. A-23.

68. Ibid.

69. *Jean v. Nelson*, 11 C.A. No. 82-5772 Apr. 12, 1983).

70. "Haitian Lawyers Hail Court Ruling," *New York Times*, April 14, 1983, p. A-24.

71. *Jean v. Nelson*, No. 82-5772, 11th Circuit Court of Appeals (Feb. 28, 1984).

72. Peter Slevin, "Haitians Lose Ruling on Rights," *Miami Herald*, February 29, 1984, p. A-15.

73. Taft, North, and Ford, *Refugee Resettlement in the U.S.*, p. 55.

74. Senate Committee on the Judiciary, *U.S. Refugee Resettlement Programs*, p. 20.

75. "Florida Officials Tell Refugees of States with More Benefits," *New York Times*, May 5, 1982, p. B-11.

76. Ibid.

77. Ibid.

78. "Florida Worries about Crime Wave As Federal Funds for Refugees End," *New York Times*, June 3, 1982, p. D-18.

79. North, "The Non-sense of Immigration and Welfare Policies," p. 31.

80. "National Governors' Association Resolution," *Immigration Report*, March 1982, p. 2.

81. Barry M. Stein, "Occupational Adjustment of Refugees: The Vietnamese in the United States," *International Migration Review*, Spring 1979, p. 38.

82. Taft, North, and Ford, *Refugee Resettlement in the U.S.*, p. 56.

83. Ibid., pp. 60, 61.

84. Ibid., p. 87.

85. Bach, "The New Cuban Immigrants," pp. 39–46.

86. Ibid., p. 42.

87. Report by the U.S. Department of Health and Human Services, Office of Refugee Resettlement, Cuban-Haitian Task Force (Washington, D.C., June 30, 1981, mimeographed).

88. Taft, North, and Ford, *Refugee Resettlement in the U.S.*, p. 103.

89. Robert L. Bach and Jennifer B. Bach, "Employment Patterns of Southeast Asian Refugees," *Monthly Labor Review*, October 1980, p. 34.

90. Ibid.

91. Senate Committee on the Judiciary, *U.S. Refugee Programs, 1981*, pp. 95–96.

92. Select Commission on Immigration and Refugee Policy, *U.S. Immigration Policy* (final report), pp. 157–64.

93. Werner, "Requests for Asylum," p. B-6.

94. Ibid.

95. "Refugees and Refoulement," *New York Times*, May 12, 1983, p. A-22.

96. U.S. Congress, Senate Committee on the Judiciary, *Immigration Reform and Control: Report on S. 2222* (Washington, D.C.: GPO, 1982), p. 12.

97. "To Judge a Plea for Asylum Fairly and Speedily" (letter to the editor from Alan C. Nelson, Commissioner of the Immigration and Naturalization Service), *New York Times*, May 24, 1983, p. A-26.

98. Michael S. Teitelbaum, "Right versus Right: Immigration and Refugee Policy in the United States," *Foreign Affairs,* Fall 1980, pp. 52–53.

99. Ibid., p. 53.

100. Ronald S. Scheinman and Norman L. Zucker, "Refugee Policy," *New York Times,* May 24, 1981, p. E-19.

101. Barbara Crossitte, "Haitians in U.S. May Be Offered Land in Belize," *New York Times,* March 28, 1982, p. A-18.

102. Irving Howe, "Belize: Will It Be Another Falkland Islands?" *New York Times Magazine,* September 19, 1982, pp. 82ff.

103. Bernard Gwertzman, "Reagan Announces Aid for Caribbean and Assails Cuba," *New York Times,* February 25, 1982, pp. A-1, A-15.

104. Roger J. LeMaster and Barnaly Zall, "Compassion Fatigue: The Expansion of Refugee Admissions to the United States," *Boston College International and Comparative Law Review* 6, no. 2 (1983): 471–73.

CHAPTER 7. IMMIGRATION-RELATED POLICIES AND U.S.-MEXICAN BORDER LABOR MARKETS

1. House Select Committee on Population, *Legal and Illegal Immigration to the United States,* p. 53.

2. Victor Urquidi and Sofia M. Villarreal, "Economic Importance of Mexico's Northern Border Region," in *Views Across the Border,* ed. Ross, p. 161.

3. Ellwyn Stoddard, *Patterns of Poverty Along the U.S.-Mexico Border* (El Paso: Organization of United States Border Cities and Counties, 1978), p. 1.

4. Kathleen Brook and James T. Peach, "Income, Employment, and Population Growth in the U.S.-Mexico Border Counties," *Texas Business Review,* May–June 1981, p. 138.

5. For example, see Edward Y. George, "The Effect of the Border on the El Paso Economy," *Texas Business Review,* March–April 1982, p. 82.

6. Brook and Peach, "U.S.-Mexico Border Counties," p. 139.

7. Urquidi and Villarreal, "Mexico's Northern Border Region," p. 141. See also Raul A. Fernandez, *The United States–Mexico Border* (Notre Dame, Ind.: University of Notre Dame Press, 1977), pp. 113–18.

8. Urquidi and Villarreal, "Mexico's Northern Border Region," p. 143.

9. Ibid., pp. 143, 152.

10. Ibid., p. 142.

11. John A. Garcia, "Political Integration of Mexican Immigrants: Explorations into the Naturalization Process," *International Migration Review,* Winter 1981, p. 611.

12. 54 Stat. 670.

13. The figures and percentages in this paragraph are drawn from a review of the *Annual Reports* of the Immigration and Naturalization Service.

14. David S. North, *The Border Crossers: People Who Live in Mexico and Work in the United States* (Washington, D.C.: TransCentury Corp., 1970).

15. U.S. Department of Justice, Immigration and Naturalization Service, "Commuters" (paper prepared for the Select Commission on Western Hemisphere Immigration), printed in U.S. Congress, Senate Committee on Labor and Public Welfare, Subcommittee on Migratory Labor, *Hearings on Migrant and Seasonal Farmworker Powerlessness* (May 1969), pt. 5-B (Washington, D.C.: GPO 1969), p. 2623.

16. Michael V. Miller, "Industrial Development and an Expanding Labor Force in Brownsville," *Texas Business Review,* November–December 1982, p. 261.

17. Anna-Stina Ericson, "The Impact of Commuters on the Mexican-American Border Area," *Monthly Labor Review,* August 1970, p. 18.

18. U.S. Department of Labor, "The 'Commuter Problem' and Low Wages and Unemployment in American Cities on the Mexican Border" (paper prepared for the Select Commission on Western Hemisphere Immigration, 1967), printed in Senate Committee on Labor and Public Welfare, *Migrant and Seasonal Farmworker Powerlessness,* pt. 5-B, pp. 2630–31. See also Michael V. Miller, *Economic Change Along the U.S.-Mexican Border: The Case of Brownsville, Texas* (Austin, Tex.: Bureau of Business Research, 1982).

19. North, *The Border Crossers.*

20. Ibid., chap. 5.

21. *Karnuth v. Albro,* 279 U.S. 231 (1929).

22. Sheldon L. Greene, "Public Agency Distortion of Congressional Will: Federal Policy toward Non-Resident Alien Labor," *George Washington Law Review,* March 1972, p. 442, citing 8 C.F.R. 211.1 (b) (1) (1971).

23. Ibid., p. 443, citing 8 U.S. 65 (1974).

24. *Saxbe v. Bustos,* 419 U.S. 65 (1974).

25. U.S. Congress, House Committee on the Judiciary, Subcommittee No. 1, *Study of Population and Immigration Problems,* no. 11 (Washington, D.C.: GPO, 1963), p. 62.

26. Fred H. Schmidt, *Spanish Surnamed American Employment in the Southwest* (Washington, D.C.: U.S. Equal Employment Opportunity Commission, 1970), p. 62.

27. *Espinoza v. Farah Manufacturing Co.,* 414 U.S. 86 (1973).

28. *Cabell v. Chavez-Salido,* appeal docketed, No. 80-990, Sup. Ct., Jan. 1982.

29. North, *The Border Crossers,* pp. 180–82. See also Gilberto Cardenas, "Manpower Impact and Problems of Mexican Illegal Aliens in an Urban Labor Market" (Ph.D. diss., University of Illinois, December 1976), p. 31.

30. For example, see "Violence, Often Unchecked, Pervades U.S. Border Patrol," *New York Times,* January 14, 1980, p. D-8.

31. North, *The Border Crossers,* p. 180.

32. U.S. Congress, Senate Committee on Labor and Public Welfare, Subcommittee on Migratory Labor, *Hearings on Migrant and Seasonal Farmworker Powerlessness* (May 1969), pt. 5-A (Washington, D.C.: GPO, 1969), p. 2145.

33. House Select Committee on Population, *Legal and Illegal Immigration to the United States,* p. 11.

34. Grebler, Moore, and Guzman, *The Mexican-American People,* p. 73.

35. Senate Committee on Labor and Public Welfare, *Migrant and Seasonal Farmworker Powerlessness,* pt. 5-A, p. 2148.

36. Donald W. Barrensen, "Mexico's Assembly Program: Implications for the United States," *Texas Business Review,* November–December 1981, p. 253.

37. Liborio Villalobos Calderon, "Foreign Assembly Industries in Mexico: A Necessary Evil of an Underdeveloped Society" (paper presented at the Conference on Economic Relations between Mexico and the United States, Institute of Latin American Studies, University of Texas at Austin, April 16–20, 1973), pp. 5–9.

38. Barrensen, "Mexico's Assembly Program," p. 256. See also Susan C. Fouts, "Mexican Border Industrialization: An Analogy and a Comment" (paper presented to the Conference on Economic Relations between Mexico and the United States, Institute of Latin American Studies, University of Texas at Austin, April 16–20, 1973), p. 9.

39. U.S. Tariff Commission, *Economic Factors Affecting the Use of Items 807.00 and 806.30 of the Tariff Schedules of the United States* (Washington, D.C.: GPO, September 1970).

40. Texas Good Neighbor Commission, *Texas Migrant Labor: Annual Report, 1972* (Austin: Texas Good Neighbor Commission, 1972), pp. 25–26. See also "Spread of U.S. Plants to Mexico Brings a Boom—and Complaints," *U.S. News and World Report,* March 27, 1972, p. 59.

41. Barrensen, "Mexico's Assembly Program," p. 254.

42. See Niles Hansen, "Interdependence Along the U.S.-Mexico Border," *Texas Business Review,* November–December 1983, p. 251–52.

43. Urquidi and Villarreal, "Mexico's Northern Border Region," p. 160.

44. George, "The Effect of the Border on the El Paso Economy," p. 81.

45. See Wayne King, "Peso's Turmoil Shakes Economics of Cities of Mexican-U.S. Border," *New York Times,* August 22, 1982, pp. A-1, and A-25; Lydia Chavez, "Mexico Curbs: Border Suffers," ibid., September 25, 1982, pp. D-1, D-41; "Mexico's Controls Are Felt in El Paso," ibid., September 25, 1982, p. D-41; "Down and Out in Laredo," *Fortune,* November 1982, pp. 139–45; and Donald W. Barrensen, "Devaluation and Merchandising in Texas Border Cities," *Texas Business Review,* September–October, 1982, pp. 229–31.

46. Brook and Peach, "U.S.-Mexico Border Counties," pp. 136–40.

47. Fouts, "Mexican Border Industrialization," p. 8; and Barrensen, "Mexico's Assembly Program," p. 256.

48. Mitchell A. Seligson and Edward J. Williams, *Maquiladoras and Migration* (Tucson: Department of Political Science, University of Arizona, 1980), chap. 3. See also Fernandez, *The United States–Mexico Border,* p. 141.

CHAPTER 8. U.S. IMMIGRATION POLICY IN THE 1980s

1. Select Commission on Immigration and Refugee Policy, *U.S. Immigration Policy* (final report), p. 2.

2. Deborah P. Klein, "Labor Force Data: The Impact of the 1980 Census," *Monthly Labor Review,* July 1982, pp. 39–43.

3. Howard N. Fullerton, "How Accurate Were Projections of the 1980 Labor Force?" *Monthly Labor Review,* July 1982, pp. 15–21.

4. Howard N. Fullerton, "The 1995 Labor Force: A First Look," *Monthly Labor Review,* December 1980, p. 21.

5. Ibid.

6. Howard N. Fullerton and John Tschetter, "The 1995 Labor Force: A Second Look," *Monthly Labor Review,* November 1983, pp. 3–10.

7. Fullerton and Tschetter, "The 1995 Labor Force: A First Look," p. 17.

8. See Arvil V. Adams, *The Lingering Crisis of Youth Unemployment* (Kalamazoo, Mich.: W. E. Upjohn Institute, 1978); and Paul Osterman, *Getting Started: The Youth Labor Market* (Cambridge: MIT Press, 1980).

9. Walter Guzzardi, "Demography's Good News for the 1980s," *Fortune,* November 1979, pp. 92ff.

10. Fullerton, "The 1995 Labor Force," p. 17.

11. Ibid.

12. See Vernon M. Briggs, Jr., Walter Fogel, and Fred H. Schmidt, *The Chicano Worker* (Austin: University of Texas Press, 1977).

13. Fullerton, "The 1995 Labor Force," p. 12.

14. National Commission on Excellence in Education, *Nation at Risk: The Imperative for Educational Reform,* prepared for the U.S. Department of Education (Washington, D.C.: GPO, 1983).

15. Charles C. Killingsworth, "The Fall and Rise of the Idea of Structural Unemployment," *Proceedings of the Thirty-first Meeting of the Industrial Relations Research Association* (University of Wisconsin, Madison, 1979), pp. 1–13.

16. Eli Ginzberg, "The Mechanization of Work," *Scientific American,* September 1982, pp. 66–75. In the same issue see also Robert Marovelli and John Karhnak, "The Mechanization of Mining," pp. 90–113; and Thomas Gunn, "The Mechanization of Design and Manufacturing," pp. 114–31.

17. Carol N. Leon, "Occupation Winners and Losers: Who They Were during 1972–80," *Monthly Labor Review,* June 1982, pp. 18–28.

18. Philip L. Rones, "Moving to the Sun: Regional Job Growth, 1968–1978," *Monthly Labor Review,* March 1980, pp. 12–19.

19. Ibid., p. 16.

20. Robert Pear, "Aliens Who Stay in Clusters Are Said to Do Better," *New York Times,* March 11, 1982, p. A-24.

21. Ray Marshall, Allan G. King, and Vernon M. Briggs, Jr., *Labor Economics: Wages Employment and Trade Unionism,* 5th ed. (Homewood, Ill.: Richard D. Irwin, 1984), chap. 3.

APPENDIX C

1. Carlos H. Zazueta and Rodolfo Corona, *Los Trabajadores Mexicanos en los Estados Unidos: Primeros Resultados de la Encuesta Nacional de Emigración* (Mexico City: Centro Nacional de Información y Estadísticas del Trabajo, 1979).

2. Manuel Garcia y Griego, *El Volumen de la Migración de Mexicanos No Documentados a los Estados Unidos: Nuevas Hipótesis* (Mexico City: Centro Nacional de Información y Estadísticas del Trabajo, 1979).

Index

VERNON M. BRIGGS, JR., is a labor economist in the New York State School of Industrial and Labor Relations at Cornell University and has written extensively on various aspects of low-wage labor markets in the United States. His books include *Chicanos and Rural Poverty* (also from Johns Hopkins) and, most recently, *Labor Economics: Wages, Employment, and Trade Unionism.*